THE ENVIRONMENT

ISSN 2332-3825

THE ENVIRONMENT

Kim Masters Evans

INFORMATION PLUS® REFERENCE SERIES
Formerly Published by Information Plus, Wylie, Texas

GALE
CENGAGE Learning·

Farmington Hills, Mich • San Francisco • New York • Waterville, Maine
Meriden, Conn • Mason, Ohio • Chicago

The Environment

Kim Masters Evans

Kepos Media, Inc.: Steven Long and Janice Jorgensen, Series Editors

Project Editors: Tracie Moy, Laura Avery

Rights Acquisition and Management: Ashley Maynard, Carissa Poweleit

Composition: Evi Abou-El-Seoud, Mary Beth Trimper

Manufacturing: Rita Wimberley

For product information and technology assistance, contact us at
Gale Customer Support, 1-800-877-4253.
For permission to use material from this text or product,
submit all requests online at **www.cengage.com/permissions**.
Further permissions questions can be e-mailed to
permissionrequest@cengage.com

Cover photograph: © Yvonne Pijnenburg-Schonewille/Shutterstock.com.

While every effort has been made to ensure the reliability of the information presented in this publication, Gale, a part of Cengage Learning, does not guarantee the accuracy of the data contained herein. Gale accepts no payment for listing; and inclusion in the publication of any organization, agency, institution, publication, service, or individual does not imply endorsement of the editors or publisher. Errors brought to the attention of the publisher and verified to the satisfaction of the publisher will be corrected in future editions.

Gale
27500 Drake Rd.
Farmington Hills, MI 48331-3535

ISBN-13: 978-0-7876-5103-9 (set)
ISBN-13: 978-1-5730-2668-0

ISSN 2332-3825

This title is also available as an e-book.
ISBN-13: 978-1-5730-2709-0 (set)
Contact your Gale sales representative for ordering information.

Printed in the United States of America
1 2 3 4 5   20 19 18 17 16

TABLE OF CONTENTS

Public opinion and knowledge about environmental issues have evolved over time and have led to federal and state laws protecting environmental resources. These laws have been debated on their economic impact and on how well they protect citizens from environmental hazards. Various political factors affect the implementation of such laws. The international community is also concerned about the environment and has, with varying degrees of success, instituted environmental standards of protection.

Emissions of chemicals from transportation vehicles, industrial facilities, and power plants are mostly to blame for air pollution, which can make people sick and harm the environment. Government regulation, along with the implementation of new technologies, is designed to promote clean air. Although some people believe these measures are too restrictive, others believe the measures do not go far enough.

Scientists generally agree that the earth is getting warmer because of anthropogenic (human-caused) emissions of greenhouse gases that can bring about climate change. These gases include carbon dioxide, methane, nitrous oxide, and engineered gases, and their continued emissions could have severe environmental effects on the earth. Many nations have committed themselves to reducing greenhouse gas emissions, with varying levels of success.

Ozone can be either a health hazard or a health protectant, depending on where in the atmosphere it is located. Human-made chemicals, such as chlorofluorocarbons, can deplete the protective layer of ozone found in the upper atmosphere, which shields humans, plants, and animals from excess ultraviolet radiation exposure. The international community plays an important role in safeguarding environmental health by protecting the ozone layer.

The combustion of fossil fuels emits sulfur oxides and nitrogen oxides into the atmosphere, leading to acid rain. Acid rain can harm human health and damage ecosystems. Politicians and environmental groups in the United States and throughout the world have attempted, through legislation and other measures, to reduce pollution that causes acid rain.

The vast majority of waste generated by modern society is not inherently hazardous. It includes paper, wood, plastics, glass, and nonhazardous metals and chemicals. Landfilling, incineration, and combustion are the most common disposal methods for nonhazardous waste. Nevertheless, these methods have environmental consequences that must be mitigated through design and control techniques.

Problems associated with the disposal of nonhazardous wastes have created a greater need for the recovery of materials through recycling and composting. These methods save landfill space, conserve energy that would be used for incineration, reduce environmental degradation, and minimize the use of new resources. Their implementation and success, however, depend on public participation, government regulation, and economic factors.

The most toxic and dangerous waste materials are those classified by the government as hazardous or radioactive. The storage, transport, and disposal of these wastes require special consideration, subjecting them to strict regulatory control and intense public scrutiny. Federal and state governments try to ensure that these wastes are managed in a way that protects both the environment and public health.

Water is an essential resource that is necessary for sustaining all forms of life, but human alteration of the environment and patterns of water usage can have a devastating effect on the water supply. Legislation, including the Clean Water Act, seeks to improve and protect the integrity of U.S. surface water, groundwater, oceans, coastal water, and drinking water. The effectiveness of such laws remains a matter of debate.

CHAPTER 10
Many of the substances found naturally in the environment or released by modern, industrialized society are poisonous at certain dosages. Such substances may be found in the home, workplace, or backyard; in the foods people eat and in the water they drink; and in consumer products. Common toxins include metals and other chemicals; radiation, particularly from radon exposure; indoor air pollutants, such as asbestos; and foodborne contaminants, including pathogens. These toxins can have damaging effects on human health and the environment.

CHAPTER 11
Forests and wetlands are rich and valuable ecosystems that are endangered by the activities of humans. The diversity of life on the earth (biodiversity) is also at risk, with many species facing extinction. Although domestic production of minerals and fossil fuels is important economically, it also has environmental consequences that must be addressed.

PREFACE

The Environment is part of the *Information Plus Reference Series*. The purpose of each volume of the series is to present the latest facts on a topic of pressing concern in modern American life. These topics include the most controversial and studied social issues of the 21st century: abortion, capital punishment, care for senior citizens, crime, health care, immigration, national security, sports, weight, women, youth, and many more. Although this series is written especially for high school and undergraduate students, it is an excellent resource for anyone in need of factual information on current affairs.

By presenting the facts, it is the intention of Gale, Cengage Learning, to provide its readers with everything they need to reach an informed opinion on current issues. To that end, there is a particular emphasis in this series on the presentation of scientific studies, surveys, and statistics. These data are generally presented in the form of tables, charts, and other graphics placed within the text of each book. Every graphic is directly referred to and carefully explained in the text. The source of each graphic is presented within the graphic itself. The data used in these graphics are drawn from the most reputable and reliable sources, such as from the various branches of the U.S. government and from private organizations and associations. Every effort has been made to secure the most recent information available. Readers should bear in mind that many major studies take years to conduct and that additional years often pass before the data from these studies are made available to the public. Therefore, in many cases the most recent information available in 2016 is dated from 2013 or 2014. Older statistics are sometimes presented as well if they are landmark studies or of particular interest and no more-recent information exists.

Although statistics are a major focus of the *Information Plus Reference Series*, they are by no means its only content. Each book also presents the widely held positions and important ideas that shape how the book's

subject is discussed in the United States. These positions are explained in detail and, where possible, in the words of their proponents. Some of the other material to be found in these books includes historical background, descriptions of major events related to the subject, relevant laws and court cases, and examples of how these issues play out in American life. Some books also feature primary documents or have pro and con debate sections that provide the words and opinions of prominent Americans on both sides of a controversial topic. All material is presented in an evenhanded and unbiased manner; readers will never be encouraged to accept one view of an issue over another.

HOW TO USE THIS BOOK

The condition of the world's environment is an issue of great concern both to Americans and to other people worldwide. Since the late 19th century, humankind's ability to alter the natural world, both deliberately and unintentionally, has increased. Many people fear that without proper restraint, humankind's actions could forever alter, or even eliminate, life on the earth. There are others, however, who believe that these fears are exaggerated and that the substantial cost to business and industry for environmental protection should be minimized. The conflict between these two positions has serious economic, environmental, and political ramifications, within the United States and worldwide. This book examines the steps that have been taken to protect the earth's natural environment and the controversies that surround them.

The Environment consists of 11 chapters and three appendixes. Each chapter is devoted to a particular aspect of the environment. For a summary of the information that is covered in each chapter, please see the synopses that are provided in the Table of Contents. Chapters generally begin with an overview of the basic facts and background information on the chapter's topic, then proceed to examine subtopics of particular interest. For example, Chapter 9: Water Issues begins with an examination of water use trends and presents data on water usage by different sectors of society. Water quality considerations are then addressed, including the Clean Water Act and the regulatory programs that govern discharges to the nation's water bodies. Data on specific water contaminants are presented and discussed based on surveys conducted by state agencies. Water quality stressors, such as mercury, and sources of impairment, such as atmospheric deposition, are described. National water quality assessment reports prepared by the U.S. Environmental Protection Agency and the U.S. Geological Survey are also reviewed. The chapter ends with an overview of issues affecting ocean and coastal waters, beaches, and the nation's drinking water supply. Readers can find their way through a chapter by looking for the section and subsection headings, which are clearly set off from the text. They can also refer to the book's extensive Index if they already know what they are looking for.

Statistical Information

The tables and figures featured throughout *The Environment* will be of particular use to readers in learning about this issue. The tables and figures represent an extensive collection of the most recent and important statistics on the environment, as well as related issues—for example, graphics cover the amounts of different kinds of pollutants that are found in the air across the United States; probable sources of impairment to assessed water bodies; the amounts of wetlands that are destroyed each year; and public opinion on whether environmental protection or economic considerations should have priority. Gale, Cengage Learning, believes that making this information available to readers is the most important way to fulfill the goal of this book: to help readers understand the issues and controversies surrounding the environment and reach their own conclusions about them.

Each table or figure has a unique identifier appearing above it, for ease of identification and reference. Titles for the tables and figures explain their purpose. At the end of each table or figure, the original source of the data is provided.

To help readers understand these often complicated statistics, all tables and figures are explained in the text. References in the text direct readers to the relevant statistics. Furthermore, the contents of all tables and figures are fully indexed. Please see the opening section of the Index at the back of this volume for a description of how to find tables and figures within it.

Appendixes

Besides the main body text and images, *The Environment* has three appendixes. The first is the Important Names and Addresses directory. Here, readers will find contact information for a number of government and private organizations that can provide further information on aspects of the environment. The second appendix is the Resources section, which can also assist readers in conducting their own research. In this section, the author and editors of *The Environment* describe some of the sources that were most useful during the compilation of this book. The final appendix is the detailed Index. It has been greatly expanded from previous editions and should make it even easier to find specific topics in this book.

COMMENTS AND SUGGESTIONS

The editors of the *Information Plus Reference Series* welcome your feedback on *The Environment*. Please direct all correspondence to:

Editors
Information Plus Reference Series
27500 Drake Rd.
Farmington Hills, MI 48331-3535

CHAPTER 1

THE STATE OF THE ENVIRONMENT: AN OVERVIEW

Photographs from outer space impress on the world that humankind shares one planet, and a small one at that. (See Figure 1.1.) The earth is one ecosystem. There may be differences in race, nationality, religion, and language, but everyone resides on the same orbiting planet.

General concern about the environment is a relatively recent phenomenon. It arose in the United States during the turbulent 1960s and early 1970s, when social activism was a major force for change. Environmentalism was truly a grassroots movement in which public outcry spurred politicians to act. The result was a flurry of government regulations that were aimed at cleaning up the worst excesses of industrialism. Over the following decades the environmental movement continued to wield social and political influence, but the initial zeal for aggressive action faded as Americans turned their attention to other challenges. The economy, energy, and terrorism took precedence in the public consciousness. Around the turn of the millennium, environmental activism experienced a rebirth that was driven by concern about a "new" threat facing the world: climate change. This latest revolution in attitudes unleashed a fresh passion about environmental issues, particularly among young people. Nevertheless, this "green" surge was dampened during the latter half of the first decade of the 21st century by the so-called Great Recession (which lasted from late 2007 to mid-2009). A turbulent public debate emerged over the often conflicting priorities of environmental protection versus economic growth. It remains to be seen how this philosophical and political battle will shape future U.S. environmental policy.

HISTORICAL ATTITUDES TOWARD THE ENVIRONMENT

The Industrial Revolution

Humankind has always altered the environment around itself. For much of human history, however, these changes were fairly limited. The world was too vast and people too few to have more than a minor effect on the environment, especially as they had only primitive tools and technology to aid them. All this began to change during the 1800s. First in Europe and then in the United States, powerful new machines, such as steam engines, were developed and put into use. These new technologies led to great increases in the amount and quality of goods that could be manufactured and the amount of food that could be harvested. As a result, the quality of life rose substantially and the population began to boom. The so-called Industrial Revolution was under way.

Although the Industrial Revolution enabled people to live better in many ways, it also increased pollution. For many years pollution was thought to be an insignificant side effect of growth and progress. In fact, at one time people looked on the smokestacks belching black soot as a healthy sign of economic growth. The reality was that pollution, along with the increased demands for natural resources and living space that resulted from the Industrial Revolution, was beginning to have a significant effect on the environment.

The Environmental Revolution

For much of the early 20th century Americans accepted pollution as an inevitable cost of economic progress. During the 1940s and 1950s, however, more and more incidents involving pollution made people aware of the environmental problems that were caused by human activities. In Los Angeles, California, smog (a smoky haze of pollution that forms like a fog in the city; the word was made by combining the words *smoke* and *fog*) contributed a new word to the English language. According to the South Coast Air Quality Management District, in "The Southland's War on Smog: Fifty Years of Progress toward Clean Air" (May 1997, http://www.aqmd.gov/home/library/public-information/publications/50-years-of-progress#The%20Arrival%20of%20Air%20Pollution), "World War II dramatically

FIGURE 1.1

Space view of earth, photograph. *U.S. National Aeronautics and Space Administration (NASA).*

increased the region's industrial base and resulting air pollution. The city's population and motor vehicle fleet grew rapidly as well. As a result, according to weather records, visibility declined rapidly from 1939 to 1943. Angelenos grew increasingly alarmed at the smoke that clouded their vision and the fumes that filled their lungs." In 1947 public pressure spurred local officials to create the country's first air pollution control program. This is an example of grassroots activism—actions by ordinary people that are designed to bring about change.

One influential person in the modern environmental movement was Rachel Carson (1907–1964), a prolific writer and biologist who specialized in raising public awareness about natural resources and conservation. In *Silent Spring* (1962), Carson described the environmental toll of the chemical insecticide dichloro-diphenyl-trichloroethane (DDT) and other persistent (long-lasting in the environment) synthetic pesticides. Extensive DDT use had begun during World War II (1939–1945). Its effectiveness in killing insects greatly reduced the number of deaths from diseases such as malaria. However, DDT also had a negative affect on the environment. Carson alleged that the synthetic chemicals and their residues had become persistent and were found widely in rivers, lakes, groundwater, soil, and in the bodies of fish, birds, reptiles, other animals, and even humans.

Carson cited the results of scientific studies indicating the lethal effects of DDT on songbirds, bald eagles, pheasants, ducks, and other fish-eating fowl. She made

the case that DDT spreads throughout the food chain and the environment, poisoning organisms along the way. From a human health standpoint, she argued that the chemicals build up in human tissues and likely cause long-term damage to the liver and kidneys. At the time, the lethal effects of acute exposure (short-term exposure to a large dose) of DDT to humans were well documented. Although a cause-and-effect relationship between long-term, low-level exposure and human illness had not been established, Carson contended that chronic exposure must certainly be detrimental to human health. Her work is considered to be one of the driving forces behind the environmental movement.

According to the U.S. Environmental Protection Agency (EPA), in the press release "DDT Ban Takes Effect" (December 31, 1972, http://www2.epa.gov/aboutepa/ddt-ban-takes-effect), approximately 675,000 tons (612,000 t) of the pesticide were applied in the United States between the 1940s and the 1972 ban, mostly to agricultural crops, such as cotton. The EPA notes, however, that insects began developing resistance to the pesticide. (This happens as naturally resistant individuals survive pesticide applications and pass their resistance to their offspring. Eventually, resistant individuals outnumber susceptible individuals, and the insecticide is no longer effective.) In addition, the EPA cites growing public and government concern about the toxic effects of the pesticide and the development of effective alternatives as reasons for the U.S. ban in 1972 on almost all domestic uses of DDT.

The United States' environmental problems at the time were not limited to air pollution and chemical toxins. In 1969 the Cuyahoga River near Cleveland, Ohio, burst into flames because of pollutants in the water. Clearly, strong and decisive action was needed.

LAWS AND LAWSUITS. In 1970 Congress passed and President Richard M. Nixon (1913–1994) signed a series of unprecedented laws to protect the environment. Nixon proposed and Congress approved the creation of a new federal agency, the EPA, which combined many smaller federal agencies. The EPA was charged with setting limits on water and air pollutants and investigating the environmental impact of proposed, federally funded projects. In the years that followed, many more environmental laws were passed, setting basic rules for interaction with the environment. Most notable among these laws were the Clean Air Act (CAA) of 1970, the Clean Water Act (CWA) of 1972, the Endangered Species Act of 1973, the Safe Drinking Water Act of 1974, and the Resource Conservation and Recovery Act of 1976.

A significant feature of many of these federal laws was the so-called citizen-suit provision. This provision allows ordinary citizens to file lawsuits in civil court against businesses or federal government agencies for failing to meet standards or follow orders laid out by Congress in the laws. For example, Section 505 of the CWA (http://www2.epa.gov/enforcement/clean-water-act-cwa-section-505-effect-prior-citizen-suit-adjudications-or-settlement) states that "any citizen may commence a civil action on his own behalf." Of course, there are legal technicalities and expenses involved in filing citizen suits. As a result, they are mostly pursued by environmental organizations with the legal savvy and funds to do so.

The late 1960s and early 1970s witnessed the birth of some influential environmental organizations, such as the Environmental Defense Fund, the Union of Concerned Scientists, Greenpeace, and the Natural Resources Defense Council. These groups and long-standing conservation organizations, such as the Sierra Club and the National Audubon Society, quickly realized the power of citizen suits to further their environmental goals. The Environmental Defense Fund's legal battles against DDT played a major role in the banning of the pesticide. In 1971 the Sierra Club founded a legal defense fund that was later renamed Earthjustice (2015, http://earthjustice.org/about/our_history).

By the 1960s many states had already established agencies that were charged with conserving land or protecting health-related resources, such as drinking water. As environmental awareness grew, so did state laws and protection schemes. Small agencies, often operating under a Department of Health, were merged, or brand-new agencies were created to focus solely on pollution control. The EPA (August 26, 2015, http://www.epa.gov/epahome/state.htm) maintains an online listing with links to the environmental agencies in every state.

EARTH DAY. There are actually two dates that have been celebrated annually as Earth Day. The better-known date is April 22. The idea for this Earth Day began to evolve during the early 1960s. Nationwide "teach-ins" were being held on university campuses across the country to protest the Vietnam War (1954–1975). The U.S. senator Gaylord Nelson (1916–2005; D-WI), troubled by the apathy of U.S. leaders toward the environment, announced that a grassroots demonstration on behalf of the environment would be held during the spring of 1970, and he invited everyone to participate. On April 22, 1970, 20 million people participated in massive rallies on university campuses and in large cities. Earth Day went on to become an annual event.

A lesser-known Earth Day was initiated in 1970 by John McConnell (1915–2012), a peace activist. It was often called the equinox Earth Day because it was celebrated on the vernal equinox (March 21, the first day of spring in the Northern Hemisphere). The United Nations (UN) traditionally celebrated the equinox Earth Day with the ringing of a peace bell. In April 2009 the UN General Assembly officially declared April 22 of each year to be International Mother Earth Day.

RADICAL ENVIRONMENTALISM. The environmental movement inspired some adherents to engage in acts of civil disobedience, such as by chaining themselves to trees that were going to be cut down. More radical actions including sabotage and the destruction of property have also taken place. These acts are known broadly as ecoterrorism or ecotage. Since the late 1970s several environmental groups have allegedly engaged in ecoterrorism, including the Environmental Life Force, the Sea Shepherd Conservation Society, Earth First, the Earth Liberation Front (ELF), and the Animal Liberation Front (ALF).

The ELF and the ALF are perhaps the most active and well-known of the groups. In February 2002 James F. Jarboe of the Federal Bureau of Investigation (FBI; http://www.fbi.gov/news/testimony/the-threat-of-eco-terrorism) testified before the U.S. House of Representatives, Resources Committee, Subcommittee on Forests and Forest Health, noting, "During the past several years, special interest extremism, as characterized by the Animal Liberation Front (ALF) and the Earth Liberation Front (ELF), has emerged as a serious terrorist threat." Officials suggest that the ELF and the ALF are not so much organizations as an ideology with which many ecoterrorists claim allegiance. The letters "ELF" are often found spray painted near sites that are suspected of being victimized by ecoterrorists. New luxury housing developments in or near sensitive environments have been a frequent target of such crimes. One of the most famous cases occurred in 1998, when arsonists set fire to the Vail Ski Resort in Vail, Colorado. In "Eco-terror Indictments" (January 20, 2006, http://www.fbi.gov/news/stories/2006/january/elf012006), the FBI indicates the attack did $12 million in damages. In a May 2004 hearing before the U.S. Senate Committee on the Judiciary, John E. Lewis (http://www.fbi.gov/news/testimony/animal-rights-extremism-and-ecoterrorism), the deputy assistant director of the FBI, stated, "The FBI estimates that the ALF/ELF and related groups have committed more than 1,100 criminal acts in the United States since 1976, resulting in damages conservatively estimated at approximately $110 million."

In 2004 the FBI launched Operation Backfire, a comprehensive and focused investigation of suspected ecoterrorists. According to the bureau, in "Putting Intel to Work: Against ELF and ALF Terrorists" (June 30, 2008, http://www.fbi.gov/news/stories/2008/june/ecoterror_063008), by 2008 the FBI had obtained indictments against 30 people. As of November 2015, two people believed to be affiliated with the ELF/ALF were listed on the FBI's "wanted" website (http://www.fbi.gov/wanted/dt) for domestic terrorism: Joseph Mahmoud Dibee and Josephine Sunshine Overaker. Both were accused of various ecoterrorism crimes, including arson.

A Change in Attitude toward Environmentalism

Widespread public concern about the nation's serious (and obvious) environmental problems during the 1960s and 1970s pushed politicians to take decisive action. This resulted in major improvements in the condition of the environment. Many of the most dangerous chemicals that once polluted the air and water were banned or their emissions into the environment were greatly reduced. As the highly visible dangers—belching smokestacks and burning rivers—were improved, the initial zeal for environmental action began to fade.

One factor was money. The U.S. economy was booming during the 1960s and early 1970s, when environmental activism began. By the end of the 1970s, however, the economy was burdened with high unemployment and high inflation rates—problems that lasted well into the 1980s. Americans fearing for their jobs rallied against environmental restrictions, believing that the restrictions threatened their livelihood. This war of attitudes came to a head in 1990, when the northern spotted owl was declared a threatened species in the Pacific Northwest. Millions of acres of forestland were set aside as habitat for the species, and logging was banned on federal lands within the area. Loggers bitterly protested the loss of jobs, an argument that won sympathy from the American public. Although the national economy improved tremendously during the 1990s, it did not eliminate people's concerns about the potential negative effects of environmental regulations on the economy.

The impact of environmental protection on private property rights also played a role in the change in attitudes. The Endangered Species Act and the wetlands provisions of the CWA spurred a grassroots private property rights movement. Many people became concerned that these acts, as well as other legislation, allowed the government to take or devalue properties without compensation. For example, if federal regulations prohibit construction on a plot of land that is protected by law, then the landowner may feel that the government is unfairly limiting the use of his or her property. At the very least, the landowner may want government compensation for decreasing the monetary value of the land.

Partisan Politics

During the 1960s and 1970s political support for environmental issues was largely bipartisan (shared by both major political parties). However, this condition was not to last. Over the latter decades of the 20th century the Republican Party adopted a more conservative stance that embraced limited government as one of its main platforms. This position favors freer economic markets, such as through less regulation of industry and businesses. However, the nation's environmental policy had long been based on a command-and-control scheme in which the EPA established increasingly stricter regulations on industry. During the 1980s the Republican Party began arguing that this approach was too burdensome on industry because of the high compliance costs involved. It was a message that resonated with some sectors of society.

In 1990 Congress performed a major overhaul of the CAA. As is explained in Chapter 2, lawmakers incorporated new market-based programs that give businesses more options in how they achieve pollution control goals. This approach represents a major departure from the traditional command-and-control regulatory scheme. The chief outcome has been the Acid Rain Program (ARP), which is described in detail in Chapter 4. The ARP features a cap-and-trade program in which a cap or maximum limit is set for total emissions of a particular pollutant across an industry group. However, individual emitters operating below emissions limits are allowed to sell credits to other companies that are having trouble meeting the limits. An example is shown in Figure 1.2. Initially, the three plants that make up the regulated industry collectively emitted 30 tons (27.2 t). A new overall cap of 15 tons (13.6 t) was established for the industry; equating to an average limit of 5 tons (4.5 t) per plant. Plant A reduced its emissions by 5 tons, Plant B by 7 tons (6.4 t), and Plant C by 3 tons (2.7 t). Plant A met the new limit. Plant B was 2 tons (1.8 t) below the new limit and Plant C was 2 tons above the new limit. Under a cap-and-trade system Plant B could sell its 2-ton allowance to Plant C. In this way all three plants would meet the new limit overall. The ARP cap-and-trade system has proven effective at curbing the problems with acid rain that were quite evident during the 1980s.

By the 1990s many of the cheapest and easiest environmental problems to fix had already been resolved. Most of the remaining problems were so large or complicated that it was believed that tremendous amounts of money would have to be spent before even modest improvements would be realized. In a way, the environmental movement was a victim of its own success. Emerging issues, such as atmospheric ozone depletion, were less obvious and more difficult to comprehend than environmental problems of the past and aroused less widespread public passion. Nevertheless, a new era of activism was dawning and would have a profound effect on the environmental movement.

Being Green

During the 1990s new waves of social activism began emerging around the world. The so-called antiglobalism or anticapitalism movement captured headlines with demonstrations, and sometimes violent riots, during meetings of the world's industrialized countries, including a summit of the World Trade Organization in Seattle,

FIGURE 1.2

Diagram of cap-and-trade scheme

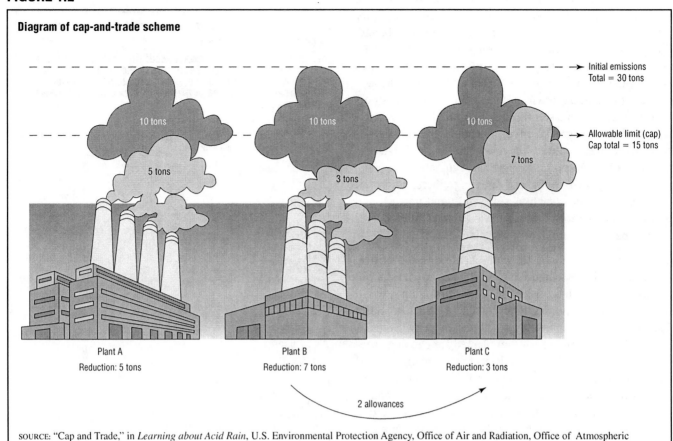

SOURCE: "Cap and Trade," in *Learning about Acid Rain*, U.S. Environmental Protection Agency, Office of Air and Radiation, Office of Atmospheric Programs, Clean Air Markets Division, April 2008, http://www.epa.gov/acidrain/education/teachersguide.pdf (accessed August 28, 2015)

Washington, in 1999. The movement presented a variety of grievances involving environmental, labor, and social issues. At the same time, public awareness was growing about an emerging environmental problem called global warming. As is explained in Chapter 3, a scientific consensus slowly developed that human-related emissions of carbon dioxide and other gases (primarily from the burning of fossil fuels) were causing the atmosphere to hold too much heat and raising the earth's temperature. Concern rose that continued global warming could have climatic consequences, including rising sea levels, stronger storms, and habitat loss and extinction.

In 1997 many countries joined the Kyoto Protocol to the UN Framework on Climate Change (UNFCC), an international agreement brokered by the UN, in which carbon emissions limits were placed on some countries. The U.S. government refused to enter into the agreement because the emissions from China and India—two of the United States' biggest economic competitors—were not limited. This failure by some countries to hold themselves to higher environmental standards while expecting the United States to do so inflamed antienvironmental sentiment in the United States. As is explained in Chapter 3, U.S. politicians feared that the international agreement would place an undue economic burden on the United

States. These concerns were strengthened during the latter years of the first decade of the 21st century, when the Great Recession weakened the U.S. economy.

In 2004 the movie *The Day after Tomorrow* dramatized the disastrous consequences of unchecked global warming. Two years later the former vice president Albert Gore Jr. (1948–) released the book *An Inconvenient Truth: The Planetary Emergency of Global Warming and What We Can Do about It*, which reached number one on the *New York Times* best-seller list. A companion documentary film was also highly successful and significantly raised public awareness about the issue.

By that point global warming and climate change had firmly installed some new concepts to the environmental movement:

- Carbon footprint—the amount of carbon that is emitted into the environment by a particular activity

- Carbon offsetting—reducing one's carbon footprint by taking action to reduce carbon emissions, such as by planting trees (growing, healthy trees biologically soak up carbon dioxide from the atmosphere)

- Carbon neutral—a condition in which an activity's carbon footprint is completely offset

Carbon offsetting or reducing one's carbon footprint became a popular activity for many people who were concerned about the consequences of climate change. Companies and organizations sprang up that offered customers opportunities to purchase offsetting options (such as tree plantings). During the 1990s and the first decade of the 21st century environmentalism at the grassroots level was also expressed through two other means: recycling and buying green (environmentally friendly) products. Examples include recycled-content and energy-saving goods, natural (as opposed to synthetic) products, organically grown foods and clothing fibers, nonfossil fuel energy sources (such as solar and wind power), and ecotourism (vacations that are designed to minimize negative impact on ecologically sensitive areas).

Green consumerism has both champions and critics. Advocates believe it helps raise public awareness about environmental issues and is a good first step toward achieving social and political change. Detractors claim that consumerism in itself is bad for the environment. Economic development is often blamed for causing environmental problems. As a result, there is growing support for sustainability, which is the result of economic development that does not harm the environment (or society). The goal of environmental sustainability is to ensure that natural resources are not irreversibly destroyed, but maintained and even enhanced for the future. The recycling of paper to prevent the destruction of trees is an example of sustainability.

ENVIRONMENTALISM IN THE 21ST CENTURY

Competing national priorities and deeply divisive political partisanship have shaped U.S. policy on multiple issues since the turn of the 21st century. The terrorist attacks of September 11, 2001, and the subsequent wars in Iraq and Afghanistan greatly heightened security concerns and federal spending on national defense. The Great Recession, which plagued the country from 2007 through 2009, brought historically high unemployment rates and lingering financial woes. Energy challenges, including high prices and controversy over how best to ensure the nation's energy security, also preoccupied the nation. As is explained in Chapter 11, domestic energy production has environmental consequences. This is true for established technologies, such as offshore drilling, and for newer methods, such as hydraulic fracturing. The reality is that the nation's environmental protection goals continue to come into conflict with economic and energy security goals.

The Gallup Organization conducts polling to gauge U.S. public opinion on various environmental issues. In polls dating back to 1984 Gallup has asked respondents to choose whether environmental protection or economic growth should take priority when the two conflict. As

TABLE 1.1

Public opinion on whether the environment or the economy should be given priority, 1984–2015

WITH WHICH ONE OF THESE STATEMENTS ABOUT THE ENVIRONMENT AND THE ECONOMY DO YOU MOST AGREE—PROTECTION OF THE ENVIRONMENT SHOULD BE GIVEN PRIORITY, EVEN AT THE RISK OF CURBING ECONOMIC GROWTH (OR) ECONOMIC GROWTH SHOULD BE GIVEN PRIORITY, EVEN IF THE ENVIRONMENT SUFFERS TO SOME EXTENT?

	Environment	Economic growth	Equal priority (vol.)	No opinion
	%	%	%	%
2015 Mar 5–8	46	42	6	5
2014 Mar 6–9	50	41	4	5
2013 Mar 7–10	43	48	4	5
2012 Mar 8–11	41	49	6	4
2011 Mar 3–6	36	54	6	4
2010 Mar 24–25	50	43	4	3
2010 Mar 4–7	38	53	4	5
2009 Mar 5–8	42	51	5	3
2008 Mar 6–9	49	42	5	3
2007 Mar 11–14	55	37	4	4
2006 Mar 13–16	52	37	6	4
2005 Mar 7–10	53	36	7	4
2004 Mar 8–11	49	44	4	3
2003 Mar 3–5	47	42	7	4
2002 Mar 4–7	54	36	5	5
2001 Mar 5–7	57	33	6	4
2000 Apr 3–9	67	28	2	3
2000 Jan 13–16	70	23	—	7
1999 Apr 13–14	67	28	—	5
1999 Mar 12–14	65	30	—	5
1998 Apr 17–19	68	24	—	8
1997 Jul 25–27	66	27	—	7
1995 Apr 17–19	62	32	—	6
1992 Jan 5–Mar 31	58	26	8	8
1991 Apr 11–14	71	20	—	9
1990 Apr 5–8	71	19	—	10
1984 Sep 28–Oct 1	61	28	—	11

—No responses.

SOURCE: "With which one of these statements about the environment and the economy do you most agree—protection of the environment should be given priority, even at the risk of curbing economic growth (or) economic growth should be given priority, even if the environment suffers to some extent?" in *Environment*, The Gallup Organization, 2015, http://www.gallup.com/poll/1615/Environment.aspx#1 (accessed August 28, 2015). Copyright © 2015 Gallup, Inc. All rights reserved. The content is used with permission; however, Gallup retains all rights of republication.

shown in Table 1.1, environmental protection was the clear favorite for more than two decades. However, during the latter half of the first decade of the 21st century public opinion began to shift. In 2009 economic growth was named the preferred objective for the first time. In 2015 the two goals had near equal preference, with 42% of respondents choosing economic growth and 46% choosing environmental protection.

Since 2001 Gallup pollsters have posed a similar question pitting environmental protection against development of domestic energy supplies, such as oil, gas, and coal. (See Table 1.2.) The results indicate that environmental protection was the favorite (but not by much) until early 2009. Thereafter, public opinion went back and forth between the two objectives. In 2015 environmental protection had the support of 49% of respondents, compared with 39% of respondents who supported development of U.S. energy supplies.

Gallup finds that concern about the quality of the environment ranks very low in comparison with other national problems. In *Racism Edges Up Again as Most Important U.S. Problem* (July 16, 2015, http://www.gallup.com/poll/184193/racism-edges-again-important-problem.aspx), Rebecca Riffkin of the Gallup Organization notes that a July 2015 poll found "environment/pollution" ranked 16th out of 17 national problems named by Americans. The list was dominated by concerns about the economy, government, and race relations.

In March 2015 Gallup asked poll participants to rate specific environmental issues in regards to the amount of concern they personally feel about them: a great deal, a fair amount, only a little, or none at all. As shown in Table 1.3, pollution of drinking water had the highest percentage of respondents expressing a great deal of concern. It topped the list with 55%, followed by pollution of rivers, lakes, and reservoirs

with 47%. In general, water-related issues garnered the most amount of concern in 2015.

The Political Party Divide

Although Republicans and Democrats differ on many principles, the divide on environmental issues is particularly wide. As stated earlier and shown in Table 1.2, in 2015 Gallup pollsters found that 49% of Americans favored environmental protection over development of U.S. energy supplies when the two are in conflict. Table 1.4 shows the responses broken down by political party identification. Republicans favored

TABLE 1.2

Public opinion on whether the environment or energy production should be given priority, 2001–15

WITH WHICH ONE OF THESE STATEMENTS ABOUT THE ENVIRONMENT AND ENERGY PRODUCTION DO YOU MOST AGREE—[ROTATED: PROTECTION OF THE ENVIRONMENT SHOULD BE GIVEN PRIORITY, EVEN AT THE RISK OF LIMITING THE AMOUNT OF ENERGY SUPPLIES—SUCH AS OIL, GAS, AND COAL—WHICH THE UNITED STATES PRODUCES (OR) DEVELOPMENT OF U.S. ENERGY SUPPLIES—SUCH AS OIL, GAS, AND COAL—SHOULD BE GIVEN PRIORITY, EVEN IF THE ENVIRONMENT SUFFERS TO SOME EXTENT]?

	Environment	Development of U.S. energy supplies	Both equally (vol.)	Neither/ other (vol.)	No opinion
	%	%	%	%	%
2015 Mar 5–8	49	39	4	2	5
2014 Mar 6–9	51	40	4	2	3
2013 Mar 7–10	45	46	3	3	3
2012 Mar 8–11	44	47	3	2	4
2011 Mar 3–6	41	50	4	1	4
2010 May 24–25	55	39	3	1	2
2010 Mar 4–7	43	50	2	2	3
2009 Mar 5–8	47	46	3	1	3
2008 Mar 6–9	50	41	4	2	3
2007 Mar 11–14	58	34	3	2	3
2006 Mar 13–16	49	42	4	2	3
2005 Mar 7–10	52	39	4	2	3
2004 Mar 8–11	48	44	3	1	4
2003 Mar 3–5	49	40	5	2	4
2002 Mar 4–7	52	40	3	2	3
2001 Mar 5–7	52	36	6	2	4

SOURCE: "With which one of these statements about the environment and energy production do you most agree—[ROTATED: protection of the environment should be given priority, even at the risk of limiting the amount of energy supplies—such as oil, gas, and coal—which the United States produces (or) development of U.S. energy supplies—such as oil, gas, and coal—should be given priority, even if the environment suffers to some extent]?" in *Environment*, The Gallup Organization, 2015, http://www.gallup.com/poll/1615/Environment.aspx#1 (accessed August 28, 2015). Copyright © 2015 Gallup, Inc. All rights reserved. The content is used with permission; however, Gallup retains all rights of republication.

TABLE 1.3

Poll respondents expressing their level of worry regarding environmental problems, March 2015

2015 Mar 5–8 (sorted by "a great deal")	Great deal	Fair amount	Only a little/not at all
Pollution of drinking water	55	22	23
Pollution of rivers, lakes, and reservoirs	47	32	21
Air pollution	38	33	29
Extinction of plant and animal species	36	28	36
The loss of tropical rain forests	33	30	37
Global warming/global warming or climate change	32	23	45

SOURCE: Jeff Jones and Lydia Saad, "I'm going to read you a list of environmental problems. As I read each one, please tell me if you personally worry about this problem a great deal, a fair amount, only a little, or not at all. First, how much do you personally worry about—[RANDOM ORDER]?" in *Gallup Poll Social Series: Environment—Final Topline*, The Gallup Organization, March 5–8, 2015, http://www.gallup.com/file/poll/182111/150325EnviroWorries.pdf (accessed August 28, 2015). Copyright © 2015 Gallup, Inc. All rights reserved. The content is used with permission; however, Gallup retains all rights of republication.

TABLE 1.4

Public opinion on whether the environment or energy production should be given priority, by political party, March 2015

WITH WHICH ONE OF THESE STATEMENTS ABOUT THE ENVIRONMENT AND ENERGY PRODUCTION DO YOU MOST AGREE—[ROTATED: PROTECTION OF THE ENVIRONMENT SHOULD BE GIVEN PRIORITY, EVEN AT THE RISK OF LIMITING THE AMOUNT OF ENERGY SUPPLIES—SUCH AS OIL, GAS AND COAL—WHICH THE UNITED STATES PRODUCES (OR) DEVELOPMENT OF U.S. ENERGY SUPPLIES—SUCH AS OIL, GAS AND COAL—SHOULD BE GIVEN PRIORITY, EVEN IF THE ENVIRONMENT SUFFERS TO SOME EXTENT]?

	Environment	Development of U.S. energy supplies
	%	%
Democrats	72	18
Independents	48	39
Republicans	27	62

SOURCE: Andrew Dugan, "Environment vs. Energy Trade-Off, by Party Identification," in *Americans Choose the Environment over Energy Development*, The Gallup Organization, April 13, 2015, http://www.gallup.com/poll/182402/americans-choose-environment-energy-development.aspx?utm_source=environment&utm_medium=search&utm_campaign=tiles (accessed August 28, 2015). Copyright © 2015 Gallup, Inc. All rights reserved. The content is used with permission; however, Gallup retains all rights of republication.

development of U.S. energy supplies (62%) by a large margin over environmental protection (27%). Independents leaned toward environmental protection, but only by nine percentage points. By contrast, Democrats strongly preferred environmental protection (72%) over development of U.S. energy supplies (18%).

Gallup has asked Americans to rate the overall quality of the U.S. environment as excellent, good, only fair, or poor. As shown in Figure 1.3, between 2001 and 2015, 39% to 50% of respondents rated the environment as excellent or good each year. In 2015 the value was 50%. However, there were sharp differences between members of differing political parties. In 2015, 62% of Republicans said the environment was in excellent or good condition, compared with 40% of Democrats. (See Figure 1.4.) Overall, 44% to 66% of Republicans asked each year between 2001 and 2015 held this high opinion of the quality of the environment, compared with only 14% to 42% of Democrats. There is a noticeable dip in the data in 2008, when only 44% of Republicans, 24% of independents, and 14% of Democrats gave the environment an excellent or good rating. Since 2008 poll participants—particularly Democrats—have had more favorable views on the quality of the environment.

Gallup has occasionally gauged public opinion regarding the appropriateness of government action on environmental protection. In 1992, when respondents were first asked about this topic, 68% said the government was doing too little to protect the environment, 26% said government action was about right, and 4% said the government was doing too much. (See Table 1.5.) Over time, lower percentages said the government was doing too little for the environment. For example, in 2015 just under half (48%) of the respondents shared this view. Around one-third (34%) said the government was doing about the right amount, and 16% said the government was doing too much. As noted earlier, Republicans, particularly conservative Republicans, believe in limited government. In 2015 only 30% of Republicans thought the government was doing too little to protect the environment, compared with 64% of Democrats. (See Figure 1.5.)

In earlier polls, Gallup asked participants their opinion on specific pollution control measures. According to Frank Newport of the Gallup Organization, in *Smaller Majorities in U.S. Favor Gov't Pollution Controls* (June 4, 2014, http://www.gallup.com/poll/170885/smaller-majorities-favor-gov-pollution-controls.aspx), in 2014 nearly two-thirds (65%) of Americans favored "setting higher emissions and pollution standards for business and industry." Support was down considerably from the first decade of the 21st century, when 77% to 84% of those asked between 2001 and 2007 favored this measure. Also, in 2014, 63% of respondents expressed support for "imposing mandatory controls on carbon dioxide emissions and other greenhouse gases." These gases are widely believed by scientists to contribute to

FIGURE 1.3

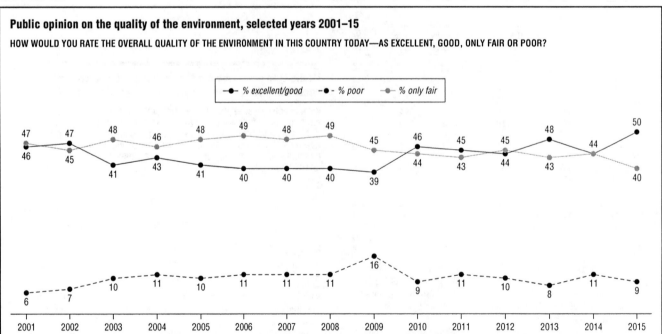

Public opinion on the quality of the environment, selected years 2001–15

HOW WOULD YOU RATE THE OVERALL QUALITY OF THE ENVIRONMENT IN THIS COUNTRY TODAY—AS EXCELLENT, GOOD, ONLY FAIR OR POOR?

SOURCE: Rebecca Riffkin, "Views of the Quality of the Environment Highest since 2001," in *Americans' Rating of Environment Inches up to Record High*, The Gallup Organization, March 24, 2015, http://www.gallup.com/poll/182108/americans-rating-environment-inches-record-high.aspx?utm_source=environment&utm_medium=search&utm_campaign=tiles (accessed August 28, 2015). Copyright © 2015 Gallup, Inc. All rights reserved. The content is used with permission; however, Gallup retains all rights of republication.

FIGURE 1.4

Poll respondents rating the quality of the environment as excellent or good, by political party, selected years 2001–15

HOW WOULD YOU RATE THE OVERALL QUALITY OF THE ENVIRONMENT IN THIS COUNTRY TODAY—AS EXCELLENT, GOOD, ONLY FAIR OR POOR? (% EXCELLENT/GOOD)

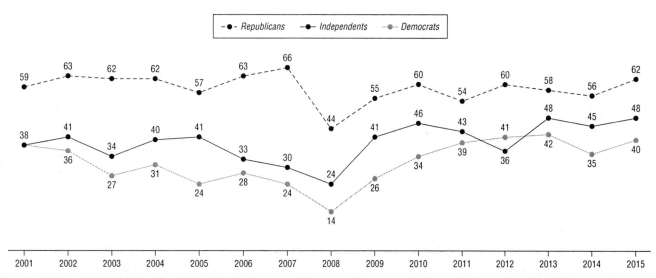

SOURCE: Rebecca Riffkin, "Views of the Quality of the Environment—by Party ID," in *Americans' Rating of Environment Inches up to Record High,* The Gallup Organization, March 24, 2015, http://www.gallup.com/poll/182108/americans-rating-environment-inches-record-high.aspx?utm_source= environment&utm_medium=search&utm_campaign=tiles (accessed August 28, 2015). Copyright © 2015 Gallup, Inc. All rights reserved. The content is used with permission; however, Gallup retains all rights of republication.

TABLE 1.5

Public opinion on the adequacy of the government's environmental protection measures, selected years 1992–2015

DO YOU THINK THE U.S. GOVERNMENT IS DOING TOO MUCH, TOO LITTLE, OR ABOUT THE RIGHT AMOUNT IN TERMS OF PROTECTING THE ENVIRONMENT?

	Too much	Too little	About the right amount	No opinion
	%	%	%	%
2015 Mar 5–8	16	48	34	1
2014 Mar 6–9	17	48	34	1
2013 Mar 7–10	16	47	35	2
2012 Mar 8–11	17	51	30	2
2011 Mar 3–6	16	49	33	2
2010 Mar 4–7	15	46	35	4
2006 Mar 13–16*	4	62	33	1
2005 Mar 7–10*	5	58	34	3
2004 Mar 8–11*	5	55	37	3
2003 Mar 3–5*	7	51	37	5
2000 Apr 3–9	10	58	30	2
1992 Jan 5–Mar 31	4	68	26	2

*Asked of a half sample.

SOURCE: "Do you think the U.S. government is doing too much, too little, or about the right amount in terms of protecting the environment?" in *Environment*, The Gallup Organization, 2015, http://www.gallup.com/poll/1615/Environment.aspx#1 (accessed August 28, 2015). Copyright © 2015 Gallup, Inc. All rights reserved. The content is used with permission; however, Gallup retains all rights of republication.

global warming. There was greater support for controls on these gases between 2003 and 2007, when 75% to 79% favored such a measure. Newport notes that support for both measures dropped considerably between 2007 and 2014, possibly because of economic concerns and the election of President Barack Obama (1961–), a Democrat. Newport suggests that "some Americans may be less likely to favor government regulation of the environment when a Democrat, rather than a Republican, is in office."

Science and Environmental Protection

U.S. environmental policies and decisions are supposed to be based on science. For example, the CAA states, "Air quality criteria for an air pollutant shall accurately reflect the latest scientific knowledge." Thus, the EPA and other environmental agencies rely on scientific data to craft their approaches to solving environmental problems. However, in reality science does not always provide clear black-and-white answers on issues; there can be many caveats, conditions, and levels of uncertainty attached to scientific findings. Thus, the ways in which the findings are interpreted and used to set policy become paramount concerns.

U.S. environmental regulation is based on risk analysis, or more specifically risk-benefit analysis, which at its simplest is a scientific assessment of the risk of something and the benefits that could be achieved by reducing or even eliminating the risk. In theory, the exercise can provide stark choices. For example, the environment would clearly benefit if all pollutant discharges, no matter how small, were outlawed. Numerous benefits to

FIGURE 1.5

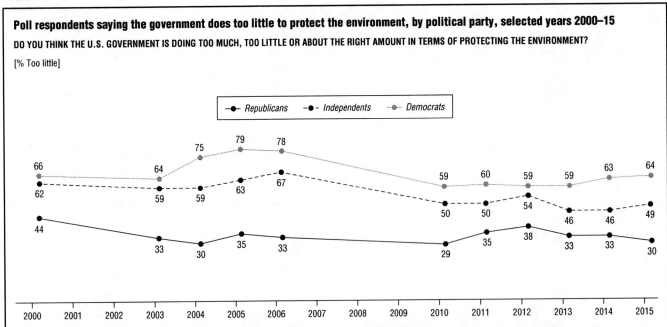

Poll respondents saying the government does too little to protect the environment, by political party, selected years 2000–15

DO YOU THINK THE U.S. GOVERNMENT IS DOING TOO MUCH, TOO LITTLE OR ABOUT THE RIGHT AMOUNT IN TERMS OF PROTECTING THE ENVIRONMENT?

[% Too little]

● Republicans   ● Independents   ● Democrats

environmental quality and public health would result. However, the regulatory and economic burden to society would be massive. Policy makers seek compromise solutions that are based on sound science and reduce risks and therefore reap benefits, but minimize undesirable consequences. This is a very challenging undertaking. In addition, environmental policy decisions are not made in a political vacuum; political considerations influence which environmental problems receive priority and which do not.

This is particularly true for global warming. As is described in Chapter 3, there is widespread international scientific consensus that climate change, in part due to global warming, is caused by human activities, particularly the burning of fossil fuels. As a result, policy makers around the world (particularly in Europe) have focused on reducing emissions that are believed to cause global warming. These decision makers find that the scientific knowledge on the subject convincingly illuminates the risks of the emissions to the world's climate and public health. They believe the benefits of taking aggressive action against global warming outweigh the economic consequences of doing so. U.S. policy makers have been far less likely to share this thinking.

DDT REVISITED. Since the 1962 publication of *Silent Spring*, scientific studies have provided much new (and sometimes conflicting) information on the environmental and human health risks of DDT. For example, some studies indicate that DDT causes thinning of bird eggshells and link it to cancer in humans. Other studies, however, contradict or limit these findings. What is known for certain is that DDT effectively kills the mosquitoes that can carry malaria, a serious and often deadly disease. In "Elimination of Malaria in the United States (1947–1951)" (November 9, 2012, http://www.cdc.gov/malaria/about/history/elimination_us.html), the Centers for Disease Control and Prevention (CDC) notes that malaria once plagued mosquito-ridden areas of the U.S. South and territorial islands. The disease was eliminated in the United States during the late 1940s and early 1950s by widespread use of DDT. However, other areas of the world have continued to suffer. According to the CDC (August 17, 2015, http://www.cdc.gov/Malaria), in 2013 an estimated 198 million cases of malaria occurred worldwide, and 500,000 people died from it, mostly children in Africa. The volume of human suffering and the evolving scientific knowledge about DDT have combined to change some opinions about the risk-benefit analysis of the pesticide.

For example, in 2006 the World Health Organization (WHO) and the UN began re-promoting DDT for use in combating malaria after many years of opposing the pesticide. The WHO notes in the press release "Reversing Its Policy, UN Agency Promotes DDT to Combat the Scourge of Malaria" (September 15, 2006, http://www.un.org/apps/news/story.asp?NewsID=19855#.Uf-KK5LlYy4) that "extensive research and testing has since demonstrated that well-managed indoor residual spraying programmes using DDT pose no harm to wildlife or to humans."

The Status of Environmental Protection

In subsequent chapters the various factors that shape U.S. policies on environmental protection for specific resources, such as air and water, are examined in depth. Overall, there are three interacting forces that greatly affect policy decisions in the 21st century: legislation, litigation, and political priorities.

Most of the major environmental laws were written many decades ago and have not been substantially changed in years. For example, the last major amendments to the CAA took place in 1990. Thus, the laws reflect the environmental priorities and goals of their times. In some cases the goals have proven difficult to achieve given the political and economic realities that have developed. In *Clean Air Act: EPA Should Improve the Management of Its Air Toxics Program* (June 2006, http://www.gao.gov/new.items/d06669.pdf), the U.S. Government Accountability Office (GAO) describes the ambitious goals laid out in the 1990 CAA amendments for the nation's hazardous air pollutants (or air toxics) program. Nearly 200 air toxins emitted by tens of thousands of facilities in hundreds of different industries around the country are to be regulated. The GAO notes that the EPA has been very slow at issuing the regulations and meeting the deadlines laid out in the act, in part, because of budget constraints and lack of resources.

The major environmental laws assign many specific tasks to the EPA and lay out deadlines that Congress set for the agency to meet. When the EPA fails to do so, the citizen lawsuit provisions of the acts allow parties to sue the agency. As a result, litigation has become a major driving factor behind EPA actions. Environmental groups are often the plaintiffs in these cases, but the states also litigate against the EPA when they have competing interests. For example, Chapter 3 describes the long legal battle that California waged against the federal government to set tougher carbon emissions and fuel economy standards than those desired by the EPA. The EPA maintains a website (http://www.epa.gov/ogc/noi.html) that lists the notices the agency has received regarding intents to sue the EPA over alleged failures to perform acts or duties required by law.

Of course, not all litigation against the EPA is driven by the desire for tougher environmental protection. Industry groups and states also sue the agency seeking to prevent control measures from being put into place. Numerous such lawsuits are discussed in subsequent chapters. For example, Chapter 9 describes how 31 states sued the EPA in 2015 over the Clean Water Rule, a regulation that would expand the types of water bodies that are subject to the CWA. It should be noted that the vast majority of the states that were party to the lawsuits had Republican governors.

As described earlier, environmental policy making is often characterized by political partisanship. Republicans and Democrats have sharply differing views on many environmental issues. As of November 2015, two presidents had served during the 21st century. George W. Bush (1946–), a Republican, was in office from January 2001 through January 2009. He was succeeded by Obama (1961–), a Democrat, who was in office as of November 2015. The environmental policies of both presidents represent, in general, the views of their primary voting blocs. Bush's policies reflected the limited government and free-market approach favored by Republicans. As such, the EPA under his administration was subject to extreme criticism by environmental advocates. By the last full year (2008) of Bush's second term in office, Gallup polls show that the American public had a fairly negative view about the quality of the nation's environment. As shown in Figure 1.4, in 2008 historically low percentages of Republicans (44%), independents (24%), and Democrats (14%) rated environmental quality as excellent or good. Overall, only about a quarter of all respondents in 2006, 2007, and 2008 thought the quality of the nation's environment was "getting better." (See Figure 1.6.)

Environmental advocates had high hopes that Obama would usher in a "green revolution," including aggressive actions against global warming. Obama's policies have reflected the traditional command-and-control approach favored by Democrats. However, he has made concessions based on the nation's economic conditions. For example, in 2010 the EPA proposed stricter air quality standards for ozone. This proposal elicited fierce political opposition from Republican leaders, who argued it would place a financial burden on industry and lead to layoffs. Such arguments were particularly persuasive as the nation struggled to recover from the lingering effects of the Great Recession. Obama withdrew the proposal, greatly disappointing environmental advocates. In 2015, with the economy improving, the EPA finally implemented the stricter standards, which are described in Chapter 2.

In general, Gallup polls show that opinions about the quality of the nation's environment, especially among independents and Democrats, improved dramatically after Obama took office in 2009. (See Figure 1.4 and Figure 1.7.) In 2015, 62% of Republicans, 48% of independents, and 40% of Democrats rated the quality of the nation's environment as excellent or good. (See Figure 1.4.) Overall, 41% of Americans polled in 2015 said the quality of the nation's environment is "getting better," whereas 51% said it is "getting worse." (See Figure 1.6.) Although the percentage rating the environment as "getting worse" was higher than the percentage

Public opinion on whether the nation's environment as a whole is getting better or getting worse, 2001–15

RIGHT NOW, DO YOU THINK THE QUALITY OF THE ENVIRONMENT IN THE COUNTRY AS A WHOLE IS GETTING BETTER OR GETTING WORSE?

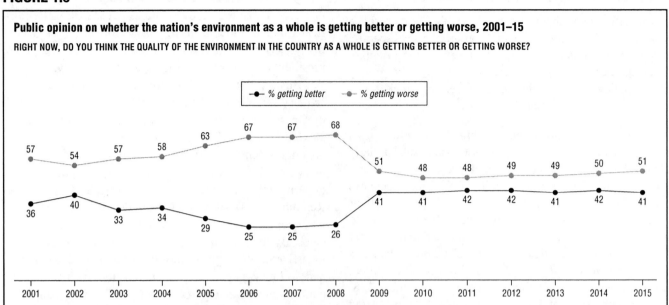

SOURCE: Rebecca Riffkin, "Views of the Outlook of the Environment Stable since 2009," in *Americans' Rating of Environment Inches up to Record High*, The Gallup Organization, March 24, 2015, http://www.gallup.com/poll/182108/americans-rating-environment-inches-record-high.aspx?utm_source= environment&utm_medium=search&utm_campaign=tiles (accessed August 28, 2015). Copyright © 2015 Gallup, Inc. All rights reserved. The content is used with permission; however, Gallup retains all rights of republication.

Poll respondents saying the environment is getting better, by political party, selected years 2001–15

RIGHT NOW, DO YOU THINK THE QUALITY OF THE ENVIRONMENT IN THE COUNTRY AS A WHOLE IS GETTING BETTER OR GETTING WORSE?

[% Getting better]

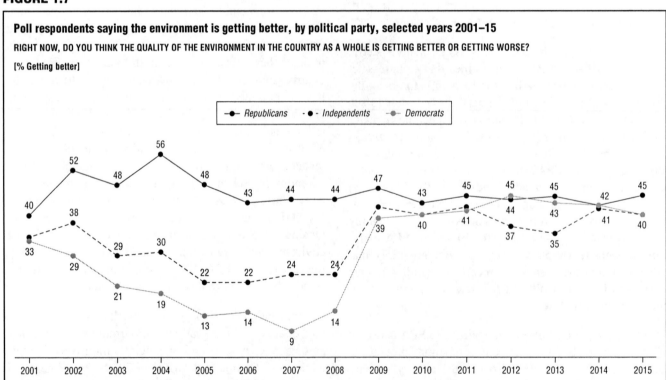

SOURCE: Rebecca Riffkin, "Views of the Outlook of the Environment—by Party ID," in *Americans' Rating of Environment Inches up to Record High*, The Gallup Organization, March 24, 2015, http://www.gallup.com/poll/182108/americans-rating-environment-inches-record-high.aspx?utm_source= environment&utm_medium=search&utm_campaign=tiles (accessed August 28, 2015). Copyright © 2015 Gallup, Inc. All rights reserved. The content is used with permission; however, Gallup retains all rights of republication.

rating the environment as "getting better," the values indicate greater optimism about the nation's environment in 2015 than between 2001 and 2008 (the years of the Bush administration).

The EPA's Budget

Early each year (usually in February) the president presents to Congress a proposed budget request for the federal government for the upcoming fiscal year (FY), which lasts from October 1 (of that year) to September 30 (of the next year). It can take Congress many months and sometimes over a year to approve budget. Figure 1.8 shows the EPA's enacted budgets for FYs 2004 to 2015 and Obama's budget request for FY 2016. In general, the agency's enacted budget was in the range of $7.5 billion to $8.7 billion per year during this period. The exception was FY 2010, which had a budget of $10.3 billion.

The president's budget request for FY 2016 was $8.6 billion. The amount is broken down by broad agency goal in Figure 1.9. Overall, the largest chunk of the budget ($4.1 billion or 47.2%) was devoted to protecting the nation's water resources. The next two largest expenditures were for cleaning up communities ($2 billion or 22.7%) and taking action on climate change and improving air quality ($1.1 billion or 13%). Table 1.6 shows the budget request broken down by expense category. More than two-fifths ($3.6 billion or 41.9%) of the total was slated for state and tribal assistance grants. According to the U.S. House of Representatives, in "State and Tribal Assistance Grants" (2012,

http://thomas.loc.gov/cgi-bin/cpquery/?&sid=cp112IbClz &r_n=hr151.112&dbname=cp112&&sel=TOC_258258&), the grants provide funding for infrastructure projects, primarily at the local level, that support environmental protection and for environmental programs operated by state and tribal governments.

THE INTERNATIONAL RESPONSE TO ENVIRONMENTAL PROBLEMS

Environmental issues have never been neatly bound by national borders. Activities taking place in one country often affect the environment of other countries, if not that of the entire planet. In fact, many of the most important aspects of environmental protection involve areas that are not located within any particular country, such as the oceans, or that belong to no one, such as the atmosphere. In an attempt to deal with these issues, the international community has held a number of conferences and developed many declarations, agreements, and treaties.

In 1972 the UN met in Stockholm, Sweden, for a conference on the environment. Delegates from 113 countries gathered, with each reporting the state of his or her nation's environment—forests, water, farmland,

FIGURE 1.8

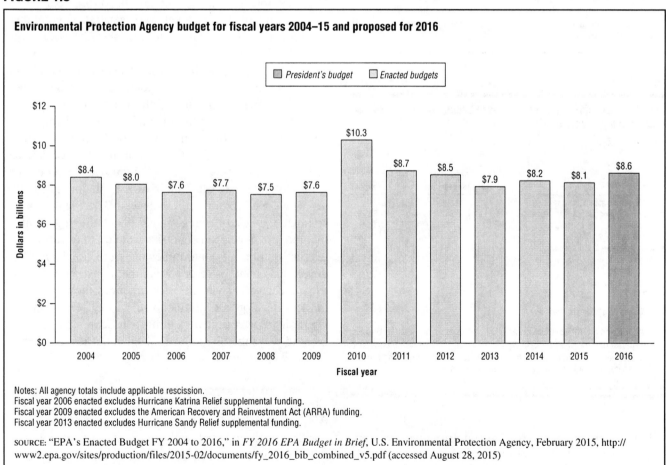

Environmental Protection Agency budget for fiscal years 2004–15 and proposed for 2016

Notes: All agency totals include applicable rescission.
Fiscal year 2006 enacted excludes Hurricane Katrina Relief supplemental funding.
Fiscal year 2009 enacted excludes the American Recovery and Reinvestment Act (ARRA) funding.
Fiscal year 2013 enacted excludes Hurricane Sandy Relief supplemental funding.

SOURCE: "EPA's Enacted Budget FY 2004 to 2016," in *FY 2016 EPA Budget in Brief*, U.S. Environmental Protection Agency, February 2015, http://www2.epa.gov/sites/production/files/2015-02/documents/fy_2016_bib_combined_v5.pdf (accessed August 28, 2015)

FIGURE 1.9

Breakdown by goal of proposed budget for the Environmental Protection Agency for fiscal year 2016

[Total agency: $8,592 million]

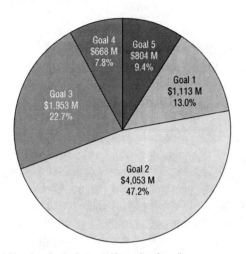

Goal 4 $668 M 7.8%
Goal 5 $804 M 9.4%
Goal 1 $1,113 M 13.0%
Goal 3 $1,953 M 22.7%
Goal 2 $4,053 M 47.2%

Goal 1: Addressing climate change and improving air quality.
Goal 2: Protecting America's waters.
Goal 3: Cleaning up communities and advancing sustainable development.
Goal 4: Ensuring the safety of chemicals and preventing pollution.
Goal 5: Protecting human health and the environment by enforcing laws and assuring compliance.

M = Million.
Note: Values do not sum to 100% due to rounding.

SOURCE: "Environmental Protection Agency's FY 2016 Budget by Goal," in *FY 2016 EPA Budget in Brief*, U.S. Environmental Protection Agency, February 2015, http://www2.epa.gov/sites/production/files/2015-02/documents/fy_2016_bib_combined_v5.pdf (accessed August 28, 2015)

TABLE 1.6

Breakdown by appropriation of proposed budget for Environmental Protection Agency for fiscal year 2016

[Total agency: $8,592 million]

	Amount in millions of dollars	Percent
State & tribal assistance grants	3,599	41.9%
Environmental programs & management	2,842	33.1%
Superfund	1,154	13.4%
Science & technology	769	9.0%
Leaking underground storage tanks	95	1.1%
Buildings & facilities	52	0.6%
Inspector general	50	0.6%
Inland oil spill programs	23	0.3%
eManifest	7	0.1%

Notes: Values do not sum to 100% due to rounding.

SOURCE: Adapted from "Environmental Protection Agency's FY 2016 Budget by Appropriation," in *FY 2016 EPA Budget in Brief*, U.S. Environmental Protection Agency, February 2015, http://www2.epa.gov/sites/production/files/2015-02/documents/fy_2016_bib_combined_v5.pdf (accessed August 28, 2015)

and other natural resources. The countries that were represented essentially fell into two groups. The industrialized countries were primarily concerned about how to protect the environment by preventing pollution and overpopulation and conserving natural resources. The less developed countries were more concerned about problems of widespread hunger, disease, and poverty that they all faced. They did consider the environment important, however, and were willing to protect it as long as doing so did not have a major negative economic impact on their citizens.

By the end of the two-week meeting, the delegates had agreed that the human environment had to be protected, even as industrialization proceeded in the less developed countries. They established the UN Environment Programme (UNEP), which included Earthwatch, a program to monitor changes in the physical and biological resources of the earth. The most important outcome of the conference was awareness of the earth's ecology as a whole. For the first time in global history, the environmental problems of both rich and poor nations were put into perspective. General agreement emerged to protect natural resources, to encourage family planning and population control, and to protect against the negative effects of industrialization.

Since the 1972 conference, hundreds of environmental treaties and agreements have been signed. The United States is a party to most of them; one major exception is the Kyoto Protocol to the UNFCC. The international and U.S. positions on this agreement related to global warming are explained in Chapter 3. In general, international agreements have had limited success at effecting environmental improvements worldwide. Part of the problem lies in differing opinions about what roles should be played by developed and developing countries. Less developed countries are generally unwilling to alter their laws and economy to end environmentally destructive ways, because a shift to environmentally friendly practices would be too expensive, they claim, for their economies to handle. In contrast, the richer, industrialized countries generally refuse to alter their own behavior unless the less developed countries do so as well. Their reason is not so much the cost of change rather than believing it unfair that the less developed countries want them to carry most of the burden of environmental protection. The less developed countries respond that the industrialized countries became rich via the very practices they now want the less developed countries to stop using. They claim it is unfair to be expected to limit their economic development in ways that the industrialized countries themselves never would have done.

ENVIRONMENTAL JUSTICE: AN EVOLVING ISSUE

The environmental justice issue stems from concerns that poor people and racial minorities are disproportionately subject to environmental hazards. The EPA

(May 24, 2012, http://www.epa.gov/environmentaljustice/basics/index.html) defines environmental justice as "fair treatment and meaningful involvement of all people regardless of race, color, national origin, or income with respect to the development, implementation, and enforcement of environmental laws, regulations, and policies."

The environmental justice movement gained national attention in 1982 with a demonstration against the construction of a hazardous waste landfill in Warren County, North Carolina, a county with a predominantly African American population. A resulting congressional study—*Siting of Hazardous Waste Landfills and Their Correlation with Racial and Economic Status of Surrounding Communities* (June 1983, http://archive.gao.gov/d48t13/121648.pdf)—found that, for three out of four landfills surveyed, African Americans made up most of the population living nearby and that at least 26% of the population in those communities was below the poverty level. In 1987 the United Church of Christ published the nationwide study *Toxic Waste and Race in the United States*, reporting that race was the most significant factor among the variables tested in determining locations of hazardous waste facilities.

In June 1992 the EPA concluded in *Environmental Equity: Reducing Risk for All Communities* (http://www3.epa.gov/environmentaljustice/resources/reports/annual-project-reports/reducing_risk_com_vol1.pdf) that racial minorities and low-income people bore a disproportionate burden of environmental risk. These groups were exposed to lead, air pollutants, hazardous waste facilities, contaminated fish, and agricultural pesticides in far greater frequencies than the general population.

Similar findings were reported by Robert D. Bullard et al. in *Toxic Wastes and Race at Twenty: 1987–2007—Grassroots Struggles to Dismantle Environmental Racism in the United States* (March 2007, http://www.ejnet.org/ej/twart.pdf). The report, which was prepared for the United Church of Christ, found that racial minorities make up the majority of the population in neighborhoods near hazardous waste facilities and that poverty rates in the neighborhoods are 1.5 times greater than the rates in nonhost neighborhoods. Bullard et al. conclude that the evidence supporting environmental racism is strong, noting that "race continues to be an independent predictor of where hazardous wastes are located, and it is a stronger predictor than income, education and other socioeconomic indicators."

According to the EPA (http://www.epa.gov/environmentaljustice/basics/ejbackground.html), the Office of Environmental Justice was established in 1992 to address environmental impacts that affect minority and low-income communities. In February 1994 President Bill Clinton (1946–) issued Executive Order 12898, Federal Actions to Address Environmental Justice in Minority Populations and Low-Income Populations (http://www.epa.gov/environmentaljustice/resources/policy/exec_order_12898.pdf), which required federal agencies to develop a comprehensive strategy for including environmental justice in their decision making. Also in 1994 the Office of Environmental Justice established a grants program to provide funds to local groups that address environmental justice issues. In "Environmental Justice Small Grants Program" (October 20, 2015, http://www3.epa.gov/environmentaljustice/grants/ej-smgrants.html), the EPA notes that it has issued more than 1,400 grants since 1994, totaling more than $26 million.

ENVIRONMENTAL EDUCATION

Many states require schools to incorporate environmental concepts, such as ecology, conservation, and environmental law, into many subjects at all grade levels. Some even require special training in environmentalism for teachers. The EPA indicates in "Environmental Education (EE) Grants" (October 21, 2015, http://www2.epa.gov/education/environmental-education-ee-grants) that since 1992 it has awarded grants to more than 3,600 projects at a cost of $2 million to $3.5 million per year.

Although the mandating of environmental education pleases environmentalists, some people have concerns. Critics claim that most environmental education in the schools is based on flawed information, biased presentations, and questionable objectives. Critics also say it leads to brainwashing and pushing a regulatory mind-set on students. Some critics contend that, at worst, impressionable children are being trained to believe that the environment is in immediate danger of catastrophe because of consumption, economic growth, and free-market capitalism.

CHAPTER 2

AIR QUALITY

THE AIR PEOPLE BREATHE

According to the U.S. Environmental Protection Agency (EPA; October 26, 2015, http://www.epa.gov/air/basic.html), the average adult breathes in more than 3,000 gallons (11,400 L) of air each day. Because air is so essential to life, it is important that it be free of pollutants. Poor air quality contributes to disease and premature death, to dying forests and lakes, and to the corrosion of stone buildings and monuments. Air quality is also important to quality of life and recreation because air pollution causes haze that decreases visibility during outdoor activities.

Air pollutants are generated by natural and anthropogenic (human-related) sources. Fossil fuels and chemicals have played a major role in society's pursuit of economic growth and higher standards of living. However, burning fossil fuels and releasing toxic chemicals into the air alter the earth's chemistry and can threaten the very air on which life depends.

Air quality plays a major and complex role in public health. Among the factors that must be considered are the levels of pollutants in the air, the levels of individual exposure to these pollutants, individual susceptibility to toxic substances, and the time of exposure that is related to the ill effects from certain substances. Blaming health effects on specific pollutants is also complicated by the health impact of nonenvironmental causes (such as heredity or poor diet).

Scientists do know that air pollution is related to a number of respiratory diseases and other problems, including bronchitis, pulmonary emphysema, lung cancer, bronchial asthma, eye irritation, weakened immune system, and premature lung tissue aging. In addition, lead contamination causes neurological and kidney disease and can be responsible for impaired fetal and mental development.

THE HISTORY OF AIR POLLUTION LEGISLATION

By the late 1940s smog had become a serious problem in many urban areas of the United States. Extensive industrial growth during World War II (1939–1945), a boom in car ownership, and unregulated outdoor burning were the primary culprits. Los Angeles, California, and other large U.S. cities suffered from smog during hot summer months. In 1952 London, England, experienced an episode of smog so severe that thousands of people prematurely died from respiratory illnesses that were aggravated by poor air quality. The incident was a wake-up call for many governments. Air pollution legislation was quickly passed in England and across Europe.

U.S. Air Pollution Legislation

In the United States concerns about smog led to the passage of the Air Pollution Control Act of 1955. It provided grants to public health agencies to research the threats posed to human health by air pollution. In 1963 the first Clean Air Act (CAA) was passed. It set aside even more grant money for research and data collection and encouraged the development of emissions standards for major sources of pollution. The act was amended several times through the remainder of the decade to expand research priorities and local air pollution control agencies and to set national emissions standards for some sources.

THE CAA OF 1970. In 1970 the CAA received a major overhaul. It required the newly established EPA to establish the National Ambient Air Quality Standards (NAAQS) for major pollutants. These standards are divided into two classes:

- Primary standards are designed to protect public health, with special focus on so-called sensitive populations, including children, the elderly, and people with chronic respiratory problems, such as asthma.

- Secondary standards are designed to protect the overall welfare of the public by reducing air pollution that impairs visibility and damages resources, such as crops, forests, animals, monuments, and buildings.

State environmental agencies have to prepare state implementation plans to show how they intend to achieve compliance with the NAAQS. Counties that consistently meet the NAAQS for a particular pollutant over several years are called attainment areas for that pollutant; counties that consistently do not meet the NAAQS over several years are called nonattainment areas. Nonattainment areas are classified into five categories: marginal, moderate, serious, severe, or extreme, depending on the air quality concentrations. Nonattainment areas can be upgraded to attainment status when air quality data improve and so long as the affected county has an EPA-approved state implementation plan in place. The upgraded areas are called maintenance areas.

The revised CAA also required the setting of National Emissions Standards for Hazardous Air Pollutants (NESHAPs) and resulted in the New Source Performance Standards. These are technology-based standards that apply when certain types of facilities are first constructed or undergo major modifications. Although the New Source Performance Standards are set by the EPA, state governments are responsible for enforcing them.

In 1977 the CAA was amended again. One major change was expansion of a program called the Prevention of Significant Deterioration. The program is designed to ensure that new facilities built in attainment areas do not significantly degrade the air quality. In addition, the amended law required the formation of an independent technical and scientific committee—the Clean Air Scientific Advisory Committee (CASAC)—to advise the EPA administrator on the setting of the NAAQS standards. The CAA also mandated that the EPA review the standards for appropriateness every five years.

THE CLEAN AIR ACT AMENDMENTS OF 1990. In 1990 the CAA was substantially revised to better address three issues of growing concern: acid rain, urban air pollution (particularly smog), and emissions of toxic air pollutants. In addition, a national permits program was established and enforcement and compliance procedures were strengthened. The revised law included new and innovative approaches to air pollution legislation. Market-based programs allow businesses more choices in how they achieve pollution control goals. Economic incentives are also included to reduce the reliance on regulations to obtain certain goals. As of November 2015, the CAA consisted of six major sections:

- Title I—Air Pollution Prevention and Control
- Title II—Emission Standards for Moving Sources

- Title III—General
- Title IV—Acid Deposition Control
- Title V—Permits
- Title VI—Stratospheric Ozone Protection

PRIORITY AIR POLLUTANTS

The EPA establishes the NAAQS for six major air pollutants:

- Carbon monoxide
- Lead
- Nitrogen dioxide
- Ozone
- Particulate matter
- Sulfur dioxide

These are called the priority or criteria pollutants and are identified as serious threats to human health. Although the EPA sets the standards for the NAAQS pollutants, it does not have the authority under the CAA to directly regulate individual emitters, such as factories. That authority belongs to the states, which develop state implementation plans to carry out and maintain the standards. The states can have stricter standards than the federal program but not more lenient ones.

The EPA has documented air pollution trends in the United States since 1970. Two kinds of trends are tracked for the priority pollutants: emissions and air quality concentrations. Emissions are calculated estimates of the total tonnage of pollutants that are released into the air annually. All the priority pollutants except ozone are emitted directly into the air. Ozone forms due to atmospheric interactions between other chemicals, mainly volatile organic compounds (VOCs), that are emitted into the air. Thus, VOCs are said to be ozone precursors, and VOC emissions are tracked rather than ozone emissions. The EPA maintains a database called the National Emissions Inventory (http://www3.epa.gov/ttn/chief/trends/index.html) that characterizes the emissions of air pollutants in the United States based on data input from state and local agencies.

Table 2.1 compares emissions of five of the principal air pollutants and VOCs for various years between 1980 and 2013. Note that fire emissions and dust are not included. The table shows that the emissions of common pollutants and their precursors declined between 1980 and 2013. Nonetheless, the EPA estimates that in 2013 approximately 94 million tons (85.3 million t) of the air pollutants were emitted into the atmosphere in the United States.

The EPA also tracks air quality concentrations based on data collected at thousands of monitoring sites around

TABLE 2.1

Trends in national emissions of air pollutants, selected years, 1980–2013

[For common pollutants and their precursors]

	Millions of tons per year						
	1980	1985	1990	1995	2000	2005	2013
Carbon monoxide (CO)	178	170	144	120	102	81	59
Lead	0.074	0.023	0.005	0.004	0.002	0.001	0.001
Nitrogen oxides (NO$_x$)	27	26	25	25	22	20	13
Volatile organic compounds (VOC)	30	27	23	22	17	16	14
Particulate matter (PM)							
PM$_{10}$	6	4	3	3	3	4	3
PM$_{2.5}$	NA	NA	2	2	3	3	2
Sulfur dioxide (SO$_2$)	26	23	23	19	16	14	5
Totals	**267**	**250**	**218**	**189**	**160**	**135**	**94**

Notes: NEI = National Emissions Inventory. For CO, NO$_x$, SO$_2$, and VOC emissions, fires are excluded because they are highly variable; for direct PM emissions, both fires and dust are excluded. PM estimates do not include condensible PM. The estimates for 2008 and beyond are based on the final version 3 of the 2008 NEI. PM$_{2.5}$ emissions are not included when calculating the emissions totals because they are included in the PM$_{10}$ emissions number. EPA did not estimate PM$_{2.5}$ emissions prior to 1990. The 1999 estimate for lead was used to represent 2000; the 2002 estimate for lead was used to represent 2005; and the 2008 estimate for lead was used to represent 2013.

SOURCE: "National Emissions Estimates (Fires and Dust Excluded) for Common Pollutants and Their Precursors," in *Air Quality Trends*, U.S. Environmental Protection Agency, October 8, 2014, http://www.epa.gov/airtrends/aqtrends.html (accessed August 31, 2015)

TABLE 2.2

Percentage change in concentrations of air pollutants, 1980 vs. 2013, 1990 vs. 2013, and 2000 vs. 2013

	1980 vs. 2013	1990 vs. 2013	2000 vs. 2013
Carbon monoxide (CO)	−84	−76	−59
Ozone (O$_3$) (8-hr)	−33	−23	−18
Lead (Pb)	−92	−87	−60
Nitrogen dioxide (NO$_2$) (annual)	−58	−50	−40
Nitrogen dioxide (NO$_2$) (1-hour)	−60	−46	−29
PM$_{10}$ (24-hr)	—	−34	−30
PM$_{2.5}$ (annual)	—	—	−34
PM$_{2.5}$ (24-hr)	—	—	−34
Sulfur dioxide (SO$_2$) (1-hour)	−81	−76	−62

—Trend data not available.
Notes: Negative numbers indicate improvements in air quality. In 2010, EPA established new 1-hour average National Ambient Air Quality standards for NO$_2$ and SO$_2$.

SOURCE: "Percent Change in Air Quality," in *Air Quality Trends*, U.S. Environmental Protection Agency, October 8, 2014, http://www.epa.gov/airtrends/aqtrends.html (accessed August 31, 2015)

the country. As shown in Table 2.2, the concentrations of the principal air pollutants declined significantly between 1980 and 2013. Nevertheless, 75.4 million people lived in counties with air quality concentrations that were consistently above the level of at least one NAAQS in 2013. (See Figure 2.1.)

Carbon Monoxide

Carbon monoxide (CO) is a colorless, odorless gas created when the carbon in certain fuels is not burned completely. These fuels include coal, gasoline, natural gas, oil, and wood.

EMISSIONS AND SOURCES. As shown in Table 2.1, the EPA estimates that carbon monoxide emissions decreased from 178 million tons (161.5 million t) in 1980 to 59 million tons (53.5 million t) in 2013, a decrease of 67%.

Yearly emissions and source data for carbon monoxide are available from the EPA's National Emissions Inventory database (http://www.epa.gov/ttn/chief/trends/trends06/national_tier1_caps.xlsx). Transportation vehicles have historically been the largest source of the emissions. For 2013 the source breakdown was as follows:

- Highway vehicles—34%
- Off-highway vehicles (e.g., bulldozers)—21%
- Wildfires—18%
- Stationary fuel combustion (e.g., power plants)—7%
- Industrial and other processes—4%
- Miscellaneous—16%

AIR QUALITY. The national air quality concentrations of carbon monoxide between 1990 and 2013 are shown in Figure 2.2 based on monitoring data from 134 sites around the country. According to the EPA, in "Carbon Monoxide" (September 21, 2015, http://www.epa.gov/airtrends/carbon.html), the national average declined 76% during this period. In 2013 the measured eight-hour average carbon monoxide concentration at the monitoring sites was less than 1.5 parts per million (ppm). This was well below the national standard of 9 ppm. In "National Ambient Air Quality Standards" (September 3, 2015, http://www3.epa.gov/ttn/naaqs/criteria.html), the EPA indicates that a primary national standard of 35 ppm (one-hour period) was also in effect, but there were no secondary standards for carbon monoxide.

As noted earlier, the CAA requires the EPA to review the NAAQS every five years and update them as necessary.

FIGURE 2.1

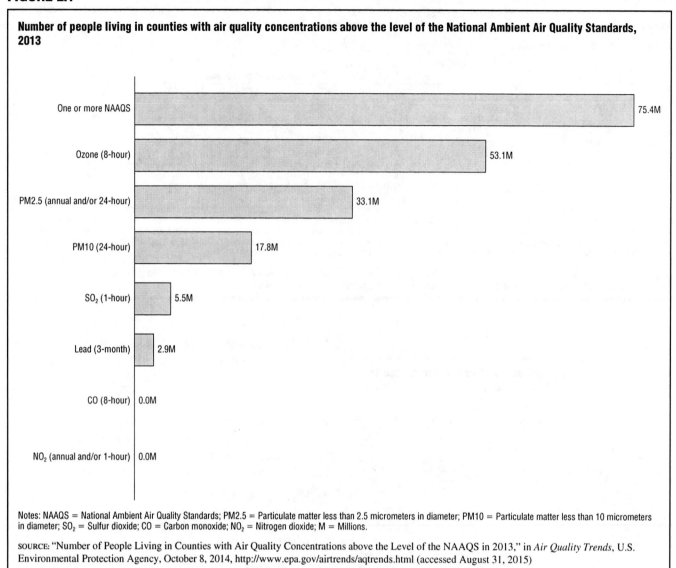

Number of people living in counties with air quality concentrations above the level of the National Ambient Air Quality Standards, 2013

Notes: NAAQS = National Ambient Air Quality Standards; PM2.5 = Particulate matter less than 2.5 micrometers in diameter; PM10 = Particulate matter less than 10 micrometers in diameter; SO_2 = Sulfur dioxide; CO = Carbon monoxide; NO_2 = Nitrogen dioxide; M = Millions.

SOURCE: "Number of People Living in Counties with Air Quality Concentrations above the Level of the NAAQS in 2013," in *Air Quality Trends*, U.S. Environmental Protection Agency, October 8, 2014, http://www.epa.gov/airtrends/aqtrends.html (accessed August 31, 2015)

In early 2011 the agency (September 29, 2015, http://www.epa.gov/ttn/naaqs/standards/co/s_co_history.html) proposed maintaining the national standards for carbon monoxide at their previous levels. The proposal became final in August 2011.

As shown in Figure 2.1, no areas of the country in 2013 had air quality concentrations of carbon monoxide consistently above the NAAQS. Previous nonattainment areas for carbon monoxide have been upgraded to maintenance areas that are classified similarly to nonattainment areas in terms of increasing order of air quality concentrations—marginal, moderate, serious, severe, or extreme. As of October 2015, the EPA (http://www3.epa.gov/airquality/greenbk/cmc.html) listed 43 maintenance areas. None was classified as "extreme." Seven areas were considered "serious" carbon monoxide maintenance areas: Anchorage and Fairbanks, Alaska; Phoenix, Arizona; Los Angeles South Coast Air Basin, California;

Denver-Boulder, Colorado; Las Vegas, Nevada; and Spokane, Washington.

ADVERSE HEALTH EFFECTS. Carbon monoxide is a dangerous gas that enters a person's bloodstream through the lungs. It reduces the ability of blood to carry oxygen to the body's cells, organs, and tissues. The health danger is highest for people suffering from cardiovascular diseases.

Lead

Lead (Pb) is a metal that can enter the atmosphere via the combustion or industrial processing of lead-containing materials.

EMISSIONS AND SOURCES. The EPA estimates that lead emissions declined from 74,000 tons (67,130 t) in 1980 to 1,000 tons (907.2 t) in 2013, a decrease of 99%. (See Table 2.1.) Before 1985 the major source of lead emissions in the United States was leaded gasoline used

FIGURE 2.2

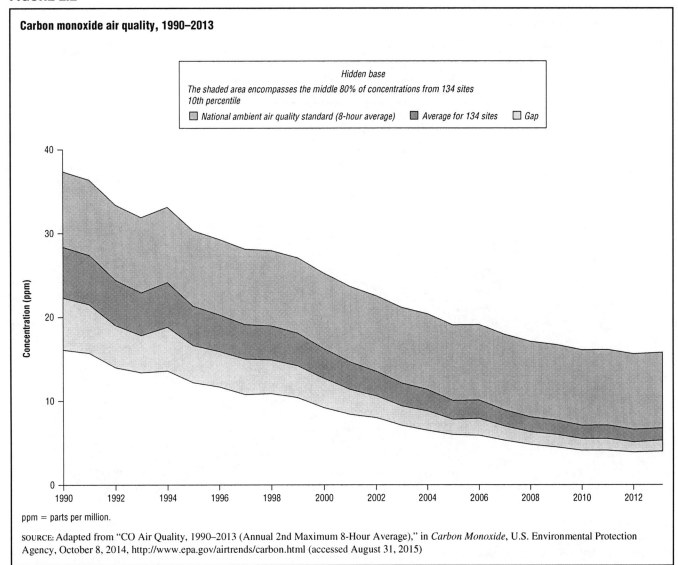

Carbon monoxide air quality, 1990–2013

Hidden base
The shaded area encompasses the middle 80% of concentrations from 134 sites
10th percentile

☐ *National ambient air quality standard (8-hour average)* ■ *Average for 134 sites* ☐ *Gap*

ppm = parts per million.

SOURCE: Adapted from "CO Air Quality, 1990–2013 (Annual 2nd Maximum 8-Hour Average)," in *Carbon Monoxide*, U.S. Environmental Protection Agency, October 8, 2014, http://www.epa.gov/airtrends/carbon.html (accessed August 31, 2015)

in automobiles. Conversion to unleaded gasoline produced a dramatic reduction in lead emissions. As a result, ground transportation has virtually been eliminated as a source of lead emissions in the United States. According to the EPA, in "Lead in Air" (September 14, 2015, http://www3.epa.gov/airquality/lead), most of the nation's lead emissions are from facilities that process ores or metals (such as lead smelters) and from small aircraft that burn leaded aviation gasoline.

The continued use of lead in aviation gasoline (avgas) in the United States is highly controversial. Rebecca Kessler explains in "Sunset for Leaded Aviation Gasoline?" (*Environmental Health Perspectives*, vol. 121, no. 2, February 2013) that avgas is typically used by small airplanes with piston engines (as opposed to jet engines). Various grades of unleaded and leaded avgas are available. According to Kessler, the "most widely available avgas" at U.S. general aviation airports is 100LL, which contains lead to help the fuel burn evenly.

Since 2003 environmental groups have been petitioning the EPA to ban leaded avgas based on studies that show lead levels are higher than background in the air above and around some airports. A 2011 study conducted by Duke University researchers found higher blood lead levels among children living near airports in North Carolina. As of July 2015, the EPA (http://www3.epa.gov/otaq/aviation.htm) indicated that it would issue a decision on the matter by 2018.

AIR QUALITY. The air quality concentrations of lead based on monitoring data from 27 sites between 1990 and 2013 are shown in Figure 2.3. According to the EPA, in "Lead" (September 21, 2015, http://www.epa.gov/airtrends/lead.html), the national average declined 87% during this period. In 2013 the three-month average lead concentration at the monitoring sites was less than 0.2 micrograms per cubic meter ($\mu g/m^3$). The national standard was 0.15 $\mu g/m^3$. This standard was finalized in 2008 and is significantly lower than the previous standard of

FIGURE 2.3

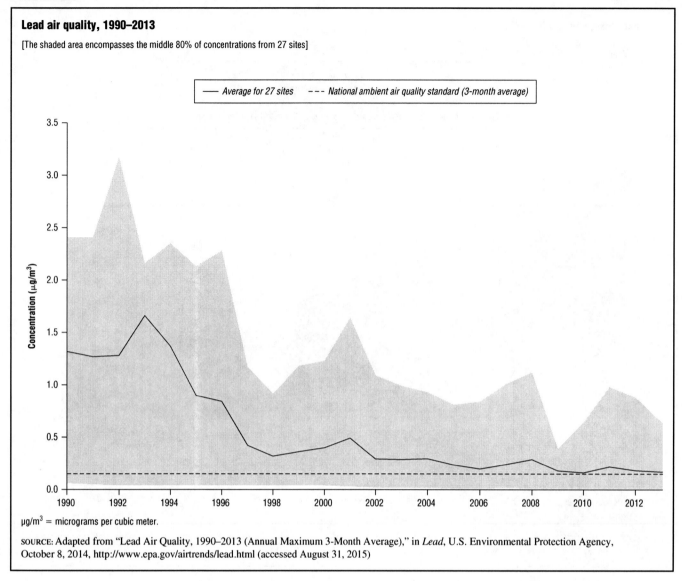

Lead air quality, 1990–2013

[The shaded area encompasses the middle 80% of concentrations from 27 sites]

— Average for 27 sites   - - - National ambient air quality standard (3-month average)

μg/m³ = micrograms per cubic meter.

SOURCE: Adapted from "Lead Air Quality, 1990–2013 (Annual Maximum 3-Month Average)," in *Lead*, U.S. Environmental Protection Agency, October 8, 2014, http://www.epa.gov/airtrends/lead.html (accessed August 31, 2015)

1.5 μg/m³. In "Lead in Air," the EPA notes that in December 2014 it proposed to retain the existing NAAQS for lead. As of November 2015, the proposal had not been finalized.

Despite great progress in lead reduction, Figure 2.1 shows that 2.9 million people lived in counties with air quality concentrations consistently above the NAAQS for this pollutant in 2013. The EPA (http://www3.epa.gov/airquality/greenbook/mnc.html) reports that as of October 2015 there were 21 lead nonattainment areas around the country.

ADVERSE HEALTH EFFECTS. Lead is a particularly dangerous pollutant because it accumulates in the blood, bones, and soft tissues of the body. It can adversely affect the nervous system, kidneys, liver, and other organs. Excessive concentrations are associated with neurological impairments, mental retardation, and behavioral disorders. Even low doses of lead can damage the brain and nervous system of fetuses and young children. Atmospheric lead that falls onto vegetation poses an ingestion hazard to humans and animals.

Nitrogen Dioxide

Nitrogen dioxide (NO_2) is a reddish-brown gas that forms in the atmosphere when nitrogen oxide is oxidized. Inhalation of even low concentrations of nitrogen dioxide for short periods can be harmful to the human body's breathing functions. Longer exposures are considered damaging to the lungs and may cause people to be more susceptible to certain respiratory problems, such as infections.

The chemical formula NO_x is used collectively to refer to nitrogen oxide, nitrogen dioxide, and other nitrogen oxides.

EMISSIONS AND SOURCES. As shown in Table 2.1, NO_x emissions declined from 27 million tons (24.5 million t) in 1980 to 13 million tons (11.8 million t) in

2013, a decrease of 52%. Most of this improvement occurred after the 1990s.

Nitrogen oxides primarily come from burning fuels such as coal, gasoline, natural gas, and oil. Yearly emissions and source data are available from the EPA's National Emissions Inventory database. For 2013 the source breakdown for NO_x was as follows:

- Highway vehicles—38%
- Stationary fuel combustion—28%
- Off-highway vehicles—21%
- Industrial and other processes—10%
- Wildfires—1%
- Miscellaneous—2%

AIR QUALITY. Nitrogen dioxide is a major precursor of smog and contributes to acid rain and haze. It can also undergo reactions in the air that lead to the formation of particulate matter and ozone. Figure 2.4 illustrates the air quality concentrations of nitrogen dioxide based on monitoring data from 98 sites around the country between 1990 and 2013. According to the EPA, in "Nitrogen Dioxide" (September 21, 2015, http://www.epa.gov/air trends/nitrogen.html), the national average declined 46% during this period. In 2013 the maximum average one-hour measured nitrogen dioxide concentration at the monitoring sites was around 42 parts per billion (ppb). This was well below the national standard of 100 ppb. The EPA indicates that the 100 ppb (one-hour) standard was implemented in 2010. In "Fact Sheet: Final Revisions to the National Ambient Air Quality Standards for Nitrogen Dioxide" (May 18, 2011, http://www3.epa.gov/airquality/nitrogenoxides/pdfs/20100122fs.pdf), the agency notes that the new standard "will protect against adverse health effects associated with short-term exposure to NO_2, including respiratory effects that can result in admission to a hospital." Another primary and secondary national standard of 53 ppb (annual average) has been in effect since 1971.

As shown in Figure 2.1, no areas of the country had air quality concentrations of nitrogen dioxide consistently above the NAAQS in 2013. As of October 2015, the EPA (http://www3.epa.gov/airquality/greenbook/nmcs.html)

FIGURE 2.4

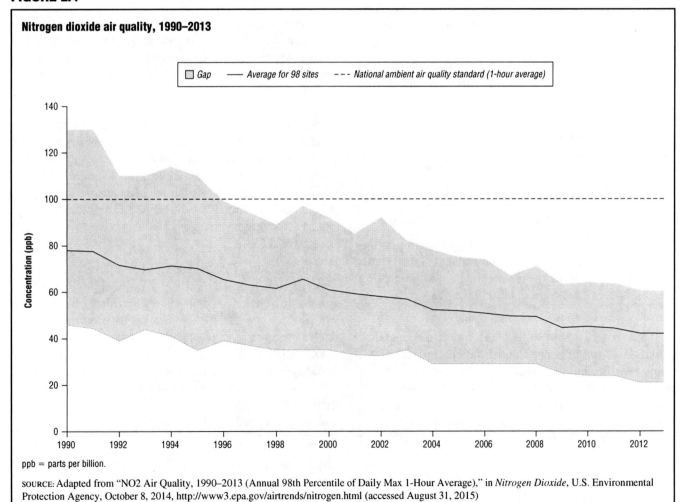

Nitrogen dioxide air quality, 1990–2013

Gap — Average for 98 sites − − − National ambient air quality standard (1-hour average)

Concentration (ppb)

ppb = parts per billion.

SOURCE: Adapted from "NO2 Air Quality, 1990–2013 (Annual 98th Percentile of Daily Max 1-Hour Average)," in *Nitrogen Dioxide*, U.S. Environmental Protection Agency, October 8, 2014, http://www3.epa.gov/airtrends/nitrogen.html (accessed August 31, 2015)

classified the Los Angeles South Coast Air Basin as a nitrogen dioxide maintenance area.

ADVERSE HEALTH EFFECTS. Nitrogen dioxide reacts with ammonia and water droplets in the atmosphere to form nitric acid and other chemicals that are potentially harmful to human health. Inhalation of these particles can interfere with respiratory processes and damage lung tissue. Particles that are inhaled deeply into the lungs can cause or aggravate respiratory conditions such as bronchitis and emphysema.

Ozone

Ozone is a gas naturally present in the earth's upper atmosphere. The National Oceanic and Atmospheric Administration indicates in "Science: Ozone Basics" (March 20, 2008, http://www.ozonelayer.noaa.gov/science/basics.htm) that approximately 90% of the earth's ozone lies in the stratosphere at altitudes greater than about 9.3 miles (15 km) up to approximately 22.8 miles (35 km). Ozone molecules at this level absorb ultraviolet radiation from the sun and prevent it from reaching the ground. Thus, stratospheric ozone (the ozone layer) is good for the environment. Beneath the stratosphere is the troposphere. Tropospheric (ground-level) ozone is a potent air pollutant with serious health consequences. It is the most complex, pervasive, and difficult to control of the six priority pollutants.

Ground-level ozone is the primary component in smog. It retards crop and tree growth, impairs health, and limits visibility. When temperature inversions occur (the warm air stays near the ground instead of rising) and winds are calm, such as during the summer, smog may hang over a huge area for days at a time. As traffic and other pollution sources add more pollutants to the air, the smog gets worse. Wind often blows smog-forming pollutants away from their sources; this is why smog can be miles away from where the pollutants were created.

Ground-level ozone is harmful to ecosystems, particularly vegetation. Ozone exposure reduces forest yields by stunting the growth of seedlings and increasing stresses on trees. Such damage can take years to become evident.

EMISSIONS AND SOURCES. Unlike other air pollutants, ground-level ozone is not emitted directly into the air. It forms mostly on sunny, hot days because of complex chemical reactions that take place when the atmosphere contains other pollutants, primarily VOCs and NO_x. These pollutants are called ozone precursors because their presence in the atmosphere leads to the creation of ozone.

VOCs are carbon-containing chemicals that easily become vapors or gases. Paint thinners, degreasers, and other solvents contain a great number of VOCs, which are also released from burning fuels such as coal, gasoline, natural gas, and wood.

According to the EPA, VOC emissions dropped from 30 million tons (27.2 million t) in 1980 to 14 million tons (12.7 million t) in 2013, a decline of 53%. (See Table 2.1.) The EPA's National Emissions Inventory database provides yearly emissions and source data. For 2013 the source breakdown was as follows:

- Industrial and other processes—41%
- Wildfires—17%
- Highway vehicles—14%
- Off-highway vehicles—11%
- Stationary fuel combustion—4%
- Miscellaneous—14%

Note that the individual percentages do not sum to 100% due to rounding.

AIR QUALITY. Ozone has different health and environmental effects, depending on the time of exposure. Ozone concentrations can vary greatly from year to year, depending on the emissions of ozone precursors and weather conditions.

The setting of ozone standards has been fraught with controversy. According to the EPA (October 8, 2015, http://www.epa.gov/ttn/naaqs/standards/ozone/s_o3_history.html), a one-hour ozone standard was in effect from the 1970s through the 1990s. In 1997 the agency proposed replacing the standard with a new eight-hour standard of 0.08 ppm. This is equivalent to 80 ppb. The proposal was challenged in court by industry groups and some states who argued that the compliance costs necessary to achieve the standard would be too high. The legal battle reached the U.S. Supreme Court, which ruled in *Whitman v. American Trucking Associations Inc.* (531 U.S. 457 [2001]) that the EPA does not have to consider compliance costs when setting ambient air standards.

In 2006 the CASAC completed a five-year review and recommended to the EPA that the eight-hour standard be lowered to within the range of 60 to 70 ppb. However, when the EPA published its proposed rule in 2007, the agency called for the standard to be 70 to 75 ppb. This set off another legal battle. Some states and industry groups argued that the proposal was too strict, whereas other states and environmental and health groups criticized it as not being strict enough. A standard of 75 ppb was finalized in March 2008.

In January 2010 the EPA proposed a new primary eight-hour ozone standard of 60 to 70 ppb and a secondary ozone standard of 7 to 15 ppm-hours. However, in September 2011 the administration of President Barack Obama (1961–) withdrew the proposed ozone standards.

In a statement (http://www.whitehouse.gov/the-press-office/2011/09/02/statement-president-ozone-national-ambient-air-quality-standards), President Obama lauded the EPA for its work to reduce air pollution, but noted, "At the same time, I have continued to underscore the importance of reducing regulatory burdens and regulatory uncertainty, particularly as our economy continues to recover." This statement referred to the lingering effects of the Great Recession, a sharp economic decline that lasted from late 2007 to mid-2009. Obama decided to wait for the results of the required five-year review of the ozone standard that was due to be completed by 2013. That review resulted in a CASAC recommendation that the standard be set at 60 to 70 ppb.

In December 2014 the EPA (https://www.federalregister.gov/articles/2014/12/17/2014-28674/national-ambient-air-quality-standards-for-ozone) proposed primary and secondary eight-hour ozone standards within the range of 65 to 70 ppb. In October 2015 the agency (http://www3.epa.gov/airquality/ozonepollution/actions.html) finalized both standards at 70 ppb. In "EPA Sets Stricter Standard for Ozone" (WSJ.com, October 1, 2015), Amy Harder calls the new standard "an attempted compromise

that left some businesses relieved and environmental and health leaders upset the initiative wasn't stronger."

Figure 2.5 illustrates the eight-hour air quality concentrations of ozone based on monitoring data from 466 sites around the country between 1990 and 2013. According to the EPA, in "Ozone" (September 21, 2015, http://www3.epa.gov/airtrends/ozone.html), the national average declined 23% during this period. In 2013 the eight-hour average measured ozone concentration at the monitoring sites was 0.068 ppm (68 ppb), which was below the national standard of 75 ppb.

In 2013, 53.1 million people lived in counties with ozone concentrations above the level of the NAAQS. (See Figure 2.1.) The EPA (http://www3.epa.gov/airquality/greenbook/hnc.html) reports that as of October 2015 there were 45 locations around the country that were designated nonattainment for ozone air quality. Two areas were classified as "extreme" nonattainment for the eight-hour ozone standard: the Los Angeles South Coast Air Basin and the San Joaquin Valley in California. Many other areas in and around major cities were also classified as nonattainment.

FIGURE 2.5

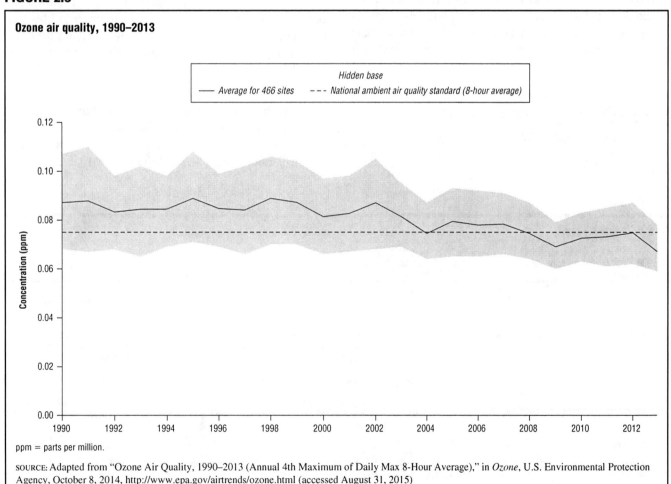

Ozone air quality, 1990–2013

Hidden base
—— Average for 466 sites – – – National ambient air quality standard (8-hour average)

ppm = parts per million.

SOURCE: Adapted from "Ozone Air Quality, 1990–2013 (Annual 4th Maximum of Daily Max 8-Hour Average)," in *Ozone*, U.S. Environmental Protection Agency, October 8, 2014, http://www.epa.gov/airtrends/ozone.html (accessed August 31, 2015)

ADVERSE HEALTH EFFECTS. Even the smallest amounts of ozone can cause breathing difficulties. Ozone exposure can cause serious problems with lung functions, leading to infections, chest pain, and coughing. According to the EPA, ozone exposure is linked to increased emergency department visits and hospital admissions because of respiratory problems such as lung inflammation and asthma. Ozone causes or aggravates these problems, particularly in people working outdoors, the elderly, and children. Children are especially susceptible to the harmful effects of ozone because they spend a great deal of time outside and because their lungs are still developing.

The EPA maintains the Air Quality Index (AQI) as a means for warning the public when air pollutants (particularly ozone) exceed unhealthy levels. The AQI values range from 0 to 500. Higher values correspond to greater levels of air pollution and increased risk to human health. An AQI value of 100 is assigned to the concentration of an air pollutant equal to its NAAQS. Table 2.3 shows the ozone AQI. Index values are commonly reported during summertime radio and television newscasts to warn people about the dangers of ozone exposure.

In *State of the Air: 2015: Most Polluted Cities* (2015, http://www.stateoftheair.org/2015/city-rankings/most-polluted-cities.html), the American Lung Association ranks metropolitan areas and counties in terms of their ozone pollutant levels. The 10 metropolitan areas with the worst ozone pollution in 2015 were:

- Los Angeles–Long Beach, California
- Visalia-Porterville-Hanford, California
- Bakersfield, California
- Fresno-Madera, California
- Sacramento-Roseville, California
- Houston–The Woodlands, Texas
- Dallas–Fort Worth, Texas
- Modesto-Merced, California
- Las Vegas–Henderson, Nevada
- Phoenix-Mesa-Scottsdale, Arizona

Particulate Matter

Particulate matter (PM) is the general term for the mixture of solid particles and/or liquid droplets that are found in the air. The primary particles are those that are emitted directly to the atmosphere—for example, dust, dirt, and soot (black carbon). Secondary particles form in the atmosphere because of complex chemical reactions among gaseous emissions and include sulfates, nitrates, ammoniums, and organic carbon compounds. For example, sulfate particulates can form when sulfur dioxide emissions from industrial facilities and power plants undergo chemical reactions in the atmosphere.

The EPA tracks two sizes of PM: PM_{10} and $PM_{2.5}$. PM_{10} particles are those less than or equal to 10 micrometers in diameter. This is roughly one-seventh the diameter of a human hair and small enough to be breathed into the lungs. $PM_{2.5}$ are the smallest of these particles (less than or equal to 2.5 micrometers in diameter). $PM_{2.5}$ is also called fine PM. The particles ranging in size between 2.5 and 10 micrometers in diameter are known as coarse PM. Most coarse PM consists of primary particles, whereas most fine PM consists of secondary particles.

EMISSIONS AND SOURCES. Table 2.1 shows direct PM emissions from sources other than fires and dust. PM_{10} emissions decreased from 6 million tons (5.4 million t) in 1980 to 3 million tons (2.7 million t) in 2013, a decline of

TABLE 2.3

Air quality index: ozone

Levels of health concern because air quality conditions are:	Air quality index color	Air quality index range	Meaning
Good	Green	0–50	Air quality is considered satisfactory, and air pollution poses little or no risk.
Moderate	Yellow	51–100	Air quality is acceptable; however, for some pollutants there may be a moderate health concern for a very small number of people. For example, people who are unusually sensitive to ozone may experience respiratory symptoms.
Unhealthy for sensitive groups	Orange	101–150	Although the general public is not likely to be affected at this AQI range, people with lung disease, older adults and children are at a greater risk from exposure to ozone, whereas persons with heart and lung disease, older adults and children are at greater risk from the presence of particles in the air.
Unhealthy	Red	151–200	Everyone may begin to experience some adverse health effects, and members of the sensitive groups may experience more serious effects.
Very unhealthy	Purple	201–300	This would trigger a health alert signifying that everyone may experience more serious health effects.
Hazardous	Maroon	301–500	This would trigger a health warning of emergency conditions. The entire population is more likely to be affected.

AQI = Air Quality Index.

SOURCE: Adapted from "Understanding the AQI" and "AQI Colors," in *Air Quality Index (AQI) Basics*, U.S. Environmental Protection Agency, March 16, 2015, http://www.airnow.gov/?action=aqibasics.aqi (accessed August 31, 2015)

50%. $PM_{2.5}$ emissions were 2 million tons (1.8 million t) in both 1990 and 2013.

Yearly emissions and source data for PM are available from the EPA's National Emissions Inventory database. For 2013 the source breakdown was as follows:

- Wildfires—6%

- Industrial and other processes—5%

- Stationary fuel combustion—5%

- Highway vehicles—2%

- Off-highway vehicles—1%

- Miscellaneous—81%

AIR QUALITY. When PM hangs in the air, it creates a haze, limiting visibility. PM is one of the major components of smog and can have adverse effects on vegetation and sensitive ecosystems. Long-term exposure to PM can damage painted surfaces, buildings, and monuments.

Figure 2.6 shows the historical trend in PM_{10} air quality based on data collected by the EPA from 207 monitoring sites. According to the EPA, in "Particulate Matter" (September 21, 2015, http://www3.epa

.gov/airtrends/pm.html), the national average declined 34% between 1990 and 2013. The 24-hour average in 2013 was around 56 $\mu g/m^3$, well below the national standard of 150 $\mu g/m^3$.

As shown in Figure 2.1, 17.8 million people lived in counties with 24-hour PM_{10} concentrations above the NAAQS in 2013. The EPA (http://www3.epa.gov/airquality/greenbook/pnc.html) reports that as of October 2015, 39 areas around the country were nonattainment for PM_{10} concentrations. Areas classified "serious" nonattainment were in Southern California and in parts of Nevada and Arizona.

In 1999 the EPA began nationwide tracking of $PM_{2.5}$ air quality concentrations. Figure 2.7 shows the historical trend based on data collected by the EPA from 537 monitoring sites. In 2013 the annual average $PM_{2.5}$ concentration was around 9 $\mu g/m^3$, less than the standard of 12 $\mu g/m^3$. In "National Ambient Air Quality Standards (NAAQS)," the EPA indicates that as of 2015, a primary national standard of 35 $\mu g/m^3$ (24-hour period) was also in effect.

According to the EPA (September 29, 2015, http://www.epa.gov/ttn/naaqs/standards/pm/s_pm_history.html),

FIGURE 2.6

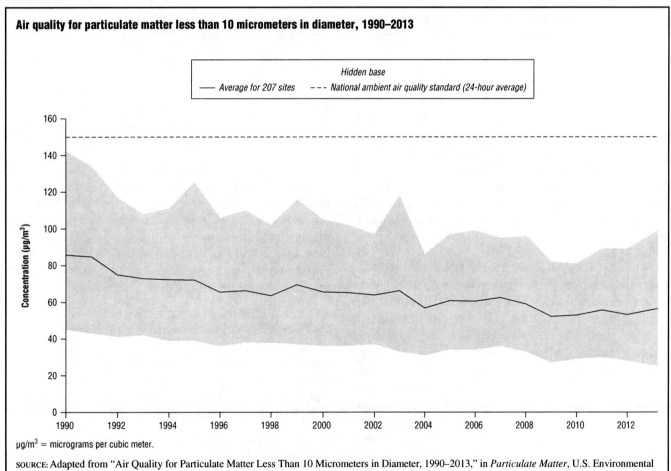

Air quality for particulate matter less than 10 micrometers in diameter, 1990–2013

Hidden base
—— Average for 207 sites   - - - National ambient air quality standard (24-hour average)

$\mu g/m^3$ = micrograms per cubic meter.

SOURCE: Adapted from "Air Quality for Particulate Matter Less Than 10 Micrometers in Diameter, 1990–2013," in *Particulate Matter*, U.S. Environmental Protection Agency, October 16, 2014, http://www.epa.gov/airtrends/pm.html (accessed August 31, 2015)

FIGURE 2.7

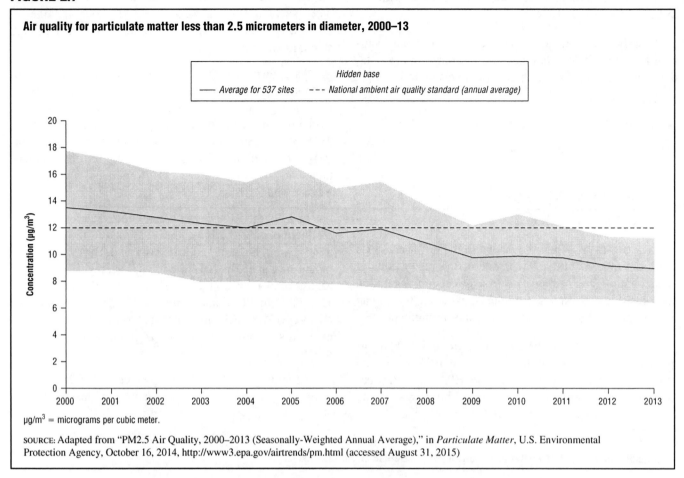

Air quality for particulate matter less than 2.5 micrometers in diameter, 2000–13

$\mu g/m^3$ = micrograms per cubic meter.

SOURCE: Adapted from "PM2.5 Air Quality, 2000–2013 (Seasonally-Weighted Annual Average)," in *Particulate Matter*, U.S. Environmental Protection Agency, October 16, 2014, http://www3.epa.gov/airtrends/pm.html (accessed August 31, 2015)

NAAQS standards for $PM_{2.5}$ were first issued in 1997 and revised as needed in 2006 and 2012.

In 2013, 33.1 million people lived in counties with $PM_{2.5}$ concentrations above the level of the annual and/or 24-hour NAAQS. (See Figure 2.1.) The EPA (http://www3.epa.gov/airquality/greenbook/rnc.html) notes that as of October 2015 there were 17 locations around the country that were designated nonattainment for $PM_{2.5}$ air quality. Most were major- and medium-sized metropolitan areas.

ADVERSE HEALTH EFFECTS. PM can irritate the nostrils, throat, and lungs and aggravate respiratory conditions such as bronchitis and asthma. PM exposure can also endanger the circulatory system and is linked to cardiac arrhythmias (episodes of irregular heartbeats) and heart attacks. $PM_{2.5}$ particles are the most damaging because their small size allows them access to deeper regions of the lungs. These small particles have been linked to the most serious health effects in humans. Particulates pose the greatest health risk to those with heart or lung problems, the elderly, and especially children, who are particularly susceptible because of the greater amount of time they spend outside and the fact that their lungs are not fully developed.

Sulfur Dioxide

Sulfur dioxide (SO_2) is a gas composed of sulfur and oxygen. The chemical formula SO_x is used collectively to describe sulfur oxide, sulfur dioxide, and other sulfur oxides.

EMISSIONS AND SOURCES. One of the primary sources of sulfur dioxide is the combustion of fossil fuels containing sulfur. Coal (particularly high-sulfur coal, which is common to the eastern United States) and oil are the major fuel sources associated with sulfur dioxide. Power plants have historically been the main source of sulfur dioxide emissions. Some industrial processes and metal smelting also cause sulfur dioxide to form.

Sulfur dioxide emissions have decreased since the 1980s because of greater reliance on cleaner fuels with lower sulfur content and the increased use of pollution-control devices, such as scrubbers, to clean emissions. As shown in Table 2.1, between 1980 and 2013 sulfur dioxide emissions declined from 26 million tons (23.6 million t) to 5 million tons (4.5 million t), a decrease of 81%.

The EPA's National Emissions Inventory database provides yearly emissions and source data for sulfur dioxide. Fuel combustion in stationary sources (e.g., power plants) has traditionally produced the most sulfur

FIGURE 2.8

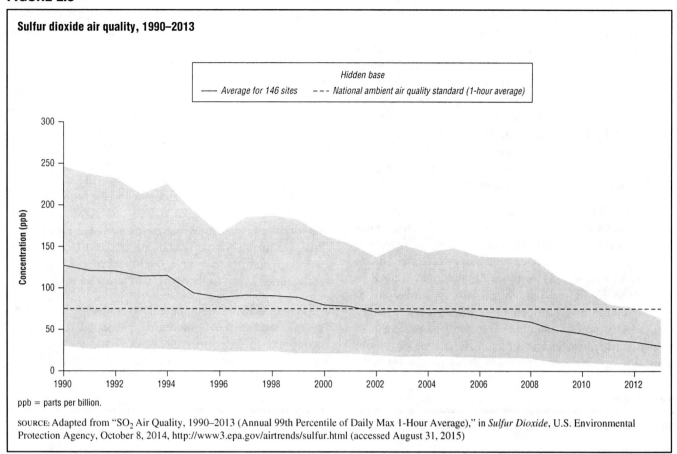

Sulfur dioxide air quality, 1990–2013

Hidden base

—— Average for 146 sites   - - - National ambient air quality standard (1-hour average)

ppb = parts per billion.

SOURCE: Adapted from "SO₂ Air Quality, 1990–2013 (Annual 99th Percentile of Daily Max 1-Hour Average)," in *Sulfur Dioxide*, U.S. Environmental Protection Agency, October 8, 2014, http://www3.epa.gov/airtrends/sulfur.html (accessed August 31, 2015)

dioxide emissions. For 2013 the source breakdown was as follows:

- Stationary fuel combustion—82%

- Industrial and other processes—12%

- Off-highway vehicles—2%

- Wildfires—2%

- Highway vehicles—0.5%

- Miscellaneous—2%

Note that the individual percentages do not sum to 100% due to rounding.

AIR QUALITY. Figure 2.8 shows the historical trend in sulfur dioxide air quality based on data collected by the EPA from 146 monitoring sites. According to the EPA, in "Sulfur Dioxide" (September 21, 2015, http://www.epa.gov/airtrends/sulfur.html), the national average declined 76% between 1990 and 2013. In 2013 the average one-hour measured concentration at the monitoring sites was around 30 ppb. This was well below the national standard of 75 ppb.

As shown in Figure 2.1, in 2013, 5.5 million people lived in nonattainment areas based on the one-hour sulfur dioxide standard. The EPA (http://www3.epa.gov/airquality/greenbook/tnc.html) reports that as of October 2015 there were 29 nonattainment areas around the country.

Sulfur dioxide is a major contributor to acid rain, haze, and PM. Acid rain is of particular concern because of its negative impacts on the environment. Acid rain control measures are described in detail in Chapter 5.

ADVERSE HEALTH EFFECTS. Inhaling sulfur dioxide in polluted air can impair breathing in those with asthma or even in healthy adults who are active outdoors. As with other air pollutants, children, the elderly, and those with preexisting respiratory and cardiovascular diseases and conditions are the most susceptible to adverse effects from breathing this gas.

CROSS-STATE AIR POLLUTION

One of the difficulties in regulating air pollution is that emissions can travel far from their sources, including across state lines. This can result in a situation in which a state's air quality meets the NAAQS, but emissions from within its borders contribute to another state not meeting the standards. As part of the 1990 amendments to the CAA, Congress added what is called the "Good Neighbor" Provision. According to the EPA, in "Interstate Air Pollution Transport" (March 30, 2015, http://www3.epa.gov/airtransport), the provision "requires EPA and states to address interstate transport of air pollution that affects downwind states' ability to attain and maintain National Ambient Air Quality Standards (NAAQS)." However, finding a suitable solution to cross-state air pollution has proved challenging. Part of the difficulty lies in quantifying the emissions from upwind states that negatively affect downwind states. In addition, as noted earlier, although the EPA has the statutory authority (authority granted by law, in this case the CAA) to set national air quality limits, it cannot tell individual states how to achieve the limits. Multiple lawsuits have been filed over the decades regarding the complex issues involved.

In 2005 the EPA issued the Clean Air Interstate Rule (CAIR) to tackle problems in the eastern United States with air pollutants that move across state boundaries. The program was to be carried out using a cap-and-trade system, as was already in place for the Acid Rain Program. The CAIR put permanent caps on emissions of sulfur dioxide and nitrogen oxide in 28 eastern states and the District of Columbia. The rule was projected to reduce sulfur dioxide emissions in these states by more than 70% and reduce nitrogen oxide emissions by more

than 60% compared with 2003 levels. Control of these pollutants was expected to reduce the formation of fine PM, acid rain, and ground-level ozone across the country.

The CAIR was subjected to legal challenges after its issuance. In July 2008 the U.S. Court of Appeals for the District of Columbia Circuit vacated (revoked) the CAIR in *North Carolina v. EPA* (531 F.3d 896). Later that year the court ordered the EPA to issue a new rule to replace the CAIR. In July 2011 the EPA finalized the Cross-State Air Pollution Rule (CSAPR; July 28, 2015, http://www3.epa.gov/crossstaterule) to replace the CAIR. The CSAPR imposes new restrictions on the emissions of sulfur dioxide and nitrogen oxide from power plants in many eastern and midwestern states. (See Table 2.4.) These pollutants in particular are prone to cross state lines and contribute to air quality problems, such as ozone, miles away from where they are generated.

The CSAPR was immediately challenged in court. The rule was stayed (temporarily prevented from going into effect) in December 2011 while the legal process played out. In the meantime, the CAIR remained in

TABLE 2.4

States subject to the Cross-State Air Pollution Rule

State	Required to reduce emissions of NO$_x$ during the Ozone Season (1997 Ozone NAAQS)	Required to reduce annual emissions of SO$_2$ and NO$_x$ (1997 annual PM2.5 NAAQS)	Required to reduce annual emissions of SO$_2$ and NO$_x$ (2006 24-hour PM2.5 NAAQS)	SO$_2$ group*
Alabama	X	X	X	2
Arkansas	X			
Florida	X			
Georgia	X	X	X	2
Illinois	X	X	X	1
Indiana	X	X	X	1
Iowa	X	X	X	1
Kansas			X	2
Kentucky	X	X	X	1
Louisiana	X			
Maryland	X	X	X	1
Michigan	X	X	X	1
Minnesota			X	2
Mississippi	X			
Missouri	X	X	X	1
Nebraska			X	2
New Jersey	X		X	1
New York	X	X	X	1
North Carolina	X	X	X	1
Ohio	X	X	X	1
Oklahoma	X			
Pennsylvania	X	X	X	1
South Carolina	X	X		2
Tennessee	X	X	X	1
Texas	X	X		2
Virginia	X		X	1
West Virginia	X	X	X	1
Wisconsin	X	X	X	1
Number of states	**25**	**18**	**21**	

NO$_x$ = Nitrogen oxides. SO$_2$ = Sulfur dioxide.
NAAQS = National Ambient Air Quality Standards.
PM2.5 = Particulate matter less than 2.5 micrometers in diameter.
*The final Cross-State Air Pollution Rule CSAPR divides the states required to reduce SO$_2$ into two groups. Both groups must reduce their SO$_2$ emissions beginning in Phase I. Group 1 states must make significant additional reductions in SO$_2$ emissions for Phase II in order to eliminate their significant contribution to air quality problems in downwind areas.

SOURCE: "States That Are Included in the Cross-State Air Pollution Rule (CSAPR)," in *Cross-State Air Pollution Rule (CSAPR): Resources for Implementation*, U.S. Environmental Protection Agency, May 28, 2015, http://www.epa.gov/crossstaterule/stateinfo.html#states (accessed September 1, 2015)

TABLE 2.5

Projected annual number of adverse health effects that will be avoided due to implementing the Cross-State Air Pollution Rule

Health effect	Number of cases avoided
Premature mortality	13,000 to 34,000
Non-fatal heart attacks	15,000
Hospital and emergency department visits	19,000
Acute bronchitis	19,000
Upper and lower respiratory symptoms	420,000
Aggravated asthma	400,000
Days when people miss work or school	1.8 million

Note: Impacts avoided due to improvements in PM2.5 and ozone air quality. PM2.5 = particulate matter less than 2.5 micrometers in diameter. Impacts avoided due to improvements in PM2.5 and ozone air quality.

SOURCE: "Estimated Annual Number of Adverse Health Effects Avoided Due to Implementing the CSAPR," in *Cross-State Air Pollution Rule (CSAPR)*, U.S. Environmental Protection Agency, July 28, 2015, http://www.epa.gov/crossstaterule/ (accessed September 1, 2015)

effect. In August 2012 the U.S. Court of Appeals for the District of Columbia Circuit ruled in *EME Homer City Generation, L.P v. EPA* (696 F.3d 7) that the EPA had overstepped its authority with the CSAPR. In particular, the court found that the "EPA has used the good neighbor provision to impose massive emissions reduction requirements on upwind States without regard to the limits imposed by the statutory text." The agency appealed the decision, and in April 2014 the U.S. Supreme Court in *EPA v. EME Homer City Generation* (No. 12-1182) ruled in the EPA's favor.

As noted in Table 2.4, the rule includes two phases for sulfur dioxide emissions. All of the covered power plants must reduce their emissions during the first phase. A subset of the covered power plants must then make additional emissions cuts during the second phase. The EPA explains in "Cross-State Air Pollution Rule" (July 28, 2015, http://www3.epa.gov/crossstaterule) that it began implementing phase one of the rule in 2015. Phase two is scheduled to begin in 2017. Table 2.5 lists the health benefits that the agency expects will result from lower power plant emissions under the CSAPR. Overall, it is projected to prevent tens of thousands of premature deaths and illnesses associated with breathing contaminated air.

HAZARDOUS AIR POLLUTANTS

Hazardous air pollutants (HAPs), or air toxics, are pollutants that can cause severe health effects and/or ecosystem damage. Examples of HAPs are arsenic, benzene, beryllium, dioxins, mercury, and vinyl chloride. Serious health risks linked to HAPs include cancer, immune system disorders, neurological problems, reproductive effects, and birth defects. In "About Air Toxics" (June 21, 2012, http://www3.epa.gov/ttn/atw/allabout.html), the EPA notes that it focuses on 187 HAPs. These chemicals are listed in the CAA and are targeted for regulation under

Section 112. As noted earlier, the EPA does not have to consider compliance costs when setting ambient air quality standards. This is not the case for HAP standards. Section 112 specifically directs the agency to set them while "taking into consideration the cost of achieving such emission reduction." This distinction has made the setting of NESHAPs very challenging and fraught with political difficulties.

The major sources of HAP emissions include transportation vehicles, construction equipment, power plants, factories, and refineries. Some air toxics come from common sources. For example, benzene emissions are associated with gasoline. Air toxics are not subject to intensive national monitoring. The EPA, through its National Air Toxics Trends Station Network (http://www3.epa.gov/ttnamti1/natts.html), operated 27 monitoring sites around the country as of August 2015.

National Air Toxics Assessments

As of November 2015, the EPA had conducted four National Air Toxics Assessments (http://www3.epa.gov/nata): in 1996, 1999, 2002, and 2005. The results were typically published six to seven years later. In 2011 the EPA released the 2005 National-Scale Air Toxics Assessment (http://www3.epa.gov/ttn/atw/nata2005). It evaluates 177 HAPs plus PM from the burning of diesel fuel. The EPA notes in *Summary of Results for the 2005 National-Scale Assessment* (February 17, 2011, http://www.epa.gov/ttn/atw/nata2005/05pdf/sum_results.pdf) that the assessment indicates which of the air toxics pose the greatest potential cancer and noncancer risks to humans. Overall, the EPA concludes:

> All 285 million people in the U.S. have an increased cancer risk of greater than 10 in one million. 13.8 million people (less than 5 percent of the total U.S. population based on the 2000 census) have an increased cancer risk of greater than 100 in a million. The average, national, cancer risk for 2005 is 50 in a million. This means that, on average, approximately 1 in every 20,000 people have an increased likelihood of contracting cancer as a result of breathing air toxics from outdoor sources if they were exposed to 2005 emission levels over the course of their lifetime.

The agency also includes maps that show the levels of cancer and noncancer risks using census tracts from the 2000 census.

NESHAPs for Power Plants

Section 112 of the CAA singles out electric utility steam generating units for special consideration. The law defines an electric utility steam generating unit as "any fossil fuel fired combustion unit of more than 25 megawatts that serves a generator that produces electricity for sale." Fossil fuels include coal, oil, and natural gas. When the CAA was amended in 1990, Congress directed the EPA to perform a study of emissions from electric utility steam generating units and determine whether the units should be subject to regulation under Section 112. Specifically, the law states: "The [EPA] Administrator shall regulate electric utility steam generating units under this section, if the Administrator finds such regulation is appropriate and necessary after considering the results of the study required by this subparagraph." In December 2000 the agency issued its findings in "Regulatory Finding on the Emissions of Hazardous Air Pollutants from Electric Utility Steam Generating Units" (*Federal Register*, vol. 65, no. 245), which supported the regulation of electric utility steam generating units for air toxics under Section 112. Specifically, the EPA noted that "coal- and oil-fired electric utility steam generating units are significant emitters of HAP, including mercury which is emitted from coal-fired units, and which EPA identified as the HAP of greatest concern to public health from the industry."

Mercury is naturally present in the earth's crust, such as in rocks and fossil fuels, particularly coal. When the fuels are burned, the mercury enters the atmosphere. From there, it can fall into water supplies, where it is absorbed by fish and shellfish. The consumption of contaminated fish and shellfish is the primary source of mercury exposure to humans.

According to the EPA, in *Reducing Toxic Pollution from Power Plants: EPA's Proposed Mercury and Air Toxics Standards* (March 16, 2011, http://www.epa.gov/airquality/powerplanttoxics/pdfs/presentation.pdf), three sources accounted for approximately two-thirds of the nation's total mercury emissions in 1990: power plants, municipal waste combustors, and medical waste incinerators. Emissions from the latter two sources were reduced by more than 96% between 1990 and 2005. However, mercury emissions from power plants declined only 10% during the same period. Figure 2.9 shows the portion of air pollution that is attributed by the EPA to coal- and oil-fired power plants. These sources contribute approximately 50% of mercury, 60% of sulfur dioxide, and 62% of arsenic. Arsenic and mercury are air toxics.

In 2005 the EPA issued the Clean Air Mercury Rule (CAMR) to limit and reduce mercury emissions nationwide from coal-fired power plants. The CAMR was immediately unpopular with some state governments, particularly those in the eastern United States, where many coal-fired power plants operate. In February 2008 the U.S. Court of Appeals for the District of Columbia Circuit ruled in *New Jersey v. EPA* (517 F.3d 574) that the regulatory approach of the CAMR was invalid. In March 2011 the EPA (September 25, 2015, http://www3.epa.gov/mats) proposed mercury and air toxics standards under Section 112. The standards were finalized later that year and cover emissions of mercury and other HAPs. Figure 2.10 shows a map of the power plants around the country that are subject to the mercury and air

FIGURE 2.9

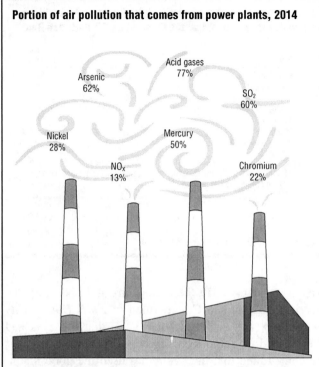

Portion of air pollution that comes from power plants, 2014

Acid gases 77%

Arsenic 62%

SO₂ 60%

Nickel 28%

Mercury 50%

NOₓ 13%

Chromium 22%

SOURCE: "Portion of U.S. Air Pollution That Comes from Power Plants," in *Cleaner Power Plants*, U.S. Environmental Protection Agency, February 11, 2014, http://www.epa.gov/mats/powerplants.html (accessed August 31, 2015)

toxics standards rule. In "Cleaner Power Plants" (September 25, 2015, http://www3.epa.gov/mats/powerplants.html), the EPA notes that the new standards are expected to provide the following environmental benefits:

- Prevent approximately 90% of the mercury in the coal from entering the atmosphere

- Reduce acid gas emissions by 88%

- Reduce sulfur dioxide emissions by 41% beyond the reductions expected from implementation of the CSAPR

HAP Rules for Boilers and Process Heaters

The EPA (September 28, 2015, http://www.epa.gov/ttn/atw/mactfnlalph.html) has established NESHAPs for dozens of sources that are specific to certain industries, such as boat manufacturing and pesticide production. Huge controversy erupted in 2003, when the agency proposed NESHAPs for industrial, commercial, and institutional boilers and process heaters. These devices are quite common and are used not only at industrial facilities, such as refineries and chemical plants, but also at many universities, hospitals, and commercial facilities.

In 2007 the EPA's final standards for this source category were struck down by a court order, and the agency was ordered to rewrite them. A revised proposal

FIGURE 2.10

Locations of power plants covered by the Mercury and Air Toxics Standards (MATS) Rule

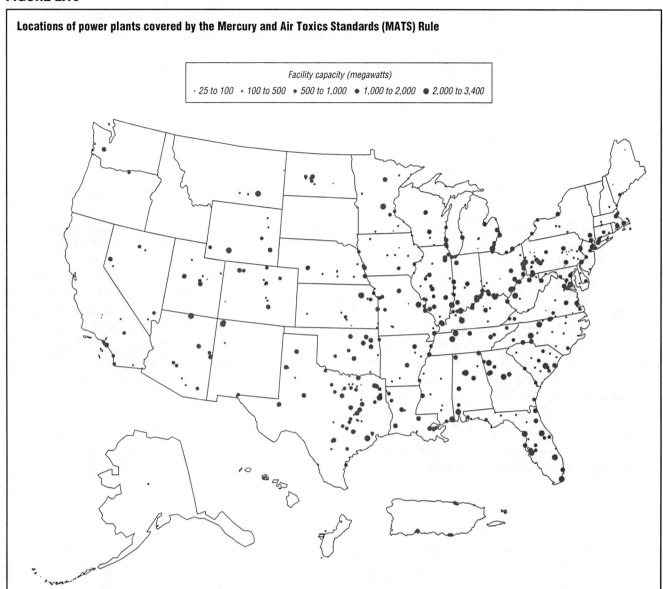

Facility capacity (megawatts)

· 25 to 100   · 100 to 500   • 500 to 1,000   ● 1,000 to 2,000   ● 2,000 to 3,400

National Electric Energy Data System (NEEDS 4.10 MATS) (EPA, December 2011) and EPA's Information Collection Request (ICR) for New and Existing Coal-And Oil-Fired Electric Utility Stream Generation Units (2010)

SOURCE: "The Toxics Rule Facilities," in *Where You Live: Power Plants Likely Covered by the Mercury and Air Toxics Standards (MATS) for Power Plants*, U.S. Environmental Protection Agency, December 2011, http://www.epa.gov/mats/pdfs/20111221facilitiesmap.pdf (accessed August 31, 2015)

in 2010 expanded the number of sources that were subject to the new rules, setting off a political firestorm. In "Rolling Onward" (RecyclingToday.com, May 15, 2012), Curt Harler notes that the EPA received nearly 5,000 public comments regarding the proposed rules. Industrial groups and conservative Republicans fiercely criticized the rules as too wide-sweeping and costly. At the time, the nation was beginning to recover from the Great Recession. During the midterm elections in November 2010 Republicans gained majority control in the U.S. House of Representatives. They began putting intense pressure on the Obama administration not to implement regulatory measures that some viewed as economically damaging to businesses.

In March 2011 the EPA published the revised final rule in the *Federal Register*, the legal archive of the federal government. However, months later the EPA stayed the effective date, thereby giving itself more time to truly finalize the rule. Environmentalists were furious about the decision and accused the Obama administration of bowing to political pressure from right-wing Republicans. In late 2011 the EPA again proposed revised standards and then finalized them in December 2012. However, environmentalists complained that the standards had been weakened. For example, in "U.S. EPA Softens Rules on Industrial Boiler Emissions" (ChicagoTribune.com, December 21, 2012), Valerie Volcovici quotes Frank O'Donnell of Clean Air Watch, who stated,

"These watered-down rules suggest the Obama administration will collaborate more with industry in the second [presidential] term."

In January 2015 the EPA proposed in "National Emission Standards for Hazardous Air Pollutants for Area Sources: Industrial, Commercial, and Institutional Boilers" (*Federal Register*, vol. 80, no. 13) changes to the standards. The agency noted that it received three petitions that raised five issues regarding the final rule that bore reconsideration. As a result, the EPA requested public comments on the proposed changes. As of November 2015, the standards had not been finalized.

THE AUTOMOBILE'S CONTRIBUTION TO AIR POLLUTION

For several decades following the passage of the original CAA in 1970, air pollution from industrial sources was the primary focus of lawmakers and the public. As dramatic achievements in air quality were obtained in this sector, more attention was focused on air pollutants that were associated with transportation vehicles. Figure 2.11 provides a breakdown of highway vehicle production by vehicle type for model years 1975 to 2014. Although cars still account for the majority of

highway vehicles, their share has declined dramatically as sports utility vehicles have grown in popularity. As noted earlier in this chapter, the EPA estimates that highway vehicles accounted for significant percentages of some of the criteria air pollutant emissions in 2013, including 34% of carbon monoxide, 38% of nitrous oxide, and 14% of VOCs. In addition, highway vehicles are minor sources of other pollutant emissions, including ammonia, PM, and sulfur dioxide.

Exhaust Emissions Limits

The 1990 amendments to the CAA included a program to control air pollution from new motor vehicles. The so-called EPA Tier 1 emissions standards were issued in 1991 and took effect during the mid-1990s. These standards applied to all new light-duty vehicles weighing less than 8,500 pounds (3,900 kg). This included cars, pickup trucks, and sport-utility vehicles. There were different emissions standards by weight class within Tier 1. In 1997 the EPA issued regulations for the National Low Emission Vehicle program, a voluntary program that was modeled after California standards for emissions reductions from motor vehicles.

FIGURE 2.11

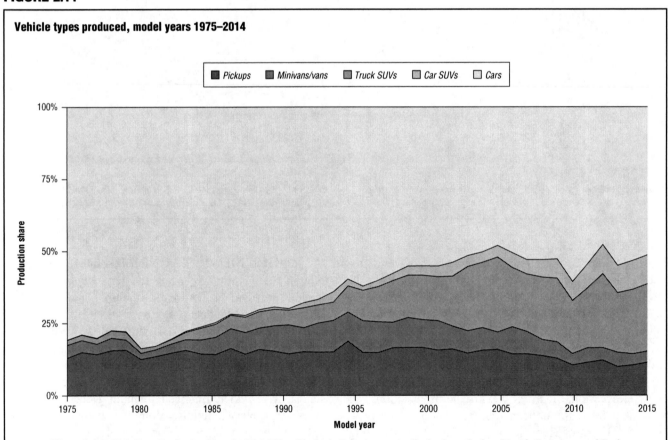

SOURCE: "Figure 3.4. Vehicle Type Production Share by Model Year," in *Light-Duty Automotive Technology, Carbon Dioxide Emissions, and Fuel Economy Trends: 1975 through 2014*, U.S. Environmental Protection Agency, October 2014, http://www.epa.gov/fueleconomy/fetrends/1975-2014/420r14023a.pdf (accessed September 11, 2015)

Because of California's extreme air pollution problems, the 1990 amendments to the CAA allowed states to set stricter emissions standards than those that were required by the amendments, which California did. These included strict new laws on automobile pollution. The California low-emission vehicle (LEV) regulations were originally adopted in 1991 and became applicable in 1994. LEV II regulations were passed in 1998 and became applicable with 2004 model year vehicles. LEV III amendments were adopted in 2012. According to the California Air Resources Board, in *The California Low-Emission Vehicle Regulations* (April 2013, http://www.arb.ca.gov/msprog/levprog/cleandoc/cleancomplete%20lev-ghg%20regs%204-13.pdf), the LEV III regulations will be phased in over the 2015 through 2025 model years.

The remaining 49 states have the option of choosing either the California standards or the standards set under the CAA. Some states have tougher tests for auto emissions than others. In most major metropolitan areas, owners of cars and light trucks are required to pay for exhaust emissions tests. For those that do not pass, repairs must be made to bring them into compliance.

In 1999 the EPA introduced its Tier 2 federal emissions limits for new vehicles. They took effect in 2004 and were completely implemented by 2009. Emissions limits apply to carbon monoxide, formaldehyde, NO_x, nonmethane organic gases, and PM. Manufacturers are allowed the flexibility to certify new vehicles to different sets of exhaust emissions standards called bins. The manufacturers must choose bins for their vehicles that ensure that their corporate sales fleet emits an average of no more than 0.07 grams of NO_x per mile.

In 2014 the EPA (October 6, 2015, http://www3.epa.gov/otaq/tier3.htm) finalized its Tier 3 Vehicle Emission and Fuel Standards Program, which imposes new emissions standards for vehicles and requires lower sulfur content for gasoline beginning in 2017. The agency notes in "EPA Sets Tier 3 Motor Vehicle Emission and Fuel Standards" (March 2014, http://www3.epa.gov/otaq/documents/tier3/420f14009.pdf) that the standards will supplement California's LEV III standards and the fuel economy and carbon dioxide emissions standards that were issued jointly in 2010 by the U.S. Department of Transportation's National Highway Traffic Safety Administration (NHTSA) and the EPA. The latter standards are described later in this chapter. Greenhouse gas emissions and standards are discussed in detail in Chapter 3.

THE VOLKSWAGEN EMISSIONS SCANDAL. In 2015 a major scandal erupted over allegations that the Volkswagen Group (VW) had deceived regulators about the emissions from some of its vehicles. The article "VW Scandal: Engineer's Testing 'Opened a Can of Worms' for Automaker" (Reuters, September 24, 2015) indicates that from late 2012 through early 2013 researchers at West Virginia University tested the emissions from several different car models with diesel engines. The tests were done while the cars were stationary and under real-life driving conditions. The researchers noticed that two VW models, a Passat and a Jetta, produced much higher emissions during the highway tests than during the stationary tests. They notified the EPA and the California Air Resources Board. According to the article, those two agencies confirmed the test results.

In "Everything We Know about Volkswagen Emissions Scandal" (Freep.com, September 22, 2015), the *Detroit Free Press* notes that the agencies asked VW to explain the discrepancies, and the corporation eventually admitted that it had purposely rigged some of its cars to provide deceptive test results. This was achieved through use of a so-called defeat device. The *Detroit Free Press* explains, "The device would activate the cars' emission controls during testing, but deactivate them in real-world driving." As many as 11 million VW cars worldwide are believed to have been rigged with the defeat devices.

VW's chief executive officer resigned after apologizing for the scandal. The corporation faces large fines from U.S. agencies, such as the EPA, and could face criminal charges from the U.S. Department of Justice.

Gasoline Formulations

During the 1980s lead was phased out of gasoline to provide substantial improvements in air quality. A variety of other federal and state standards have gone into effect that dictate particular properties of gasoline, such as volatility (tendency to evaporate) and levels of NO_x, heavy metals, toxic compounds, sulfur, and oxygen. The CAA requires the use of specially blended gasoline in areas of the country that are deemed nonattainment for ozone or carbon monoxide levels. Attainment areas can choose to opt-in to these requirements.

All the varying standards have resulted in the creation of many so-called boutique gasolines that greatly complicate the distribution dynamics for gasoline in the country. Critics complain that a gasoline shortage in one area can often not be relieved by shipping in gasoline from another part of the country because of the highly varying standards.

Corporate Average Fuel Economy Standards

In 1973 some of the nations belonging to the Organization of the Petroleum Exporting Countries imposed an oil embargo that provided a painful reminder to Americans of how dependent the country had become on foreign sources of fuel. Congress passed the 1975 Automobile Fuel Efficiency Act, which set the initial Corporate Average Fuel Economy (CAFE) standards. The NHTSA is responsible for establishing the standards and promulgating the regulations concerning them. The EPA is responsible for calculating the average fuel economy that is achieved by each vehicle manufacturer.

CAFE standards have varied over the decades, but have generally increased with time. In 2010 the NHTSA and the EPA issued a joint rulemaking that established a new program to regulate fuel economy and greenhouse gas emissions, such as carbon dioxide, for model years 2012 to 2016 of cars and light-duty trucks. (See Table 2.6.) Two years later the agencies finalized standards for model years 2017 to 2025. The targets are based on vehicle size or footprint (the distance between the axles times the distance between the wheels on the same axle). Table 2.7 shows the emissions and fuel economy targets in effect in 2025 for some example cars and light-duty trucks.

Alternative Fuels

Early pollution-reducing efforts by vehicle manufacturers focused on reducing tailpipe emissions instead of eliminating their formation in the first place. Automakers introduced lighter engines, fuel injection systems, catalytic converters, and other technological improvements. Since the 1970s concerns about U.S. dependence on foreign oil supplies and environmental issues have focused attention on the development of alternative fuels for transportation vehicles. The Energy Policy Act of 1992 defines alternative fuels as those that are "substantially not petroleum and would yield substantial energy security benefits and substantial environmental benefits." Under the act the following are designated as alternative fuels:

- Coal-derived liquid fuels

- Liquefied petroleum gas (propane)

- Natural gas and liquid fuels domestically produced from natural gas

- Methanol, ethanol, and other alcohols

- Blends of 85% or more of alcohol with gasoline

- Biodiesel and other fuels derived from biological materials

- Electricity

- Hydrogen

- P-series fuels (blends of natural gas liquids, ethanol, and the biomass-derived cosolvent methyltetrahydrofuran)

Although alternative fuels offer energy security advantages over gasoline, their use may substitute one environmental problem for another. Alternative fuels can also have trade-offs in terms of economic and energy effects. This is particularly true for ethanol.

TABLE 2.6

Fuel economy and carbon dioxide emissions standards for cars and light trucks, model years 2012–25

Year	Cars	Light trucks	Combined cars and light trucks
	Average required fuel economy (miles per gallon)		
2012	33.3	25.4	29.7
2013	34.2	26.0	30.5
2014	34.9	26.6	31.3
2015	36.2	27.5	32.6
2016	37.8	28.8	34.1
2017	40.1	29.4	35.4
2018	41.6	30.0	36.5
2019	43.1	30.6	37.7
2020	44.8	31.2	38.9
2021	46.8	33.3	41.0
2022	49.0	34.9	43.0
2023	51.2	36.6	45.1
2024	53.6	38.5	47.4
2025	56.2	40.3	49.7
	Average projected emissions compliance levels under the footprint-based carbon dioxide standards (grams per mile)		
2012	263	346	295
2013	256	337	286
2014	247	326	276
2015	236	312	263
2016	225	298	250
2017	212	295	243
2018	202	285	232
2019	191	277	222
2020	182	269	213
2021	172	249	199
2022	164	237	190
2023	157	225	180
2024	150	214	171
2025	143	203	163

Note: The required fuel economy, along with projections of CO$_2$ emissions, shown here use a model year 2008 baseline. The presented rates of increase in stringency for National Highway Traffic Safety Administration Corporate Average Fuel Economy (NHTSA CAFE) standards are lower than the Environmental Protection Agency (EPA) rates of increase in stringency for greenhouse gas (GHG) standards. One major difference is that NHTSA's standards, unlike EPA's, do not reflect the inclusion of air conditioning system refrigerant and leakage improvements, but EPA's standards would allow consideration of such improvements which reduce GHGs but generally do not affect fuel economy. The 2025 EPA GHG standard of 163 grams/mile would be equivalent to 54.5 mpg, if the vehicles were to meet this level all through fuel economy improvements. The agencies expect, however, that a portion of these improvements will be made through reductions in air conditioning leakage, which would not contribute to fuel economy.

SOURCE: Stacy C. Davis, Susan W. Diegel, and Robert G. Boundy, "Table 4.18. Fuel Economy and Carbon Dioxide Emissions Standards, MY 2012–2015," in *Transportation Energy Data Book, Edition 33*, Oak Ridge National Laboratory, July 2014

THE ETHANOL DEBATE. Ethanol is an alcohol that can be derived from sugar-containing plants. A variety of plants can be used, but corn is, by far, the sugar source of choice for U.S.-produced ethanol. Ethanol is used as a motor vehicle fuel through two primary means. It can be added to regular gasoline at concentrations of up to 10% ethanol with 90% gasoline. This mixture is known as E10 and can be used in any regular gasoline-powered vehicle. Another product, E85, is a blend of 85% ethanol with 15% gasoline. E85 can only be used in so-called flex-fuel vehicles that are specially designed to combust either gasoline or gasoline/ethanol mixtures containing up to 85% ethanol. Ethanol has a lower energy content than

TABLE 2.7

Fuel economy and carbon dioxide emissions targets for cars and light trucks, model years 2025

Vehicle type	Example models	Example model footprint (square feet)	CO_2 emissions target (grams per mile)	Fuel economy target (miles per gallon)
		Example passenger cars		
Compact car	Honda Fit	40	131	61.1
Midsize car	Ford Fusion	46	147	54.9
Fullsize car	Chrysler 300	53	170	48.0
		Example light-duty trucks		
Small SUV	4WD Ford Escape	44	170	47.5
Midsize crossover	Nissan Murano	49	188	43.4
Minivan	Toyota Sienna	55	209	39.2
Large pickup truck	Chevy Silverado	67	252	33.0

Note: Examples use model year 2012 vehicle specifications. The fuel economy from this table will not match the fuel economy listed on the window sticker of a new vehicle. Window sticker fuel economy is calculated by a different methodology than the Corporate Average Fuel Economy. CO_2 = Carbon dioxide.

The target levels for the fuel economy and carbon dioxide emission standards for vehicles manufactured in model years 2012-on are assigned based on a vehicle's "footprint." Each footprint has a different target.

The vehicle footprint is calculated as:

footprint = track width × wheelbase, where track width = lateral distance between the centerlines of the base tires at ground, and wheelbase = longitudinal distance between the front and rear wheel centerlines.

SOURCE: Stacy C. Davis, Susan W. Diegel, and Robert G. Boundy, "Table 4.19. Fuel Economy and Carbon Dioxide Targets for Model Year 2025," in *Transportation Energy Data Book, Edition 33*, Oak Ridge National Laboratory, July 2014

gasoline. This means that a gallon of E85 gets fewer miles to the gallon than a gallon of gasoline.

Because ethanol is relatively expensive to produce, the federal government has encouraged its production since the 1970s with tax incentives. In addition, the federal government and some state governments have issued mandates (legal requirements) that their fleets of government-owned vehicles increasingly use alternative fuels. At the federal level, the Energy Policy Act of 2005 and the Energy Independence and Security Act of 2007 mandated increased use of biofuels (such as ethanol) through the early 2020s. These mandates have spurred manufacturers to produce more flex-fuel vehicles for government and private customers.

Ethanol is touted by its proponents as an environmentally friendly alternative to gasoline. For example, the Renewable Fuels Association, a national trade association for the ethanol industry, states in "Why Is Ethanol Important?" (2015, http://www.ethanolrfa.org/consumers/why-is-ethanol-important) that "ethanol use reduces greenhouse gas emissions by 40–50% compared to gasoline. Ethanol also reduces emissions of particulate matter, carbon monoxide, and volatile organic compounds, displacing toxic aromatics such as benzene and toluene." The U.S. Department of Energy's (DOE) Alternative Fuels Data Center notes in "Ethanol Vehicle Emissions" (December 16, 2014, http://www.afdc.energy.gov/vehicles/flexible_fuel_emissions.html) that although ethanol is an alternative fuel, it still produces emissions of "regulated pollutants, toxic chemicals, and greenhouse gases." The Alternative Fuels Data Center points out, however, that "when compared to gasoline, the use of high-level ethanol blends, such as E85, generally result in lower emissions levels."

ALTERNATIVE FUEL VEHICLES AND STATIONS. Alternative fuels cannot become a viable transportation option unless a fuel supply is readily available to consumers. Ideally, the infrastructure for supplying alternative fuels will be developed simultaneously with the vehicles. Table 2.8 estimates the number of alternative fuel highway vehicles in use between 1995 and 2011. Overall, E85 vehicles were the most abundant, accounting for 72% of the total in 2011.

As shown in Table 2.9, an estimated 40,578 alternative fuel stations and electric charging outlets were operating around the country in 2014. The vast majority of them—22,747 charging outlets and 9,794 stations—serviced electric vehicles. California (8,876) had the largest number of offerings, followed by Texas (3,153), Washington (2,100), Florida (1,835), and New York (1,647).

Market success of alternative fuels depends on public acceptance. People are accustomed to using gasoline as their main transportation fuel, and it is readily available. As federal and state requirements for alternative fuels increase, so should the availability of such fuels as well as their acceptance by the general public. Although E85 is heavily marketed by the ethanol industry and supported by government mandates, it is generally not expected to satisfy the United States' long-term need for an environmentally friendly vehicle fuel. In the long run, hydrogen and electricity seem the most promising of the alternative fuels for vehicles.

HYDROGEN-FUELED VEHICLES ON THE HORIZON. As the simplest and most abundant naturally occurring element, hydrogen can be found in materials such as coal,

TABLE 2.8

Number of alternative fuel highway vehicles in use, 1995–2011

Year	LPG	CNG	LNG	M85	M100	E85[a]	E95	Electricity[b]	Hydrogen	Total
1995	172,806	50,218	603	18,319	386	1,527	136	2,860	0	246,855
1996	175,585	60,144	663	20,265	172	4,536	361	3,280	0	265,006
1997	175,679	68,571	813	21,040	172	9,130	347	4,453	0	280,205
1998	177,183	78,782	1,172	19,648	200	12,788	14	5,243	0	295,030
1999	178,610	91,267	1,681	18,964	198	24,604	14	6,964	0	322,302
2000	181,994	100,750	2,090	10,426	0	87,570	4	11,830	0	394,664
2001	185,053	111,851	2,576	7,827	0	100,303	0	17,847	0	425,457
2002	187,680	120,839	2,708	5,873	0	120,951	0	33,047	0	471,098
2003	190,369	114,406	2,640	0	0	176,799	0	47,485	9	531,708
2004	182,864	118,532	2,717	0	0	211,800	0	49,536	43	565,492
2005	173,795	117,699	2,748	0	0	246,363	0	51,398	119	592,122
2006	164,846	116,131	2,798	0	0	297,099	0	53,526	159	634,559
2007	158,254	114,391	2,781	0	0	364,384	0	55,730	223	695,763
2008	151,049	113,973	3,101	0	0	450,327	0	56,901	313	775,664
2009	147,030	114,270	3,176	0	0	504,297	0	57,185	357	826,315
2010	143,037	115,863	3,354	0	0	618,506	0	57,462	421	938,643
2011	139,477	118,214	3,436	0	0	862,837	0	67,295	527	1,191,786
					Average annual percentage change					
1995–2011	−1.3%	5.5%	11.5%	−100.0%	−100.0%	48.6%	−100.0%	21.8%		10.3%

[a]Includes only those E85 vehicles believed to be used as alternative-fuels vehicles (AFVs), primarily fleet-operated vehicles; excludes other vehicles with E85-fueling capability. In 1997, some vehicle manufacturers began including E85-fueling capability in certain model lines of vehicles. For 2007, the Energy Information Administration (EIA) estimates that the number of E85 vehicles that are capable of operating on E85, motor gasoline, or both, is about 7.1 million. Many of these AFVs are sold and used as traditional gasoline-powered vehicles.
[b]Excludes hybrid and electric vehicles.
Note: Vehicles in Use represent accumulated acquisitions, less retirements, as of the end of each calendar year. They do not include concept and demonstration vehicles. LPG = Liquified Petroleum Gas. CNG = Compressed Natural Gas. LNG = Liquefied Natural Gas.

SOURCE: Stacy C. Davis, Susan W. Diegel, and Robert G. Boundy, "Table 6.1. Estimates of Alternative Fuel Highway Vehicles in Use, 1995–2011," in *Transportation Energy Data Book, Edition 33*, Oak Ridge National Laboratory, July 2014

natural gas, and water. For decades advocates of hydrogen have promoted it as the fuel of the future because it is abundant, clean, and cheap. However, challenges with technology, economics, and safety issues have stymied its commercialization potential.

In 2003 President George W. Bush (1946–) announced the creation of the Hydrogen Fuel Initiative (HFI). The goal of this five-year $1.2 billion program was to develop the technology needed for commercially viable hydrogen-powered fuel cells for transportation vehicles and home/business use by 2020. The Energy Policy Act of 2005 extended the HFI beyond the initial five-year program through 2020.

In November 2014 the DOE issued *DOE Hydrogen and Fuel Cells Program: 2014 Annual Progress Report* (http://www.hydrogen.energy.gov/annual_progress14.html). The department notes that the technologies are advancing and that some hydrogen-fueled equipment has been adopted commercially, such as forklifts powered by fuel cells. It does not, however, provide an estimated schedule for when hydrogen-fueled passenger vehicles will become widely available.

ELECTRIC VEHICLES: PROMISE AND REALITY. The electric vehicle is not a new invention. Popular during the 1890s, the quiet, clean, and simple vehicle was expected to dominate the automotive market of the 20th century. Instead, it quietly disappeared as automakers

chose to invest billions of dollars in the internal combustion engine. It has taken a century, but the electric vehicle has returned.

Electric vehicles run on one or more electric motors that are powered by a battery pack. Because they do not burn or combust a fuel, electric cars have zero tailpipe emissions. However, the production of electricity at utility plants likely generates air pollutants. This is particularly true for coal-fired plants. According to the DOE, in "All-Electric Vehicles" (2015, http://www.fueleconomy.gov/Feg/evtech.shtml), electric cars do have several operational drawbacks. Most of the cars have a range of only about 100 to 200 miles (160 to 320 km) before they need a battery recharge. This is roughly half of the mileage achievable with a gasoline-powered vehicle before it needs refueling. The time required to fully recharge the battery pack of many electric cars ranges from four to eight hours. This is a substantial amount of time to people used to filling their cars with gasoline in a matter of minutes. In addition, the battery packs used in electric cars are large, heavy, and expensive to replace.

According to the DOE (http://www.fueleconomy.gov/feg/PowerSearch.do?action=noform&path=1&year1=1984&year2=2016&vtype=Electric), as of November 2015 there were 95 all-electric car models available to consumers covering model years 1984 to 2016. Examples include the Chevrolet Spark, Ford Focus, Honda Fit, and Nissan Leaf. Tesla Motors also had a few of its models on

TABLE 2.9

Alternative fuel sites, by state and fuel type, 2014

State	B20 sites	CNG sites	E85 sites	Electric stations	Electric charging outlets	Hydrogen sites	LNG sites	LPG sites	Totals by state*
Alabama	10	23	33	62	82	0	2	115	327
Alaska	0	1	0	0	0	0	0	6	7
Arizona	79	34	30	302	749	1	6	64	1,265
Arkansas	5	10	39	32	44	0	1	37	168
California	82	275	93	2,100	6,028	24	44	230	8,876
Colorado	17	36	89	170	351	1	0	47	711
Connecticut	2	15	1	161	278	1	1	15	474
Delaware	1	1	2	13	20	1	0	6	44
Dist. of Columbia	7	2	3	61	139	0	0	0	212
Florida	17	34	55	544	1,115	0	1	69	1,835
Georgia	25	27	60	249	467	0	1	60	889
Hawaii	9	1	3	184	414	3	0	3	617
Idaho	4	10	9	14	21	0	6	25	89
Illinois	12	44	225	360	696	1	1	104	1,443
Indiana	7	21	178	123	207	0	1	175	712
Iowa	9	5	184	53	93	0	0	18	362
Kansas	6	8	25	75	127	0	0	37	278
Kentucky	4	4	60	39	100	0	0	48	255
Louisiana	2	23	5	45	65	0	1	34	175
Maine	3	1	0	20	25	0	0	10	59
Maryland	9	9	34	263	598	0	0	19	932
Massachusetts	13	23	8	243	582	1	0	17	887
Michigan	16	22	196	291	736	4	0	74	1,339
Minnesota	11	12	282	167	355	0	0	30	857
Mississippi	4	6	2	35	38	0	0	117	202
Missouri	4	14	108	100	181	1	0	65	473
Montana	6	2	3	4	2	0	0	43	60
Nebraska	4	9	78	20	33	0	0	22	166
Nevada	5	8	20	83	216	1	2	38	373
New Hampshire	4	3	0	38	53	0	0	11	109
New Jersey	5	30	5	130	233	0	0	9	412
New Mexico	8	11	15	22	54	0	0	45	155
New York	36	110	79	435	916	9	0	62	1,647
North Carolina	134	36	22	276	618	0	0	98	1,184
North Dakota	3	1	58	5	6	0	0	19	92
Ohio	18	32	113	153	224	2	3	65	610
Oklahoma	5	94	28	30	41	0	0	153	351
Oregon	24	14	8	403	957	0	1	31	1,438
Pennsylvania	7	55	35	197	308	2	0	73	677
Rhode Island	6	6	0	62	147	0	0	6	227
South Carolina	60	10	83	141	230	2	1	45	572
South Dakota	2	0	87	11	23	0	0	18	141
Tennessee	44	11	58	375	893	0	0	103	1,484
Texas	19	76	100	692	1,774	1	12	479	3,153
Utah	3	89	4	59	102	0	7	27	291
Vermont	2	3	1	33	68	0	0	2	109
Virginia	12	20	19	211	527	1	0	60	850
Washington	33	25	24	523	1,426	0	1	68	2,100
West Virginia	2	4	5	26	98	0	0	13	148
Wisconsin	4	53	131	153	274	0	1	55	671
Wyoming	13	12	9	6	13	0	0	17	70
Totals by fuel	**817**	**1,375**	**2,709**	**9,794**	**22,747**	**56**	**93**	**2,987**	**40,578**

*Totals by state is the total number of fuel types available at stations. Stations are counted once for each type of fuel available.
B20 = A blend of 20% biodiesel with 80% petroleum diesel.
CNG = Compressed natural gas.
E85 = A blend of 85% ethanol with 15% gasoline.
LNG = Liquefied natural gas.
LPG = Liquefied petroleum gas.
Note: This list includes public and private refuel sites; therefore, not all of these sites are available to the public.

SOURCE: Stacy C. Davis, Susan W. Diegel, and Robert G. Boundy "Table 6.8. Number of Alternative Refuel Sites by State and Fuel Type, 2014," in *Transportation Energy Data Book, Edition 33*, Oak Ridge National Laboratory, July 2014

the list. The company (http://www.teslamotors.com/super charger) is notable for its innovative charging technology that allows its cars to be charged to 80% battery capacity in about 30 minutes at special charging stations. Tesla Motors is also known for the luxuriousness of its all-electric cars. Alanna Petroff reports in "Porsche Plans Electric Car to Challenge Tesla" (CNN.com, September 15, 2015) that in 2015 Porsche and Audi announced plans to market luxury all-electric cars with fast-charging capabilities.

ADVANCED TECHNOLOGY VEHICLES. Many experts believe the most feasible solution in the near future is the use of vehicles that use a combination of gasoline and one of the alternative fuel sources. These are called advanced technology vehicles or hybrid vehicles. Gasoline-electric hybrids have proven to be the most commercially viable option. In fact, the term *hybrid* is now associated almost entirely with the gasoline-electric vehicle. These hybrids rely on a small internal combustion engine and electricity (from batteries). As such, their tailpipe emissions are lower than those of comparable vehicles that are powered fully by gasoline.

The DOE (May 2015, http://www.afdc.energy.gov/uploads/data/data_source/10301/10301_hev_sales.xlsx) estimates that approximately 3.6 million of the vehicles were sold in the United States between 1999 and 2014. The Toyota Prius was introduced in 2000 and was the top-selling model on an annual basis through 2014.

THE CAA: COSTS AND BENEFITS

In 1970 Congress passed the landmark CAA, proclaiming that it would restore urban air quality. It was no coincidence that the law was passed during a 14-day smog alert in the District of Columbia. The act was amended several times over the following decades, including a massive overhaul in 1990. Although the act has had mixed results, and many goals remain to be met, most experts credit it with making great strides toward cleaning up the air. As of October 2015, the EPA (http://www2.epa.gov/clean-air-act-overview/benefits-and-costs-clean-air-act) had published three comprehensive reports mandated by the CAA on the monetary costs and benefits of controlling air pollution.

In *The Benefits and Costs of the Clean Air Act, 1970 to 1990* (October 1997, http://www2.epa.gov/sites/production/files/2015-06/documents/contsetc.pdf), the EPA concludes that the economic value of clean air programs was 42 times greater than the total costs of air pollution control during the 20-year period. The agency finds that many positive consequences occurred in the U.S. economy because of CAA programs and regulations. The CAA affected industrial production, investment, productivity, consumption, employment, and economic growth. In fact, the agency estimates that total agricultural benefits from the CAA were almost $10 billion. The EPA compares benefits with direct costs or expenditures. The total costs of the CAA were $523 billion for the 20-year period, whereas the total benefits equaled $22.2 trillion—a net benefit of approximately $21.7 trillion.

According to the EPA, in *The Benefits and Costs of the Clean Air Act, 1990 to 2010* (November 1999, http://www2.epa.gov/sites/production/files/2015-07/documents/fullrept.pdf), the second mandated review of the CAA, the act produced major reductions in pollution that causes illness and disease, smog, acid rain, haze, and damage to the environment. Using a sophisticated array of computer models and the latest cost data, the EPA finds that by 2010 the act had prevented 23,000 Americans from dying prematurely and averted more than 1.7 million asthma attacks. The CAA prevented 47,000 episodes of acute bronchitis, 91,000 occurrences of shortness of breath, 4.1 million lost workdays, and 31 million days in restricted activity because of illness. Another 22,000 respiratory-related hospital admissions were averted, as well as 42,000 admissions for heart disease and 4,800 emergency department visits for asthma.

The EPA estimates that the benefits of CAA programs in the reduction of illness and premature death alone totaled about $110 billion. By contrast, the agency finds that the cost of achieving these benefits was only $27 billion, which was a fraction of the value of the benefits. In addition, the agency reports that there were other benefits that scientists and economists cannot quantify and express in monetary terms, such as controlling cancer-causing air toxins and bringing benefits to crops and ecosystems by reducing pollutants.

At the same time, many cities were still not in compliance with the law. One reason efforts to clean the air were only partly successful was that they focused on specific measures to combat individual pollutants rather than on addressing the underlying social and economic structures that create the problem—for example, the distance between many Americans' residences and their places of work.

In April 2011 the EPA issued *The Benefits and Costs of the Clean Air Act from 1990 to 2020* (http://www2.epa.gov/sites/production/files/2015-07/documents/fullreport_rev_a.pdf), the third mandated review of the benefits and costs of the CAA. The agency estimates that by 2020 the CAA as amended will have prevented more than 230,000 early deaths and provided approximately $2 trillion in economic benefits. The vast majority (85%) of these benefits will be attributed to a reduction in premature mortality due to decreased air quality concentrations of PM. Other benefits include decreased premature mortality due to ozone exposure, prevention of health problems (such as myocardial infarctions and chronic bronchitis), and improved environmental conditions, particularly visibility.

PUBLIC OPINION ABOUT AIR POLLUTION

Every year the Gallup Organization conducts a poll on the environment around the time of the nation's celebration of Earth Day. In March 2015, 38% of those asked expressed a great deal of concern about air pollution, compared with 33% who expressed a fair amount of concern. (See Table 2.10.) Another 19% indicated only a little concern and 10% expressed no concern. The percentage of poll respondents indicating a great deal of concern about air pollution has dropped dramatically in recent years, from a high of 63% in May 1989.

TABLE 2.10

Public concern about air pollution, selected years 1989–2015

	Great deal	Fair amount	Only a little	Not at all	No opinion
2015 Mar 5–8	38	33	19	10	*
2014 Mar 6–9	46	27	21	7	—
2013 Mar 7–10	40	30	20	9	—
2012 Mar 8–11	36	35	22	7	*
2011 Mar 3–6	36	36	20	8	*
2010 Mar 4–7	38	32	22	8	*
2009 Mar 5–8	45	31	18	6	*
2008 Mar 6–9	43	35	17	6	—
2007 Mar 11–14	46	33	15	5	*
2006 Mar 13–16	44	34	15	7	*
2004 Mar 8–11	39	30	23	8	*
2003 Mar 3–5	42	32	20	6	*
2002 Mar 4–7	45	33	18	4	*
2001 Mar 5–7	48	34	14	4	*
2000 Apr 3–9	59	29	9	3	*
1999 Apr 13–14	52	35	10	3	*
1999 Mar 12–14	47	33	16	4	*
1997 Oct 27–28	42	34	18	5	1
1991 Apr 11–14	59	28	10	4	*
1990 Apr 5–8	58	29	9	4	*
1989 May 4–7	63	24	8	4	*

*Less than 0.5%.
—No responses.

SOURCE: Jeff Jones and Lydia Saad, "I'm going to read you a list of environmental problems. As I read each one, please tell me if you personally worry about this problem a great deal, a fair amount, only a little, or not at all. First, how much do you personally worry about—air pollution?" in *Gallup Poll Social Series: Environment—Final Topline*, The Gallup Organization, March 5–8, 2015, http://www.gallup.com/file/poll/182111/150325EnviroWorries.pdf (accessed August 28, 2015). Copyright © 2015 Gallup, Inc. All rights reserved. The content is used with permission; however, Gallup retains all rights of republication.

CHAPTER 3
CLIMATE CHANGE

DEFINING CLIMATE AND CLIMATE CHANGE

Climate and weather are not the same thing. Both describe conditions in the lower atmosphere—for example, wet or dry, cold or warm, stormy or fair, and cloudy or clear. Weather is the short-term local state of the atmosphere. Weather conditions can change from moment to moment and can differ in two places that are relatively close together. Climate describes the average pattern of weather conditions that are experienced by a region over a long period. For example, Florida has a warm climate but can experience days and even weeks of cold weather.

The earth's climate as a whole has not changed much over the last several thousand years. In general, most of the planet has been warm enough for humans, animals, and plants to thrive. This was not so in the distant past, when the climate fluctuated between long periods of cold and warmth, each lasting for many thousands of years. Scientists are not sure what triggered these major climate changes. A variety of factors are believed to have been involved, including movement of the tectonic plates, changes in the earth's orbit around the sun, and variations in atmospheric gases.

The earth's temperature depends on a delicate balance of energy inputs and outputs, chemical processes, and physical phenomena. As shown in Figure 3.1, solar radiation passes through the earth's atmosphere and warms the earth. The earth emits infrared radiation. Some outgoing infrared radiation is not allowed to escape into outer space but is trapped beneath the atmosphere. The amount of energy that is trapped depends on many variables. One major factor is atmospheric composition. Some gases, such as water vapor, carbon dioxide, and methane, act to trap heat beneath the atmosphere in the same way that glass panels trap heat in a greenhouse. The panels allow sunlight into the greenhouse, but prevent heat from escaping.

The earth's surface temperature is about 60 degrees Fahrenheit (33 degrees C) warmer than it would be if natural greenhouse gases were not present. Without this natural warming process, the earth would be much colder and could not sustain life as it now exists.

It is necessary, however, to distinguish between the "natural" and the "enhanced" greenhouse effect. The natural greenhouse effect provides a warm atmosphere for the earth that is necessary for life. The theory behind the enhanced greenhouse effect is that human activities have loaded the atmosphere with too much carbon dioxide and other heat-trapping gases. This has increased the earth's temperature above that expected from the natural greenhouse effect, which is known as global warming. Global warming is one aspect of climate change, which poses numerous consequences to the earth's environment and inhabitants. These consequences include rising sea levels, stronger storms, and habitat loss and extinction. (See Figure 3.2.) The primary human activities blamed for inducing climate change are the burning of fossil fuels (mainly coal and oil) and their derivatives (such as gasoline) and the destruction of large amounts of vegetation that normally absorb carbon dioxide.

A GLOBAL PROBLEM

The global nature and consequences of climate change have prompted an international effort to analyze the problem and its possible remedies. In 1988 the World Meteorological Organization (WMO), a nongovernmental agency under the United Nations Environment Programme (UNEP), established the Intergovernmental Panel on Climate Change (IPCC). As of November 2015, the IPCC (http://www.ipcc.ch/publications_and _data/publications _and_data_reports.shtml) had published several assessment reports that provide many data used in this chapter:

- *Climate Change*, which was published in 1990

- *Climate Change 1995*

- *Climate Change 2001*

- *Climate Change 2007*

- *Climate Change 2013: The Physical Science Basis*

FIGURE 3.1

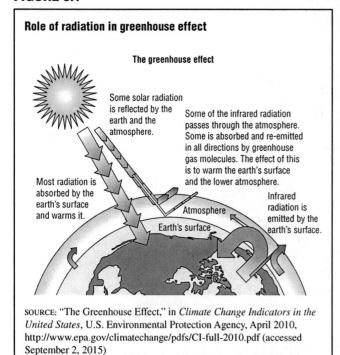

Role of radiation in greenhouse effect

The greenhouse effect

Some solar radiation is reflected by the earth and the atmosphere.

Some of the infrared radiation passes through the atmosphere. Some is absorbed and re-emitted in all directions by greenhouse gas molecules. The effect of this is to warm the earth's surface and the lower atmosphere.

Most radiation is absorbed by the earth's surface and warms it.

Infrared radiation is emitted by the earth's surface.

Atmosphere

Earth's surface

SOURCE: "The Greenhouse Effect," in *Climate Change Indicators in the United States*, U.S. Environmental Protection Agency, April 2010, http://www.epa.gov/climatechange/pdfs/CI-full-2010.pdf (accessed September 2, 2015)

GREENHOUSE GASES

Greenhouse gases are gases in the atmosphere that allow shortwave radiation (sunlight) from the sun to pass through to the earth but that absorb and reradiate long-wave infrared radiation (heat) coming from the earth's surface. (See Figure 3.1.) This process serves to warm the lower atmosphere (the troposphere). The troposphere extends from the earth's surface up to approximately 5.5 to 7.5 miles (9 to 12 km) above the surface. (See Figure 3.3.)

Water Vapor

Water vapor is part of the natural water cycle that takes place on and around the earth. Water evaporates from the surface, condenses into clouds, and then returns to the surface as precipitation. The water cycle is also a heat cycle in that it transfers heat around the earth and back and forth between the surface and the atmosphere. Water vapor cycles quickly through the atmosphere, lingering for a few days at most.

FIGURE 3.2

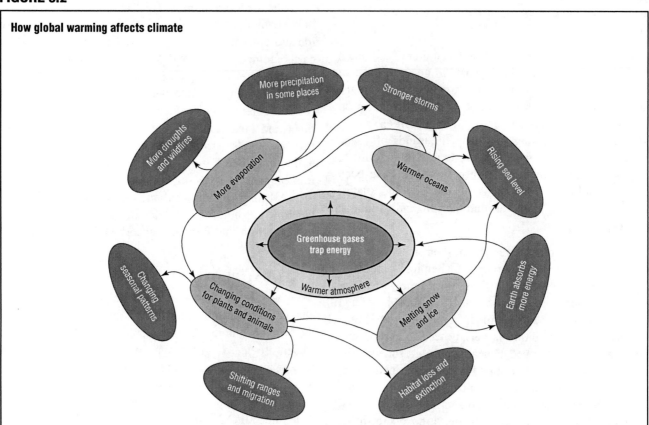

How global warming affects climate

More precipitation in some places

Stronger storms

More droughts and wildfires

More evaporation

Warmer oceans

Rising sea level

Greenhouse gases trap energy

Changing seasonal patterns

Changing conditions for plants and animals

Warmer atmosphere

Melting snow and ice

Earth absorbs more energy

Shifting ranges and migration

Habitat loss and extinction

SOURCE: "Climate Connections," in *A Student's Guide to Global Climate Change: Climate Concepts*, U.S. Environmental Protection Agency, August 28, 2014, http://www.epa.gov/climatechange/kids/basics/concepts.html (accessed September 2, 2015)

FIGURE 3.3

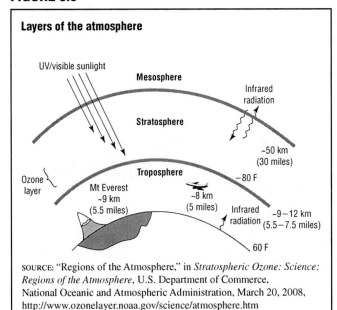

Layers of the atmosphere

UV/visible sunlight

Mesosphere

Stratosphere

Infrared radiation

Troposphere

~50 km (30 miles)

–80 F

Ozone layer

Mt Everest ~9 km (5.5 miles)

~8 km (5 miles)

Infrared radiation

~9–12 km (5.5–7.5 miles)

60 F

SOURCE: "Regions of the Atmosphere," in *Stratospheric Ozone: Science: Regions of the Atmosphere*, U.S. Department of Commerce, National Oceanic and Atmospheric Administration, March 20, 2008, http://www.ozonelayer.noaa.gov/science/atmosphere.htm (accessed September 2, 2015)

Scientists know that water vapor is the most prevalent greenhouse gas in the atmosphere and is responsible for the vast majority of the natural greenhouse effect. However, its role in the enhanced greenhouse effect and corresponding climate change has been a matter of debate.

Carbon Dioxide

Carbon dioxide (CO_2) is a heavy colorless gas. It is a respiration product from most living things. It is also released during the decay or combustion of organic materials. Huge amounts of carbon dioxide are cycled back and forth between the oceans and the atmosphere. Likewise, vegetation, algae, and some types of bacteria absorb carbon dioxide from the air. The result of all these processes is a global carbon cycle that maintains carbon dioxide at suitable levels in the atmosphere to sustain the natural greenhouse effect.

Before the 1800s humans had little impact on atmospheric carbon dioxide levels. The Industrial Revolution ushered in widespread use of fossil fuels, primarily coal, oil, and natural gas. Combustion of these carbon-loaded fuels releases large amounts of carbon dioxide. As shown in Figure 3.4 and Table 3.1, the United States emitted 6,673 teragrams (Tg) of greenhouse gases in 2013. Figure 3.4 provides a breakdown of total emissions by gas. Carbon dioxide accounted for the largest portion of the total.

The burning of fossil fuels by industry and motor vehicles is, by far, the leading source of carbon dioxide emissions in the United States and accounted for 5,505.2 Tg, or 82% of the nation's total greenhouse gas emissions

in 2013. (See Table 3.1). Other anthropogenic (human-caused) sources of carbon dioxide include deforestation, burning of biomass (combustible organic materials, such as wood scraps and crop residues), and certain industrial processes.

The atmospheric lifetime (how long a gas stays in the atmosphere) of carbon dioxide cannot be determined exactly because the gas is continuously cycled back and forth between the atmosphere and the oceans. Mason Inman reports in "Carbon Is Forever" (Nature.com, November 20, 2008) that climate scientists believe that approximately 20% of emitted carbon dioxide can stay in the atmosphere for "many thousands of years." The remainder has an atmospheric lifetime of several decades to several centuries. In "Carbon and Other Biogeochemical Cycles" (*Climate Change 2013: The Physical Science Basis*, http://www.ipcc.ch/pdf/assessment-report/ar5/wg1/WG1AR5_ALL_FINAL.pdf), Philippe Ciais et al. state, "Involvement of extremely long time scale processes into the removal of a pulse of CO_2 emissions into the atmosphere complicates comparison with the cycling of the other [greenhouse gases]. This is why the concept of a single, characteristic atmospheric lifetime is not applicable to CO_2."

Scientists use the global warming capacity of carbon dioxide as a benchmark against which the global warming capacity of other long-lived gases is compared. The so-called global warming potential (GWP) of carbon dioxide is arbitrarily assigned a value of 1. The GWP of other long-lived greenhouse gases is then calculated based on their relative capacity to trap heat in the atmosphere over the same period.

Methane

Methane (CH_4) is a colorless gas found in trace (extremely small) amounts in the atmosphere. It is the primary component of natural gas—the gas trapped beneath the earth's crust that is mined and burned for energy. Methane is an important component of greenhouse emissions, second only to carbon dioxide. (See Figure 3.4.) According to the IPCC, in *Climate Change 2013: The Physical Science Basis*, methane has a GWP of 28 for a 100-year period, meaning that methane is 28 times more effective at trapping heat in the atmosphere over 100 years than the same mass of carbon dioxide. Human sources of atmospheric methane include landfills, natural gas systems, agricultural activities, coal mining, and wastewater treatment processes.

Methane emissions between 1990 and 2013 are listed in Table 3.1 for selected years. Note that the units are Tg CO_2 equivalents. In "Glossary of Climate Change Terms" (October 26, 2015, http://epa.gov/climatechange/glossary.html), the U.S. Environmental Protection Agency (EPA) explains

FIGURE 3.4

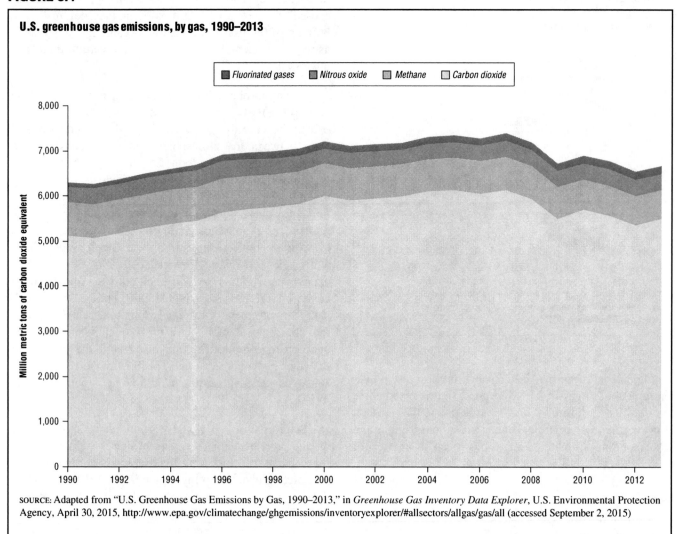

U.S. greenhouse gas emissions, by gas, 1990–2013

SOURCE: Adapted from "U.S. Greenhouse Gas Emissions by Gas, 1990–2013," in *Greenhouse Gas Inventory Data Explorer*, U.S. Environmental Protection Agency, April 30, 2015, http://www.epa.gov/climatechange/ghgemissions/inventoryexplorer/#allsectors/allgas/gas/all (accessed September 2, 2015)

that carbon dioxide equivalents are calculated by multiplying the tons of a gas by the GWP of the gas.

Methane emissions in 2013 totaled 636.3 Tg CO_2 equivalents. (See Table 3.1.) Natural gas systems, enteric fermentation, and landfills were the primary contributors. Enteric fermentation is a natural digestive process that occurs in domestic animals, such as cattle and sheep, that releases methane.

Humans contribute to atmospheric methane levels through activities that concentrate and magnify biological decomposition. This includes landfilling organic materials, raising livestock, cultivating rice in paddies, collecting sewage for treatment, and constructing artificial wetlands. In addition, methane is a by-product of the combustion of biomass and is vented (intentionally and unintentionally) during the extraction and processing of fossil fuels. It also results from incomplete combustion of fossil fuels. The IPCC notes that methane is believed to break down in the atmosphere after approximately 12 years.

Ozone

Ozone (O_3) is a blue-tinted gas naturally found in the earth's atmosphere. In "Science: Ozone Basics" (March 20, 2008, http://www.ozonelayer.noaa.gov/science/basics.htm), the National Oceanic and Atmospheric Administration (NOAA) indicates that approximately 90% of the earth's ozone lies in the stratosphere, the atmospheric layer lying above the troposphere. The so-called ozone layer absorbs harmful ultraviolet radiation from the sun, preventing it from reaching the ground. Scientists believe stratospheric ozone is being depleted by the introduction of certain industrial chemicals, primarily chlorine and bromine. (See Chapter 4.) This depletion has serious consequences in terms of ultraviolet radiation effects and probably lessens the warmth-trapping capability of ozone at this level.

Tropospheric ozone is believed to be a potent greenhouse gas and is the primary component in smog, a key air pollutant. It is not emitted directly into the air but forms because of complex reactions that occur when

TABLE 3.1

Trends in U.S. greenhouse gas emissions and sinks, selected years 1990–2013

Gas/source	1990	2005	2009	2010	2011	2012	2013
	5,123.7	6,134.0	5,500.6	5,704.5	5,568.9	5,358.3	5,505.2
Fossil fuel combustion	4,740.7	5,747.7	5,197.1	5,367.1	5,231.3	5,026.0	5,157.7
Electricity generation	1,820.8	2,400.9	2,145.7	2,258.4	2,157.7	2,022.2	2,039.8
Transportation	1,493.8	1,887.8	1,720.3	1,732.0	1,711.5	1,700.8	1,718.4
Industrial	842.5	827.8	727.7	775.7	774.1	784.2	817.3
Residential	338.3	357.8	336.4	334.7	327.2	283.1	329.6
Commercial	217.4	223.5	223.5	220.2	221.0	197.1	220.7
U.S. territories	27.9	49.9	43.5	46.2	39.8	38.6	32.0
Non-energy use of fuels	117.7	138.9	106.0	114.6	108.4	104.9	119.8
Iron and steel production & metallurgical coke production	99.8	66.7	43.0	55.7	60.0	54.3	52.3
Natural gas systems	37.6	30.0	32.2	32.3	35.6	34.8	37.8
Cement production	33.3	45.9	29.4	31.3	32.0	35.1	36.1
Petrochemical production	21.6	28.1	23.7	27.4	26.4	26.5	26.5
Lime production	11.7	14.6	11.4	13.4	14.0	13.7	14.1
Ammonia production	13.0	9.2	8.5	9.2	9.3	9.4	10.2
Incineration of waste	8.0	12.5	11.3	11.0	10.5	10.4	10.1
Petroleum systems	4.4	4.9	4.7	4.2	4.5	5.1	6.0
Liming of agricultural soils	4.7	4.3	3.7	4.8	3.9	5.8	5.9
Urea consumption for non-agricultural purposes	3.8	3.7	3.4	4.7	4.0	4.4	4.7
Other process uses of carbonates	4.9	6.3	7.6	9.6	9.3	8.0	4.4
Urea fertilization	2.4	3.5	3.6	3.8	4.1	4.2	4.0
Aluminum production	6.8	4.1	3.0	2.7	3.3	3.4	3.3
Soda ash production and consumption	2.7	2.9	2.5	2.6	2.6	2.7	2.7
Ferroalloy production	2.2	1.4	1.5	1.7	1.7	1.9	1.8
Titanium dioxide production	1.2	1.8	1.6	1.8	1.7	1.5	1.6
Zinc production	0.6	1.0	0.9	1.2	1.3	1.5	1.4
Phosphoric acid production	1.6	1.4	1.0	1.1	1.2	1.1	1.2
Glass production	1.5	1.9	1.0	1.5	1.3	1.2	1.2
Carbon dioxide consumption	1.5	1.4	1.8	1.2	0.8	0.8	0.9
Peatlands remaining peatlands	1.1	1.1	1.0	1.0	0.9	0.8	0.8
Lead production	0.5	0.6	0.5	0.5	0.5	0.5	0.5
Silicon carbide production and consumption	0.4	0.2	0.1	0.2	0.2	0.2	0.2
Magnesium production and processing	+	+	+	+	+	+	+
Land use, land-use change, and forestry (sink)[a]	(775.8)	(911.9)	(870.9)	(871.6)	(881.0)	(880.4)	(881.7)
Wood biomass and ethanol consumption[b]	219.4	229.8	250.5	265.1	268.1	267.7	283.3
International bunker fuels[c]	103.5	113.1	106.4	117.0	111.7	105.8	99.8
CH$_4$	**745.5**	**707.8**	**709.5**	**667.2**	**660.9**	**647.6**	**636.3**
Enteric fermentation	164.2	168.9	172.7	171.1	168.7	166.3	164.5
Natural gas systems	179.1	176.3	168.0	159.6	159.3	154.4	157.4
Landfills	186.2	165.5	158.1	158.1	121.8	121.3	114.6
Coal mining	96.5	64.1	79.9	82.3	71.2	66.5	64.6
Manure management	37.2	56.3	59.7	60.9	61.4	63.7	61.4
Petroleum systems	31.5	23.5	21.5	21.3	22.0	23.3	25.2
Wastewater treatment	15.7	15.9	15.6	15.5	15.3	15.2	15.0
Rice cultivation	9.2	8.9	9.4	11.1	8.5	9.3	8.3
Stationary combustion	8.5	7.4	7.4	7.1	7.1	6.6	8.0
Abandoned underground coal mines	7.2	6.6	6.4	6.6	6.4	6.2	6.2
Forest fires	2.5	8.3	5.8	4.7	14.6	15.7	5.8
Mobile combustion	5.6	3.0	2.3	2.3	2.3	2.2	2.1
Composting	0.4	1.9	1.9	1.8	1.9	1.9	2.0
Iron and steel production & metallurgical coke production	1.1	0.9	0.4	0.6	0.7	0.7	0.7
Field burning of agricultural residues	0.3	0.2	0.3	0.3	0.3	0.3	0.3
Petrochemical production	0.2	0.1	+	0.1	+	0.1	0.1
Ferroalloy production	+	+	+	+	+	+	+
Silicon carbide production and consumption	+	+	+	+	+	+	+
Peatlands remaining peatlands	+	+	+	+	+	+	+
Incineration of waste	+	+	+	+	+	+	+
International bunker fuels[c]	0.2	0.1	0.1	0.1	0.1	0.1	0.1

other air pollutants, primarily volatile organic compounds and nitrogen oxides, are present. The primary sources of these ozone precursors are industrial chemical processes and fossil fuel combustion. The atmospheric lifetime of ozone ranges from weeks to months.

Nitrous Oxide

Nitrous oxide (N$_2$O) is a colorless gas found in trace amounts in the atmosphere. Soils naturally release the gas as a result of bacterial processes called nitrification and denitrification. Soils found in tropical areas and moist

TABLE 3.1

Trends in U.S. greenhouse gas emissions and sinks, selected years 1990–2013 [CONTINUED]

Gas/source	1990	2005	2009	2010	2011	2012	2013
N_2O	**329.9**	**355.9**	**356.1**	**360.1**	**371.9**	**365.6**	**355.2**
Agricultural soil management	224.0	243.6	264.1	264.3	265.8	266.0	263.7
Stationary combustion	11.9	20.2	20.4	22.2	21.3	21.4	22.9
Mobile combustion	41.2	38.1	24.6	23.7	22.5	20.2	18.4
Manure management	13.8	16.4	17.0	17.1	17.3	17.3	17.3
Nitric acid production	12.1	11.3	9.6	11.5	10.9	10.5	10.7
Wastewater treatment	3.4	4.3	4.6	4.7	4.8	4.9	4.9
N_2O from product uses	4.2	4.2	4.2	4.2	4.2	4.2	4.2
Adipic acid production	15.2	7.1	2.7	4.2	10.2	5.5	4.0
Forest fires	1.7	5.5	3.8	3.1	9.6	10.3	3.8
Settlement soils	1.4	2.3	2.2	2.4	2.5	2.5	2.4
Composting	0.3	1.7	1.7	1.6	1.7	1.7	1.8
Forest soils	0.1	0.5	0.5	0.5	0.5	0.5	0.5
Incineration of waste	0.5	0.4	0.3	0.3	0.3	0.3	0.3
Semiconductor manufacture	+	0.1	0.1	0.1	0.2	0.2	0.2
Field burning of agricultural residues	0.1	0.1	0.1	0.1	0.1	0.1	0.1
Peatlands remaining peatlands	+	+	+	+	+	+	+
International bunker fuels[b]	0.9	1.0	0.9	1.0	1.0	0.9	0.9
HFCs	**46.6**	**131.4**	**142.9**	**152.6**	**157.4**	**159.2**	**163.0**
Substitution of ozone depleting substances[d]	0.3	111.1	136.0	144.4	148.4	153.5	158.6
HCFC-22 production	46.1	20.0	6.8	8.0	8.8	5.5	4.1
Semiconductor manufacture	0.2	0.2	0.2	0.2	0.2	0.2	0.2
Magnesium production and processing	0.0	0.0	+	+	+	+	0.1
PFCs	**24.3**	**6.6**	**3.9**	**4.4**	**6.9**	**6.0**	**5.8**
Aluminum production	21.5	3.4	1.9	1.9	3.5	2.9	3.0
Semiconductor manufacture	2.8	3.2	2.0	2.6	3.4	3.0	2.9
SF_6	**31.1**	**14.0**	**9.3**	**9.5**	**10.0**	**7.7**	**6.9**
Electrical transmission and distribution	25.4	10.6	7.3	7.0	6.8	5.7	5.1
Magnesium production and processing	5.2	2.7	1.6	2.1	2.8	1.6	1.4
Semiconductor manufacture	0.5	0.7	0.3	0.4	0.4	0.4	0.4
NF_3	**+**	**0.5**	**0.4**	**0.5**	**0.7**	**0.6**	**0.6**
Semiconductor manufacture	+	0.5	0.4	0.5	0.7	0.6	0.6
Total emissions	**6,301.1**	**7,350.2**	**6,722.7**	**6,898.8**	**6,776.6**	**6,545.1**	**6,673.0**
Total sinks[a]	**(775.8)**	**(911.9)**	**(870.9)**	**(871.6)**	**(881.0)**	**(880.4)**	**(881.7)**
Net emissions (sources and sinks)	**5,525.2**	**6,438.3**	**5,851.9**	**6,027.2**	**5,895.6**	**5,664.7**	**5,791.2**

+ = Does not exceed 0.05 MMT CO_2 Eq.

[a]Parentheses indicate negative values or sequestration. Sinks (i.e., CO_2 removals) are only included in the net emissions total.

[b]Emissions from wood biomass and ethanol consumption are not included specifically in summing energy sector totals. Net carbon fluxes from changes in biogenic carbon reservoirs are accounted for in the estimates for land use, land-use change, and forestry.

[c]Emissions from international bunker fuels are not included in totals. Small amounts of PFC emissions also result from this source.

MMT CO_2 Eq. = Million metric tons of carbon dioxide equivalent; CO_2 = Carbon dioxide; CH_4 = Methane; N_2O = Nitrous oxide; HFCs = Hydrofluorocarbons; PFCs = Perfluorocarbons; SF_6 = Sulfur hexafluoride; NF_3 = Nitrogen trifluoride; IPCC = Intergovernmental Panel on Climate Change; AR4 = 4th Assessment Report (*Climate Change 2007*); GWP = Global Warming Potential.

Note: Emissions values are presented in CO_2 equivalent mass units using IPCC AR4 GWP values. Totals may not sum due to independent rounding.

SOURCE: "Table ES-2. Recent Trends in U.S. Greenhouse Gas Emissions and Sinks (MMT CO_2 Eq.)," in *Inventory of U.S. Greenhouse Gas Emissions and Sinks: 1990–2013*, U.S. Environmental Protection Agency, April 15, 2015, http://www.epa.gov/climatechange/Downloads/ghgemissions/US-GHG-Inventory-2015-Main-Text.pdf (accessed September 2, 2015)

forests are believed to be the largest contributors. Oxygen-poor waters and sediments in oceans and estuaries are also natural sources. Although nitrous oxide makes up a much smaller portion of greenhouse gases than carbon dioxide, it is much more powerful than carbon dioxide at trapping heat. The IPCC notes in *Climate Change 2013: The Physical Science Basis* that nitrous oxide has an atmospheric lifetime of 121 years and a 100-year GWP of 265, meaning that over 100 years nitrous oxide is 265 times more effective at trapping atmospheric heat than the same mass of carbon dioxide.

Agriculture has been the major source of nitrous oxide emissions in the United States, followed by energy and industrial sources. As shown in Table 3.1, agricultural soil management accounted for 263.7 Tg CO_2 equivalents of the total 355.2 Tg CO_2 equivalents of nitrous oxide emissions in 2013, or 74% of the total.

Humans have significantly increased the release of nitrous oxide from soils through the use of nitrogen-rich fertilizers. Other anthropogenic sources include combustion of fossil fuels and biomass, wastewater treatment, and certain manufacturing processes, particularly the production of nylon and nitric acid.

Engineered Gases

Engineered gases are synthetic gases specially designed for modern industrial and commercial purposes.

They are also known as "high GWP gases" because they have a high GWP when compared with carbon dioxide. They include hydrofluorocarbons (HFCs), perfluorocarbons (PFCs), and sulfur hexafluoride (SF_6).

HFCs are chemicals that contain hydrogen, fluorine, and carbon. They are popular substitutes in industrial applications for chlorofluorocarbons (CFCs). CFCs are commonly used in cooling equipment and fire extinguishers. They are one of the culprits blamed for the depletion of stratospheric ozone. PFCs are a class of chemicals that contain fluorine and carbon. They are also increasingly being used by industry as substitutes for ozone-depleting CFCs. Sulfur hexafluoride is a colorless, odorless gas commonly used as an insulating medium in electrical equipment and as an etchant (an etching agent) in the semiconductor industry.

Although emissions of these chemicals are small in comparison to other greenhouse gases, they are of particular concern because of their long life in the atmosphere. The IPCC indicates in *Climate Change 2013: The Physical Science Basis* that many PFCs and sulfur hexafluoride are actually far more potent greenhouse gases than carbon dioxide, with GWP values in the thousands.

Indirect Greenhouse Gases

There are several gases that are considered to be indirect greenhouse gases because of their effects on the chemical environment of the atmosphere. These gases include reactive nitrogen oxides, carbon monoxide, and volatile organic compounds. Most of their emissions are from anthropogenic sources, primarily combustion and industrial processes.

U.S. Greenhouse Gases and Sources

Figure 3.5 shows the annual percent change in U.S. greenhouse gas emissions between 1991 and 2013. Emissions generally increased on a year-to-year basis through 2007. There were sharp declines in 2008 (down 2.8%) and 2009 (down 6.5%). These declines resulted from the so-called Great Recession that occurred during these years. The U.S. Energy Information Administration (EIA) explains in "U.S. Carbon Dioxide Emissions in 2009: A Retrospective Review" (May 5, 2010, http://www.eia.gov/oiaf/environment/emissions/carbon) that the Great Recession significantly reduced demand for fossil fuel–derived energy. This decline was severe in the industrial sector, particularly in energy-intensive industries such as metals and minerals processing, and in the transportation sector. The latter sector was also hit hard by high gasoline prices that further dampened consumer demand. As shown in Figure 3.5, U.S. greenhouse gas emissions rose in 2010, but then experienced two years of decline, before rebounding in 2013.

Figure 3.6 shows trends in the emissions of carbon dioxide between 1990 and 2013 by the major economic sectors in the United States. The electricity generating sector was the largest emitter, followed by the transportation and industry sectors. The agricultural, commercial, and residential sectors were much smaller contributors.

International Emissions of Greenhouse Gases

In "International Energy Statistics" (2015, http://www.eia.gov/cfapps/ipdbproject/IEDIndex3.cfm?tid=90&pid=44&aid=8), the EIA presents data collected on carbon dioxide emissions related to energy consumption around the world. As shown in Table 3.2, Asia and

FIGURE 3.5

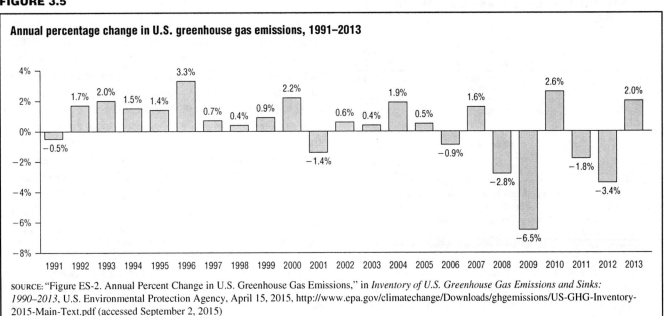

Annual percentage change in U.S. greenhouse gas emissions, 1991–2013

SOURCE: "Figure ES-2. Annual Percent Change in U.S. Greenhouse Gas Emissions," in *Inventory of U.S. Greenhouse Gas Emissions and Sinks: 1990–2013*, U.S. Environmental Protection Agency, April 15, 2015, http://www.epa.gov/climatechange/Downloads/ghgemissions/US-GHG-Inventory-2015-Main-Text.pdf (accessed September 2, 2015)

FIGURE 3.6

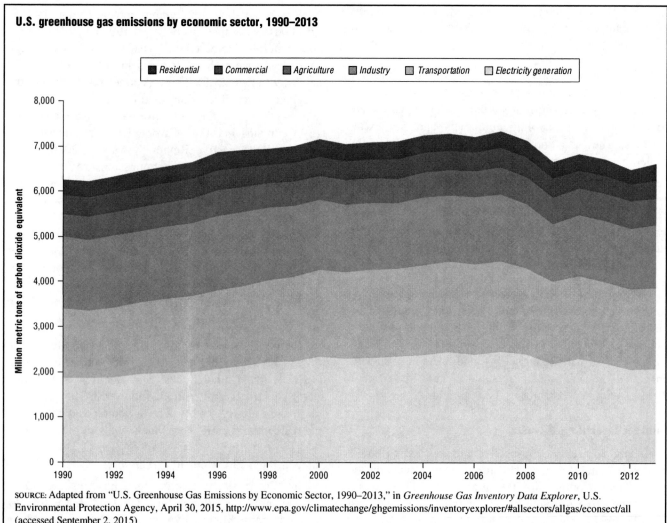

U.S. greenhouse gas emissions by economic sector, 1990–2013

■ Residential   ■ Commercial   ■ Agriculture   ■ Industry   ■ Transportation   □ Electricity generation

SOURCE: Adapted from "U.S. Greenhouse Gas Emissions by Economic Sector, 1990–2013," in *Greenhouse Gas Inventory Data Explorer*, U.S. Environmental Protection Agency, April 30, 2015, http://www.epa.gov/climatechange/ghgemissions/inventoryexplorer/#allsectors/allgas/econsect/all (accessed September 2, 2015)

TABLE 3.2

World carbon dioxide emissions from the consumption of energy, by region, 2012

	Emissions (million metric tons)	Percentage of world total
North America	6,298.3	19.5%
Central & South America	1,399.6	4.3%
Europe	4,263.3	13.2%
Eurasia	2,672.0	8.3%
Middle East	2,035.7	6.3%
Africa	1,205.7	3.7%
Asia & Oceania	14,435.8	44.7%
World	**32,310.3**	**100.0%**

SOURCE: Adapted from "Total Carbon Dioxide Emissions from the Consumption of Energy (Million Metric Tons)," in *International Energy Statistics*, U.S. Department of Energy, Energy Information Administration, 2015, http://www.eia.gov/cfapps/ipdbproject/IEDIndex3.cfm?tid=90&pid=44&aid=8 (accessed September 2, 2015)

Table 3.3. The top-five emitters were China, the United States, India, Russia, and Japan.

In its energy and emissions analyses, the EIA assesses countries based on whether they are members of the Organisation for Economic Co-operation and Development (OECD). The OECD was founded in 1961 and is an international organization of democratic countries with free-market economies (such as the United States). OECD countries are developed countries that are characterized by mature economies and industries and relatively slow rates of growth in population and fuel usage. Non-OECD countries include developing countries in which population, industrial base, and fuel usage are growing quickly. Examples include China, India, Russia, and most other areas of Central and South America, Asia, the Middle East, and Africa.

As shown in Table 3.4, non-OECD countries are expected to greatly outpace OECD countries in terms of energy-related carbon dioxide emissions through 2040. China and other developing countries are heavily reliant

Oceania (44.7%) were responsible for the largest portion of such emissions in 2013, followed by North America (19.5%) and Europe (13.2%). The 20 countries with the largest carbon dioxide emissions in 2013 are listed in

TABLE 3.3

Top-20 countries in terms of carbon dioxide emissions from the consumption of energy, 2012

	Emissions (million metric tons)	Percentage of world total
China	8,106.4	25.1%
United States	5,270.4	16.3%
India	1,830.9	5.7%
Russia	1,781.7	5.5%
Japan	1,259.1	3.9%
Germany	788.3	2.4%
Korea, South	657.1	2.0%
Iran	603.6	1.9%
Saudi Arabia	582.7	1.8%
Canada	550.8	1.7%
Brazil	500.2	1.5%
United Kingdom	498.9	1.5%
South Africa	473.2	1.5%
Indonesia	456.2	1.4%
Mexico	453.8	1.4%
Australia	420.6	1.3%
Italy	385.8	1.2%
France	364.5	1.1%
Spain	312.4	1.0%
Taiwan	307.1	1.0%
World	**32,310.3**	**100.0%**

SOURCE: Adapted from "Total Carbon Dioxide Emissions from the Consumption of Energy (Million Metric Tons)," in *International Energy Statistics*, U.S. Department of Energy, Energy Information Administration, 2015, http://www.eia.gov/cfapps/ipdbproject/IEDIndex3.cfm?tid=90&pid=44&aid=8 (accessed September 2, 2015)

on coal to fuel their industrial development and electricity production, whereas developed countries, such as the United States, rely more on cleaner burning fuels such as natural gas. Environmentalism as a social and political force is also much more mature in developed countries.

CHANGES IN THE ATMOSPHERE

The earth's atmosphere was first compared to a glass vessel in 1827 by the French mathematician Jean-Baptiste-Joseph Fourier (1768–1830). During the 1850s the British physicist John Tyndall (1820–1893) tried to measure the heat-trapping properties of various components of the atmosphere. By the 1890s scientists had concluded that the great increase in combustion during the Industrial Revolution had the potential to change the atmosphere's load of carbon dioxide. In 1896 the Swedish chemist Svante Arrhenius (1859–1927) made the revolutionary suggestion that human activities could actually disrupt this delicate balance. He theorized that the rapid increase in the use of coal as a result of the Industrial Revolution could increase carbon dioxide concentrations and cause a gradual rise in temperatures. For almost six decades his theory stirred little interest.

In 1957 studies at the Scripps Institute of Oceanography in California suggested that half the carbon dioxide

TABLE 3.4

World energy-related carbon dioxide emissions, 1990 and 2010 and predicted for selected years 2020–40

Region/country	1990	2010	2020	2030	2040	Average annual percent change 1990–2010	Average annual percent change 2010–2040
OECD							
OECD Americas	5,832	6,657	6,627	6,880	7,283	0.7	0.3
United States	5,032	5,608	5,454	5,523	5,691	0.5	0.0
Canada	466	546	574	609	654	0.8	0.6
Mexico/Chile	334	503	599	748	937	2.1	2.1
OECD Europe	4,195	4,223	4,097	4,151	4,257	0.0	0.0
OECD Asia	1,585	2,200	2,296	2,340	2,358	1.7	0.2
Japan	1,047	1,176	1,220	1,215	1,150	0.6	−0.1
South Korea	242	581	627	666	730	4.5	0.8
Australia/New Zealand	296	443	449	460	478	2.0	0.3
Total OECD	**11,612**	**13,079**	**13,020**	**13,373**	**13,897**	**0.6**	**0.2**
Non-OECD							
Non-OECD Europe and Eurasia	4,199	2,645	2,898	3,249	3,526	−2.3	1.0
Russia	2,368	1,595	1,749	1,945	2,018	−2.0	0.8
Other	1,831	1,050	1,149	1,304	1,508	−2.7	1.2
Non-OECD Asia	3,652	11,538	15,812	19,392	21,668	5.9	2.1
China	2,270	7,885	11,532	14,028	14,911	6.4	2.1
India	569	1,695	2,109	2,693	3,326	5.6	2.3
Other	814	1,958	2,171	2,671	3,431	4.5	1.9
Middle East	669	1,649	2,126	2,419	2,756	4.6	1.7
Africa	657	1,070	1,224	1,474	1,815	2.5	1.8
Central and South America	663	1,202	1,366	1,556	1,793	3.0	1.3
Brazil	235	450	547	632	771	3.3	1.8
Other	428	752	819	924	1,022	2.9	1.0
Total non-OECD	**9,840**	**18,104**	**23,426**	**28,092**	**31,558**	**3.1**	**1.9**
World total	**21,452**	**31,183**	**36,446**	**41,464**	**45,453**	**1.9**	**1.3**

Note: OECD = Organisation for Economic Co-operation and Development.

SOURCE: "Table 21. World Carbon Dioxide Emissions by Region and Country in the Reference Case, 1990–2040 (Million Metric Tons)," in *International Energy Outlook 2013*, U.S. Department of Energy, Energy Information Administration, July 2013, http://www.eia.gov/forecasts/ieo/pdf/0484(2013).pdf (accessed September 2, 2015)

released by industry was being permanently trapped in the atmosphere. The studies showed that atmospheric concentrations of carbon dioxide in the previous 30 years were greater than in the previous two centuries and that the gas had reached its highest level in 160,000 years. Scientists can estimate the makeup of the earth's atmosphere dating back several hundred thousand years by testing air pockets in ice sheets that are believed to have formed around the same time.

Findings during the 1980s and 1990s provided more disturbing evidence of atmospheric changes. Scientists detected increases in other, even more potent gases that contribute to the greenhouse effect, notably CFC-11 and CFC-12, methane, nitrous oxide, and halocarbons (CFCs, methyl chloroform, and hydrochlorofluorocarbons).

T. J. Blasing of the Carbon Dioxide Information Analysis Center estimates in "Recent Greenhouse Gas Concentrations" (February 2014, http://cdiac.ornl.gov/pns/current_ghg.html) that the average "natural" background atmospheric concentration of carbon dioxide immediately before 1750 was 280 parts per million. Likewise, the average methane level immediately before 1750 was around 722 parts per billion. Increases in these gases as well as in nitrous oxide, CFC-11, and CFC-12—also potent greenhouse gases—are shown in Figure 3.7. These data were collected by NOAA, which compiles long-term records on air quality and solar radiation data. Figure 3.8 shows that global monthly mean (average) carbon dioxide concentrations grew from around 390 parts per million in 2011 to around 400 parts per million in mid-2015.

Scientists agree that atmospheric concentrations of gases known to play a role in the natural greenhouse effect are increasing. There is scientific consensus that this increase is driving up the earth's temperature. As

FIGURE 3.7

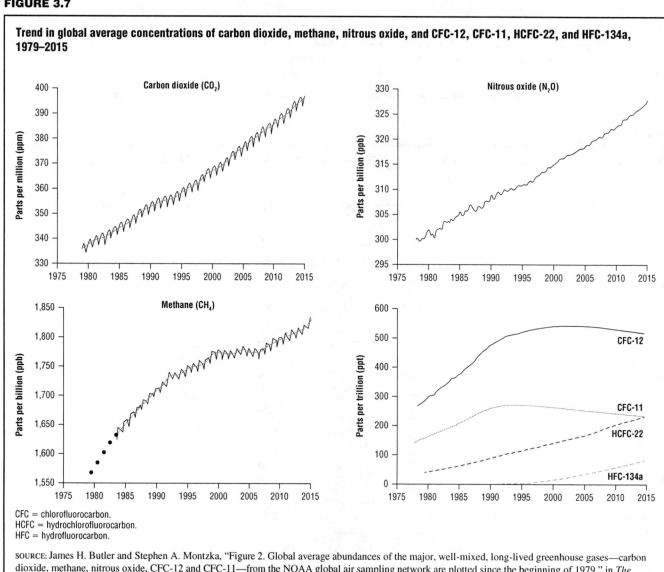

Trend in global average concentrations of carbon dioxide, methane, nitrous oxide, and CFC-12, CFC-11, HCFC-22, and HFC-134a, 1979–2015

CFC = chlorofluorocarbon.
HCFC = hydrochlorofluorocarbon.
HFC = hydrofluorocarbon.

SOURCE: James H. Butler and Stephen A. Montzka, "Figure 2. Global average abundances of the major, well-mixed, long-lived greenhouse gases—carbon dioxide, methane, nitrous oxide, CFC-12 and CFC-11—from the NOAA global air sampling network are plotted since the beginning of 1979," in *The NOAA Annual Greenhouse Gas Index (AGGI)*, U.S. Department of Commerce, National Oceanic and Atmospheric Administration, Earth System Research Laboratory, Spring 2015, http://www.esrl.noaa.gov/gmd/aggi/aggi.html (accessed September 2, 2015)

FIGURE 3.8

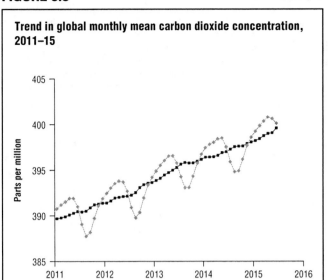

Trend in global monthly mean carbon dioxide concentration, 2011–15

SOURCE: "Recent Global Monthly Mean CO2," in *Trends in Atmospheric Carbon Dioxide*, U.S. Department of Commerce, National Oceanic and Atmospheric Administration, Earth System Research Laboratory, August 2015, http://www.esrl.noaa.gov/gmd/webdata/ccgg/trends/co2_trend_gl.pdf (accessed September 2, 2015)

FIGURE 3.9

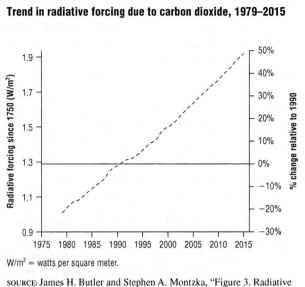

Trend in radiative forcing due to carbon dioxide, 1979–2015

W/m² = watts per square meter.

SOURCE: James H. Butler and Stephen A. Montzka, "Figure 3. Radiative Forcing, Relative to 1750, Due to Carbon Dioxide Alone since 1979," in *The NOAA Annual Greenhouse Gas Index (AGGI)*, U.S. Department of Commerce, National Oceanic and Atmospheric Administration, Earth System Research Laboratory, Spring 2015, http://www.esrl.noaa.gov/gmd/aggi/aggi.html (accessed September 2, 2015)

noted earlier, the earth's temperature depends on a balance between incoming and outgoing infrared radiation. Various factors have either warming or cooling effects. Radiative forcing is the term used to describe these effects. Figure 3.9 shows radiative forcing that is attributed only to carbon dioxide between 1979 and 2015. The forcing increased from just over 1 watt per square meter in 1979 to more than 1.9 watts per square meter in 2015.

A RECENT WARMING TREND

Scientists do not know how much the global temperature has varied on its own in the last 1,000 years. Temperature records based on thermometers go back only about 150 years. Therefore, investigators have turned to proxy (indirect) means of measuring past temperatures. These methods include chemical evidence of climatic change contained in fossils, corals, ancient ice, and growth rings in trees.

During the late 1990s Michael E. Mann, Raymond S. Bradley, and Malcolm K. Hughes published two reports based on their survey of proxy evidence of temperatures over the previous millennium. The reports were "Global-Scale Temperature Patterns and Climate Forcing over the Past Six Centuries" (*Nature*, vol. 392, April 23, 1998) and "Northern Hemisphere Temperatures during the Past Millennium: Inferences, Uncertainties, and Limitations" (*Geophysical Research Letters*, vol. 26, no. 6, 1999). They concluded that in the Northern Hemisphere the 20th century was the warmest century of the millennium and that 1998 was the warmest year of the millennium.

They also noted that the warming trend seems to be closely connected to the emissions of greenhouse gases by humans.

However, some experts questioned the validity of the proxy evidence that was cited in the reports, particularly for the oldest portion of the historical record. In response, Congress asked the National Research Council (NRC) of the National Academy of Sciences to analyze and report on available scientific data regarding historical surface temperatures. The resulting report, *Surface Temperature Reconstructions for the Last 2,000 Years* (http://www.nap.edu/catalog/11676.html), was published in 2006. The NRC concluded "with a high level of confidence" that the scientific evidence indicates that in the Northern Hemisphere the last few decades of the 20th century were warmer than any comparable period over the last four centuries.

In "Why So Many Global Temperature Records?" (January 21, 2015, http://www.giss.nasa.gov/research/features/201501_gistemp), Adam Voiland of the National Aeronautics and Space Administration (NASA) notes that four agencies around the world are considered keepers of the "major global temperature record":

- Japanese Meteorological Agency (the national weather service of Japan) in Tokyo, Japan

- Met Office (the national weather service of the United Kingdom) in Exeter, United Kingdom

- NOAA's National Climatic Data Center in Asheville, North Carolina, United States

• NASA's Goddard Institute for Space Studies (GISS) in New York City, United States

According to Voiland, the agencies rely on data from weather stations around the world. However, some areas of the planet (particularly the oceans) have relatively few weather stations. The agencies use slightly different analytical methods to account for missing information. Consequently, they do not always agree on their rankings of the hottest years on record. Even so, Voiland explains that "despite some differences in the year-to-year rankings, the trends observed by all the groups are roughly the same. They all show warming. They all find the most recent decade to be warmer than previous decades."

Voiland indicates that in early 2015 the Japanese Meteorological Agency, the National Climatic Data Center, and the GISS all declared 2014 to be the hottest year on record for the planet. In "2014 One of the Warmest Years on Record Globally" (January 26, 2015, http://www.metoffice.gov.uk/news/release/archive/2015/2014-global-temperature), the Met Office proclaims that 2014 and 2010 are tied for the hottest year on record.

NASA notes in "2014 Was the Warmest Year in the Modern Record" (2015, http://earthobservatory.nasa.gov/NaturalHazards/view.php?id=85083) that "with the exception of 1998, the ten warmest years in the instrumental record (dating to 1880) have all occurred since 2000." The agency continues, "Since 1880, Earth's average surface temperature has warmed by about 0.8 degrees Celsius (1.4 degrees Fahrenheit), a trend largely driven by the increase in carbon dioxide and other human emissions into the atmosphere."

Figure 3.10 shows the anomaly (deviation from the normal) for global mean surface temperatures between 1880 and 2014, compared with the mean between 1951 and 1980 as reported by the GISS. There was a strong warming trend from around 1910 through 1940 and then a relatively level period through the mid-1970s. Warming was dramatic through 2002 and then flattened somewhat over the following decade.

Puzzling Temperature Data

There are people known as global warming deniers, doubters, skeptics, or contrarians. They argue that global warming is either not occurring or, if it is occurring, is driven by natural factors rather than by anthropogenic factors. As is explained later in this chapter, contrarians make up a minority of climate scientists; however, the contrarian viewpoint enjoys some popular support among the public at large.

The apparent stabilization of global temperatures between approximately 2002 and 2012 was seized on by contrarians as evidence that anthropogenic global warming is not as certain and inevitable as many scientists have

FIGURE 3.10

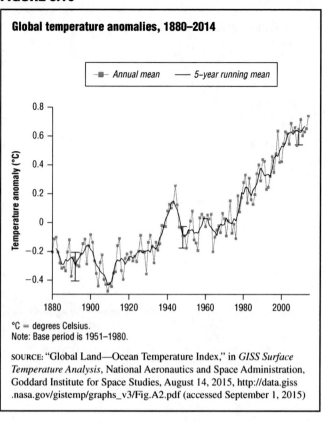

Global temperature anomalies, 1880–2014

°C = degrees Celsius.
Note: Base period is 1951–1980.

SOURCE: "Global Land—Ocean Temperature Index," in *GISS Surface Temperature Analysis*, National Aeronautics and Space Administration, Goddard Institute for Space Studies, August 14, 2015, http://data.giss.nasa.gov/gistemp/graphs_v3/Fig.A2.pdf (accessed September 1, 2015)

insisted. As shown in Figure 3.7, carbon dioxide concentrations continued to rise between 2002 and 2012, as did the concentrations of other potent greenhouse gases. Thus, it is puzzling why global temperatures appeared to flatten somewhat during this period. In *Climate Change 2013: The Physical Science Basis*, the IPCC describes the warming slowdown a "hiatus" and notes that "the observed global mean surface temperature ... has shown a much smaller increasing linear trend over the past 15 years than over the past 30 to 60 years."

In "Science Challenges Claim That Global Warming Took a Hiatus" (NationalGeographic.com, June 4, 2015), Marianne Lavelle calls the hiatus "a mystery that has vexed scientists and delighted contrarians." Scientists have put forth various theories to explain the phenomenon. Lavelle indicates that more than 80 papers on the subject were published in peer-reviewed journals. In June 2015, however, scientists with NOAA and a private research organization argued in the journal *Science* that no hiatus actually occurred. Thomas R. Karl et al. assert in "Possible Artifacts of Data Biases in the Recent Global Surface Warming Hiatus" (*Science*, vol. 348, no. 6242) that a reanalysis conducted with more extensive and appropriate data shows that "the rate of warming during the first 15 years of the 21st century is at least as great as the last half of the 20th century."

Not all climate scientists agreed with Karl et al.'s conclusions. For example, Met Office scientists continued to state that a "slowdown" had occurred in global warming rates. Adam Scaife et al. discuss in *Big Changes Underway in the Climate System?* (September 2015, http://www.metoffice.gov.uk/media/pdf/8/c/Changes_In_The_Climate_System.pdf) the effects of regional climatic events, such as atmospheric and oceanic circulation changes, on the global climate. The researchers state, "Some of these patterns of climate variability fluctuate over years and decades and can even affect global average surface temperature, as appears to have occurred in recent years with changes in the Pacific [Ocean] implicated in the slowdown in the rate of global surface warming."

INTERNATIONAL ANALYSES

At the 1972 Stockholm Conference, the world's first ecological summit, climate change was not even listed among the threats to the environment. However, many scientists and meteorologists were becoming alarmed about the growing evidence supporting the notion of an enhanced greenhouse effect. Data collection and research efforts intensified through the late 1970s and into the 1980s. In 1988 the WMO and the UNEP established the IPCC, which created three working groups to assess available scientific information on climate change, estimate the expected impacts of climate change, and formulate strategies for responding to the problem.

The IPCC's First Assessment Report

The first IPCC assessment report, *Climate Change*, was issued in 1990. Several signs of climate change were noted by the IPCC:

- The average warm-season temperature in Alaska had risen nearly 3 degrees Fahrenheit (1.7 degrees C) in the previous 50 years.

- Glaciers had generally receded and become thinner on average by about 30 feet (9.1 m) in the previous 40 years.

- There was approximately 5% less sea ice in the Bering Sea than during the 1950s.

- Permafrost was thawing, causing the ground to subside (sink), opening holes in roads, producing landslides and erosion, threatening roads and bridges, and causing local floods.

- Ice cellars in northern villages had thawed and become useless.

- More precipitation was falling as rain than as snow in northern areas, and the snow was melting faster, causing more running and standing water.

Using computer models, IPCC researchers predicted that the global mean temperature would increase by 0.5 degrees Fahrenheit (0.3 degrees C) each decade during the 21st century. They also predicted that the global mean

sea level would rise by 2.4 inches (6.1 cm) per decade. However, the scientists noted that there were a number of uncertainties in their assumptions due to a lack of data.

The IPCC's Second Assessment Report

In 1995 the IPCC reassessed the state of knowledge about climate change and published its findings in its second assessment report, *Climate Change 1995*. The IPCC reaffirmed its earlier conclusions and updated its forecasts, predicting that, if no further action is taken to curb emissions of greenhouse gases, temperatures will increase between 1.4 degrees and 6.3 degrees Fahrenheit (0.8 degrees and 3.5 degrees C) by 2100. The panel concluded that the evidence suggests a human influence on global climate. The cautiously worded statement was a compromise following intense discussions. Nonetheless, it was a landmark conclusion because the panel, until then, had maintained that global warming and climate changes could be the result of natural variability.

The IPCC's Third Assessment Report

In 2001 the IPCC released its third assessment report, *Climate Change 2001*, which actually consisted of four reports that addressed various aspects of climate change and its impacts. The IPCC's assessment covered the adaptability and vulnerability of North America to climate change impacts likely to occur from global warming. Among the suggested possible effects of global warming were:

- Expansion of some diseases in North America

- Increased erosion, flooding, and loss of wetlands in coastal areas

- Risk to "unique natural ecosystems"

- Changes in seasonal snowmelts, which would have effects on water users and aquatic ecosystems

- Some initial benefits for agriculture, but those benefits would decline over time and possibly "become a net loss"

The IPCC's Fourth Assessment Report

In 2007 the IPCC released its fourth assessment report, *Climate Change 2007*. Actually, the three working groups of the IPCC each released a report, as follows:

- Working Group I—*Climate Change 2007: The Physical Science Basis*

- Working Group II—*Climate Change 2007: Impacts, Adaptation, and Vulnerability*

- Working Group III—*Climate Change 2007: Mitigation of Climate Change*

In addition, the IPCC published a synthesis report that integrates information from all three working group reports.

In *Climate Change 2007: The Physical Science Basis*, the IPCC concluded that there is *"very high confidence* that the global average net effect of human activities since 1750 has been one of warming." The panel defined "very high confidence" as meaning that there is over a nine out of 10 chance that a hypothesis is correct. This was the strongest wording yet from the IPCC indicting human activities for global warming. Various emissions modeling scenarios predicted that the earth will continue to warm by approximately 0.4 degrees Fahrenheit (0.2 degrees C) per decade over the next 20 years.

The IPCC noted in *Climate Change 2007: Impacts, Adaptation, and Vulnerability* that "observational evidence from all continents and most oceans shows that many natural systems are being affected by regional climate changes, particularly temperature increases." These effects included an earlier occurrence of springtime events and a poleward movement in the ranges of plant and animal species. In addition, many changes were reported in ice and snow ecosystems near the earth's poles. Warming water body temperatures were linked to range changes for algae, plankton, and fish species.

Estimated future impacts of global warming included the loss of freshwater store because of melting glaciers, greater extent of drought areas coupled with more frequent "heavy precipitation" events that tend to cause flooding, and acidification of the earth's oceans because of greater carbon take-up. The latter effect is particularly troubling for ocean coral, which is sensitive to acidity changes. An estimated 20% to 30% of plant and animal species were deemed to be at increased risk of extinction if the global average temperature increases by more than 2.7 degrees to 4.5 degrees Fahrenheit (1.5 degrees to 2.5 degrees C).

Sea level rises were expected to expose millions of people to increased risk of flooding, exacerbate coastal erosion, and endanger coastal ecosystems. Although increasing temperatures would help lower the number of deaths caused by cold exposure in far northern and southern regions, this benefit was expected to be more than offset by higher death rates in the temperate regions of the earth, particularly in developing countries.

The 2007 Nobel Peace Prize

In 2007 the IPCC and Albert Gore Jr. (1948–), the former U.S. vice president, were jointly awarded the Nobel Peace Prize for their work on climate change. During his time in office (1993–2001), Gore was very vocal about the dangers of anthropogenic global warming and traveled around the country to speak about it. His efforts were captured in the Academy Award–winning documentary *An Inconvenient Truth*, which premiered in 2006.

The IPCC's Fifth Assessment Report

Over 2013 and 2014 the IPCC released four reports that are collectively referred to as the organization's fifth assessment report. They are:

- *Climate Change 2013: The Physical Science Basis*
- *Climate Change 2014: Impacts, Adaptation, and Vulnerability*
- *Climate Change 2014: Mitigation of Climate Change*
- *Climate Change 2014: Synthesis Report*

In *Climate Change 2013: The Physical Science Basis*, the IPCC states, "Human influence has been detected in warming of the atmosphere and the ocean, in changes in the global water cycle, in reductions in snow and ice, in global mean sea level rise, and in changes in some climate extremes." The IPCC goes on to state, "This evidence for human influence has grown since [the fourth assessment report]. It is *extremely likely* that human influence has been the dominant cause of the observed warming since the mid-20th century." The organization indicates that the phrase "extremely likely" corresponds with 95% to 100% probability.

The IPCC uses five nonnumeric qualifiers (very low, low, medium, high, and very high) to indicate its level of confidence in various statements in the report. It notes that it has medium confidence that over the period 2016–35 the global mean surface temperature change relative to 1986–2005 will "likely" be in the range of 0.5 to 1.3 degrees Fahrenheit (0.3 to 0.7 degrees C). The organization indicates that the phrase "likely" corresponds with 66% to 100% probability.

The IPCC provides in *Climate Change 2014: Impacts, Adaptation, and Vulnerability* an overview of the major environmental impacts that are associated with global warming, including melting ice and snow, sea level rise and associated flooding, ocean acidification, and extreme weather events (such as droughts). The threats to human health and livelihoods, food security, and plant and animal ecosystems are examined. For North America, the IPCC lists risks that it has high confidence will occur due to specific climate-related drivers:

- Warming and drying trend—threats to human health and well-being and to ecosystems; property damage and losses associated with wildfires

- Extreme temperature events—increased risk of human deaths due to high heat

- Extreme precipitation, damaging hurricanes, and rising sea levels—public health risks; impaired water quality; property and infrastructure damage due to flooding; disruption of ecosystems, supply chains, and social systems

In *Climate Change 2014: Mitigation of Climate Change*, the IPCC defines mitigation as "human intervention to reduce the sources or enhance the sinks of greenhouse gases." The panel calls on governments to work together to achieve mitigation, noting that "climate change has the characteristics of a collective action problem at the global scale, because most greenhouse gases (GHGs) accumulate over time and mix globally, and emissions by any agent (e.g., individual, community, company, country) affect other agents. International cooperation is therefore required to effectively mitigate GHG emissions and address other climate change issues."

INTERNATIONAL AGREEMENTS

In 1992 the United Nations (UN) adopted the UN Framework Convention on Climate Change (UNFCCC; July 18, 2000, http://unfccc.int/cop3/fccc/climate/fact18.htm). The UNFCCC was an international agreement that was presented for signatures at the 1992 Earth Summit in Rio de Janeiro, Brazil. The stated objective of the agreement was: "Stabilization of greenhouse gas concentrations in the atmosphere at a level that would prevent dangerous anthropogenic (man-made) interference with the climate system. Such a level should be achieved within a time-frame sufficient to allow ecosystems to adapt naturally to climate change, to ensure that food production is not threatened and to enable economic development to proceed in a sustainable manner."

The agreement set specific goals for developed countries to track and publish detailed inventories of their greenhouse gas emissions. However, it did not include specific emissions targets that countries had to meet. The UNFCCC (2015, http://unfccc.int/parties_and_observers/items/2704.php) categorized countries based on their level of economic development as follows:

- Annex 1—developed countries that were members of the OECD as of 1992 and countries with economies in transition (EIT), such as Russia and other members of the former Soviet Union

- Annex 2—the OECD members listed under Annex 1 but not the EIT countries

- Non-Annex 1—developing countries, such as China and India

The UNFCCC was signed by more than 100 countries, including the United States. Many environmentalists criticized the treaty as being too weak because it did not establish specific emissions targets that countries had to meet. The treaty did not include specific emissions targets mainly because the United States refused to accept them. The U.S. Senate ratified (formally approved into law) the UNFCCC. The treaty went into effect in 1994.

In 1995, 120 parties to the UNFCCC met in Berlin, Germany, in what became known as the Berlin Mandate, to determine the success of existing treaties and to embark on discussions of emissions after 2000. Differences persisted along North-South lines, with developing countries making essentially a moral argument for requiring more of the richer countries. They pointed out that the richer countries are responsible for most of the pollution. The Berlin talks essentially failed to endorse binding timetables for reductions in greenhouse gases.

The Kyoto Protocol

In 1997 delegates from 166 countries met in Kyoto, Japan, at the UN Climate Change Conference to negotiate actions to reduce global warming. Some developed countries, including the United States, wanted to require all countries to reduce their emissions. Developing countries, however, felt the industrialized countries had caused, and were still causing, most global warming and therefore should bear the brunt of economic sacrifices to clean up the environment. The conference developed an agreement known as the Kyoto Protocol to the UNFCCC. Countries listed in Annex B to the Kyoto Protocol were those listed under Annex 1 to the UNFCCC; they agreed to meet specific greenhouse gas emissions reduction targets by 2008–12 (the first commitment period) as compared with a base year, which was 1990 for most countries.

Overall, different targets were set for different countries taking into account their economic and social circumstances. Most countries committed to reduce their emissions, while others could hold their emissions steady or could actually increase their emissions compared with the base year. The Kyoto Protocol was set up to take effect when two conditions were met:

- It was ratified by at least 55 countries

- The ratifying countries accounted for at least 55% of carbon dioxide emissions based on 1990 levels

In 2002 the treaty was ratified by several major entities, including the European Union (EU), Canada, China, India, and Japan. It went into effect in February 2005 following ratification by Russia in late 2004. At the time, Australia and the United States were the major holdouts. In December 2007 Australia ratified the treaty following national elections. The UNFCCC indicates in "Status of Ratification of the Kyoto Protocol" (http://unfccc.int/kyoto_protocol/background/status_of_ratification/items/2613.php) that as of November 2015 the Kyoto Protocol had been ratified by 192 countries. The notable exception was the United States.

As noted earlier, Annex B countries committed to meet specific emissions targets by 2008–12 compared with a base year, which was 1990 in most cases. Nearly two-thirds of the Annex B countries are members of the EU, which as of 2015 included 28 countries. Only the EU members Cyprus and Malta did not have emissions targets for the first commitment period. In 1997, when the Kyoto Protocol was adopted, the EU consisted of 15 members: Austria, Belgium, Denmark, Finland, France, Germany, Greece, Ireland, Italy, Luxembourg, the Netherlands, Portugal, Spain, Sweden, and the United Kingdom. The EU-15 agreed to reduce its overall emissions by 8% under an umbrella agreement through which it set different emissions targets for its member-nations; individual countries within the EU-15, however, had differing emissions targets.

Overall, the Kyoto Protocol was expected to effect a total reduction in greenhouse gas emissions by the Annex B parties of at least 5% by 2012, compared with 1990 levels. Although China and India were not required to commit to specific limits, they did have to pledge to develop national programs for dealing with climate change.

THE UNITED STATES' POSITION ON THE KYOTO PROTOCOL. The U.S. Constitution grants the president the power to make treaties with foreign powers, but only with the consent of two-thirds of the Senate. In other words, the president or a designee (such as the vice president) can sign treaties, but they do not become binding under U.S. law until they are approved by the Senate. The administration of George H. W. Bush (1924–) supported and signed the UNFCCC, which was ratified by the Senate, but opposed precise deadlines for carbon dioxide limits, arguing that the extent of the problem was too uncertain to justify painful economic measures.

In 1998 Vice President Gore signed the Kyoto Protocol on behalf of the United States, but this was a symbolic gesture. President Bill Clinton (1946–) never submitted it to the Senate for ratification. The political climate at the time was unfavorable for a treaty that bound the United States to specific emissions limits but did not set limits on developing countries, such as China and India. In "Global Climate Change Update" (December 29, 1998, http://www.agiweb.org/legis105/climate.html), the American Geological Institute indicates that at the time Gore noted, "We will not submit the Protocol for ratification without the meaningful participation of key developing countries in efforts to address climate change." The Senate had already made clear through a nonbinding, but unanimous resolution passed in 1997 that it would not ratify the Kyoto Protocol as written because some countries were excluded from emissions limits and the treaty was deemed damaging to U.S. economic interests. The resolution was sponsored by Senators Robert C. Byrd (1917–2010; D-WV) and Chuck Hagel (1946–; R-NE) and is often referred to as the Byrd-Hagel Resolution.

When George W. Bush (1946–) took office in 2001, he affirmed his administration's steadfast opposition to the Kyoto Protocol. His successor, Barack Obama (1961–), has a more complicated history on the issue. According to Ken Dilanian, in "Obama Shifts Stance on Environmental Issues" (USAToday.com, July 18, 2008), in 1998, when Obama was an Illinois state senator, he voted in support of legislation "condemning the Kyoto global warming treaty and forbidding state efforts to regulate greenhouse gases."

During his first presidential campaign in 2008, Obama talked about anthropogenic global warming and expressed support for greater U.S. involvement in international actions related to climate change. For example, in "Obama Vows Climate 'Engagement'" (BBC.co.uk, November 18, 2008), Richard Black provides a quote from Obama regarding an upcoming UNFCCC summit: "Once I take office, you can be sure that the United States will once again engage vigorously in these negotiations, and help lead the world toward a new era of global co-operation on climate change." European observers interpreted such statements as hopeful news that the United States intended to finally become a party to the Kyoto Protocol. However, this was not the case.

In December 2009 President Obama attended the UN's Copenhagen Summit in Denmark. Environmentalists were hopeful that he would broker a deal with China and the other major developing countries for a new post-Kyoto agreement on greenhouse gas emissions. Negotiations proved fruitless, however, and the main outcome of the conference was a nonbinding agreement called the Copenhagen Accord, in which countries pledged to voluntarily meet target emissions reductions by 2020. According to the UN (2015, http://unfccc.int/meetings/copenhagen_dec_2009/items/5264.php), the U.S. target was "in the range of 17%, in conformity with anticipated U.S. energy and climate legislation, recognizing that the final target will be reported to the Secretariat in light of enacted legislation." The base year for the U.S. target was 2005.

The political realities of Obama's time in office, including the Great Recession and its lingering aftereffects, have not been conducive to Senate approval of the Kyoto Protocol. Instead, Obama has focused his efforts on domestic regulations and legislation related to global warming. As a result, as of November 2015, the United States had not ratified the Kyoto Protocol and was not expected to do so. Nonetheless, an emissions target limit of minus 7% is listed for the United States under the Kyoto Protocol. This value is a suggested target because it is not actually binding.

CANADA'S POSITION ON THE KYOTO PROTOCOL. Canada was active in the negotiations that produced the Kyoto Protocol and ratified the agreement in 2002, agreeing to a 6% reduction in greenhouse gas emissions for the first commitment period. However, over the first decade of the 21st century the nation elected more conservative leaders and experienced an oil boom due to the extraction of large-scale deposits of crude oil in the midwestern part of the country. A combination of political and economic factors prevented the nation from making significant progress toward its emissions target goal. In 2011 Canada officially notified the UN that it was withdrawing from the Kyoto Protocol.

MARKET-BASED MECHANISMS. In *Fact Sheet: The Kyoto Protocol* (February 2011, http://unfccc.int/files/press/backgrounders/application/pdf/fact_sheet_the_kyoto_protocol.pdf), the UN indicates that the Annex B countries must "first and foremost take domestic action against climate change," such as by reducing domestic greenhouse gas emissions. However, the Kyoto Protocol also established market-based mechanisms through which Annex B parties can reduce their emissions. The key component is an emissions trading scheme in which Annex B parties that reduce their emissions by more than their targets can sell their extra emissions units (expressed in tonnes of carbon dioxide equivalent) to other Annex B parties. The UN explains in "Emissions Trading" (2014, http://unfccc.int/kyoto_protocol/background/items/2880.php) that "countries not meeting their commitments will be able to 'buy' compliance ... but the price may be steep. The higher the cost, the more pressure they will feel to use energy more efficiently and to research and promote the development of alternative sources of energy that have low or no emissions."

This mechanism is broadly known as carbon trading; however, it is not limited to emissions units. According to the UN, parties can also buy and sell removal units, which are units achieved through planting or expanding forests. In addition, projects conducted through the Joint Implementation (JI) and Clean Development Mechanism (CDM) programs can also count toward carbon trading. The JI program concerns projects that are conducted by Annex B parties in concert with other Annex B parties (primarily EIT countries). The CDM program involves Annex B parties that invest in sustainable development projects in developing countries. The projects must be designed to reduce greenhouse gas emissions.

At the time the Kyoto Protocol went into effect, the EU already had a program called the Emissions Trading System, which became part of the international agreement's carbon market program.

PROGRESS AT MEETING KYOTO EMISSIONS GOALS. Determining the progress (or lack thereof) of the Annex B countries toward meeting their Kyoto Protocol emissions targets is difficult. It is not simply a matter of calculating the difference between greenhouse gas emissions between 1990 and 2012 because the various debits and credits under the carbon trading mechanisms must

also be taken into account. According to the UN, in *Kyoto Protocol Reference Manual on Accounting of Emissions and Assigned Amount* (2008, http://unfccc.int/resource/docs/publications/08_unfccc_kp_ref_manual.pdf), the final compliance assessment is expected to take place in 2015 after the parties submit a "true-up period" report. The UN (http://unfccc.int/kyoto_protocol/true-up_process/items/9023.php) indicates that the true-up period was scheduled to begin in November 2015.

Reports required under the UNFCCC provide some clues about how parties are faring at meeting Kyoto Protocol goals. Occasional reports called national communications detail the steps the parties are taking to implement the convention. As of November 2015, all UNFCCC Annex 1 parties had submitted a sixth national communications (NC6; http://unfccc.int/national_reports/annex_i_natcom/submitted_natcom/items/7742.php). The NC6 reports provide a comprehensive overview of each country's greenhouse gas emissions and sources.

In December 2014 the UN published a summation of the NC6 reports for the 43 Annex 1 parties. This includes the 40 Kyoto Protocol Annex B parties plus Cyprus, Malta, and Turkey. Turkey ratified the Kyoto Protocol in 2009; however, it did not commit to a binding emissions target for the first commitment period. In *National Greenhouse Gas Inventory Data for the Period 1990–2012* (November 17, 2014, http://unfccc.int/resource/docs/2014/sbi/eng/20.pdf), the UN concludes that the total aggregate greenhouse gas emissions (excluding adjustments for land-use change and forestry projects) by the Annex 1 parties decreased 10.6% between 1990 and 2012. This statistic bodes very well for achievement of the desired 5% reduction by the Kyoto Protocol Annex B parties. Expectations are high that the overall emissions target of the Kyoto Protocol will be met when the final compliance assessment is conducted.

THE KYOTO PROTOCOL THROUGH 2020. The first commitment period of the Kyoto Protocol covered emissions through 2012. At the Copenhagen Summit in 2009 delegates hoped to hash out a new post-Kyoto agreement, but they were unsuccessful. Media reports indicated deep divisions at the conference between developed and developing countries over each side's level of responsibility in future target agreements. A second round of talks in Bonn, Germany, in June 2011 proved equally divisive.

In November and December 2011 the UN held a summit in Durban, South Africa. An agreement was reached to establish a second commitment period under the Kyoto Protocol to begin in 2013 and end in 2020. The EU notes in "Doha Amendment to the Kyoto Protocol" (June 4, 2015, http://www.europarl.europa.eu/RegData/etudes/ATAG/2015/559475/EPRS_ATA%282015%29559475_EN.pdf) that it has committed to reduce its greenhouse gas emissions by 20% by 2020. However, few other developed countries expressed a willingness to join the extended Kyoto Protocol. Canada, Japan, New Zealand, Russia, and the United States declined to participate. The second commitment period was officially adapted as part of an amendment to the Kyoto Protocol that was passed during a meeting held in Doha, Qatar, in December 2012. The UN (2015, http://unfccc.int/kyoto_protocol/doha_amendment/items/7362.php) indicates that the amendment will enter into force after at least 75% of the parties to the Kyoto Protocol accept it. As of November 2015, the amendment had not gone into effect.

THE LEGACY OF THE KYOTO PROTOCOL. As the first commitment period of the Kyoto Protocol came to a close in 2012, numerous media outlets examined the legacy of the international agreement. The reviews were mixed, with some observers flatly declaring it a failure and others highlighting its positive effects. Overall, it was widely agreed that the Kyoto Protocol failed to significantly lessen global emissions of greenhouse gases. In 2011 the PBL Netherlands Environmental Assessment Agency and the European Commission's Joint Research Centre commissioned the report *Long-Term Trend in Global CO$_2$ Emissions: 2011 Report* (September 2011, http://www.pbl.nl/sites/default/files/cms/publicaties/C02%20Mondiaal_%20webdef_19sept.pdf), which was written by Jos G. J. Olivier et al. The researchers indicate that global carbon dioxide emissions grew from 25 billion tons (22.7 billion t) in 1990 to 36.4 billion tons (33 billion t) in 2010, an increase of 45%. China accounted for nearly 9.9 billion tons (9 billion t), or just over a quarter of the 2010 total. Carbon dioxide emissions doubled in China between 2003 and 2010.

Quirin Schiermeier acknowledges in "The Kyoto Protocol: Hot Air" (*Nature*, vol. 491, no. 7426, November 28, 2012) the success of European nations at meeting their Kyoto Protocol targets, but notes the factors that helped them to do so. He states, "Overall, they met their target with room to spare, cutting their collective emissions by around 16%. But most of those cuts came with little or no effort, because of the collapse of greenhouse-gas producing industries in eastern Europe and, more recently, the global economic crisis." Schiermeier believes the best legacy of the Kyoto Protocol may be the market-based mechanisms, such as the carbon trading schemes, that it helped foster. These mechanisms are expected to play a major role in future greenhouse gas agreements that are reached by the international community.

A Post-Kyoto Agreement

At the Durban summit in 2011 the parties agreed to a plan of action called the Durban Platform (http://unfccc.int/files/meetings/durban_nov_2011/decisions/application/pdf/cop17_durbanplatform.pdf), which lays out the general problems and challenges associated with climate change.

The parties agreed to come up with a new international agreement regarding climate change by 2015. The 21st session of the Conference of the Parties to the UNFCCC (COP21) was scheduled to take place in Paris from November 30 to December 11, 2015. According to the UN (http://www4.unfccc.int/submissions/indc/Submission%20Pages/submissions.aspx), as of November 2015, dozens of countries had submitted their Intended Nationally Determined Contributions (INDCs). These are either greenhouse gas emissions targets or other measures that individual countries are willing to accept as part of a new international agreement. For example, the U.S. government (http://www4.unfccc.int/submissions/INDC/Published%20Documents/United%20States%20of%20America/1/U.S.%20Cover%20Note%20INDC%20and%20Accompanying%20Information.pdf) indicates it will contribute by reducing its greenhouse gas emissions by 26% to 28% by 2025 as compared to 2005 levels. The EU (http://www4.unfccc.int/submissions/INDC/Published%20Documents/Latvia/1/LV-03-06-EU%20INDC.pdf) indicates that its 28 member-nations will commit to reducing their total greenhouse gas emissions by 40% by 2030 as compared to 1990 levels.

The UN is expected to publish a synthesis report in November 2015 that summarizes all of the INDCs. It remains to be seen if the negotiators at COP21 can consolidate the many different proposed contributions into a cohesive international agreement.

THE UNITED STATES GOES ITS OWN WAY

The United States has declined to become a party to the Kyoto Protocol. Instead, it has focused on domestic policies and legislation that address global warming and climate change. These activities actually began before the Kyoto Protocol was adopted in 1997.

In 1989 President George H. W. Bush established the U.S. Global Change Research Program (USGCRP), which was authorized by Congress in the Global Change Research Act of 1990. President Clinton took office in January 1993. Later that year the United States released, in accordance with the UNFCCC, *The Climate Change Action Plan*, which called for measures to reduce emissions for all greenhouse gases to 1990 levels by 2000. However, the U.S. economy grew at a more robust rate than anticipated, which led to increased emissions. Furthermore, Congress did not provide full funding for the actions contained in the plan.

The Clinton administration implemented some policies that did not require congressional approval. These included tax incentives and investments that focused on improving energy efficiency and renewable energy technologies, coordinating federal efforts to develop renewable fuels technology, and requiring all federal government agencies to reduce greenhouse gas emissions below 1990 levels by 2010. Clinton also established the U.S.

Climate Change Research Initiative to study areas of uncertainty about global climate change science and identify priorities for public investments.

President George W. Bush took office in January 2001. He established a new cabinet-level management structure to oversee government investments in climate change science and technology. Both the U.S. Climate Change Research Initiative and the USGCRP were placed under the oversight (supervision) of the interagency U.S. Climate Change Science Program (beginning in 2009 it was renamed the U.S. Global Change Research Program).

Although numerous bills regarding global warming were introduced in Congress during the Bush administration, they failed to move forward because of a lack of consensus among legislators about how to deal with the issue. The exclusion of developing countries, such as China and India, from the Kyoto Protocol's emissions limits was a major sticking point for many U.S. politicians, who feared that the United States would be put at an economic disadvantage if it had to meet specific emissions limits. The United States' refusal to ratify the Kyoto Protocol or develop a similar control plan at the national level elicited strong criticism from foreign and domestic sources.

The Obama Administration: A New Way Forward?

As noted in Chapter 1, the November 2008 election of President Obama was hailed by many environmentalists as the beginning of a green revolution in the United States. Obama publicly expressed support for the Kyoto Protocol; however, he did not try to achieve ratification of it by the Senate. He advocated for mandatory limits on U.S. emissions of global warming gases and suggested that the federal government charge a permit fee to facilities that emit certain carbon levels. He proposed a cap-and-trade system that would include a nationwide cap (upper limit) on carbon emissions from industries. Facilities that reduced their emissions below the cap would receive credits (or allowances) that they could sell to facilities emitting carbon levels above the cap. As is described in Chapter 5, the cap-and-trade approach has been used successfully in the United States to curtail emissions of chemicals, such as sulfur dioxide, that cause acid rain. However, the United States' carbon dioxide emissions dwarf those of sulfur dioxide, meaning that many facilities would be subject to a carbon cap-and-trade system. Although mandatory limits would spur research and development into alternative fuels and emissions controls, they would also raise energy and production costs for industry. These expenses would likely be passed onto consumers, making a carbon cap-and-trade scheme a politically risky endeavor.

In June 2009 the U.S. House of Representatives passed by a thin margin (219–212) the American Clean Energy and Security Act. This legislation included a carbon cap-and-trade program that was projected to reduce emissions of greenhouse gases by 17% by 2020 compared with 2005 emissions. However, the bill was not considered by the Senate and thus did not become law. During the November 2010 midterm elections Republicans gained control of the House and made large gains in the Senate. This was viewed politically as a public rebuke of Obama's policies. Neela Banerjee reports in "EPA Delays Rule on Industrial Emissions" (LATimes.com, May 17, 2011) that following the midterm elections the Obama administration chose to "postpone controversial environmental regulations and steer a more business-friendly course."

Following his reelection in 2012, Obama adopted a much stronger stance on global warming and climate change. By that point the U.S. economy was strengthening, and the administration was emboldened to take action on greenhouse gas emissions. In June 2013 Obama released *The President's Climate Action Plan* (http://www.whitehouse .gov/sites/default/files/image/president27sclimateactionplan .pdf), which lays out a series of executive actions that are designed to reduce U.S. carbon emissions and prepare the nation for the expected impacts of climate change. The executive branch of the U.S. government includes the president and all the agencies that report to him. Thus, Obama opted not to pursue climate change action through the legislative branch, which is made up by the Senate and the House of Representatives.

In "President Obama's Plan to Fight Climate Change" (June 25, 2013, http://www.whitehouse.gov/ share/climate-action-plan), the White House summarizes the Climate Action Plan (CAP). The president makes three general assertions in the CAP:

- The weather is getting more extreme due to climate change

- Extreme weather has an economic cost and threatens public health

- Carbon pollution is the biggest driver of climate change

To cut U.S. carbon emissions, the president lists six initiatives:

- Reduce carbon emissions from power plants

- Accelerate clean energy development (e.g., advanced biofuels, nuclear power, and clean coal) and achieve greater electricity generation from renewable sources

- Reduce carbon emissions from the transportation sector

- Cut energy waste in homes, businesses, and factories via government programs that finance energy efficiency investments and encourage state and local governments to adopt waste-cutting policies

- Reduce emissions of greenhouse gases other than carbon dioxide, particularly methane, and encourage private-sector investment in alternatives to potent greenhouse gases

- Take actions within the federal government sector to reduce greenhouse gas emissions (e.g., by relying more on electricity from renewable energy sources)

In January 2015 Obama took his most aggressive actions to date against global warming. In his State of the Union speech (https://www.whitehouse.gov/the-press-office/2015/01/20/remarks-president-state-union-address-january-20-2015), he stated, "And no challenge—no challenge—poses a greater threat to future generations than climate change." Obama went on to say, "The best scientists in the world are all telling us that our activities are changing the climate, and if we don't act forcefully, we'll continue to see rising oceans, longer, hotter heat waves, dangerous droughts and floods, and massive disruptions that can trigger greater migration and conflict and hunger around the globe. The Pentagon says that climate change poses immediate risks to our national security. We should act like it." Over subsequent months the Obama administration acted through the EPA to impose carbon emissions limits on power plants and transportation vehicles.

CARBON EMISSIONS LIMITS FOR POWER PLANTS. Previously, in 2013, Obama released "Presidential Memorandum—Power Sector Carbon Pollution Standards" (June 25, 2013, http://www.whitehouse.gov/the-press-office/2013/06/25/presidential-memorandum-power-sector-carbon-pollution-standards), which directed the EPA to propose carbon pollution standards for fossil fuel–fired power plants. Republicans expressed intense disapproval over this proposal and decried the standards as energy taxes in disguise. (Under the U.S. Constitution, only Congress has the power to levy taxes.) Republicans also accused the Obama administration of waging a war on coal because the proposed standards would mostly affect coal-burning power plants. As shown in Table 3.5, coal accounted for 39% of U.S. net electricity generation in 2014, compared with 27% from natural gas, 20% from nuclear power, and smaller contributions from other fuels and generation methods.

In July 2013 a group of Republican senators introduced the Energy Tax Repeal Act, which sought to prohibit "any regulations promulgated pursuant to a presidential memorandum relating to power sector carbon pollution standards." The senators argued that such standards would be devastating to the U.S. economy. The act failed to come to a vote in the Senate, which during the 2013–14 session featured a Democratic majority. In "12 States Sue the EPA over Proposed Power Plant Regulations" (LATimes.com, August 4, 2014), Neela Banerjee notes that in 2014 a dozen states (Alabama, Indiana, Kansas, Kentucky, Louisiana, Nebraska,

TABLE 3.5

Electricity net generation by fuel type, 2014

[Million kilowatt-hours]

2014	Million Kilowatt-hours	Percentage
Coal	1,585.7	39%
Natural gas	1,121.9	27%
Nuclear	797.1	20%
Hydro	252.5	6%
Wind	181.8	4%
Other renewable	99.3	2%
Petroluem	30.5	1%
Miscellaneous	11.6	0.3%
Total	**4,080.4**	**100%**

SOURCE: Adapted from "Table 7.2a. Electricity Net Generation: Total (All Sectors)," in *Monthly Energy Review: August 2015*, U.S. Department of Energy, Energy Information Administration, August 26, 2015, http://www.eia.gov/totalenergy/data/monthly/pdf/sec7_5.pdf (accessed September 1, 2015)

Ohio, Oklahoma, South Carolina, South Dakota, West Virginia, and Wyoming) sued the EPA in a failed effort to stop implementation of the proposed rule. Many of these states have large coal industries and view carbon emissions standards as economically harmful to those industries and the people they employ.

In August 2015 the EPA finalized the standards known as the Clean Power Plan. The agency explains in the fact sheet "Components of the Clean Power Plan: Setting State Goals to Cut Carbon Pollution" (August 3, 2015, http://www2.epa.gov/sites/production/files/2015-08/documents/fs-cpp-state-goals.pdf) that it has established interim and final goals for power plants to meet. The EPA explains, "States then develop and implement customized plans that ensure that the power plants in their state—either individually, together or in combination with other measures—achieve the interim CO_2 emissions performance rates over the period of 2022 to 2029 and the final CO_2 emissions performance rates, rate-based goals or mass-based goals by 2030." The EPA notes that states have various options for meeting their emissions goals, including emissions trading.

In the fact sheet "Clean Power Plan and Carbon Pollution Standards Key Dates" (January 7, 2015, http://www2.epa.gov/cleanpowerplan/fact-sheet-clean-power-plan-carbon-pollution-standards-key-dates#print), the EPA indicates that states must submit their plans by the summer of 2016, with extensions allowed until the summer of 2018. The compliance period is scheduled to begin in 2020.

Figure 3.11 shows the locations of fossil fuel–fired electricity generating facilities around the country as of 2015. According to the EPA, in *Regulatory Impact Analysis for the Final Standards of Performance for Greenhouse Gas Emissions from New, Modified, and*

FIGURE 3.11

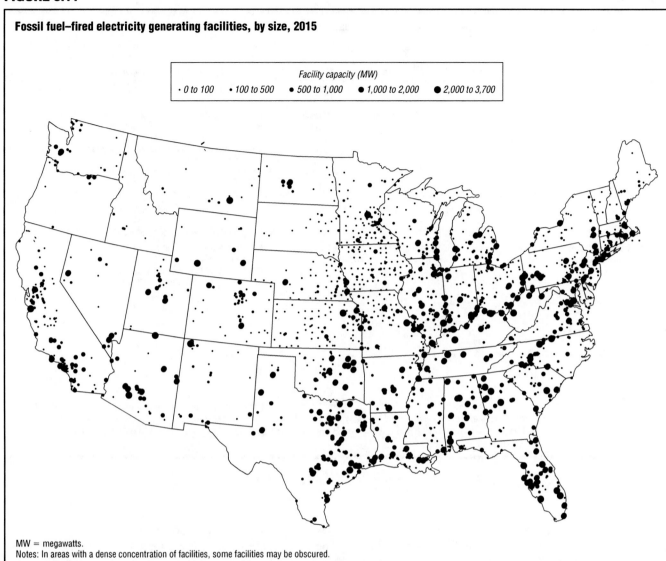

Fossil fuel–fired electricity generating facilities, by size, 2015

Facility capacity (MW)

· 0 to 100   • 100 to 500   ● 500 to 1,000   ● 1,000 to 2,000   ● 2,000 to 3,700

MW = megawatts.
Notes: In areas with a dense concentration of facilities, some facilities may be obscured.

SOURCE: "Figure 2-3. Fossil Fuel-Fired Electricity Generating Facilities, by Size," in *Regulatory Impact Analysis for the Final Standards of Performance for Greenhouse Gas Emissions from New, Modified, and Reconstructed Stationary Sources: Electric Utility Generating Units*, U.S. Environmental Protection Agency, Office of Air Quality Planning and Standards, Health and Environmental Impacts Division, August 2015, http://www2.epa.gov/sites/production/files/2015-08/documents/cps-ria.pdf (accessed September 1, 2015)

Reconstructed Stationary Sources: Electric Utility Generating Units (August 2015, http://www2.epa.gov/sites/production/files/2015-08/documents/cps-ria.pdf), the standards require new, modified, or reconstructed units to apply "the best system of emission reduction (BSER) that the EPA has determined has been adequately demonstrated for each type of unit." The types of units covered by the Clean Power Plan, the applicable BSER, and the CO_2 standards are listed in Table 3.6.

The EPA's issuance of the final rule was staunchly criticized by the coal industry and the governors of numerous states. In "Ohio Will Sue EPA over Obama's Clean Power Plan" (Cleveland.com, August 5, 2015), John Funk notes that as many as 25 states were expected to sue the EPA over the Clean Power Plan. Funk explains, "The issue? It's not about air quality or even carbon dioxide. The issue is the balance of power between federal authority and state authority." As of November 2015, no further information was available on prospective state lawsuits regarding the Clean Power Plan. It is expected that a legal battle will take place that will ultimately be decided by the U.S. Supreme Court.

CARBON EMISSIONS LIMITS FOR VEHICLES. As described in Chapter 2, in 2010 and 2012 the EPA and the National Highway Transportation Safety Administration (NHTSA) established fuel economy and carbon dioxide standards for cars and light-duty trucks for model years 2012 to 2025. Figure 3.12 shows the amounts of carbon dioxide emitted by these vehicle types between 1975 and 2014. The EPA notes in

TABLE 3.6

Standards limiting carbon dioxide emissions from fossil fuel–fired electric utility steam generating units and stationary combustion turbines

Affected EGU	BSER	Standard
Newly constructed fossil fuel-fired steam generating units	Efficient new SCPC utility boiler implementing partial CCS	1,400 lb CO_2/MWh-gross
Modified fossil fuel-fired steam generating units	Most efficient generation at the affected EGU achievable through a combination of best operating practices and equipment upgrades	Sources making modifications resulting in an increase in CO_2 hourly emissions of more than 10 percent are required to meet a unit-specific emission limit determined by the unit's best historical annual CO_2 emission rate (from 2002 to the date of the modification); the emission limit will be no more stringent than: 1. 1,800 lb CO_2/MWh-gross for sources with heat input > 2,000 MMBtu/h. or 2. 2,000 lb CO_2/MWh-gross for sources with heat input ≤ 2,000 MMBtu/h.
Reconstructed fossil fuel-fired steam generating units	Most efficient generating technology at the affected EGU.	1. 1,800 lb CO_2/MWh-gross for sources with heat input > 2,000 MMBtu/h. or 2. 2,000 lb CO_2/MWh-gross for sources with heat input ≤ 2,000 MMBtu/h.
Newly constructed and reconstructed natural gas-fired stationary combustion turbines	Efficient NGCC technology for natural gas-fired base load units and clean fuels for non-base load and multi-fuel-fired units.	4. 1,000 lb CO_2/MWh-gross or 1,030 lb CO_2/MWh-net for base load natural gas-fired units. 5. 120 lb CO_2/MMBtu for non-base load natural gas-fired units. 6. 120 to 160 lb CO_2/MMBtu for multi-fuel-fired units.

BSER = Best System of Emission Reduction.
CCS = Carbon Capture and Storage.
CO_2 = Carbon Dioxide.
EGU = Electricity Generating Units.
lb = Pounds.
MMBtu = Million British Thermal Units.
MWh = Megawatt-hour.
NGCC = Natural Gas Combined Cycle.
SCPC = Supercritical Pulverized Coal.

SOURCE: "Table 1-1. Summary of BSER and Final Standards for Affected EGUs," in *Regulatory Impact Analysis for the Final Standards of Performance for Greenhouse Gas Emissions from New, Modified, and Reconstructed Stationary Sources: Electric Utility Generating Units*, U.S. Environmental Protection Agency, Office of Air Quality Planning and Standards, Health and Environmental Impacts Division, August 2015, http://www2.epa.gov/sites/production/files/2015-08/documents/cps-ria.pdf (accessed September 1, 2015)

"Regulations & Standards: Light-Duty" (June 18, 2015, http://www3.epa.gov/otaq/climate/regs-light-duty.htm) that the standards are projected to cut 6.6 billion tons (6 billion t) of greenhouse gas emissions over the lifetime of the covered vehicles.

In 2011 the EPA and the NHTSA established fuel economy and carbon dioxide standards for medium- and heavy-duty vehicles, such as large pickup trucks, vans, buses, motor homes, and combination tractors (semi-trucks that typically pull trailers loaded with freight) for model years 2014 to 2018. In *EPA and NHTSA Adopt First-Ever Program to Reduce Greenhouse Gas Emissions and Improve Fuel Efficiency of Medium- and Heavy-Duty Vehicles* (August 2011, http://www.epa.gov/otaq/climate/documents/420f11031.pdf), the EPA notes that the standards are expected to reduce greenhouse gas emissions by approximately 297.6 million tons (270 million t) over the lifetime of the covered vehicles. Table 3.7 and Table 3.8 show standards for various classes of model year 2017 combination tractors and vocational vehicles, respectively. Vocational vehicles include delivery trucks, dump trucks, garbage trucks, transit buses, school buses, motor homes, and many other types of vehicles.

In June 2015 the EPA and the NHTSA proposed expanding the medium- and heavy-duty vehicle standards beyond model year 2018. According to the EPA, in "Cutting Carbon Pollution, Improving Fuel Efficiency, Saving Money, and Supporting Innovation for Trucks" (June 2015, http://www.epa.gov/otaq/climate/documents/420f15900.pdf), the so-called Phase 2 standards would reduce greenhouse gas emissions by 1.1 billion tons (1 billion t). As of November 2015, the proposed Phase 2 standards had not been finalized.

Recent U.S. Reports on Climate Science

Since 2000 the USGCRP (http://www.globalchange.gov/browse/reports) has published dozens of reports related to climate science, including three national climate assessments in 2000, 2009, and 2014.

In *Climate Change Impacts in the United States* (2014, https://s3.amazonaws.com/nca2014/low/NCA3_Climate_Change_Impacts_in_the_United%20States_LowRes.pdf), the USGCRP compiles and explains information from numerous publications from various U.S. government agencies. It examines existing and expected climate change impacts on the United States by economic sector and geographical region. Overall, it lists 12 key findings:

FIGURE 3.12

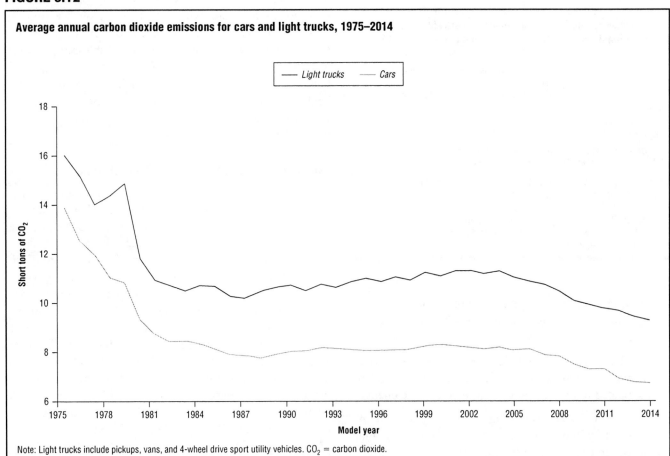

Average annual carbon dioxide emissions for cars and light trucks, 1975–2014

Note: Light trucks include pickups, vans, and 4-wheel drive sport utility vehicles. CO_2 = carbon dioxide.

SOURCE: Stacy C. Davis, et al., "Figure 7. Average Carbon Footprint for Cars and Light Trucks Sold, 1975–2014," in *2014 Vehicle Technologies Market Report*, Oak Ridge National Laboratory, March 27, 2015, http://cta.ornl.gov/vtmarketreport/pdf/2014_vtmarketreport_full_doc.pdf (accessed September 11, 2015)

TABLE 3.7

Fuel economy and carbon dioxide emissions standards for heavy-duty combination tractors (semitrucks), model year 2017

	EPA emissions standards (g CO_2/ton-mile)			NHTSA fuel consumption standards (gal/1,000 ton-mile)		
	Low roof	Mid roof	High roof	Low roof	Mid roof	High roof
Day cab class 7	104	115	120	10.2	11.3	11.8
Day cab class 8	80	86	89	7.8	8.4	8.7
Sleeper cab class 8	66	73	72	6.5	7.2	7.1

CO_2 = Carbon dioxide; EPA = Environmental Protection Agency; g = Grams; NHTSA = National Highway Traffic Safety Administration.

SOURCE: "Table 1. MY 2017 Combination Tractor Standards," in *EPA and NHTSA Adopt First-Ever Program to Reduce Greenhouse Gas Emissions and Improve Fuel Efficiency of Medium-and Heavy-Duty Vehicles*, U.S. Environmental Protection Agency, Office of Transportation and Air Quality, August 2011, http://www.epa.gov/otaq/climate/documents/420f11031.pdf (accessed September 3, 2015)

1. Global climate is changing and this is apparent across the United States in a wide range of observations. The global warming of the past 50 years is primarily due to human activities, predominantly the burning of fossil fuels.

2. Some extreme weather and climate events have increased in recent decades, and new and stronger evidence confirms that some of these increases are related to human activities.

3. Human-induced climate change is projected to continue, and it will accelerate significantly if global emissions of heat-trapping gases continue to increase.

4. Impacts related to climate change are already evident in many sectors and are expected to become increasingly disruptive across the nation throughout this century and beyond.

5. Climate change threatens human health and well-being in many ways, including through more

TABLE 3.8

Fuel economy and carbon dioxide emissions standards for heavy-duty vocational vehicles (trucks and buses), model year 2017

	EPA full useful life emissions standards (g CO₂/ton-mile)	NHTSA fuel consumption standards (gal/1,000 ton-mile)
Light heavy class 2b–5	373	36.7
Medium heavy class 6–7	225	22.1
Heavy heavy class 8	222	21.8

CO₂ = Carbon dioxide; EPA = Environmental Protection Agency; g = Grams; NHTSA = National Highway Traffic Safety Administration.

SOURCE: "Table 2. MY 2017 Vocational Vehicle Standards," in *EPA and NHTSA Adopt First-Ever Program to Reduce Greenhouse Gas Emissions and Improve Fuel Efficiency of Medium-and Heavy-Duty Vehicles*, U.S. Environmental Protection Agency, Office of Transportation and Air Quality, August 2011, http://www.epa.gov/otaq/climate/documents/420f11031.pdf (accessed September 3, 2015)

extreme weather events and wildfire, decreased air quality, and diseases transmitted by insects, food, and water.

6. Infrastructure is being damaged by sea level rise, heavy downpours, and extreme heat; damages are projected to increase with continued climate change.

7. Water quality and water supply reliability are jeopardized by climate change in a variety of ways that affect ecosystems and livelihoods.

8. Climate disruptions to agriculture have been increasing and are projected to become more severe over this century.

9. Climate change poses particular threats to Indigenous Peoples' health, well-being, and ways of life.

10. Ecosystems and the benefits they provide to society are being affected by climate change. The capacity of ecosystems to buffer the impacts of extreme events like fires, floods, and severe storms is being overwhelmed.

11. Ocean waters are becoming warmer and more acidic, broadly affecting ocean circulation, chemistry, ecosystems, and marine life.

12. Planning for adaptation (to address and prepare for impacts) and mitigation (to reduce future climate change, for example by cutting emissions) is becoming more widespread, but current implementation efforts are insufficient to avoid increasingly negative social, environmental, and economic consequences.

In June 2015 the EPA published *Climate Change in the United States: Benefits of Global Action* (http://www2.epa.gov/sites/production/files/2015-06/documents/cirareport.pdf). The agency states, "The goal of this work is to estimate to what degree climate change impacts and damages to multiple U.S. sectors (e.g., human health,

infrastructure, and water resources) may be avoided or reduced in a future with significant global action to reduce GHG emissions, compared to a future in which current emissions continue to grow." Table 3.9 provides an overview of the results with a listing of the expected benefits of mitigation in 2050 and 2100 to the nation's health and well-being and to various major resources and economic sectors. Overall, hundreds of billions of dollars in benefits are projected to occur.

Local and State Governments Take Action

During the first decade of the 21st century growing concern about climate change and the federal government's lack of involvement in the Kyoto Protocol spurred some local and state governments to establish their own campaigns against greenhouse gases. In 2007 the Sierra Club launched the Cool Counties Initiative for county governments that were committed to reducing their contributions to global warming. Some state and local governments adopted specific emissions targets. For example, in June 2008 the city of Miami developed MiPlan (http://carbonn.org/uploads/tx_carbonndata/MiPlan%20Final%20062608.pdf), a climate action plan in which Miami pledged to reduce its greenhouse gas emissions to 25% below 2006 levels by 2020. However, the subsequent economic challenges of the Great Recession hindered many such plans. In "Miami's Climate Vice: Budget Woes Stunt Urban Resilience" (GreenBiz.com, September 17, 2015), Mike Hower reports that as of 2015 "a lack of funding" had prevented Miami from fully implementing its climate action plan or even updating it.

Dozens of states joined with other states (and some Canadian provinces) in regional initiatives to reduce greenhouse gas emissions. These collaborations include the Western Climate Initiative (2013, http://www.westernclimateinitiative.org) and the Regional Greenhouse Gas Initiative (2015, http://www.rggi.org). This initiative is particularly notable because it is "the first market-based regulatory program in the United States to reduce greenhouse gas emissions." The collaborating states are Connecticut, Delaware, Maine, Maryland, Massachusetts, New Hampshire, New York, Rhode Island, and Vermont. They have agreed to a regional cap on emissions (in total tons) that declines each year. The states use an auction trading program through which power plants with lower emissions sell emissions credits to power plants with higher emissions.

According to the Center for Climate and Energy Solutions (2015, http://www.c2es.org/what_s_being_done/targets), 17 states (Arizona, California, Connecticut, Florida, Hawaii, Illinois, Maine, Massachusetts, Minnesota, New Hampshire, New Jersey, New Mexico, New York, Oregon, Rhode Island, Vermont, and Washington) established specific carbon emissions target goals during

TABLE 3.9

National benefits expected in 2050 and 2100 from limiting global temperature rise to approximately 3.6 degrees Fahrenheit (2 degrees Celsius) above preindustrial levels

	In the year 2050, global GHG mitigation is projected to result in...	In the year 2100, global GHG mitigation is projected to result in...
Health		
Air quality	An estimated 13,000 fewer deaths from poor air quality, valued at $160 billion.[a]	An estimated 57,000 fewer deaths from poor air quality, valued at $930 billion.[a]
Extreme temperature	An estimated 1,700 fewer deaths from extreme heat and cold in 49 major U.S. cities, valued at $21 billion.	An estimated 12,000 fewer deaths from extreme heat and cold in 49 major U.S. cities, valued at $200 billion.
Labor	An estimated avoided loss of 360 million labor hours, valued at $18 billion.	An estimated avoided loss of 1.2 billion labor hours, valued at $110 billion.
Water quality	An estimated $507–$700 million in avoided damages from poor water quality.[b]	An estimated $2.6–$3.0 billion in avoided damages from poor water quality.[b]
Infrastructure		
Bridges	An estimated 160–960 fewer bridges made structurally vulnerable, valued at $0.12–$1.5 billion.[b]	An estimated 720–2,200 fewer bridges made structurally vulnerable, valued at $1.1–$1.6 billion.[b]
Roads	An estimated $0.56–$2.3 billion in avoided adaptation costs.[b]	An estimated $4.2–$7.4 billion in avoided adaptation costs.[b]
Urban drainage	An estimated $56 million to $2.9 billion in avoided adaptation costs from the 50-year, 24-hour storm in 50 U.S. cities.[b]	An estimated $50 million to $6.4 billion in avoided adaptation costs from the 50-year, 24-hour storm in 50 U.S. cities.[b]
Coastal property	An estimated $0.14 billion in avoided damages and adaptation costs from sea level rise and storm surge.	An estimated $3.1 billion in avoided damages and adaptation costs from sea level rise and storm surge.
Electricity		
Demand and supply	An estimated 1.1%–4.0% reduction in energy demand and $10–$34 billion in savings in power system costs.[c]	Not estimated.
Water resources		
Inland flooding	An estimated change in flooding damages ranging from $260 million in damages to $230 million in avoided damages.[b]	An estimated change in flooding damages ranging from $32 million in damages to $2.5 billion in avoided damages.[b]
Drought	An estimated 29%–45% fewer severe and extreme droughts, with corresponding avoided damages to the agriculture sector of approximately $1.2–$1.4 billion.[b]	An estimated 40%–59% fewer severe and extreme droughts, with corresponding avoided damages to the agriculture sector of $2.6–$3.1 billion.[b]
Water supply and demand	An estimated $3.9–$54 billion in avoided damages due to water shortages.[b]	An estimated $11–$180 billion in avoided damages due to water shortages.[b]
Agriculture & forestry		
Agriculture	An estimated $1.5–$3.8 billion in avoided damages.	An estimated $6.6–$11 billion in avoided damages.
Forestry	Estimated damages of $9.5–$9.6 billion.	An estimated $520 million to $1.5 billion in avoided damages.
Ecosystems		
Coral reefs	An estimated avoided loss of 53% of coral in Hawaii, 3.7% in Florida, and 2.8% in Puerto Rico. These avoided losses are valued at $1.4 billion.	An estimated avoided loss of 35% of coral in Hawaii, 1.2% in Florida, and 1.7% in Puerto Rico. These avoided losses are valued at $1.2 billion.
Shellfish	An estimated avoided loss of 11% of the U.S. oyster supply, 12% of the U.S. scallop supply, and 4.6% of the U.S. clam supply, with corresponding consumer benefits of $85 million.	An estimated avoided loss of 34% of the U.S. oyster supply, 37% of the U.S. scallop supply, and 29% of the U.S. clam supply, with corresponding consumer benefits of $380 million.
Freshwater fish	An estimated change in recreational fishing ranging from $13 million in avoided damages to $3.8 million in damages.[b]	An estimated $95–$280 million in avoided damages associated with recreational fishing.[b]
Wildfire	An estimated 2.1–2.2 million fewer acres burned and corresponding avoided wildfire response costs of $160–$390 million.[†]	An estimated 6.0–7.9 million fewer acres burned and corresponding avoided wildfire response costs of $940 million to $1.4 billion.[†]
Carbon storage	An estimated 26–78 million fewer metric tons of carbon stored, and corresponding costs of $7.5–$23 billion.[b]	An estimated 1–26 million fewer metric tons of carbon stored, and corresponding costs of $880 million to $12 billion.[b]

[a]These results do not reflect additional benefits to air quality and human health that would stem from the co-control of traditional air pollutants along with GHG emissions.
[b]For sectors sensitive to changes in precipitation, the estimated range of results is generated using projections from two climate models showing different patterns of future precipitation in the contiguous U.S. The IGSM-CAM model projects a relatively "wetter" future for most of the contiguous U.S. compared to the "drier" MIROC model.
[c]Estimated range of benefits from the reduction in demand and system costs resulting from lower temperatures associated with GHG mitigation. The electricity section in this report presents an analysis that includes the costs to the electric sector of reducing GHG emissions.
Notes: GHG = Greenhouse gas.

SOURCE: "National Highlights," in *Climate Change in the United States: Benefits of Global Action*, U.S. Environmental Protection Agency, June 2015, http://www2.epa.gov/sites/production/files/2015-06/documents/cirareport.pdf (accessed September 3, 2015)

the first decade of the 21st century. For example, in 2007 Florida pledged to reduce its emissions by 2017 to those which it had in 2000. However, the state elected more conservative Republican leaders in 2010 who rejected limits on carbon emissions.

Climate action plans have also been stymied by legal challenges. In 2014 a federal court overturned portions of Minnesota's Next Generation Energy Act of 2007. According to David Shaffer, in "Judge Strikes Down Minnesota's Anti-coal Energy Law" (StarTribune.com,

April 18, 2014), the judge ruled that the law—which put restrictions on energy from coal-fired power plants—violates the commerce clause of the U.S. Constitution.

However, some state and local governments have persisted in their efforts to limit carbon emissions within their jurisdictions. In "Malloy 'Recommits' State to Climate Change Battle" (Courant.Com, April 22, 2015), Brian Dowling indicates that during the early 1990s Connecticut became the first state "to pass legislation requiring actions to control carbon emissions." This was followed by adoption of a climate change action plan in 2005 and passage of the Global Warming Solutions Act of 2008. The law commits the state to reducing its greenhouse gas emissions by 2020 to 10% below 1990 levels and by 2050 to 80% of 2001 levels. Dowling notes that as of April 2015, Connecticut was "on pace" to meet the 2020 goal. The 2050 goal is expected to be quite challenging; however, the state's efforts would be aided by implementation in 2020 of the federal Clean Power Plan, which limits carbon emissions from the nation's power plants.

CALIFORNIA LEADS WITH LEGISLATION. California has been the most aggressive of the states in implementing legislation related to global warming and climate change. In 2005 it set targets for greenhouse gas emissions under an executive order issued by Governor Arnold Schwarzenegger (1947–). He also created a Climate Action Team under the direction of the California Environmental Protection Agency to coordinate the state's climate policy.

In August 2006 the California legislature passed AB 32, the Global Warming Solutions Act, which adopted Schwarzenegger's plans into law. It calls for the state to reduce its greenhouse gas emissions to 1990 levels by 2020. This represents an approximate 25% reduction, compared with what emissions would be without the act. The act also includes a cap-and-trade program and a market-based trading program in which industries emitting greenhouse gases can buy or sell credits among themselves to meet the limits. The state's carbon market began trading in 2012 and quickly grew to be the second largest in the world, behind the EU's Emissions Trading System. Lynn Doan reports in "California Adopts Regulation to Link Carbon Markets with Quebec" (Bloomberg.com, April 19, 2013) that in April 2013 the state modified its cap-and-trade program to align it with Quebec, a Canadian province with an aggressive policy toward reducing greenhouse gas emissions.

Opponents to AB 32 worry about its economic consequences, fearing that it will drive businesses from California and raise consumer prices, particularly for gasoline. Advocates counter that California companies will create profitable technological innovations for the world marketplace that will ultimately offset and even surpass the short-term costs of tighter emissions limits.

California has also targeted carbon emissions from transportation vehicles. The state's Low Carbon Fuel Standard (http://www.arb.ca.gov/fuels/lcfs/lcfs.htm) was implemented in April 2009 through a new regulation that targets providers, refiners, importers, and blenders of transportation fuels. It is designed to reduce greenhouse gas emissions from transportation fuels and encourage development and investment in alternative fuels other than gasoline.

MITIGATING CARBON BUILDUP IN THE ATMOSPHERE

To mitigate means to relieve or reduce in harshness. Limiting greenhouse gas emissions is one way to mitigate carbon buildup in the atmosphere and the main method that is focused on in legislation and government policy, such as through cap-and-trade programs or other emissions controls.

Carbon Sequestration

Besides emissions controls, scientists are increasingly exploring techniques for long-term storage of carbon to keep it out of the atmosphere. This is known as carbon sequestration. Carbon storage media are known as repositories or sinks.

NATURAL SINKS: OCEANS, VEGETATION, AND SOILS. The earth's oceans, vegetation (particularly forests), and soils act naturally to mitigate the effect of carbon buildup by absorbing and storing carbon. The oceans are, by far, the largest reservoir of carbon in the earth's carbon cycle. Some scientists believe the oceans can absorb between 1 billion and 2 billion tons (907 million and 1.8 billion t) of carbon dioxide per year. Living vegetation, especially trees, also naturally absorbs and neutralizes carbon dioxide. Deforestation (the clearing of forests) reduces natural carbon sequestration. The burning of the Amazon rain forest and other forests has had a twofold effect: the immediate release of large amounts of carbon dioxide into the atmosphere from the fires and the loss of trees to absorb the carbon dioxide in the atmosphere. Natural disasters can also destroy large swaths of trees, as happened during Hurricane Katrina in 2005. Soil can also be a carbon sink due to the presence of tiny carbon-storing microbes. Disturbing the soil, for example, through plowing, releases the carbon.

PURPOSEFUL CARBON CAPTURE. Purposeful carbon capture is carbon sequestration facilitated by humans. Afforestation (establishing new forest) is one method. However, massive amounts of forested land are required to offset anthropogenic emissions.

Geological sequestration is the injection of carbon dioxide into sealed formations or reservoirs deep beneath the earth's surface. These include already tapped oil and natural gas reservoirs, saline formations (formations of porous rock that is saturated with saltwater), unmineable deep coal seams, and basalt formations (formations of solidified lava). According to the U.S. Department of Energy's National Energy Technology Laboratory, the use of tapped oil reservoirs could be particularly beneficial because the injection of carbon dioxide would help push hard-to-pump oil out of the reservoir. This process is known as CO_2-enhanced oil recovery and is already being used by the petroleum industry. The laboratory believes that widespread use of CO_2-enhanced oil recovery could significantly boost U.S. oil production while sequestering away a potent greenhouse gas.

The Department of Energy is engaged in public-private partnerships to further research and development of carbon sequestration in the commercial power industry. The National Carbon Capture Center (http://national carboncapturecenter.com) was launched in May 2009 to develop and test technologies that can be used to capture carbon dioxide emissions from coal-based power plants. The FutureGen Industrial Alliance (2015, http://future genalliance.org/futuregen-2-0-project) is a private-public project with the goal of building a coal-fired power plant in Meredosia, Illinois, that will use geological sequestration for most of its carbon dioxide emissions. As of November 2015, engineering design work continued on the project.

GLOBAL WARMING SKEPTICS

Although there is widespread agreement among scientists that the earth's temperature has warmed in recent years, there is lingering debate over the causes of this warming. Some scientists believe major climate events should be viewed in terms of thousands of years, not just a century. A record of only the past century may indicate, but not prove, that a major change has occurred. Is it caused by anthropogenic greenhouse gases or is it natural variability?

Critics of global warming contend that there are several reasons for the change in climate, including:

- Climate has been known to change dramatically within a relatively short period without any human influence.

- Temperature readings already showed increased temperatures before carbon dioxide levels rose significantly (before 1940).

- Natural variations in climate may exceed any human-caused climate change.

- Some of the increase in temperatures can be attributed to sunspot activity.

- Although clouds are crucial to climate predictions, so little is known about them that computer models cannot produce accurate predictions.

There are a handful of scientists notably known for their criticism of the IPCC and its conclusions about anthropogenic causes of global warming. They believe modeling results exaggerate the role of carbon dioxide emissions on climate and attack what they see as environmental hysteria on a subject about which much is still unknown by the scientific community.

PUBLIC OPINION ABOUT GLOBAL WARMING

Polling conducted by the Gallup Organization indicates that a majority of Americans recognize that many scientists believe that global warming is taking place. In 2015 nearly two-thirds (62%) of poll respondents expressed their agreement with the statement "Most scientists believe that global warming is occurring." (See Table 3.10.) However, 27% of the respondents said they are "unsure," and 8% agreed with the statement "Most scientists believe that global warming is not occurring." The remaining 3% of respondents had no opinion on the matter. Thus, there is far from universal acceptance in the United States that most scientists believe that global warming is taking place.

Americans have doubts about the science underpinning the purported cause of global warming. As shown in Table 3.11, a 2015 Gallup poll found that 55% of Americans believe global warming is due to "the effects of pollution from human activities," whereas 41% blame global warming on "natural changes in the environment." In *Conservative Republicans Alone on Global*

TABLE 3.10

Public opinion on the belief in global warming by scientists, selected years 1997–2015

JUST YOUR IMPRESSION, WHICH ONE OF THE FOLLOWING STATEMENTS DO YOU THINK IS MOST ACCURATE—MOST SCIENTISTS BELIEVE THAT GLOBAL WARMING IS OCCURRING, MOST SCIENTISTS BELIEVE THAT GLOBAL WARMING IS NOT OCCURRING, OR MOST SCIENTISTS ARE UNSURE ABOUT WHETHER GLOBAL WARMING IS OCCURRING OR NOT?

	Is occurring	Not occurring	Unsure	No opinion
	%	%	%	%
2015 Mar 5–8	62	8	27	3
2014 Mar 6–9	60	8	29	3
2013 Mar 7–10	62	6	28	4
2012 Mar 8–11	58	7	32	3
2011 Mar 3–6	55	8	33	4
2010 Mar 4–7	52	10	36	2
2008 Mar 6–9	65	7	26	3
2006 Mar 13–16	65	3	29	3
2001 Mar 5–7	61	4	30	5
1997 Nov 21–23	48	7	39	6

SOURCE: "Just your impression, which one of the following statements do you think is most accurate—most scientists believe that global warming is occurring, most scientists believe that global warming is NOT occurring, or most scientists are unsure about whether global warming is occurring or not?" in *Environment*, The Gallup Organization, 2015, http://www.gallup.com/poll/1615/Environment.aspx#1 (accessed August 28, 2015). Copyright © 2015 Gallup, Inc. All rights reserved. The content is used with permission; however, Gallup retains all rights of republication.

TABLE 3.11

Public opinion about the causes of Earth's increasing temperatures, selected years 2003–15

AND FROM WHAT YOU HAVE HEARD OR READ, DO YOU BELIEVE INCREASES IN THE EARTH'S TEMPERATURE OVER THE LAST CENTURY ARE DUE MORE TO—THE EFFECTS OF POLLUTION FROM HUMAN ACTIVITIES (OR) NATURAL CHANGES IN THE ENVIRONMENT THAT ARE NOT DUE TO HUMAN ACTIVITIES?

	Human activities	Natural causes	No opinion
	%	%	%
2015 Mar 5–8	55	41	4
2014 Mar 6–9	57	40	3
2013 Mar 7–10	57	39	4
2012 Mar 8–11	53	41	6
2011 Mar 3–6	52	43	5
2010 Mar 4–7	50	46	5
2008 Mar 6–9	58	38	5
2007 Mar 11–14	61	35	5
2006 Mar 13–16	58	36	6
2003 Mar 3–5	61	33	6

SOURCE: "And from what you have heard or read, do you believe increases in the Earth's temperature over the last century are due more to—the effects of pollution from human activities (or) natural changes in the environment that are not due to human activities?" in *Environment*, The Gallup Organization, 2015, http://www.gallup.com/poll/1615/Environment.aspx#1 (accessed August 28, 2015). Copyright © 2015 Gallup, Inc. All rights reserved. The content is used with permission; however, Gallup retains all rights of republication.

TABLE 3.12

Public opinion on media exaggeration of the seriousness of global warming, selected years 1997–2015

THINKING ABOUT WHAT IS SAID IN THE NEWS, IN YOUR VIEW IS THE SERIOUSNESS OF GLOBAL WARMING—GENERALLY EXAGGERATED, GENERALLY CORRECT, OR IS IT GENERALLY UNDERESTIMATED?

	Generally exaggerated	Generally correct	Generally underestimated	No opinion
	%	%	%	%
2015 Mar 5–8	42	21	35	2
2014 Mar 6–9	42	23	33	2
2013 Mar 7–10	41	24	33	2
2012 Mar 8–11	42	24	31	3
2011 Mar 3–6	43	26	29	3
2010 Mar 4–7	48	24	25	3
2009 Mar 5–8	41	29	28	2
2008 Mar 6–9	35	33	29	2
2007 Mar 11–14	33	29	35	4
2006 Mar 13–16	30	28	38	4
2005 Mar 7–10	31	29	35	5
2004 Mar 8–11	38	25	33	4
2003 Mar 3–5	33	29	33	5
2002 Mar 4–7	31	32	32	5
2001 Mar 5–7	30	34	32	4
1997 Nov 6–9*	31	34	27	8

*Based on half sample.

SOURCE: "Thinking about what is said in the news, in your view is the seriousness of global warming—generally exaggerated, generally correct, or is it generally underestimated?" in *Environment*, The Gallup Organization, 2015, http://www.gallup.com/poll/1615/Environment.aspx#1 (accessed August 28, 2015). Copyright © 2015 Gallup, Inc. All rights reserved. The content is used with permission; however, Gallup retains all rights of republication.

Warming's Timing (April 22, 2015, http://www.gallup.com/poll/182807/conservative-republicans-alone-global-warming-timing.aspx), Andrew Dugan of the Gallup Organization breaks down the responses by party affiliation and ideology. He notes that 81% of liberal Democrats agreed that global warming is due to pollution from human activities, compared with only 27% of conservative Republicans. In between these two extremes the percentages for other ideologies were 67% of conservative/moderate Democrats, 54% of nonleaning independents, and 49% of moderate/liberal Republicans. Seven out of 10 (70%) conservative Republicans attributed global warming to natural changes in the environment, compared with only 16% of liberal Democrats. The percentages for other ideologies were 29% of conservative/moderate Democrats, 38% of nonleaning independents, and 47% of moderate/liberal Republicans. There is obviously deep disbelief among Republicans that humans are the cause of global warming. Even among independents and Democrats there is some skepticism about the issue. These beliefs help explain why some U.S. policy makers have been reluctant to take aggressive action against emissions linked by many scientists to global warming.

In 2015 Gallup found that 42% of poll respondents said the seriousness of global warming has been "generally exaggerated," compared with 35% who said it has been "generally underestimated." (See Table 3.12.) The percentage of Americans believing that the seriousness of global warming has been exaggerated spiked upward during and after the Great Recession, reaching a peak of 48% in 2010. Skepticism is much higher among Republicans than among Democrats. Frank Newport and Andrew Dugan of the Gallup Organization examine in *College-Educated Republicans Most Skeptical of Global Warming* (March 26, 2015, http://www.gallup.com/poll/182159/college-educated-republicans-skeptical-global-warming.aspx) responses on this question from Gallup's 2010 through 2015 polls by political party and education level. Republican college graduates (74%) were the most likely to believe the seriousness of global warming has been exaggerated. This compares with 57% of Republicans with at least a high school education. The breakdown among Democrats was quite different. More than a quarter (27%) of Democrats with at least a high school education said the seriousness has been exaggerated, compared with only 15% of Democratic college graduates.

CHAPTER 4
A HOLE IN THE SKY: OZONE DEPLETION

THE EARTH'S PROTECTIVE OZONE LAYER

Ozone is a gas naturally present in the earth's atmosphere. Unlike ordinary oxygen, a diatomic molecule that contains two oxygen atoms (O_2), ozone, a triatomic molecule, contains three oxygen atoms (O_3). A molecule of ordinary oxygen can be converted to ozone by ultraviolet (UV) radiation, electrical discharge (such as from lightning), or complex chemical reactions. These processes split apart the two oxygen atoms, which are then free to bind with other loose oxygen atoms to form ozone.

Ozone exists in the earth's atmosphere at two levels: the troposphere and the stratosphere. (See Figure 4.1.) Tropospheric (ground-level) ozone accounts for only a small portion of the earth's total ozone, but it is a potent air pollutant with serious health consequences. Ground-level ozone is the primary component in smog and is formed via complex chemical reactions involving emissions of industrial chemicals and through fossil fuel combustion. Ozone formation is intensified during hot weather, when more radiation reaches the ground. Smog retards crop and tree growth, impairs health, and limits visibility.

Approximately 90% of the earth's ozone lies in the stratosphere at altitudes greater than about 9.3 miles (15 km). (See Figure 4.1.) Ozone molecules at this level protect life on the earth by absorbing UV radiation from the sun and preventing it from reaching the ground. The so-called ozone layer is actually a scattering of molecules constantly undergoing change from oxygen to ozone and back. Although most of the ozone changes back to oxygen, a small amount of ozone persists. As long as this natural process stays in balance, the overall ozone layer remains thick enough to protect the earth from harmful UV radiation from the sun. The amount of ozone in the stratosphere varies greatly, depending on location, altitude, and temperature.

EVIDENCE OF OZONE DEPLETION

Many scientists believe the introduction of certain chemicals into the stratosphere alters the natural ozone balance by depleting ozone molecules. Chlorine and bromine atoms are particularly destructive. They bind to loose oxygen atoms and prevent them from reforming either oxygen or ozone. Chlorine and bromine are found in the sea salt from ocean spray. Chlorine is also present in the form of hydrochloric acid, which is emitted with volcanic gases. These are natural sources of ozone-depleting chemicals.

During the mid-1970s scientists began to speculate that the ozone layer was rapidly being destroyed by reactions involving industrial chemicals that contained chlorine and bromine. Two chemists, F. Sherwood Rowland (1927–2012) and Mario J. Molina (1943–), discovered that chlorofluorocarbons (CFCs) could break down in the stratosphere, releasing chlorine atoms that could destroy thousands of ozone molecules. This discovery led to a ban on CFCs as a propellant in aerosols in the United States and in other countries.

In 1985 Joseph C. Farman, Brian G. Gardiner, and Jonathan D. Shanklin reported in "Large Losses of Total Ozone in Antarctica Reveal Seasonal ClO_x/NO_x Interaction" (*Nature*, vol. 315, no. 6016, May 16, 1985) about alarmingly low concentrations of stratospheric ozone above Halley Bay in Antarctica (the South Pole). Measurements indicated ozone levels were about 30% lower during the springs of 1980 to 1984, compared with the springs of 1957 to 1973. (The Antarctic spring coincides with the fall season in North America.)

Scientists report ozone concentrations in Dobson units. The unit is named after Gordon M. B. Dobson (1889–1976), a British scientist who invented an instrument for measuring ozone concentrations from the ground. One Dobson unit (DU) corresponds to a layer of atmospheric ozone that would be 0.001 of a millimeter

FIGURE 4.1

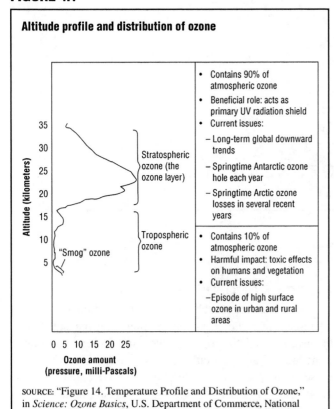

Altitude profile and distribution of ozone

- Contains 90% of atmospheric ozone
- Beneficial role: acts as primary UV radiation shield
- Current issues:
  – Long-term global downward trends
  – Springtime Antarctic ozone hole each year
  – Springtime Arctic ozone losses in several recent years

- Contains 10% of atmospheric ozone
- Harmful impact: toxic effects on humans and vegetation
- Current issues:
  –Episode of high surface ozone in urban and rural areas

SOURCE: "Figure 14. Temperature Profile and Distribution of Ozone," in *Science: Ozone Basics*, U.S. Department of Commerce, National Oceanic and Atmospheric Administration, March 20, 2008, http://www .ozonelayer.noaa.gov/science/basics.htm (accessed September 3, 2015)

thick if it was compressed into a layer at standard temperature and pressure at the earth's surface. Atmospheric ozone is considered "thin" if its concentration falls below 220 DU. A thin spot in the ozone layer is commonly called an ozone hole.

The extreme cold and unique climate conditions over the poles are thought to make the ozone layers there particularly susceptible to thinning. Where cloud and ice particles are present, reactions that hasten ozone destruction also occur on the surface of ice particles. Since 1982 an ozone hole has appeared each year over Antarctica beginning in August and lasting until November. The hole formation is linked to polar clouds that form during the dark Antarctic winter (May through September). These clouds provide reaction surfaces for chlorine-containing compounds to release their chlorine. As sunlight returns in August or September, the released chlorine begins destroying ozone molecules.

The Antarctic ozone hole increased in size throughout the 1980s. By the early 1990s it was consistently larger than the area of Antarctica. Throughout most of the first decade of the 21st century the hole was larger in size than the continent of North America. In 2002 the size of the hole dropped dramatically because of unusually warm weather at the South Pole. The 2014 hole measured 8.1 million square miles (20.9 million square km) in size.

(See Figure 4.2.) This corresponded with a minimum ozone concentration of 128.5 DU. (See Figure 4.3.) The largest ozone hole was 10.3 million square miles (26.6 million square km) in 2006. The minimum ozone concentration at that time was 98.2 DU.

Scientists also monitor stratospheric ozone levels over the Arctic (the North Pole). Historically, Arctic winters have been warmer than those in Antarctica. This helps protect the northern pole from ozone depletion. During the winter months (December to March) of 2011 the Arctic experienced an unusually low ozone level. In "NASA Pinpoints Causes of 2011 Arctic Ozone Hole" (March 11, 2013, http://www.nasa.gov/topics/earth/features/2011-ozone-hole.html), the National Aeronautics and Space Administration (NASA) notes that scientists believe a combination of very cold weather, high chlorine pollution, and unusual wind conditions combined to lower stratospheric ozone approximately 20% below its normal seasonal average. Ozone concentrations, however, did not drop below 220 DU, which is the threshold of an ozone hole. Yearly Arctic ozone maps compiled by NASA (http://ozone watch.gsfc.nasa.gov/monthly/climatology_03_NH.html) indicate that the unusually low ozone levels of 2011 were not seen in 2012 through 2015.

The World Meteorological Organization (WMO) notes in *Scientific Assessment of Ozone Depletion: 2002* (2002, http://www.esrl.noaa.gov/csd/assessments/2002) that the average total ozone column on a global basis was approximately 3% lower between 1997 and 2001 when compared with pre-1980 average values. The most dramatic changes were recorded in the polar regions and midlatitudes (between the tropics and the poles). Most of the global population lives in the midlatitudes of the Northern and Southern Hemispheres. For example, the U.S. mainland lies approximately in the range of 30 degrees to 50 degrees north latitude.

CONSEQUENCES OF OZONE DEPLETION

The sun emits radiation at a variety of wavelengths. The ozone layer acts as a protective shield against UV radiation (radiation with wavelengths of approximately 290 to 400 nanometers; a nanometer is one billionth of a meter). As the ozone layer diminishes in the upper atmosphere, the earth receives more UV radiation. In "Ozone Science: The Facts behind the Phaseout" (August 19, 2010, http://www.epa.gov/ozone/science/sc_fact.html), the U.S. Environmental Protection Agency (EPA) reports that the amount of UV radiation reaching the surface in Antarctica can double during the time of its annual ozone hole.

Scientists are particularly worried about the increased exposure to radiation in the ultraviolet-B (UVB) spectrum (wavelengths of approximately 190 to 320 nanometers). This wavelength can be damaging to human health

FIGURE 4.2

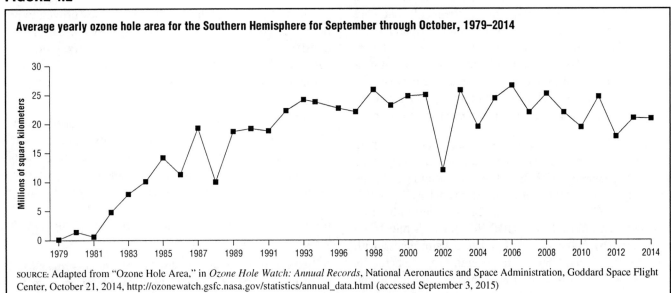

Average yearly ozone hole area for the Southern Hemisphere for September through October, 1979–2014

SOURCE: Adapted from "Ozone Hole Area," in *Ozone Hole Watch: Annual Records*, National Aeronautics and Space Administration, Goddard Space Flight Center, October 21, 2014, http://ozonewatch.gsfc.nasa.gov/statistics/annual_data.html (accessed September 3, 2015)

FIGURE 4.3

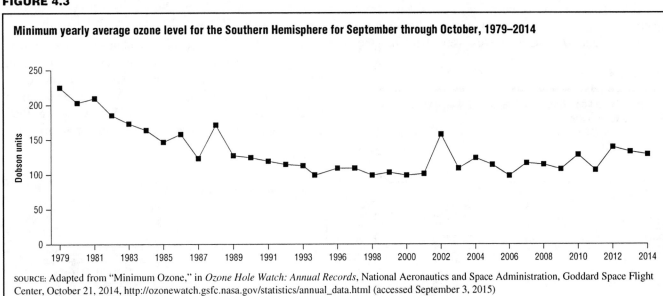

Minimum yearly average ozone level for the Southern Hemisphere for September through October, 1979–2014

SOURCE: Adapted from "Minimum Ozone," in *Ozone Hole Watch: Annual Records*, National Aeronautics and Space Administration, Goddard Space Flight Center, October 21, 2014, http://ozonewatch.gsfc.nasa.gov/statistics/annual_data.html (accessed September 3, 2015)

because it is linked with adverse effects to deoxyribonucleic acid, skin, eyes, and the immune system. In addition, excessive exposure to UV radiation can negatively affect terrestrial and aquatic ecosystems and damage synthetic materials.

UV radiation alters photosynthesis, plant yield, and growth in plant species. Phytoplankton (one-celled organisms found in the ocean) are the backbone of the marine food web. According to the EPA, excessive exposure to UVB radiation reduces the productivity and survival rate for these organisms. Diminishing phytoplankton supplies would likely harm many fish species that depend on them for food. Studies performed during the mid-1990s blamed the rise in UV radiation caused by the

thinning of the ozone layer for the decline in the number of frogs and other amphibians.

Increased UV radiation also affects synthetic materials. Plastics are especially vulnerable, tending to weaken, become brittle and discolored, and break.

OZONE-DEPLETING CHEMICALS

Most ozone destruction in the atmosphere is believed to be anthropogenic (caused by humans). In 1998 the WMO estimated in *Scientific Assessment of Ozone Depletion: 1998* (March 1999, http://www.esrl.noaa.gov/csd/assessments/1998/ExecSum98.pdf) that only 18% of the sources contributing to ozone depletion during the 1990s were natural. The remaining 82% of sources contributing to ozone depletion were industrial chemicals. The blame was largely placed on the chemicals that were developed by modern society for use as refrigerants, air conditioning fluids, solvents, cleaning agents, and foam-blowing agents. These chemicals can persist in the atmosphere for years. Thus, there is a significant lag between the time that emissions decline at the earth's surface and the time at which ozone levels in the stratosphere recover.

Table 4.1 lists the chemicals of particular concern to scientists. Each chemical is assigned a value called an ozone depletion potential (ODP) based on its harmfulness to the ozone layer. The most common depleters are CFC-11, CFC-12, and CFC-13. CFC-11 and CFC-13 are arbitrarily assigned an ODP of 1. The ODPs for other chemicals are determined by comparing their relative harmfulness with that of CFC-11 and CFC-13. In general, Class I chemicals are those with an ODP value greater than or equal to 0.1, and Class II chemicals have ODP values less than 0.1.

Class I Chemicals

Although a number of chemicals can destroy stratospheric ozone, CFCs are the main offenders because they are so prevalent. When CFCs were invented in 1928, they were welcomed as chemical wonders. Discovered by the chemist Thomas Midgley (1889–1944), they proved to be nontoxic, nonflammable, noncorrosive, stable, and inexpensive. Their artificial cooling provided refrigeration for food and brought comfort to warm climates. The CFC compound was originally marketed under the trademark Freon.

Over time, new formulations and applications were discovered. CFCs could be used not only as coolants in air conditioners and refrigerators but also as propellants in aerosol sprays, in certain plastics such as polystyrene, in insulation, in fire extinguishers, and as cleaning agents. Production grew dramatically as new uses were discovered—primarily as a solvent to clean circuit boards and computer chips.

CFCs are extremely stable; it is this stability that allows them to float intact through the troposphere and into the ozone layer. CFCs do not degrade in the lower atmosphere but, after entering the stratosphere, the sun's intense UV radiation eventually breaks them down into chlorine, fluorine, and carbon. Many scientists believe it is the chlorine that damages the ozone layer. (See Figure 4.4.)

Although CFCs are primarily blamed for ozone loss, other gases are also at fault. One of these gases is halon, which contains bromine. Halons have much higher ODP values than do CFCs. (See Table 4.1.) The bromine atoms in halons destroy ozone as shown in Figure 4.4, but they are chemically more powerful than chlorine atoms. This

TABLE 4.1

Lifetime, ozone depletion potential, and global warming potential of various chemicals

	Lifetime, in years	Ozone depletion potential	Global warming potential*
Class I			
CFC-11	45	1	4,750
CFC-12	100	0.82–1	10,900
CFC-13	640	1	14,420
CFC-113	85	0.8–0.85	6,130
CFC-114	190	0.58–1	10,000
CFC-115	1,020	0.5–0.6	7,370
Halon 1211	16	3–7.9	1,890
Halon 1301	65	10–15.9	7,140
Halon 2402	20	6–13	1,640
Carbon tetrachloride	26	0.82–1.1	1,400
Methyl bromide	0.8	0.66–0.7	5
Methyl chloroform	5	0.1–0.16	146
Class II			
HCFC-21	1.7	0.04	151
HCFC-22	11.9	0.04–0.055	1,810
HCFC-123	1.3	0.01–0.02	77
HCFC-124	5.9	0.022	609
HCFC-141b	9.2	0.11–0.12	725
HCFC-142b	17.2	0.06–0.065	2,310
HCFC-225ca	1.9	0.02–0.025	122
HCFC-225cb	5.9	0.03–0.033	595

*Global warming potential over a 100-year time horizon.
CFC = Chlorofluorocarbon; HCFC = Hydrochlorofluorocarbon.

SOURCE: Adapted from "Class I Ozone-Depleting Substances," in *Ozone-Depleting Substances*, U.S. Environmental Protection Agency, November 7, 2014, http://www.epa.gov/ozone/science/ods/classone.html (accessed September 3, 2015), and "Class II Ozone-Depleting Substances," in *Ozone-Depleting Substances*, U.S. Environmental Protection Agency, November 7, 2014, http://www.epa.gov/ozone/science/ods/classtwo.html (accessed September 3, 2015)

FIGURE 4.4

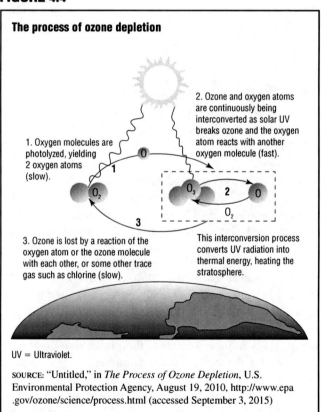

The process of ozone depletion

1. Oxygen molecules are photolyzed, yielding 2 oxygen atoms (slow).

2. Ozone and oxygen atoms are continuously being interconverted as solar UV breaks ozone and the oxygen atom reacts with another oxygen molecule (fast).

3. Ozone is lost by a reaction of the oxygen atom or the ozone molecule with each other, or some other trace gas such as chlorine (slow).

This interconversion process converts UV radiation into thermal energy, heating the stratosphere.

UV = Ultraviolet.

SOURCE: "Untitled," in *The Process of Ozone Depletion*, U.S. Environmental Protection Agency, August 19, 2010, http://www.epa.gov/ozone/science/process.html (accessed September 3, 2015)

means that the impact to ozone of a particular mass of halon is more destructive than a similar mass of a CFC. Halons are relatively long lived in the atmosphere, lingering for up to 65 years before being broken down. Halon is used primarily for fighting fires. Civilian and military firefighting training accounts for much of the halon emissions.

Other Class I ozone destroyers include carbon tetrachloride, methyl bromide, and methyl chloroform. These chemicals are commonly used as solvents and cleaning agents.

Class II Chemicals

The most common Class II ozone-depleting chemicals are hydrochlorofluorocarbons (HCFCs). HCFCs contain hydrogen. This makes them more susceptible to atmospheric breakdown than CFCs. As shown in Table 4.1, most HCFCs have a lifetime of less than six years. HCFCs have much lower ODP values than CFCs, halons, and industrial ozone depleters. HCFCs are considered good short-term replacements for CFCs. Although HCFCs are less destructive to ozone than the chemicals they are replacing, scientists believe that HCFC use must also be phased out to allow the ozone layer to fully recover.

A LANDMARK IN INTERNATIONAL DIPLOMACY: THE MONTREAL PROTOCOL

Ozone depletion was a global problem that necessitated international cooperation, but countries mistrusted one another's motives. As with the issues of climate change and pollution, developing countries resented being asked to sacrifice their economic development for a problem they believed the industrialized countries had created. To complicate matters, gaps in scientific proof led to disagreements over the extent and urgency of the ozone depletion situation.

In 1985, 20 countries signed an agreement in Vienna, Austria, known as the Convention for the Protection of the Ozone Layer (or the Vienna Convention). It called for data gathering, cooperation, and a political commitment to take action at a later date. In a 1987 negotiators' meeting in Montreal, Canada, the participants finalized a landmark in international environmental diplomacy: the Montreal Protocol on Substances That Deplete the Ozone Layer. It is generally referred to as the Montreal Protocol. The protocol was signed by 29 countries, including the United States, Australia, Canada, Japan, Mexico, all of Western Europe, and a handful of other countries.

The protocol called for industrial countries to cut CFC emissions in half by 1998 and to reduce halon emissions to 1986 levels by 1992. Developing countries were granted deferrals to compensate for their low levels of production. More importantly, the protocol also called for further amending as new data became available.

Throughout the 1990s and the first decade of the 21st century new scientific information revealed that ozone depletion was occurring faster than expected. This news spurred calls to revise the treaty. In total, four amendments to the Montreal Protocol have been adopted. These are known as the London Amendment (effective 1992), the Copenhagen Amendment (effective 1994), the Montreal Amendment (effective 1999), and the Beijing Amendment (effective 2002).

The United Nations Environment Programme (UNEP; http://ozone.unep.org/en/treaties-and-decisions) indicates that as of 2015, 197 countries (including the United States) had ratified (formally approved into law) the original Montreal Protocol and its four amendments. The final phase-out schedule for ozone-depleting substances (ODS) is shown in Table 4.2.

EPA Regulatory Programs

The EPA is responsible for ensuring that the United States meets its obligations under the Montreal Protocol. In "Specific Regulatory Programs" (November 2, 2012, http://www3.epa.gov/ozone/title6/index.html), the agency provides information about rules governing the use, import, management, and destruction of ODS. For example, technicians that service stationary refrigeration and air conditioning systems must be certified and follow specific practices for handling, labeling, and disposing of ODS. Similar requirements apply to other types of equipment, including air conditioning systems for motor vehicles and halon-based fire suppression systems.

Funding for Developing Countries

The Montreal Protocol includes special provisions for so-called Article 5 countries (developing countries). These are countries that annually produce and consume less than 0.66 of a pound (0.3 kg) per capita of ODS. The London Amendment established the Multilateral Fund for the Implementation of the Montreal Protocol. Industrial countries agreed to set up the fund to reimburse developing countries that complied with the protocol for "all

TABLE 4.2

Phase-out schedule under the Montreal Protocol for ozone-depleting substances

Ozone-depleting substance	Developed countries must phase out by:	Developing countries must phase out by:
Halons	1994	2010
Carbon tetrachloride	1996	2010
Chlorofluorocarbons (CFCs)	1996	2010
Hydrobromofluorocarbons (HBFCs)	1996	1996
Methyl chloroform	1996	2015
Bromochloromethane	2002	2002
Methyl bromide	2005	2015
Hydrochlorofluorocarbons (HCFCs)	2030	2040

SOURCE: Created by Kim Masters Evans for Gale, © 2015

agreed incremental costs," meaning all additional costs above any they would have expected to incur had they developed their infrastructure in the absence of the protocol.

The Multilateral Fund is a financial resource for developing countries that are party to the agreement. The UNEP explains in "OzonAction under the Multilateral Fund" (2015, http://www.unep.org/ozonaction/AboutTheBranch/MultilateralFundPortfolio/tabid/6183/Default.aspx) that "since 1991, the Multilateral Fund has approved activities including industrial conversion, technical assistance, training and capacity building worth over US $2 billion." In *2015 Consolidated Project Completion Report* (April 14, 2015, http://www.multilateralfund.org/74/English/1/7407.pdf), the UNEP briefly describes some of the funded projects in various countries in 2015. For example, a project in Iran was devoted to phasing out CFC use in the manufacture of refrigeration systems.

Phasing out HCFCs

In 2007 the parties to the Montreal Protocol agreed to certain changes to their commitments to phase out HCFCs. According to the UNEP, in "2007 Montreal Adjustment on Production and Consumption of HCFCs" (November 30, 2007, http://ozone.unep.org/Meeting_Documents/mop/19mop/Adjustments_on_HCFCs.pdf), the changes do not affect the final phase-out deadlines shown in Table 4.2, but the intermediate deadlines. For example, developed countries had committed to achieve a 65% reduction in HCFCs by 2010. Instead, these countries agreed to achieve a 75% reduction by 2010. They must achieve a 90% reduction by 2015 and a 99.5% reduction by 2020. Table 4.3 shows an EPA listing of U.S. milestones for the HCFC phaseout compared with the phase-out schedule of the Montreal Protocol.

Article 5 countries agreed to the following new intermediate HCFC deadlines:

- 2013—a freeze on consumption based on the average of their 2009 and 2010 production and consumption figures
- 2015—10% reduction
- 2020—35% reduction
- 2025—67.5% reduction

Technically, developing countries must achieve a 100% reduction by 2030. However, they are allowed to devote a small amount of HCFCs to servicing refrigeration and air conditioning equipment until 2040.

PROGRESS AND PROBLEMS

The Montreal Protocol has been hailed as historic—the most ambitious attempt ever to combat environmental degradation on a global scale. It ushered in a new era of environmental diplomacy. Some historians view the signing of the accord as a defining moment, the point at which the definition of international security was expanded to include environmental issues as well as military matters. In addition, an important precedent was established: that science and policy makers had a new relationship. Many observers thought that the decision to take precautionary action in the absence of complete proof of a link between CFCs and ozone depletion was an act of foresight that would now be possible with other issues.

Progress reports published by the UNEP highlight the success of the Montreal Protocol in terms of party (country) compliance and reduced ODS atmospheric levels. Researchers, however, have raised troubling questions about some types of ODS and how they are being controlled by the parties. In addition, black market trade of

TABLE 4.3

Comparison of the Montreal Protocol and U.S. phase-out schedules for hydrochlorofluorocarbons

Montreal protocol		United States	
Year to be implemented	% reduction in consumption and production, using the cap as a baseline	Year to be implemented	Implementation of HCFC phaseout through Clean Air Act regulations
2004	35.0%	2003	No production and no importing of HCFC-141b
2010	75.0%	2010	In addition to the HCFC-141b restrictions, no production and no importing of HCFC-142b and HCFC-22, except for use in equipment manufactured before 1/1/2010 (so no production or importing for NEW equipment that uses these compounds)
2015	90.0%	2015	In addition to the HCFC-141b, HCFC-142b and HCFC-22 restrictions, no production and no importing of any other HCFCs, except for use as refrigerants in equipment manufactured before 1/1/2020
2020	99.5%	2020	No production and no importing of HCFC-142b and HCFC-22
2030	100.0%	2030	No production and no importing of any HCFCs

HCFCs = hydrochlorofluorocarbons.

SOURCE: "Comparison of the Montreal Protocol and United States Phase-out Schedules," in *HCFC Phaseout Schedule*, U.S. Environmental Protection Agency, February 2, 2012, http://www.epa.gov/Ozone/title6/phaseout/hcfc.html (accessed September 3, 2015)

banned ODS is a vexing and growing problem. (ODS black market trade are discussed later in the chapter.)

Progress Reports

The UNEP marked the 20th anniversary of the Montreal Protocol with issuance of the report *Montreal Protocol on Substances That Deplete the Ozone Layer 2007: A Success in the Making* (August 2007, http://ozone.unep.org/en/Publications/MP_A_Success_in_the_making-E.pdf), which detailed the progress made through 2007. At that time, the 191 countries that had ratified the agreement had phased out the production and consumption of more than 95% of the chemicals controlled by the Montreal Protocol. The UNEP noted that it was seeing high levels of compliance in both developed and developing countries. As a result atmospheric levels of major ODS had decreased. It was expected that full implementation of the protocol would return the ozone layer to pre-1980 levels by 2050 to 2075.

In 2012 the UNEP released a progress report on the 25th anniversary of the Montreal Protocol—*OzonAction: Protecting Our Atmosphere for Generations to Come: 25 Years of the Montreal Protocol* (August 2012, http://www3.epa.gov/ozone/intpol/3139-e-OASI2012_protecting_our_atmosphere.pdf). OzonAction is a UNEP program that helps developing countries meet their obligations under the international agreement. The UNEP notes that as of 2012, 197 countries had ratified the Montreal Protocol, making it "the world's most widely ratified treaty." The developing countries reportedly met the 2010 deadline to phase out CFCs, halons, and carbon tetrachloride. The UNEP predicts that continued implementation of the Montreal Protocol by all parties will result in a return by "midcentury" to pre-1980 levels of stratospheric ozone.

Monitoring Data and Modeling Results

Article 6 of the Montreal Protocol requires that the ratifying countries base their decision making on scientific information assessed and presented by an international panel of ozone experts. This panel includes the WMO, the UNEP, the European Commission, the National Oceanic and Atmospheric Administration, and NASA. As of November 2015, the most recent comprehensive UNEP assessment was published in December 2014—*Scientific Assessment of Ozone Depletion: 2014* (http://www.esrl.noaa.gov/csd/assessments/ozone/2014/chapters/2014OzoneAssessment.pdf). This is the ninth scientific assessment of the world's ozone condition and is based on analysis of data collected from satellites, aircraft, balloons, and ground-based instruments and the results of laboratory investigations and computer modeling. The UNEP indicates that as of 2014, most of the ODS controlled under the Montreal Protocol were decreasing "largely as projected." Levels of HCFCs and halon-1301 were still increasing. The UNEP notes

that carbon tetrachloride was more abundant in the atmosphere than expected due to "unknown or unreported sources." The organization projects that full compliance with the Montreal Protocol will allow the ozone layer to recover "over most of the globe." Recovery is expected before "midcentury" over the middle latitudes and the Arctic region, and "somewhat later" over Antarctica.

In "Quantifying the Ozone and Ultraviolet Benefits Already Achieved by the Montreal Protocol" (*Nature Communications*, vol. 6, May 26, 2015), Martyn P. Chipperfield et al. report on modeling results that predict how the ozone layer would have been affected if the Montreal Protocol had not been implemented. The researchers conclude that the Antarctic ozone hole would have increased in size by 40% by 2013. Ozone layer losses over the middle latitudes of the Northern Hemisphere would have more than doubled. Chipperfield et al. note that these changes would have resulted in higher rates of skin cancer due to greater atmospheric penetration of UV rays from the sun. They predict that the ozone layer will gradually improve and that the Antarctic ozone hole will disappear sometime around 2050.

The National Oceanic and Atmospheric Administration operates the Earth System Research Laboratory (ESRL), which is headquartered in Boulder, Colorado. The ESRL collects data from its observatories around the world and does research related to global trends in air quality. Historical data on atmospheric concentrations of ODS have been collected at five ESRL observatories:

- Point Barrow, Alaska

- Niwot Ridge, Colorado

- Mauna Loa, Hawaii

- Cape Matatula, American Samoa

- South Pole, Antarctica

ESRL graphs dating back to the 1970s indicate that atmospheric concentrations of CFC-11 peaked during the early 1990s and then began declining. (See Figure 4.5.) CFC-12 concentrations peaked during the first decade of the 21st century and then slowly began decreasing. Concentrations of other ODS have also declined dramatically since 1990.

However, other monitoring data show troubling trends. Johannes C. Laube et al. report in "Newly Detected Ozone-Depleting Substances in the Atmosphere" (*Nature Geoscience*, vol. 7, no. 4, 2014) measurements for four ODS—CFC-112, CFC-112a, CFC-113a, and HCFC-133a—in the atmosphere. The researchers state, "The reported emissions are clearly contrary to the intentions behind the Montreal Protocol, and raise questions about the sources of these gases." According

FIGURE 4.5

Trends in atmospheric concentrations of controlled ozone-depleting chemicals, 1984–2015

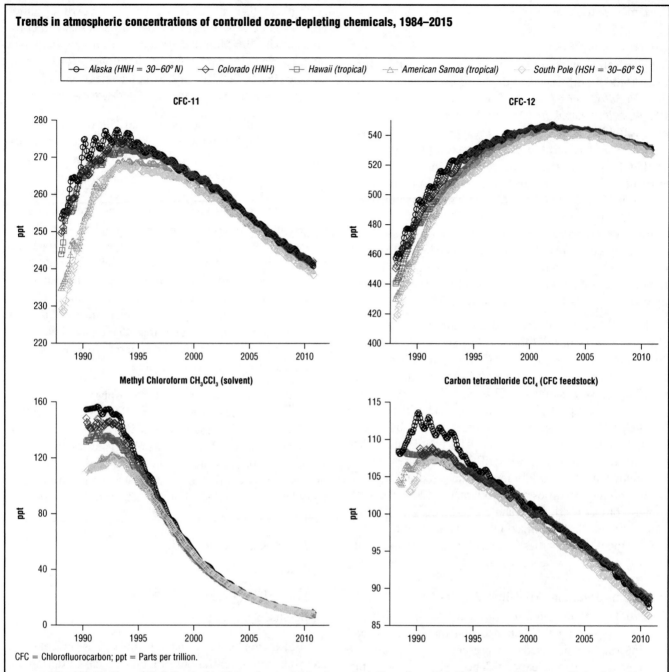

CFC = Chlorofluorocarbon; ppt = Parts per trillion.

SOURCE: "Combined In Situ and Flask Results," in *Halocarbons and Other Atmospheric Trace Gases*, U.S. Department of Commerce, National Oceanic and Atmospheric Administration, Earth System Research Laboratory, 2015, http://www.esrl.noaa.gov/gmd/hats/graphs/Combined_CFCs_2010.pdf (accessed September 3, 2015)

to Laube et al., emissions of CFC-113a have risen particularly sharply since the 1980s.

The Environmental Investigation Agency (EIA) is a London-based nonprofit organization that focuses on environmental crimes. In November 2014 the EIA provided a briefing to international representatives at the 26th Meeting of the Montreal Protocol in Paris. In *New Trends in ODS Smuggling* (https://eia-international.org/wp-content/uploads/EIA-New-Trends-in-ODS-Smuggling-lo-res.pdf), the EIA suggests that the rising CFC-113a emissions detected by Laube et al. could be related to feedstock use. CFCs and HCFCs are used as raw materials to manufacture other types of chemicals. In other words, the ODS are converted into non-ODS chemicals. This ODS usage is not restricted by the Montreal Protocol, because it has long been assumed that the emissions associated with feedstock conversion are minimal. The EIA questions if this assumption is correct and notes that "another possible explanation is that unreported use and emissions of CFC-113a are occurring."

The EIA has a similar concern about carbon tetrachloride (CCl_4), another feedstock. As shown in Figure 4.5, atmospheric concentrations of this chemical have declined since the 1990s. However, the decrease has not been as pronounced as expected. NASA notes in "Ozone-Depleting Compound Persists, NASA Research Shows" (August 20, 2014, http://www.nasa.gov/press/2014/august/ozone-depleting-compound-persists-nasa-research-shows/#.VjnhwberSUn) that "for almost a decade, scientists have debated why the observed levels of CCl_4 in the atmosphere have declined slower than expectations, which are based on what is known about how the compound is destroyed by solar radiation and other natural processes." According to Qing Liang et al., in "Constraining the Carbon Tetrachloride (CCl_4) Budget Using Its Global Trend and Inter-hemispheric Gradient" (*Geophysical Research Letters*, vol. 41, no. 14, July 28, 2014), the Montreal Protocol parties reported "near-zero" carbon tetrachloride emissions between 2007 and 2012. However, the researchers believe that "ongoing current emissions" are contributing to carbon tetrachloride levels in the atmosphere that are higher than expected. In *New Trends in ODS Smuggling*, the EIA expresses deep concern about these levels, noting, "They are an indication that either significant quantities of [carbon tetrachloride] are being emitted during their use as feedstocks or that significant non-feedstock production and use is occurring despite the Montreal Protocol ban."

Illegal Trade Problems

The black market trading of ODS became a significant challenge after implementation of the Montreal Protocol. As shown in Table 4.2, developing countries were not required to phase out many ODS, particularly CFCs, until 2010 and after. Thus, production continued in these countries well into the first decade of the 21st century.

According to Joydeep Gupta, in "India Largest Source of Smuggled CFCs: UN Official" (HindustanTimes.com, April 26, 2008), a UNEP regional coordinator in Southeast Asia reported in 2008 that India was the largest source of black market ODS. In 2006 the UNEP began Project Skyhole Patching, a collaboration with customs officers throughout the Asia Pacific region to stem the illegal trade in ODS and hazardous waste. The article "Customs Seize over 108 Tonnes of Refrigerant" (ACR-News.com, December 2, 2010) indicates that Project Skyhole Patching I, which ran through 2009, resulted in the seizure of more than 771.6 tons (700 t) of ODS. Project Skyhole Patching II was conducted during 2010 and reaped more than 119 tons (108 t) of ODS.

In *New Trends in ODS Smuggling*, the EIA describes major ODS smuggling cases dating back to 2010 involving China, India, the Philippines, Russia, and Spain. In many of the cases the product seized was believed to be of Chinese origin and had been mislabeled in an attempt to deceive customs inspectors. For example, in 2010 Russian authorities discovered 43 tons (39 t) of CFCs that had been mislabeled as "recycled." The EIA indicates that the shipment actually contained "virgin" CFCs of Chinese origin. The agency states it "is concerned that CFCs were still available for export from China, given that production was phased out in 2007. Whether the source was stockpiled material or unlicensed production is unknown." The EIA also claims that an analysis of export and import records provided by China for 2012 and 2013 shows that "on average reported imports of HCFC-22 are 32 per cent lower than China's reported exports. In many instances, the discrepancy is larger." The agency indicates that paperwork mistakes or oversights could be the cause. However, it is also possible that portions of shipments are being illegally diverted to the black market.

THE U.S. BLACK MARKET. In 1996 the ban on CFCs was implemented in the developed countries, including the United States. The CFC called Freon was widely used in automobile air conditioners before that time. After the ban went into effect, there were still millions of Americans with cars that used Freon as a refrigerant. Although alternative refrigerants were available, they were more expensive than Freon. The result was a black market for the product. This market expanded in the United States during the first decade of the 21st century with the boom in the illegal production of methamphetamine at so-called meth labs. Freon is commonly used in meth labs as part of the production process.

Several U.S. government agencies—the EPA, the U.S. Customs and Border Protection, the U.S. Departments of Commerce and Justice, and the Internal Revenue Service (IRS)—began intensive antismuggling efforts. The IRS became involved because of the Revenue Reconciliation Act of 1989, which imposes an excise tax on most U.S. manufacturers, producers, and importers of ODS. In "Enforcement Actions under Title VI of the Clean Air Act" (May 20, 2015, http://epa.gov/ozone/enforce/index.html), the EPA documents major compliance and enforcement actions related to ODS under Title VI of the Clean Air Act. Most of the cases involved alleged rules violations by companies, such as releasing ODS because of failure to repair faulty refrigeration systems. As of May 2015, the most recent completed case involving smuggling occurred in 2013, when a supplier and distributer of air conditioning and heating products pleaded guilty to receiving and selling HCFC-22 that had been smuggled into the United States. The company was sentenced to three years of probation and fined $100,000.

SUBSTITUTES AND NEW TECHNOLOGIES

As pressure increased to discontinue the use of CFCs and halons, substitute chemicals and technologies began

TABLE 4.4

Global warming potential of refrigerants with zero ozone depletion potential

Refrigerant	Ozone depletion potential	Global warming potential
HFC-134a	0	1,430
HFC-152a	0	124
HFC-227ea	0	3,220
HFC-245fa	0	1,030
HFC-365mfc	0	794
Propane (R-290)	0	3.3
R-404A	0	3,922
R-407A	0	2,107
R-410A	0	2,088
R-407C	0	1,774
R-507A	0	3,985
Isobutane (R-600a)	0	3
Ammonia (R-717)	0	0
Nitrogen (R-728)	0	0
CO_2 (R-744)	0	1

CFC = Chlorofluorocarbon; CO_2 = Carbon dioxide; HCFC = Hydrochlorofluorocarbon; HFC = Hydrofluorocarbon.

SOURCE: Adapted from "Global Warming Potentials and Ozone Depletion Potentials of Some Ozone-Depleting Substances and Alternatives Listed by the SNAP Program," in *Global Warming Potentials and Ozone Depletion Potentials of Some Ozone-Depleting Substances and Alternatives Listed by the SNAP Program*, U.S. Environmental Protection Agency, November 6, 2014, http://www.epa.gov/ozone/snap/subsgwps.html (accessed September 3, 2015)

to be developed. One of the most popular substitutes is a class of compounds called hydrofluorocarbons (HFCs). HFCs do not contain chlorine, a potent ozone destroyer. Furthermore, they are relatively short lived in the atmosphere—most survive intact for less than 12 years. This means that HFCs do not directly affect the earth's protective ozone layer. As a result, HFCs have ODP values of zero. (See Table 4.4.)

The development of effective chemical substitutes with acceptable health and environmental effects is an enormous challenge. Some experts propose returning to the refrigerant gases that were used before the invention of CFCs. These include sulfur dioxide, ammonia, and various hydrocarbon compounds. However, these chemicals have their own issues; for example, most are highly toxic.

The EPA's Significant New Alternative Policy program evaluates alternatives to ODS and determines their acceptability for use. Submissions for evaluation include those that could be used in a variety of industrial applications, including refrigeration and air conditioning, foam blowing, and fire suppression and protection.

Many industrial engineers are pursuing new technologies for cooling, including semiconductors that cool down when charged with electricity, refrigeration that uses plain water as a refrigerant, and processes that use thermoacoustics (sound energy). Extensive investment in research and development of new technologies will be required to produce cooling methods that are acceptable to industry and environmentalists.

THE CLIMATE CHANGE CONNECTION

As described in Chapter 3, the earth's climate has been warming in recent decades and is expected to continue to do so. Many scientists blame this warming on a buildup in the atmosphere of anthropogenic emissions of chemicals, such as carbon dioxide. Many ODS are believed to contribute to global warming. Table 4.1 shows the global warming potential (GWP) of some common ODS compared with a GWP value of 1 for carbon dioxide. Many of the ODS have GWP values that are several hundreds to several thousand times that of carbon dioxide.

During the 1990s the use of HFCs increased dramatically. Table 3.1 in Chapter 3 lists emissions of HFCs for various years between 1990 and 2013. NASA reports that atmospheric levels of HFCs also surged during this period. This is a concern to scientists studying global warming because HFCs are believed to enhance atmospheric heating. Also, HFC breakdown in the atmosphere produces a chemical called trifluoroacetic acid, large concentrations of which are known to be harmful to certain plants (particularly in wetlands). As shown in Table 4.4, common ODS substitutes, such as HFCs, have GWP values that are hundreds to thousands times that of carbon dioxide. Thus, increased HFC use is expected to contribute to global warming.

On the other side of the equation, global warming has a mixed effect on stratospheric ozone levels. The UNEP notes in *Scientific Assessment of Ozone Depletion: 2014* that increased carbon dioxide and methane concentrations in the atmosphere help the ozone layer, whereas increased nitrous oxide concentrations harms the ozone layer. Thus, the status of the ozone layer beginning in the late 2100s could be heavily influenced by the concentrations of these gases in the atmosphere.

Concern about the GWP of HFCs has spurred calls to amend the Montreal Protocol to add controls on HFCs. In June 2013 the White House announced (http://www.whitehouse.gov/the-press-office/2013/06/08/united-states-and-china-agree-work-together-phase-down-hfcs) that the United States and China had agreed to forge alliances with other countries to seek limits under the Montreal Protocol on the production and consumption of HFCs. However, as of November 2015, HFCs had not been added to the agreement.

PUBLIC OPINION ABOUT THE OZONE LAYER ISSUE

In March 2015 the Gallup Organization conducted its annual poll of Americans' beliefs and attitudes about environmental issues; however, the poll did not include any questions about the ozone layer. Concern about the ozone layer was last measured in March 2008. Gallup notes in *Environment* (http://www.gallup.com/poll/1615/environment.aspx) that damage to the earth's ozone layer ranked low on the list of environmental problems about which Americans were worried in 2008. Of those asked in 2008, 39% expressed a great deal of worry about damage to the ozone layer. This percentage was down from a peak of 51% in 1989. In 2008 another 29% expressed a fair amount of concern about the problem, whereas 19% acknowledged only a little concern, and 12% expressed no concern at all.

CHAPTER 5
ACID RAIN

WHAT IS ACID RAIN?

Acid rain is the common name for acidic deposits that fall to the earth from the atmosphere. The term was coined in 1872 by the Scottish chemist Robert Angus Smith (1817–1884) to describe the acidic precipitation in Manchester, England. In the 21st century scientists study both wet and dry acidic deposits. Although there are natural sources of acid in the atmosphere, acid rain is primarily caused by emissions from electric utilities that burn fossil fuels, especially coal. The main culprits are sulfur dioxide (SO_2) and nitrogen oxides (NO_x). As noted in Chapter 2, the chemical formula NO_x is used to collectively refer to nitrogen oxide, nitrogen dioxide, and other nitrogen oxides. These chemicals are converted to sulfuric acid and nitric acid, respectively, in the atmosphere and can be carried by the winds for many miles from where the original emissions took place. (See Figure 5.1.) Other chemicals contributing to acid rain include volatile organic compounds (VOCs). These are carbon-containing chemicals that easily become vapors or gases. VOC sources include paint thinners, degreasers, and other solvents and burning fuels such as coal, gasoline, natural gas, and wood. It should be noted that acid rain is an environmental problem in developed countries in North America and Europe and is becoming increasingly troublesome in developing countries that are undergoing heavy industrialization, such as China and India.

Wet deposition occurs when the acid falls in rain, snow, or ice. Dry deposition is caused by tiny particles (or particulates) in combustion emissions. They may stay dry as they fall or pollute cloud water and precipitation. Moist deposition occurs when the acid is trapped in cloud or fog droplets. This is most common at high altitudes and in coastal areas. Whatever its form, acid rain can create dangerously high levels of acidic impurities in plants, soil, and water.

Measuring Acid Rain

The acidity of any solution is measured on a potential hydrogen (pH) scale numbered from 0 to 14, with a pH value of 7 considered neutral. (See Figure 5.2.) Values higher than 7 are considered more alkaline or basic (the pH of baking soda is 8); values lower than 7 are considered acidic (the pH of lemon juice is 2). The pH scale is a logarithmic measure. This means that every pH change of one is a 10-fold change in acid content. Therefore, a decrease from pH 7 to pH 6 is a 10-fold increase in acidity; a drop from pH 7 to pH 5 is a 100-fold increase in acidity; and a drop from pH 7 to pH 4 is a 1,000-fold increase.

Pure, distilled water has a neutral pH of 7. Normal rainfall has a pH value of about 5 to 6. It is slightly acidic because it accumulates naturally occurring sulfur oxides and nitrogen oxides as it passes through the atmosphere. Acid rain has a pH of less than 5.

SOURCES OF SULFATE AND NITRATE IN THE ATMOSPHERE

Natural Sources

Natural sources of sulfate in the atmosphere include ocean spray, volcanic emissions, and readily oxidized hydrogen sulfide, which is released from the decomposition of organic matter found in the earth. Natural sources of nitrogen or nitrates include nitrogen oxides produced by microorganisms in soils, by lightning during thunderstorms, and by forest fires.

Sources Caused by Human Activity

According to the U.S. Environmental Protection Agency (EPA), in "What Is Acid Rain?" (December 4, 2012, http://www3.epa.gov/acidrain/what/index.html), the primary anthropogenic (human-related) contributors to acid rain are sulfur dioxide and nitrogen oxides, resulting

FIGURE 5.1

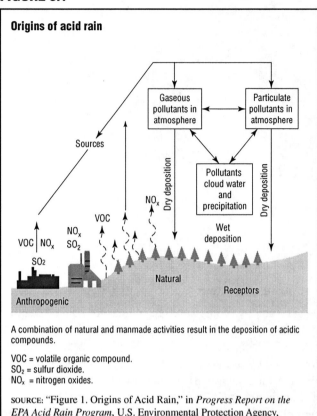

Origins of acid rain

A combination of natural and manmade activities result in the deposition of acidic compounds.

VOC = volatile organic compound.
SO₂ = sulfur dioxide.
NOₓ = nitrogen oxides.

SOURCE: "Figure 1. Origins of Acid Rain," in *Progress Report on the EPA Acid Rain Program*, U.S. Environmental Protection Agency, November 1999, http://www.epa.gov/airmarkets/documents/progressreports/1999report.pdf (accessed September 4, 2015)

FIGURE 5.2

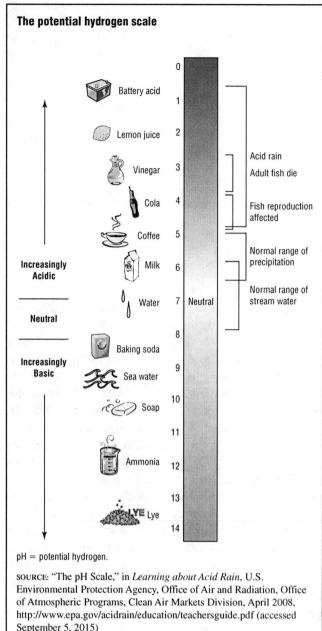

The potential hydrogen scale

pH = potential hydrogen.

SOURCE: "The pH Scale," in *Learning about Acid Rain*, U.S. Environmental Protection Agency, Office of Air and Radiation, Office of Atmospheric Programs, Clean Air Markets Division, April 2008, http://www.epa.gov/acidrain/education/teachersguide.pdf (accessed September 5, 2015)

from the burning of fossil fuels, such as coal, oil, and natural gas.

As described in Chapter 2, stationary fuel combustion (as in fossil-fueled electric utilities) accounted for 82% of sulfur dioxide emissions in 2013. Industrial and other processes contributed another 12%. Highway vehicles (38%), stationary fuel combustion (28%), and off-highway vehicles (21%) were the three largest sources of nitrous oxide emissions in 2013.

NATURAL FACTORS THAT AFFECT ACID RAIN DEPOSITION

Major natural factors that contribute to the impact of acid rain on an area include air movement, climate, topography, and geology. Transport systems—primarily the movement of air—distribute acid emissions in definite patterns around the planet. The movement of air masses transports emitted pollutants many miles, during which the pollutants are transformed into sulfuric and nitric acid by mixing with clouds of water vapor.

In drier climates, such as those of the western United States, windblown alkaline dust moves more freely through the air and tends to neutralize atmospheric acidity. The effects of acid rain can be greatly reduced by the presence of basic (also called alkali) substances. Sodium,

potassium, and calcium are examples of basic chemicals. When a basic and an acid chemical come into contact, they react chemically and neutralize each other. By contrast, in more humid climates where there is less dust, such as along the Eastern Seaboard, precipitation is more acidic.

Areas that are most sensitive to acid rain contain hard, crystalline bedrock and thin surface soils. When no alkaline-buffering particles are in the soil, runoff from rainfall directly affects surface waters, such as mountain streams. By contrast, a thick soil covering or soil with a high buffering capacity, such as flat land, neutralizes acid rain better. Lakes tend to be most susceptible to acid rain because of low alkaline content in lake beds. A lake's depth, its watershed (the area draining into the lake), and the amount of time the water has been in the lake are also factors.

EFFECTS OF ACID RAIN ON THE ENVIRONMENT

In nature the combination of rain and oxides is part of a natural balance that nourishes plants and aquatic life. However, when the balance is upset by acid rain, the results to the environment can be harmful and destructive. (See Table 5.1.)

Aquatic Systems

Although pH levels vary considerably from one body of water to another, a typical pH range for the lakes, rivers, and streams in the United States is 6 to 8. Low pH levels kill fish, their eggs, and fish food organisms. The degree of damage depends on several factors, one of which is the buffering capacity of the watershed soil—the higher the alkalinity, the more slowly the lakes and streams acidify. The exposure of fish to acidified freshwater lakes and streams has been intensely studied since the 1970s. Scientists distinguish between sudden shocks and chronic (long-term) exposure to low pH levels.

Sudden, short-term shifts in pH levels result from snowmelts, which release acidic materials that accumulated during the winter, or from sudden rainstorms that can wash residual acid into lakes and streams. The resulting acid shock can be devastating to fish and their ecosystems. Figure 5.3 shows the pH tolerance of various aquatic creatures. The darker boxes indicate safe pH levels, whereas the lighter boxes indicate life-threatening pH levels. Frogs have a high tolerance for acidic waters and can tolerate pH levels as low as 4. Clams and snails are much more sensitive and must have pH levels above 5.5 to survive.

Because many species of fish hatch in the spring, even mild increases in acidity can harm or kill the new life. Temporary increases in acidity also affect insects and other invertebrates, such as snails and crayfish, on which the fish feed. Gradual decreases of pH levels over time affect fish reproduction and spawning. In addition, excessive acid levels in female fish cause low amounts of calcium, thereby preventing the production of eggs. Even if eggs are produced, their development is often abnormal. Increased acidity can also cause the release of aluminum and manganese particles that are stored in a lake or river bottom. High concentrations of these metals are toxic to fish.

Soil and Vegetation

Acid rain is believed to harm vegetation by changing soil chemistry. Soils exposed to acid rain can gradually lose valuable nutrients, such as calcium and magnesium, and become too concentrated with dissolved inorganic aluminum, which is toxic to vegetation. Long-term changes in soil chemistry may have already affected sensitive soils, particularly in forests. Nutrient-poor trees are more vulnerable to climatic extremes, pest invasion, and the effects of other air pollutants, such as ozone.

The effect of acid rain on trees is influenced by many factors. Some trees adapt to environmental stress better than others; the type of tree, its height, and its leaf structure (deciduous or evergreen) influence how well it will adapt to acid rain. Scientists believe acid rain directly harms trees by leaching calcium from their foliage and indirectly harms them by lowering their tolerance to other stresses.

TABLE 5.1

Effects of acid rain on human health and selected ecosystems and anticipated recovery benefits

Human health and ecosystem	Effects	Recovery benefits
Human health	In the atmosphere, sulfur dioxide and nitrogen oxides become sulfate and nitrate aerosols, which increase morbidity and mortality from lung disorders, such as asthma and bronchitis, and impacts to the cardiovascular system.	Decrease emergency room visits, hospital admissions, and deaths.
Surface waters	Acidic surface waters decrease the survivability of animal life in lakes and streams and in the more severe instances eliminate some or all types of fish and other organisms.	Reduce the acidic levels of surface waters and restore animal life to the more severely damaged lakes and streams.
Forests	Acid deposition contributes to forest degradation by impairing trees' growth and increasing their susceptibility to winter injury, insect infestation, and drought. It also causes leaching and depletion of natural nutrients in forest soil.	Reduce stress on trees, thereby reducing the effects of winter injury, insect infestation, and drought, and reduce the leaching of soil nutrients, thereby improving overall forest health.
Materials	Acid deposition contributes to the corrosion and deterioration of buildings, cultural objects, and cars, which decreases their value and increases costs of correcting and repairing damage.	Reduce the damage to buildings, cultural objects, and cars, and reduce the costs of correcting and repairing future damage.
Visibility	In the atmosphere, sulfur dioxide and nitrogen oxides form sulfate and nitrate particles, which impair visibility and affect the enjoyment of national parks and other scenic views.	Extend the distance and increase the clarity at which scenery can be viewed, thus reducing limited and hazy scenes and increasing the enjoyment of national parks and other vistas.

SOURCE: "Appendix I. Effect of Acid Rain on Human Health and Selected Ecosystems and Anticipated Recovery Benefits," in *Acid Rain: Emissions Trends and Effects in the Eastern United States*, U.S. General Accounting Office, March 2000, http://www.gao.gov/archive/2000/rc00047.pdf (accessed September 5, 2015)

FIGURE 5.3

Tolerance of various aquatic species to low potential hydrogen levels

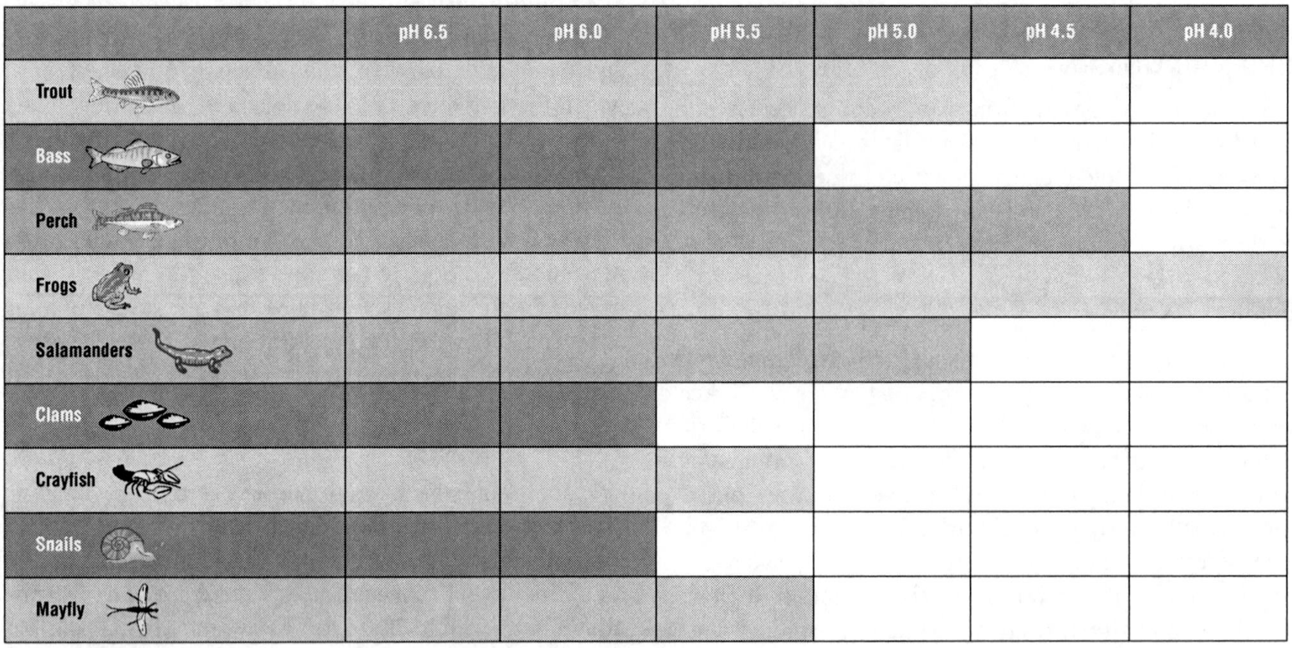

	pH 6.5	pH 6.0	pH 5.5	pH 5.0	pH 4.5	pH 4.0
Trout	▓	▓	▓	▓		
Bass	▓	▓	▓			
Perch	▓	▓	▓	▓	▓	
Frogs	▓	▓	▓	▓	▓	▓
Salamanders	▓	▓	▓	▓	▓	
Clams	▓	▓	▓			
Crayfish	▓	▓	▓	▓		
Snails	▓	▓	▓			
Mayfly	▓	▓	▓	▓	▓	

pH = potential hydrogen.

SOURCE: "pH Tolerance Chart on Aquatic Life," in *Learning about Acid Rain*, U.S. Environmental Protection Agency, Office of Air and Radiation, Office of Atmospheric Programs, Clean Air Markets Division, April 2008, http://www.epa.gov/acidrain/education/teachersguide.pdf (accessed September 5, 2015)

Birds

Increased freshwater acidity harms some species of migratory birds. Experts believe the dramatic decline of the North American black duck population since the 1950s is because of decreased food supplies in acidified wetlands. Acid rain leaches calcium out of the soil and robs snails of the calcium they need to form shells. Because some species of songbirds get most of their calcium from the shells of snails, the birds are also perishing. The eggs they lay are defective—thin and fragile. The chicks either do not hatch or have bone malformations and die.

Materials

Acid rain can also be harmful to materials, such as building stones, marble statues, metals, and paints. Historical monuments and buildings composed of these materials in the eastern United States have been affected by acid rain. For example, in "Acid Rain's Slow Dissolve" (May 22, 2012, http://www.nps.gov/nama/blogs/Acid-Rains-Slow-Dissolve.htm), Megan Nortrup of the U.S. National Park Service describes the damage done to monuments in the District of Columbia, such as the Jefferson Memorial (which is made of marble) and the Ulysses S. Grant Memorial (which is made of bronze). In both cases acid rain has caused accelerated deterioration of these monuments.

Human Health

Acid rain has several direct and indirect effects on humans. Particulates are extremely small pollutant particles that can threaten human health. Particulates related to acid rain include fine particles of sulfur oxides and nitrates. These particles can travel long distances and, when inhaled, penetrate deep into the lungs. Acid rain and the pollutants that cause it can lead to the development of bronchitis and asthma in children. Acid rain is also believed to be responsible for increasing health risks for those with asthma, chronic bronchitis, and emphysema; pregnant women; and those with histories of heart disease.

THE POLITICS OF ACID RAIN

Scientific research on acid rain was sporadic and largely focused on local problems until the late 1960s, when Scandinavian scientists began more systematic studies. Acid precipitation in North America was not identified until 1972, when scientists found that precipitation was acidic in eastern North America, especially in eastern and northeastern Canada. In 1975 the First International Symposium on Acid Precipitation and the Forest Ecosystem convened in Columbus, Ohio, to define the acid rain problem. Scientists used the meeting to propose a precipitation-monitoring network in the United States that would cooperate with the European and Scandinavian networks and set up protocols for collecting and testing precipitation.

In 1977 the Council on Environmental Quality was asked to develop a national acid rain research program. Several scientists drafted a report that eventually became the basis for the National Acid Precipitation Assessment Program. This initiative eventually translated into legislative action with the Energy Security Act of 1980. Title VII (Acid Precipitation Act of 1980) of the act produced a formal proposal that created the program and authorized federally financed support.

The first international treaty that aimed at limiting air pollution was the United Nations Economic Commission for Europe (UNECE) Convention on Long-Range Transboundary Air Pollution, which went into effect in 1983. It was ratified (formally approved into law) by 38 of the 54 UNECE members, which included not only European countries but also Canada and the United States. The treaty targeted sulfur emissions, requiring that countries reduce emissions 30% from 1980 levels—the so-called Thirty Percent Club.

The early acid rain debate centered almost exclusively on the eastern United States and Canada. The controversy was often defined as a problem of property rights. The highly valued production of electricity in coal-fired utilities in the Ohio River valley caused acid rain to fall on land in the Northeast and Canada. An important part of the acid rain controversy during the 1980s was the adversarial relationship between U.S. and Canadian government officials over emissions controls of sulfur dioxide and nitrogen dioxide. More of these pollutants crossed the border into Canada than the reverse. Canadian officials very quickly came to a consensus over the need for more stringent controls, whereas this consensus was lacking among U.S. officials.

Throughout the 1980s the major lawsuits involving acid rain all came from eastern states, and the states that passed their own acid rain legislation were those in the eastern part of the United States.

Legislative attempts to restrict emissions of pollutants were often defeated after strong lobbying by the coal industry and utility companies. These industries advocated further research for pollution-control technology rather than for placing restrictions on utility company emissions.

ACID RAIN CONTROL MEASURES

Congress created the Acid Rain Program (ARP) under Title IV (Acid Deposition Control) of the Clean Air Act Amendments of 1990. The goal of the program is to reduce annual emissions of sulfur dioxide and nitrogen oxide from electric power plants nationwide. The program set a permanent cap on the total amount of sulfur dioxide that could be emitted by these power plants. According to the EPA, in Chapter 1 of *2013 Progress Report—Clean Air Interstate Rule, Acid Rain Program, and Former NO$_x$ Budget Trading Program* (2015, http://www3.epa.gov/airmarkets/progress/reports/pdfs/chapter1_program_basics.pdf), this cap was set for 2010 at 8.95 million tons (8.1 million t), which is approximately half the number of tons of sulfur dioxide emitted by these plants in 1980. The program also established nitrogen oxide emissions limitations for certain coal-fired electric utility plants.

As described in Chapter 2, in 2005 the EPA issued the Clean Air Interstate Rule (CAIR) to address problems with cross-border contaminants, such as particulate matter, ground-level ozone, and acid rain. The CAIR put permanent caps on emissions of SO_2 and NO_x in 28 eastern states and the District of Columbia. It also includes annual and seasonal limits that apply to SO_2 and NO_x emissions.

The CAIR underwent numerous legal challenges, but remained in effect as its proposed replacement—the Cross-State Air Pollution Rule (CSAPR)—was also challenged in court. In April 2014 the U.S. Supreme Court ruled in *EPA v. EME Homer City Generation* (No. 12-1182) that the EPA could implement the CSAPR. The first phase of the rule went into effect in 2015; the second phase is scheduled to go into effect in 2017.

The ARP covers large fossil fuel–fired power plants or electric generating units. The CAIR included two programs: an annual program and a seasonal program. The annual program covered electric generating units, while the seasonal program covered electric generating units and some large industrial units that produce electricity or steam primarily for internal use. Examples include boilers and turbines at facilities, such as paper mills and petroleum refineries, and steam plants at large universities and hospitals. Table 5.2 shows the number and type of units subject to the ARP and CAIR sulfur dioxide limits in 2013. Note there is overlap between the ARP and the CAIR, with some units covered by both programs.

Both the ARP and the CAIR were designed as cap-and-trade systems featuring overall caps on emissions for an entire industry (or group of industries). Covered units have some flexibility in choosing how to achieve emissions reductions. For example, they can switch to low-sulfur coal, install pollution-control devices called scrubbers, or shut down older less-efficient plants. In addition, units that reduce their emissions below the required levels can sell their extra allowances to other units to help them meet their requirements.

TABLE 5.2

Electricity generating units and industrial units subject to the Clean Air Interstate Rule and Acid Rain Program, 2013

Fuel	ARP NO$_x$ program	ARP SO$_2$ program	CAIR NO$_x$ program	CAIR NO$_x$ ozone season program	CAIR SO$_2$ program
Coal EGUs	826	939	802	747	802
Gas EGUs	17	2,462	1,997	1,701	1,997
Oil EGUs	0	173	407	501	407
Industrial units	0	4	0	196	0
Unclassified EGUs	0	12	4	1	4
Other EGUs	4	19	29	31	29
Total units	**847**	**3,609**	**3,239**	**3,177**	**3,239**

ARP = Acid Rain Program; CAIR = Clean Air Interstate Rule; NO$_x$ = Nitrous oxides; SO$_2$ = Sulfur dioxide; EGUs = Electricity Generating Units.
Notes: "Unclassified" units have not submitted a fuel type in their monitoring plan and did not report emissions. "Other" fuel refers to units that burn waste, wood, petroleum coke, tire-derived fuel, etc.

SOURCE: "CAIR and ARP SO$_2$ Allowance Reconciliation Summary, 2013," in *2013 Program Progress—Clean Air Interstate Rule, Acid Rain Program, and Former NO$_x$ Budget Trading Program*, U.S. Environmental Protection Agency, April 2015, http://www3.epa.gov/airmarkets/progress/reports/pdfs/chapter2_affected_units.pdf (accessed September 4, 2015)

As shown in Figure 5.4, emissions of SO$_2$ from all covered units under the ARP and the CAIR declined 81.5%, from 17.3 million tons (15.7 million t) in 1980 to 3.2 million tons (2.9 million t) in 2013. The programs easily achieved the original goal of the ARP to reduce emissions to less than 8.95 million tons (8.1 million t) by 2010. The EPA (2015, http://www3.epa.gov/airmarkets/progress/reports/emissions_reductions_so2.html#figure1) indicates that units covered by the CAIR emitted 2.7 million tons (2.4 million t) of sulfur dioxide in 2013, down 70% from 2005 levels. In addition, the 2013 emissions were below the CAIR goal of 3.6 million tons (3.3 million t).

Table 5.3 shows the emissions rates in pounds of sulfur dioxide emissions per million British thermal units of heat produced. For units firing coal, gas, and oil, the emissions rates decreased between 2000 and 2013, indicating greater efficiency over time. The SO$_2$ emissions rate for units fired by other fuels increased slightly from 2000 to 2013.

FIGURE 5.4

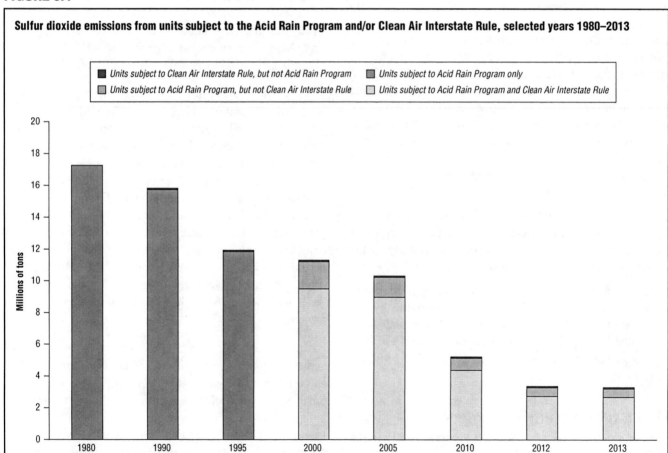

Sulfur dioxide emissions from units subject to the Acid Rain Program and/or Clean Air Interstate Rule, selected years 1980–2013

SOURCE: Adapted from "SO2 Emissions from CAIR SO2 Annual Program and ARP Sources, 1980–2013," in *2013 Program Progress—Clean Air Interstate Rule, Acid Rain Program, and Former NOx Budget Trading Program*, U.S. Environmental Protection Agency, April 2015, http://www3.epa.gov/airmarkets/progress/reports/pdfs/chapter3_SO2.pdf (accessed September 4, 2015)

TABLE 5.3

Sulfur dioxide trends under the Acid Rain Program and Clean Air Interstate Rule, selected years 2000–13

Primary fuel	SO₂ emissions (thousand tons)					SO₂ rate (lb/mmBtu)					Heat input (billion mmBtu)				
	2000	2005	2009	2010	2013	2000	2005	2009	2010	2013	2000	2005	2009	2010	2013
Coal	10,708	9,835	5,653	5,090	3,210	1.04	0.95	0.63	0.53	0.39	20.67	20.77	18.02	19.30	16.61
Gas	108	91	22	20	6	0.06	0.03	0.01	0.01	0.00	3.88	5.49	6.59	7.28	8.16
Oil	385	292	38	31	7	0.73	0.70	0.27	0.19	0.07	1.06	0.84	0.29	0.33	0.21
Other	1	4	8	26	19	0.22	0.27	0.27	0.53	0.28	0.01	0.03	0.06	0.10	0.14
Total	11,201	10,223	5,722	5,168	3,242	0.88	0.75	0.46	0.38	0.26	25.61	27.13	24.96	27.00	25.10

SO₂ = Sulfur dioxide.
lb = Pounds.
mmBtu = million British thermal units.
Notes:
The data shown here for the annual programs reflect totals for those facilities required to comply with each program in each respective year. This means that CAIR SO₂ annual program facilities are not included in the annual SO₂ data prior to 2009.
Fuel type represents primary fuel type; units might combust more than one fuel.
Totals may not reflect the sum of individual rows due to rounding.
Each year's total emission rate does not equal the arithmetic mean of the four fuel-specific rates, as each facility influences the annual emission rate in proportion to its heat input, and heat input is unevenly distributed across the fuel categories.
Unless otherwise noted, EPA data are current as of June 2014, and may differ from past of future reports as a result of resubmissions by sources and ongoing data quality assurance activities.

SOURCE: "Figure 4. CAIR and ARP Annual SO₂ Trends," in *2013 Program Progress—Clean Air Interstate Rule, Acid Rain Program, and Former NO_x Budget Trading Program*, U.S. Environmental Protection Agency, April 2015, http://www3.epa.gov/airmarkets/progress/reports/pdfs/chapter3_SO2.pdf (accessed September 4, 2015)

TABLE 5.4

Regional trends in sulfate, nitrate, acid neutralization capacity, base cations, and dissolved organic carbon, 1990–2012

Region	Water bodies covered	% of sites with improving sulfate trend	% of sites with improving nitrate trend	% of sites with improving ANC trend	% of sites with improving base cations trend	% of sites with increasing DOC trend
Adirondack Mountains	50 lakes in NY	100%	54%	76%	88%	62% (29 sites)
New England	26 lakes in ME and VT	100%	18%	43%	74%	39% (13 sites)
Catskills/N. Appalachian Plateau	9 streams in NY and PA	80%	40%	58%	90%	0% (9 sites)
Central Appalachians	66 streams in VA	15%	58%	15%	14%	NA

Notes: Trends are determined by multivariate Mann-Kendall tests. Data for 5 Pennsylvania N. Appalachian Plateau sites is unavailable for 2012. DOC was only examined in low-ANC waterbodies (acid neutralization capacity (ANC) less than 25 µeq/L). Dissolved organic carbon (DOC) is not currently measured in Central Appalachian streams.

SOURCE: "Regional Trends in Sulfate, Nitrate, ANC, Base Cations, and DOC at Long Term Monitoring Sites, 1990–2012," in *Monitoring Surface Water Chemistry*, U.S. Environmental Protection Agency, 2014, http://www.epa.gov/airmarkets/progress/surfacewater.html (accessed September 4, 2015)

According to the EPA, in Chapter 3 of *2013 Progress Report—Clean Air Interstate Rule, Acid Rain Program, and Former NO_x Budget Trading Program* (2015, http://www3.epa.gov/airmarkets/progress/reports/pdfs/chapter3_NOx.pdf), NO_x emissions under the annual programs declined from 6.4 million tons (5.8 million t) in 1990 to 1.7 million tons (1.5 million t) in 2013, a 73% decrease. The units covered by the CAIR emitted 1.2 million tons (1.1 million t) of NO_x in 2013, down 68% from 2005 levels. The 2013 emissions were below the CAIR goal of 1.5 million tons (1.4 million t).

The EPA (http://www3.epa.gov/airmarkets/progress/reports/emissions_reductions_ozone.html#figure1) notes that NO_x emissions covered by the seasonal CAIR (and its predecessor programs) declined 77% between 1990 and 2013. The 470,000 tons (426,400 t) emitted in 2013 were less than the CAIR goal of 567,744 tons (515,000 t).

ARE U.S. ECOSYSTEMS RECOVERING?

As shown in Figure 2.8 and Figure 2.4 in Chapter 2, atmospheric levels of sulfur dioxide and nitrogen dioxide averaged nationwide between 1990 and 2013 were well below the national standards for these pollutants.

Monitoring data clearly indicate decreased emissions and atmospheric concentrations of sulfur dioxide and nitrogen oxide and some reductions in deposition amounts. However, these improvements have not necessarily resulted in recovery of sensitive aquatic and terrestrial ecosystems. This is due, in part, to the long recovery times that are required to reverse damage done by acidification. The EPA reports that ecosystems harmed by acid rain deposition can take a long time to fully recover even after harmful emissions cease. The most chronic aquatic problems can take years to be resolved. Forest health is even slower to improve following decreases in emissions, taking decades to recover. Finally, soil nutrient reserves (such as calcium) can take centuries to replenish.

Table 5.4 summarizes environmental trends between 1990 and 2012 for monitoring sites at water bodies in the Adirondack Mountains, New England, the Catskills and northern Appalachian plateau, and the central Appalachians. Overall, the vast majority of sites (80% to 100%) in the first three areas showed improving sulfate trends. However, only 15% of sampled water bodies in the central Appalachians showed improvement. In *Clean Air Interstate Rule, Acid Rain Program, and Former NO$_x$ Budget Trading Program: 2012 Progress Report: Environmental and Health Results* (May 2014, http://www2 .epa.gov/sites/production/files/2015-08/documents/arpcair12 _02.pdf), the EPA notes that this area contains "highly weathered soils" that are believed to be saturated with sulfate; thus, sulfate deposits are increasingly leaching into surface waters, primarily streams.

The results were also mixed for three other environmental indicators: nitrates, acid neutralizing capacity (ANC), and dissolved organic carbon (DOC). (See Table 5.4.) Less than two-thirds of the water bodies showed improving nitrate trends. The EPA attributes these low numbers to "ecosystem factors," rather than to changes in nitrate deposition. ANC is a measure of the ability of a water body to neutralize acid. ANC trends improved significantly in the Adirondack Mountains, with 76% of sites showing improvement. Results were more modest in the other areas, particularly the central Appalachians, which saw only 15% improvement. Sites outside the central Appalachians showed improving trends for base cations. These are ions of elements such as calcium and magnesium that help prevent surface water acidification. DOC is basically a measure of dissolved organic material in the water and can have many sources. For example, the EPA notes that "increases can be indicative of reduced acidification and/or a sign of increased decomposition of organic matter in the watershed."

PUBLIC OPINION ABOUT ACID RAIN

Every year the Gallup Organization polls Americans about their attitudes regarding environmental issues. The most recent poll to assess the environment was conducted in March 2015; however, no questions about acid rain were included. Gallup notes in *Environment* (http:// www.gallup.com/poll/1615/environment.aspx) that in March 2008 participants were asked to express their level of personal concern about acid rain. Only 23% of respondents expressed a great deal of concern and 27% felt a fair amount of concern. Another 26% expressed only a little concern and 23% had no concern at all about acid rain. Analysis of historical Gallup poll results shows a dramatic decline in concern about acid rain since 1989, when 41% of respondents expressed a great deal of concern about the issue.

CHAPTER 6
NONHAZARDOUS WASTE

All waste materials that are not specifically deemed hazardous under federal law are considered nonhazardous wastes. The vast majority of waste produced in the United States is not inherently hazardous. It includes paper, wood, plastics, glass, metals, and chemicals, as well as other materials that are generated by industrial, commercial, agricultural, and residential sources. Although these wastes are not defined as hazardous, improper management of them poses significant risks to the environment and human health. Therefore, the handling, transport, and disposal of nonhazardous wastes is regulated by the government, largely at the state and local levels.

LAWS REGARDING WASTE

In 1965 the U.S. government passed the Solid Waste Disposal Act, the first of many solid waste management laws. It was amended several times, most notably in 1976 with the Resource Conservation and Recovery Act (RCRA), which is administered by the U.S. Environmental Protection Agency (EPA). The law applies to solid waste. In *RCRA Orientation Manual 2014* (October 2014, http://www2.epa.gov/sites/production/files/2015-07/documents/rom.pdf), the EPA notes that the RCRA definition of solid waste includes garbage and other materials ordinarily considered "solid," as well as sludges, semisolids, liquids, and even containers of gases.

The agency explains in "Solid Waste: Laws and Regulations" (October 14, 2015, http://www.epa.gov/region9/waste/solid/laws.html) that the RCRA's primary goal is to "protect human health and the environment from the potential hazards of waste disposal." The RCRA is also concerned with reducing the amount of solid waste that is generated, ensuring that solid wastes are managed properly, and conserving natural resources and energy.

The RCRA consists of 10 subtitles. (See Table 6.1.) Subtitle C concerns the management of hazardous waste, which makes up only a small portion of all the solid waste that is generated. Hazardous wastes are discussed in detail in Chapter 8. Subtitle D concerns the management of nonhazardous wastes. As noted earlier, nonhazardous wastes can come from many different sources, including residential, commercial, and industrial sources; agriculture; construction and demolition; and medical practices. Certain batteries and lightbulbs disposed by businesses fall under hazardous waste regulations. Thus, the extent to which a particular waste is deemed nonhazardous depends on both its physical and chemical nature and the source from which it comes.

The RCRA assigns to the states responsibility for permitting and monitoring landfills for municipal solid waste (MSW; or common garbage) and other nonhazardous wastes. Regulations established under Subtitle D describe minimum federal standards for the design, location, and operation of solid waste landfills to protect the environment. The states can develop their own permitting programs, so long as they include the federal landfill criteria. The EPA has the authority to review and approve the state programs.

State and local governments are mainly responsible for passing laws concerning nonhazardous waste, although the federal government will supply money and guidance to local governments so they can better manage their garbage systems.

It is difficult to calculate exactly how much nonhazardous waste is generated in the United States and what becomes of it. Under the RCRA the federal government collects data primarily on hazardous waste. In addition, the EPA estimates the production of MSW each year using surveys, studies, population data, and other information. However, MSW makes up only a small portion of all nonhazardous waste that is generated. The vast majority of nonhazardous waste is not tracked or

TABLE 6.1

Outline of the Resource Conservation and Recovery Act

Subtitle	Provisions
A	General provisions
B	Office of Solid Waste; authorities of the administrator and Interagency Coordinating Committee
C	Hazardous waste management
D	State or regional solid waste plans
E	Duties of the Secretary of Commerce in resource and recovery
F	Federal responsibilities
G	Miscellaneous provisions
H	Research, development, demonstration, and information
I	Regulation of underground storage tanks
J	Standards for the tracking and management of medical waste

SOURCE: "Figure 1-2. Outline of the Act," in *RCRA Orientation Manual 2011: Resource Conservation and Recovery Act*, U.S. Environmental Protection Agency, Solid Waste and Emergency Response, October 2011, http://www.epa.gov/waste/inforesources/pubs/orientat/rom.pdf (accessed September 5, 2015)

TABLE 6.2

Major pollutants associated with agriculture

- **Nutrients**—Nitrogen and phosphorus are essential plant nutrients, but can degrade water quality by causing eutrophication.
- **Ammonia**—A pungent, colorless gas that can be a health hazard to humans and animals at high concentrations, and a precursor for fine particulates (haze) in the atmosphere. It also contributes to soil acidification and eutrophication.
- **Hydrogen sulfide**—A colorless gas also hazardous to humans and animals.
- **Methane**—A nontoxic, odorless gas that contributes to global warming (greenhouse gas).
- **Odor**—A nuisance associated with animal production facilities. Odorous gases consist of a host of compounds (over 160) that originate from manure in animal housing, manure storage units, and land application.
- **Pathogens**—Threats to human health that are often contained in manure. Some of the pathogens that pose a threat to human health include the protozoan parasites *Cryptosporidium* and *Giardia* and some bacteria species such as *Salmonella*, *E. coli*, and *Campylobacter*.

SOURCE: Adapted from Marc Ribaudo and Noel Gollehon, "Animal Agriculture and the Environment," in *Agricultural Resources and Environmental Indicators, 2006 Edition*, U.S. Department of Agriculture, Economic Research Service, July 2006, http://www.ers.usda.gov/media/872940/eib16.pdf (accessed September 5, 2015)

estimated by the federal government but falls under varying state and local regulatory schemes.

NONHAZARDOUS INDUSTRIAL WASTES: SOURCES AND REGULATION

Nonhazardous industrial wastes come from a variety of sources. For example, the Texas Commission on Environmental Quality (the state's environmental agency) explains in "Nonhazardous Industrial Waste Storage, Treatment or Disposal: Am I Regulated?" (July 24, 2013, http://www.tceq.texas.gov/permitting/waste_permits/ihw_permits/NHW_Am_I_Regulated.html) that "industrial waste is waste resulting from or incidental to operations of industry, manufacturing, mining, or agriculture. For example, wastes from power generation plants, manufacturing facilities, and laboratories serving an industry are considered industrial waste while wastes from schools, hospitals, dry cleaners, most service stations, and laboratories serving the public are not considered industrial waste."

Nonhazardous industrial wastes are believed to be the largest single type of waste produced in the United States. Many big manufacturing plants have sites on their own property where they dispose of waste or treat it so it will not become dangerous. Still others ship it to private disposal sites for dumping or for treatment. Smaller manufacturers might use private waste disposal companies or even the city garbage company. State and local governments have regulatory responsibility for the management of most nonhazardous wastes.

AGRICULTURAL WASTES

Agricultural wastes are made up primarily of organic-based wastes, such as livestock manure, urine, and bedding material. The management of livestock waste, particularly on large agricultural facilities, is an issue of concern because of the potential environmental

impacts. (See Table 6.2.) The U.S. Government Accountability Office notes in *Concentrated Animal Feeding Operations: EPA Needs More Information and a Clearly Defined Strategy to Protect Air and Water Quality from Pollutants of Concern* (September 2008, http://www.gao.gov/new.items/d08944.pdf) that large farms raising thousands of animals can produce "over 2,800 tons to more than 1.6 million tons a year. To further put this in perspective, the amount of manure produced by large farms that raise animals can exceed the amount of waste produced by some large U.S. cities."

Manure is of particular concern because it is produced in huge amounts at agricultural facilities that confine large numbers of livestock in relatively small spaces. Although manure can be beneficially applied to the ground, care must be taken so that it does not adversely affect local water bodies. The runoff of nutrients from manure collection and storage facilities poses a threat to the water quality of lakes, rivers, and streams. For this reason agricultural operations that confine large numbers of animals and use manure management methods that could allow the waste to come into contact with water are regulated by the state and federal governments under water laws and regulations. (Water issues are discussed in detail in Chapter 9.)

CONSTRUCTION AND DEMOLITION DEBRIS

Construction and demolition (C&D) debris is a nonhazardous waste stream that is generated from the construction, renovation, and demolition of buildings, roads, and bridges. Table 6.3 lists typical examples of C&D wastes. Most C&D debris is managed through disposal at specially designated landfills.

TABLE 6.3

Typical components of construction and demolition debris

Material components	Content examples
Wood	Forming and framing lumber, stumps/trees, engineered wood
Drywall	Sheetrock (wallboard)
Metals	Pipes, rebar, flashing, wiring, framing
Plastics	Vinyl siding, doors, windows, flooring, pipes, packaging
Roofing	Asphalt, wood, slate, and tile shingles, roofing felt
Masonry	Cinder blocks, brick, masonry cement
Glass	Windows, mirrors, lights
Miscellaneous	Carpeting, fixtures, insulation, ceramic tile
Cardboard	From newly installed items such as appliances and tile
Concrete	Foundations, driveways, sidewalks, floors, road surfaces (all concrete containing portland cement)
Asphalt pavement	Sidewalks and road structures made with asphalt binder

SOURCE: "Table 1-1. Typical Components of C&D Materials," in *Estimating 2003 Building-Related Construction and Demolition Materials Amounts*, U.S. Environmental Protection Agency, March 2009, http://www.epa.gov/osw/conserve/imr/cdm/pubs/cd-meas.pdf (accessed September 5, 2015)

Table 6.4 shows EPA estimates of the C&D wastes generated in the United States in 2013. Overall, 530.3 million tons (481.1 million t) of materials were generated. The vast majority of the waste was demolition debris (505.9 million tons [458.9 million t]). The remainder was waste generated during construction activities. Figure 6.1 provides a breakdown of C&D composition by material for 2013. Portland cement concrete accounted for nearly two-thirds (67%) of the total. Asphalt concrete was second (18%), followed by wood products (8%). Chapter 7 discusses the recovery and reuse of C&D materials for useful purposes.

MEDICAL WASTE

Medical waste attracted widespread attention during the mid-1980s, when used needles and similar items washed up onto beaches in the Northeast. Although most medical waste is regulated by state governments, Congress responded with the Medical Waste Tracking Act of 1988. This temporary act called for better tracking and disposal methods for medical waste. The act, which expired in 1999, defined medical waste as "any solid waste that is generated in the diagnosis, treatment, or immunization of human beings or animals, in research pertaining thereto, or in the production or testing of biologicals." Thus, sources include health care facilities, medical research facilities, veterinary clinics, and medical laboratories. In "Medical Waste" (November 15, 2012, http://www.epa.gov/waste/nonhaz/industrial/medical/index.htm), the EPA gives the following as examples of medical waste under the federal definition:

- Bloody bandages

- Used surgical gloves and instruments

- Used needles (medical sharps)

TABLE 6.4

Generation of construction and demolition wastes, by material and activity, 2013

[million tons]

	Waste during construction	Demolition debris	Total C&D debris
	2013	2013	2013
Portland cement concrete	17.5	335.4	352.9
Wood products	2.5	37.7	40.2
Drywall and plasters	3.1	9.9	13.1
Steel*	0	4.3	4.3
Brick and clay tile	0.3	11.8	12.1
Asphalt shingles	1.0	11.5	12.6
Asphalt concrete	0	95.1	95.1
Total	**24.4**	**505.9**	**530.3**

*Steel consumption in buildings also includes steel consumed for the construction of roads and bridges. Data were not available to allocate steel consumption across different sources.

SOURCE: "Table ES-5. C&D Debris Generation by Material and Activity (Million Tons)," in *Advancing Sustainable Materials Management: Facts and Figures 2013*, U.S. Environmental Protection Agency, June 2015, http://www.epa.gov/wastes/nonhaz/municipal/pubs/2013_advncng_smm_rpt.pdf (accessed September 4, 2015)

FIGURE 6.1

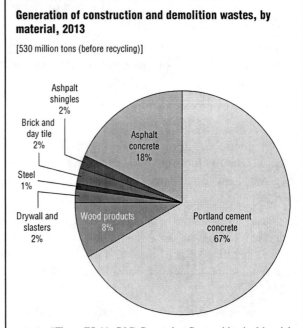

Generation of construction and demolition wastes, by material, 2013

[530 million tons (before recycling)]

Ashpalt shingles 2%
Brick and day tile 2%
Steel 1%
Drywall and slasters 2%
Wood products 8%
Asphalt concrete 18%
Portland cement concrete 67%

SOURCE: "Figure ES-11. C&D Generation Composition by Material, 2013," in *Advancing Sustainable Materials Management: Facts and Figures 2013*, U.S. Environmental Protection Agency, June 2015, http://www.epa.gov/wastes/nonhaz/municipal/pubs/2013_advncng_smm_rpt.pdf (accessed September 4, 2015)

- Biological cultures and associated equipment, such as glassware and swabs

- Surgically removed body parts, such as tonsils and limbs

- Used lancets

The EPA notes that there are varying state definitions of medical waste that can include additional waste streams not previously specified. There are different regulatory categories of medical wastes, including infectious, hazardous, radioactive, and general wastes. The EPA reports in "Medical Waste Frequent Questions" (August 17, 2015, http://www.epa.gov/waste/nonhaz/industrial/medical/mwfaqs.htm) that more than 90% of infectious medical waste is incinerated. The federal government regulates emissions from medical waste incinerators.

SPECIAL WASTES

When the RCRA regulations were promulgated in 1987, the EPA included a list of six wastes that were deemed "special wastes" and exempted them from classification as hazardous wastes until further studies could be conducted. According to the EPA, in "Special Wastes" (December 22, 2014, http://www.epa.gov/osw/nonhaz/industrial/special/index.htm), many studies on the toxicity of these wastes have been conducted, and the following are considered to be special wastes under federal law:

- Cement kiln dust, which is the fine-grained highly alkaline dust removed by air pollution control devices during the production of cement

- Wastes generated during the exploration, development, and production of crude oil, natural gas, and geothermal energy

- Certain wastes produced from the mining of uranium ore

- Wastes produced from the burning of fossil fuels (coal, oil, and natural gas) and including all ash and slag (metal waste) and any particulates removed from flue gases

- 20 waste streams from mineral processing that are generated during physical and chemical processes, such as smelting or acid treatment, and that result in wastes that are no longer considered earthen. (See Table 6.5.)

- Most wastes generated from the extraction and beneficiation (treating ore to make it more beneficial for smelting) of hard rock (metal ores and phosphate rock)

These waste streams are also known as high-volume, low-toxicity wastes. Although some components, particularly cement kiln dust, can be reused within the processes involved or sold for commercial purposes, most special wastes are disposed in land-based disposal units.

Coal Combustion Residuals

Coal combustion residuals (CCRs) or coal ash is a designated special waste that results from the combustion

TABLE 6.5

Mineral processing wastes considered "Special Wastes" under the Resource Conservation and Recovery Act

- Slag from primary copper processing
- Slag from primary lead processing
- Red and brown muds from bauxite refining
- Phosphogypsum from phosphoric acid production
- Slag from elemental phosphorous production
- Gasifier ash from coal gasification
- Process wastewater from coal gasification
- Calcium sulfate wastewater treatment plant sludge from primary copper processing
- Slag tailings from primary copper processing
- Flurogypsum from hydrofluoric acid production
- Process wastewater from hydrofluoric acid production
- Air pollution control dust/sludge from iron blast furnaces
- Iron blast furnace slag
- Treated residue from roasting/leaching of chrome ore
- Process wastewater from primary magnesium processing by the anhydrous process
- Process wastewater from phosphoric acid production
- Basic oxygen furnace and open hearth furnace air pollution control dust/sludge from carbon steel production
- Basic oxygen furnace and open hearth furnace slag from carbon steel production
- Chloride process waste solids from titanium tetrachloride production
- Slag from primary zinc processing

SOURCE: "20 Mineral Processing Wastes Covered by the Mining Waste Exclusion," in *Mining Waste*, U.S. Environmental Protection Agency, August 11, 2015, http://www.epa.gov/wastes/nonhaz/industrial/special/mining/index.htm (accessed September 4, 2015)

of coal at power plants. Table 6.6 lists the types of by-products that make up CCRs. In December 2008 more than 5 million cubic yards (3.8 million cubic m) of impounded coal ash spilled into water bodies and wetlands surrounding a power plant in Harriman, Tennessee, after an embankment failed. Over 300 acres (121 ha) were affected.

The spill prompted the EPA to propose in June 2010 the regulation of CCRs under either RCRA Subtitle C (as hazardous waste) or RCRA Subtitle D (as nonhazardous waste). Linda Luther, James E. McCarthy, and James D. Werner of the Congressional Research Service explain in *Analysis of Recent Proposals to Amend the Resource Conservation and Recovery Act (RCRA) to Create a Coal Combustion Residuals Permit Program* (March 19, 2013, http://earthjustice.org/sites/default/files/CCW-CRS-R43003.pdf) that the EPA proposals triggered a political battle in Congress over the roles that the EPA and the states should play in regulating CCRs.

In December 2014 the EPA finalized the rule regulating CCRs under Subtitle D. In "Fact Sheet: Final Rule on Coal Combustion Residuals Generated by Electric Utilities" (http://www2.epa.gov/sites/production/files/2014-12/documents/factsheet_ccrfinal_2.pdf), the agency indicates that the new rule includes specific requirements for existing and new CCR landfills and surface impoundments. For example, Table 6.7 lists the time-frames that power plants must follow for implementing minimum criteria for existing CCR landfills.

TABLE 6.6

Coal combustion residuals

Fly ash	A very fine, powdery material composed mostly of silica made from the burning of finely ground coal in a boiler.
Bottom ash	A coarse, angular ash particle that is too large to be carried up into the smoke stacks so it forms in the bottom of the coal furnace.
Boiler slag	Molten bottom ash from slag tap and cyclone type furnaces that turns into pellets that have a smooth glassy appearance after it is cooled with water.
Flue gas desulfurization material (FGD)	A material leftover from the process of reducing sulfur dioxide emissions from a coal-fired boiler that can be a wet sludge consisting of calcium sulfite or calcium sulfate or a dry powered material that is a mixture of sulfites and sulfates.

SOURCE: "What Is Coal Ash?" in *Frequent Questions about the Coal Ash Disposal Rule*, U.S. Environmental Protection Agency, July 9, 2015, http://www2.epa .gov/coalash/frequent-questions-about-coal-ash-disposal-rule (accessed September 4, 2015)

TABLE 6.7

Implementation timeframe for existing landfills holding coal combustion residuals

Requirement (Section in Title 40 of the Code of Federal Regulations)	Implementation timeframe (Number of months after publication of rule)	Description of requirement to be completed
Location restrictions (§257.64)	42 months	• Complete demonstration for unstable areas
Air criteria (§257.80)	6 months	• Prepare fugitive dust control plan
Run-on and run-off controls (§257.81)	18 months	• Prepare initial run-on and run-off control system plan
Inspections (§257.83)	6 months 9 months	• Initiate weekly inspections of the CCR unit • Complete the initial annual inspection of the CCR unit
Groundwater monitoring and corrective action (§257.90–§257.98)	30 months	• Install the groundwater monitoring system; develop the groundwater sampling and analysis program; initiate the detection monitoring program; and begin evaluating the groundwater monitoring data for statistically significant increases over background levels
Closure and post-closure care (§257.103–§257.104)	18 months	• Prepare written closure and post-closure care plans
Recordkeeping, notification, and internet requirements (§257.105–§257.107)	6 months	• Conduct required recordkeeping • Provide required notifications • Establish CCR website

Note: CCR = Coal Combustion Residuals.

SOURCE: "Table 2. Implementation Timeframes for the Minimum Criteria for Existing CCR Landfills," in *Frequent Questions about the Coal Ash Disposal Rule*, U.S. Environmental Protection Agency, July 9, 2015, http://www2.epa.gov/coalash/frequent-questions-about-coal-ash-disposal-rule (accessed September 4, 2015)

MUNICIPAL SOLID WASTE

MSW is common garbage or trash. As such, it is nonhazardous. It includes items such as food scraps, paper, containers and packaging, appliances, and yard trimmings. Table 6.8 lists example MSW products and the types of sources that generate them. MSW is generally collected and managed by local municipal agencies.

Since 1995 the EPA (http://www3.epa.gov/epawaste/nonhaz/municipal/msw99.htm) has published a report nearly every year on the generation and disposal of MSW in the United States. As of November 2015, the most recent report was *Advancing Sustainable Materials Management: Facts and Figures 2013* (June 2015, http://www2.epa.gov/sites/production/files/2015-09/documents/2013_advncng_smm_rpt.pdf), which includes data through 2013.

Determining the amount and types of MSW generated in the United States is difficult because people are not required to track or report how much MSW they produce or what it contains. The EPA uses information supplied by trade groups and industrial sources, combined with estimated product life spans and population and sales data, to estimate how much and what types of MSW are generated.

Just over 254 million tons (230.5 million t) of MSW was generated in the United States in 2013. (See Figure 6.2.) The tons of MSW generated annually increased dramatically between 1960 and 2000. Most of this increase occurred during the 1960s, 1970s, and 1980s. Between 1990 and 2000 MSW generation increased 17%, from 208.3 million tons (189 million t) to 243.5 million tons (220.9 million t). Generation then leveled off; it increased only 4% between 2000 and 2013.

The EPA indicates that in 1960 each American generated on average 2.68 pounds (1.22 kg) of MSW per day. (See Figure 6.2.) This value steadily increased until 1990, when it reached 4.57 pounds (2.07 kg) per day. The rate leveled off during the 1990s, and then began to decline after 2000. In 2013 the per capita generation was 4.4 pounds (2 kg) per day.

TABLE 6.8

Sources and examples of municipal solid waste

Sources and examples	Example products
Residential (single- and multi-family homes)	• Newspapers, clothing, disposable tableware, food packaging, cans and bottles, food, yard trimmings
Commercial (office buildings, retail and wholesale establishments, restaurants)	• Corrugated boxes, food, office papers, disposable tableware, paper napkins, yard trimmings
Institutional (schools, libraries, hospitals, prisons)	• Cafeteria and restroom trash can wastes, office papers, classroom wastes, yard trimmings
Industrial (packaging and administrative; not process wastes)	• Corrugated boxes, plastic film, wood pallets, lunchroom wastes, office papers.

SOURCE: "Untitled," in *Advancing Sustainable Materials Management: Facts and Figures 2013*, U.S. Environmental Protection Agency, June 2015, http://www
.epa.gov/wastes/nonhaz/municipal/pubs/2013_advncng_smm_rpt.pdf (accessed September 4, 2015)

FIGURE 6.2

Trends in total and per capita municipal solid waste generation, 1960–2013

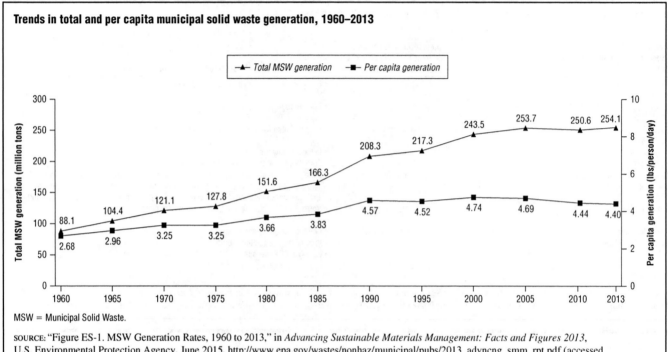

MSW = Municipal Solid Waste.

SOURCE: "Figure ES-1. MSW Generation Rates, 1960 to 2013," in *Advancing Sustainable Materials Management: Facts and Figures 2013*,
U.S. Environmental Protection Agency, June 2015, http://www.epa.gov/wastes/nonhaz/municipal/pubs/2013_advncng_smm_rpt.pdf (accessed
September 4, 2015)

MSW Composition

Figure 6.3 shows EPA estimates of the breakdown of MSW produced in 2013 by material. Paper and paperboard (boxboard and containerboard) made up the largest single component by weight, making up 27% of the waste stream. Food (14.6%), yard trimmings (13.5%), and plastics (12.8%) each also accounted for more than 10% of the total.

Another way in which the EPA characterizes MSW is by product category. The categories include durable goods (consumer items with a life expectancy in excess of three years), nondurable goods (consumer items with a life expectancy of less than three years), containers and packaging, and other wastes. In this system, a particular type of material can be classified under multiple categories. For example, steel is found in durable goods (e.g., in appliance) and in containers and packaging (e.g., in steel drums). In *Advancing Sustainable Materials Management:*

Facts and Figures 2013, the EPA provides the following breakdown of 2013 MSW by product category:

• Containers and packaging—75.8 million tons (68.7 million t) or 30% of the total

• Other wastes (includes food, yard trimmings, and miscellaneous inorganic wastes)—75.2 million tons (68.2 million t) or 30% of the total

• Durable goods—51.6 million tons (46.8 million t) or 20% of the total

• Nondurable goods—51.6 million tons (46.8 million t) or 20% of the total

CONSUMER ELECTRONICS. Consumer electronics include televisions, computers, compact disc and digital video disc players, digital and video cameras, radios, telephones and cellular phones, printers, scanners, and other miscellaneous equipment. Historically, the EPA

FIGURE 6.3

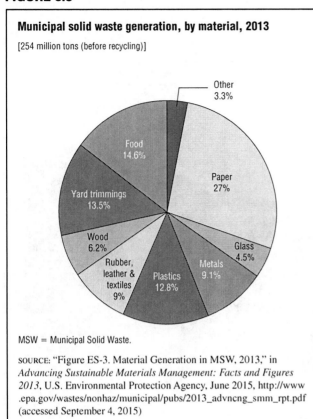

Municipal solid waste generation, by material, 2013

[254 million tons (before recycling)]

Other 3.3%
Food 14.6%
Paper 27%
Yard trimmings 13.5%
Wood 6.2%
Glass 4.5%
Rubber, leather & textiles 9%
Plastics 12.8%
Metals 9.1%

MSW = Municipal Solid Waste.

SOURCE: "Figure ES-3. Material Generation in MSW, 2013," in *Advancing Sustainable Materials Management: Facts and Figures 2013*, U.S. Environmental Protection Agency, June 2015, http://www .epa.gov/wastes/nonhaz/municipal/pubs/2013_advncng_smm_rpt.pdf (accessed September 4, 2015)

has lumped such products under the category "other miscellaneous durable goods."

In *Advancing Sustainable Materials Management: Facts and Figures 2013*, the EPA notes that beginning in 2000 consumer electronics were categorized separately, and an estimated 1.9 million tons (1.7 million t) entered the MSW stream. In 2013 this value climbed to 3.1 million tons (2.8 million t), representing 1.2% of the total 254.1 million tons (230.5 million t) of MSW generated. Although this percentage is small, it is expected to increase quickly during the 21st century as more electronic products reach the end of their useful lives.

Disposal of electronic goods in MSW poses environmental risks because of the presence of metals and other hazardous contaminants in the products. As a result, some states forbid electronic waste from MSW, as described in Chapter 8.

Historical Trends in MSW Composition

Since 1960 paper has consistently been the largest single component of MSW generated. (See Figure 6.4.) Paper's contribution grew dramatically through 2000 before leveling off and then declining through 2013. The amounts of other materials, particularly plastics and food, in the total MSW stream have grown over time. This is also true for the EPA's "all other" classification, which includes mostly wood, rubber, leather, and textiles.

Figure 6.5 provides a historical breakdown of MSW composition by product category. Between 1960 and 2013 the amount of MSW in each category type increased. The largest increases were for durable and nondurable goods, containers and packaging, and food wastes.

MSW Management

The three primary methods for the management of MSW are:

- Land disposal

- Incineration and combustion

- Recovery through recycling or composting

Land disposal involves piling or burying waste materials on or below the ground surface. This is primarily done at facilities called landfills. Incineration is a disposal method in which MSW is burned at high temperatures, and combustion is the burning of waste to produce energy. Recycling is the reuse of a material in another product or application. Composting is a method of decomposing yard trimmings and other biodegradable wastes for reuse as fertilizer or mulch. Recycling and composting are discussed at length in Chapter 7.

According to the EPA, land disposal was the most common method used to manage MSW in the United States in 2013. More than half (52.8%) of the MSW generated was discarded, going to land disposal, whereas 34.3% was recovered and 12.9% was combusted with energy recovery. (See Figure 6.6.)

As shown in Table 6.9, the EPA estimates that in 1960 each person in the United States discarded to landfills or otherwise disposed of 2.51 pounds (1.1 kg) of MSW per day. This represented 94% of the total 2.68 pounds (1.2 kg) of MSW per day that were generated. Over the decades, other types of waste management became more prominent. In 2013, each person generated 4.4 pounds (2 kg) of MSW per day. Only 2.32 pounds (1.1 kg or 53%) of this total was discarded to landfills or other disposal. The remainder was recovered for recycling, composting, or combustion.

Municipal Landfills

Municipal (or sanitary) landfills are areas where MSW waste is placed into and onto the land. Although some landfilled organic wastes will decompose, many of the wastes in MSW are not biodegradable. Landfills provide a centralized location in which these wastes can be contained.

HOW ORGANIC MATTER DECOMPOSES IN LANDFILLS. Organic material (material that was once alive, such as paper and wood products, food scraps, and clothing made of natural fibers) decomposes in the following way: first,

FIGURE 6.4

Generation of products in municipal solid waste, by material, 1960–2013

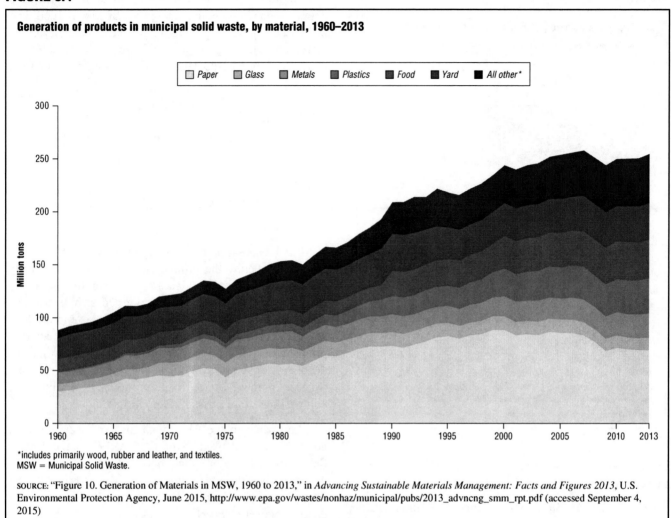

*includes primarily wood, rubber and leather, and textiles.
MSW = Municipal Solid Waste.

SOURCE: "Figure 10. Generation of Materials in MSW, 1960 to 2013," in *Advancing Sustainable Materials Management: Facts and Figures 2013*, U.S. Environmental Protection Agency, June 2015, http://www.epa.gov/wastes/nonhaz/municipal/pubs/2013_advncng_smm_rpt.pdf (accessed September 4, 2015)

aerobic (oxygen-using) bacteria use the material as food and begin the decomposition process. Principal by-products of this aerobic stage are water, carbon dioxide, nitrates, and heat. This stage lasts about two weeks. However, in compacted, layered, and covered landfills the availability of oxygen may be low.

After the available oxygen is used, anaerobic bacteria (those that do not use oxygen) continue the decomposition. They generally produce carbon dioxide and organic acids. This stage can last up to one to two years. During a final anaerobic stage of decomposition lasting several years or decades, methane gas is formed along with carbon dioxide. The duration of this stage and the amount of decomposition depend on landfill conditions, including temperature, soil permeability, and water levels.

Landfills and the Environment

METHANE. Methane, a flammable gas, is produced when organic matter decomposes in the absence of oxygen. If not properly vented or controlled, it can cause explosions and underground fires that smolder for years. Methane is also deadly to breathe. The RCRA requires landfill operators to monitor methane gas.

Methane gas can be recovered through pipes that are inserted into landfills, and the gas can be used to generate energy. The EPA indicates in "Energy Projects and Candidate Landfills" (http://www.epa.gov/lmop/projects-candidates/index.html) that as of March 2015 there were 645 operational landfill gas-to-energy projects in the United States. The EPA's Landfill Methane Outreach Program estimates that approximately 440 other landfill sites presented attractive opportunities for project development.

Landfill Design Standards

The RCRA standards require landfill operators to do several things to lessen the chance of polluting the underlying groundwater. Groundwater can become contaminated when liquid chemicals or contaminated rainfall runoff seep down through the ground underneath the landfill. This liquid is called leachate.

FIGURE 6.5

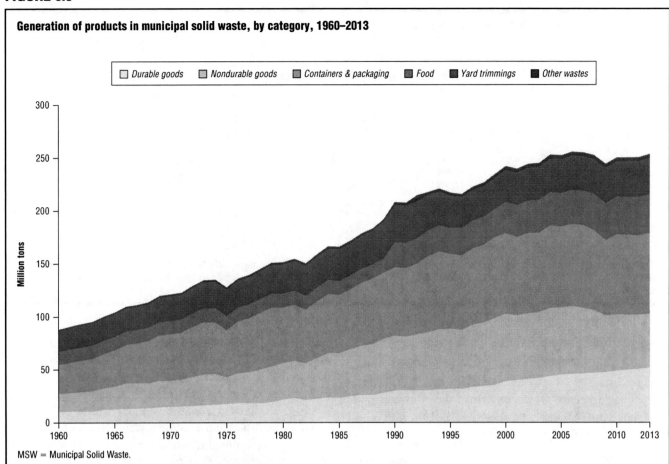

Generation of products in municipal solid waste, by category, 1960–2013

☐ Durable goods ☐ Nondurable goods ☐ Containers & packaging ☐ Food ☐ Yard trimmings ■ Other wastes

MSW = Municipal Solid Waste.

SOURCE: "Figure 14. Generation of Products in MSW, 1960 to 2013," in *Advancing Sustainable Materials Management: Facts and Figures 2013*, U.S. Environmental Protection Agency, June 2015, http://www.epa.gov/wastes/nonhaz/municipal/pubs/2013_advncng_smm_rpt.pdf (accessed September 4, 2015)

FIGURE 6.6

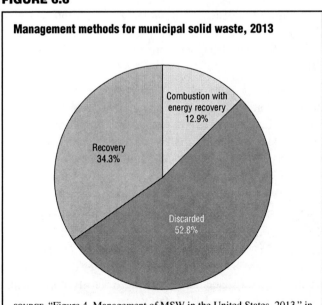

Management methods for municipal solid waste, 2013

Combustion with energy recovery 12.9%

Recovery 34.3%

Discarded 52.8%

SOURCE: "Figure 4. Management of MSW in the United States, 2013," in *Advancing Sustainable Materials Management: 2013 Fact Sheet*, U.S. Environmental Protection Agency, June 2015, http://www.epa.gov/wastes/nonhaz/municipal/pubs/2013_advncng_smm_fs.pdf (accessed September 4, 2015)

The RCRA requirements are as follows:

• Landfill operators must monitor the groundwater for pollutants. This is usually accomplished with a groundwater monitoring well system.

• Landfills must have plastic liners underneath their waste, as well as a leachate collection system. (See Figure 6.7.)

• Debris must be covered daily with soil to prevent odors and stop refuse from being blown away.

• Methane gas must be monitored, which is usually accomplished with an explosive-gas monitoring well.

• Landfill owners are responsible for cleanup of any contamination.

Landfills are not open dumps but managed facilities in which wastes are controlled. MSW is often compacted before it is placed in a landfill and covered with soil. Modern landfills have liner systems and other safeguards to prevent groundwater contamination. When they are full, landfills are usually capped with a clay liner to prevent contamination. (See Figure 6.7.)

TABLE 6.9

Generation, recovery, and discard amounts for municipal solid waste, selected years 1960–2013

[in pounds per person per day]

Activity	1960	1970	1980	1990	2000	2005	2009	2011	2012	2013
Generation	2.68	3.25	3.66	4.57	4.74	4.69	4.37	4.41	4.38	4.40
Recovery for recycling	0.17	0.22	0.35	0.64	1.03	1.10	1.10	1.17	1.14	1.12
Recovery for composting[a]	Neg.	Neg.	Neg.	0.09	0.32	0.38	0.37	0.36	0.37	0.39
Total materials recovery	**0.17**	**0.22**	**0.35**	**0.73**	**1.35**	**1.48**	**1.47**	**1.53**	**1.51**	**1.51**
Discards after recovery	2.51	3.03	3.31	3.84	3.39	3.21	2.90	2.88	2.87	2.89
Combustion with energy recovery[b]	0.00	0.01	0.07	0.65	0.66	0.58	0.52	0.56	0.56	0.57
Discards to landfill, other disposal[c]	2.51	3.02	3.24	3.19	2.73	2.63	2.38	2.32	2.31	2.32
Population (millions)	179.979	203.984	227.255	249.907	281.422	296.410	307.007	311.592	313.914	316.129

[a]Composting of yard trimmings, food and other MSW organic material. Does not include backyard composting.
[b]Includes combustion of MSW in mass burn or refuse-derived fuel form, and combustion with energy recovery of source separated materials in MSW (e.g., wood pallets, tire-derived fuel).
[c]Discards after recovery minus combustion with energy recovery. Discards include combustion without energy recovery.
Neg. = Negligible.
Notes: Details might not add to totals due to rounding.

SOURCE: "Table 30. Generation, Materials Recovery, Composting, Combustion, and Discards of Municipal Solid Waste, 1960 to 2013," in *Advancing Sustainable Materials Management: 2013 Fact Sheet*, U.S. Environmental Protection Agency, June 2015, http://www.epa.gov/wastes/nonhaz/municipal/pubs/2013_advncng_smm_fs.pdf (accessed September 4, 2015)

Interstate Imports and Exports of Garbage

The lack of landfill space has encouraged some municipalities to send their garbage to other states. Although shipments do occur across the Mexican and Canadian borders, the vast majority of U.S. MSW is managed within the United States.

Since 1989 *BioCycle* and the Earth Engineering Center at Columbia University have published occasional reports concerning MSW. As of November 2015, the most recent report available was "The State of Garbage in America" (*BioCycle*, vol. 51, no. 10, October 2010). In the report, Rob van Haaren, Nickolas Themelis, and Nora Goldstein indicate that importing and exporting MSW from state to state is common. In 2008 New York exported the most MSW (4.8 million tons [4.4 million t]), followed by Maryland (1.8 million tons [1.7 million t]) and Washington (1.3 million tons [1.2 million t]). The chief MSW importers were Michigan (5.2 million tons [4.7 million t]), Virginia (4.8 million tons [4.4 million t]), and Oregon (2.6 million tons [2.3 million t]).

Several states have tried to ban the importing of garbage into their respective state. In 1992 the U.S. Supreme Court ruled in *Chemical Waste Management v. Hunt* (504 U.S. 334) that the constitutional right to conduct commerce across state borders protects such shipments. Experts point out that newer, state-of-the-art landfills with multiple liners and sophisticated pollution control equipment have to accept waste from a wide region to be financially viable.

Trends in Landfill Development

Before using landfills, cities used open dumps—areas in which garbage and trash were simply discarded into huge piles. However, open dumps produced unpleasant odors and attracted animals. During the early 1970s the number of operating landfills in the United States was estimated at about 20,000. In 1979, as part of the RCRA, the EPA designated conditions under which solid waste disposal facilities and practices would not pose adverse effects to human health and the environment. As a result of the implementation of these criteria, open dumps had to be closed or upgraded to meet the criteria for landfills.

Additionally, many more landfills closed during the early 1990s because they could not conform to the new standards that took effect in 1993 under the 1992 RCRA amendment. Other landfills closed as they became full. According to the EPA, in *Advancing Sustainable Materials Management: Facts and Figures 2013*, there were 1,908 MSW landfills operating in the United States in 2010.

Landfilling is expected to continue to be the single most predominant MSW management method. In the coming decades it will be economically prohibitive to develop and maintain small-scale, local landfills. There will likely be fewer, larger, and more regional operations. More MSW is expected to move away from its point of generation, resulting in increased import and export rates.

Landfill protection methods will likely become stronger in the future with more options for leachate and gas recovery. To make landfills more acceptable to neighborhoods, operators will likely establish larger buffer zones, use more green space, and show more sensitivity to land-use compatibility and landscaping.

Incineration of Wastes

Incineration and combustion are popular disposal choices for nonhazardous wastes. They both involve

FIGURE 6.7

Example of a properly closed landfill

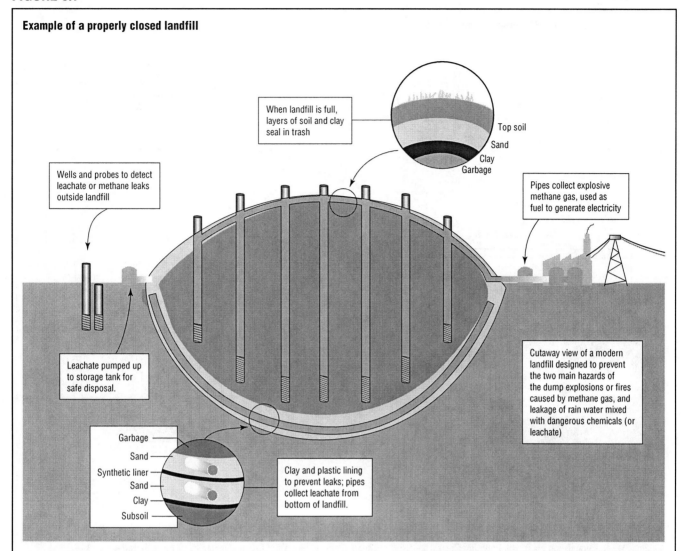

When landfill is full, layers of soil and clay seal in trash

Top soil
Sand
Clay
Garbage

Wells and probes to detect leachate or methane leaks outside landfill

Pipes collect explosive methane gas, used as fuel to generate electricity

Leachate pumped up to storage tank for safe disposal.

Cutaway view of a modern landfill designed to prevent the two main hazards of the dump explosions or fires caused by methane gas, and leakage of rain water mixed with dangerous chemicals (or leachate)

Garbage
Sand
Synthetic liner
Sand
Clay
Subsoil

Clay and plastic lining to prevent leaks; pipes collect leachate from bottom of landfill.

SOURCE: "Figure II-4. Cross-Section of a Municipal Solid Waste Landfill," in *RCRA Orientation Manual 2011: Resource Conservation and Recovery Act*, U.S. Environmental Protection Agency, Solid Waste and Emergency Response, October 2011, http://www.epa.gov/waste/inforesources/pubs/orientat/rom .pdf (accessed September 5, 2015)

heating waste to high temperatures. In the past waste was burned in incinerators primarily to reduce its volume. During the 1980s technology was developed that allowed waste to be burned for energy recovery. The use of waste as a fuel is more commonly called combustion; however, both terms are used interchangeably. The EPA refers to waste combustion as a waste-to-energy (WTE) process.

Figure 6.8 shows a typical WTE system. At this facility, the trucks dump waste into a pit. The waste is moved to the furnace by a crane. The furnace burns the waste at a high temperature, heating a boiler that produces steam for generating electricity and heat. Ash collects at the bottom of the furnace, where it is later removed and taken to a landfill for disposal. The combustion process produces both gaseous emissions and solid waste (in the form of ash).

According to the EPA, in *Advancing Sustainable Materials Management: Facts and Figures 2013*, WTE facilities operating in the United States incinerated 32.7 million tons (29.6 million t) of MSW in 2013. This represented 12.9% of the total MSW generated that year. (See Figure 6.6.) The U.S. Department of Energy reports in *Monthly Energy Review: October 2015* (October 27, 2015, http://www.eia.gov/totalenergy/data/monthly/pdf/ mer.pdf) that 0.49 quadrillion British thermal units of waste-derived energy were consumed in the United States in 2014. This was about 0.5% of the nation's total energy consumption of 98.5 quadrillion British thermal units.

MSW INCINERATION EMISSIONS. Incineration of MSW fell into disfavor during the 1980s because of concerns about air emissions from the combustion process. These emissions can include mercury and other heavy metals and acid gases (such as hydrochloric acid)

FIGURE 6.8

Waste combustion plant with pollution control system

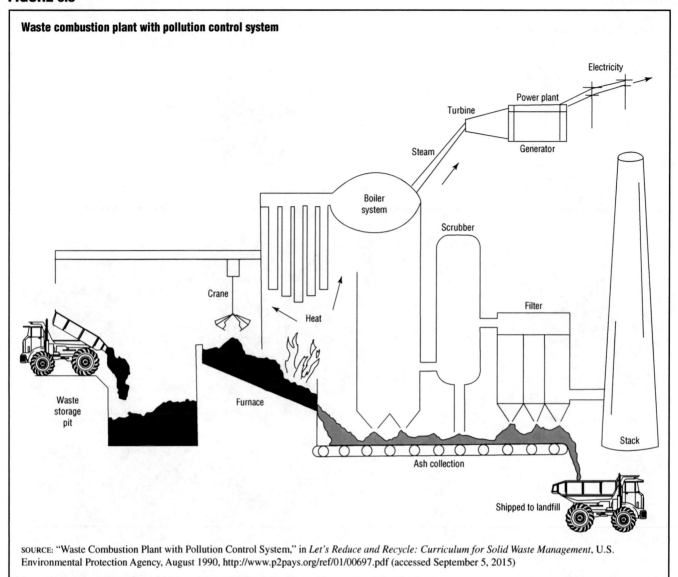

SOURCE: "Waste Combustion Plant with Pollution Control System," in *Let's Reduce and Recycle: Curriculum for Solid Waste Management*, U.S. Environmental Protection Agency, August 1990, http://www.p2pays.org/ref/01/00697.pdf (accessed September 5, 2015)

from the burning of paints, lightbulbs, electronics, and so on. Chlorine-containing chemicals within MSW are of particular concern, because their combustion can produce dioxins and furans, two groups of complex organic and toxic compounds. WTE facilities are required to use air pollution control equipment to reduce the emissions of toxic chemicals.

THE FEDERAL ROLE IN MSW MANAGEMENT

The federal government plays a key role in waste management. Its legislation has established landfill standards under the RCRA and incinerator and landfill emissions standards under the Clean Air Act.

Some waste management laws have been controversial, resulting in legal challenges. Consequently, the federal government has also had an effect on waste management programs through federal court rulings. In a series of rulings, including Supreme Court decisions such as

Chemical Waste Management v. Hunt, federal courts have held that shipments of waste are protected under the interstate commerce clause of the U.S. Constitution. As a result, state and local governments may not prohibit landfills from accepting waste from other states, nor may they impose fees on waste disposal that discriminate on the basis of origin.

Flow-Control Laws

Flow-control laws require private waste collectors to dispose of their waste in specific landfills. State and local governments institute these laws to guarantee that any new landfill they build will be used. This way, when they sell bonds to get the money to build a new landfill, the bond purchasers will not worry that they will not be repaid. In 1994 the Supreme Court held in *C & A Carbone Inc. v. Clarkstown* (511 U.S. 383) that flow-control laws violate the interstate commerce clause. However, since that time the courts have carved out various exceptions for specific circumstances. For example, in 2007 in *United Haulers Association, Inc., v. Oneida-Herkimer Solid Waste Management Authority* (550 U.S. 330), the U.S. Supreme Court upheld a local flow-control ordinance in New York. Local governments have strongly pushed for the restoration of full flow-control authority. They have appealed to Congress, which has the authority to regulate interstate commerce, to restore the use of flow control. As of November 2015, bills proposed to grant full flow control to local governments had failed to pass.

CHAPTER 7
NONHAZARDOUS MATERIALS RECOVERY:
RECYCLING AND COMPOSTING

Materials recovery is considered one of the most promising ways to reduce the amount of nonhazardous waste requiring disposal. The terms *recovery* and *recycling* are often used interchangeably. Both mean that a waste material is being reused rather than put in a landfill or incinerated. In general, reuse as a fuel does not fall under the definition of recovery, whereas composting does.

Recycling involves the sorting, collecting, and processing of wastes such as paper, glass, plastic, and metals, which are then refashioned or incorporated into new marketable products. Composting is the decomposition of organic wastes, such as food scraps and yard trimmings, in a manner that produces a humuslike substance for fertilizer or mulch.

Waste recovery offers many advantages. It conserves energy otherwise used to incinerate the waste; reduces the amount of landfill space needed for the disposal of waste; reduces possible environmental pollution because of waste disposal; generates jobs and small-scale enterprises; reduces dependence on foreign imports of raw materials; and replaces some chemical fertilizers with composting material, which further lessens possible environmental pollution. However, recycling sometimes requires more energy and water consumption than waste disposal. It depends on how far the materials must be transported and what is necessary to clean them before they can be reused. Demand for some recyclable materials is weak, making them economically unfeasible to recycle in a market-driven society.

Many Americans view waste recovery primarily as a way to help the environment. For example, if paper is recycled, fewer trees have to be cut down to make paper. State and local governments see recycling as a way to save money on waste disposal costs and prolong the life of landfill space. Thus, waste recovery has both environmental and economic components.

INDUSTRIAL WASTE RECOVERY

As noted in Chapter 6, industrial waste is believed to be the largest nonhazardous waste stream generated in the United States. It is produced by various sources including industrial facilities (e.g., factories), mines, power plants, and water and sewage treatment plants.

Industrial wastes can be recycled either within a facility or between facilities and/or companies. The use of wastes from one facility as raw materials at another facility is called by-product synergy. Examples include the recycling of industrial wastewaters, such as process rinse waters, cooling water, and scrubber water. Reuse often requires sophisticated treatment technologies to cleanse wastewaters of impurities. These technologies produce wastes, typically sludges, that contain the concentrated impurities stripped from the wastewaters. Nontoxic, industrial wastewater sludges can themselves be reused, for example, in agricultural applications or construction materials.

By-product synergy is enhanced by materials exchange services that are operated throughout the country. For example, the Materials Innovation Exchange (http://www.materialsinnovationexchange.com) facilitates by-product synergy in the Pacific Northwest and is run by the Network for Business Innovation and Sustainability, a private organization. As of November 2015, the exchange listed a variety of wastes including chemicals, packaging materials, plastics, rubber, wood products, and industrial machinery.

The Industrial Resources Council (2015, http://www.industrialresourcescouncil.org/AboutUs/tabid/360/Default.aspx), an industry organization, reports that its member industries (power generation, metal casting, steel manufacturing, construction, rubber manufacturing, and pulp and paper manufacturing) produce more than 600 million tons (544 million t) of materials annually.

These industries are particularly interested in recycling the following products:

- Coal combustion residuals—ash, boiler slag (molten ash that crystallizes as it cools), and fine solid materials collected in flue gas treatment equipment can be reused in cement and concrete production or as a filler or solidifier. (See Table 7.1 for examples of reuses.)

- Construction and demolition (C&D) wastes—wastes resulting from the construction, renovation, and demolition of buildings, roads, and bridges. Typical C&D wastes include concrete, wood, asphalt, drywall, metals, bricks, glass, and cleared trees, stumps, and earth. Figure 7.1 shows building components and materials with a high recovery potential that are typically found in buildings. C&D debris from roads, bridges, and similar infrastructures is also reusable. (See Table 7.1 for examples of reuses.)

- Foundry sand—sand used in the manufacturing of metal parts produced in molds eventually becomes degraded and can be reused in engineering applications, such as embankments, or as a component of commercially available topsoil. (See Table 7.1 for examples of reuses.)

- Metal slags—mixtures of minerals and other impurities separated from metals during melting and cooled to form glassy granules that can be ground into a powder and reused, for example, in cement and concrete.

- Pulp and paper processing residuals—sludges containing wood fibers and minerals and other pulping liquors and residues can be used as soil amendments (e.g., fertilizers) or as cover materials at landfills.

- Scrap tires—because of their high petroleum content, scrap tires are widely combusted in waste-to-energy facilities. Scrap tires are also reused in civil engineering applications, such as roads and landfills, septic tank leach fields, and other construction projects. In addition, ground rubber from scrap tires is used to produce new rubber products and as a surface material at playgrounds and sports arenas, such as running tracks.

Organic by-products encompass a variety of carbon-containing materials from agricultural, commercial, industrial, municipal, and residential sources. (See Table 7.2.) Wastes with high organic contents can be recycled, most commonly through soil-enrichment applications. Mulch, compost, and soil amendments are typical uses of organic by-products. One of the largest waste streams is biosolids, which are wastewater treatment sludges from municipal (sewage) plants or industrial facilities with organic-based processes, such as pulp and paper mills. Whatever their source, organic by-products usually require some type of treatment or processing before they can be reused.

TABLE 7.1

Industrial materials that can be recycled

Coal combustion products	**Can be recycled in**
• Fly and bottom ash	• Portland cement and concrete
• Boiler slag	• Flowable and structural fill
• Flue gas desulfurization material	• Wallboard
Construction and demolition debris	**Can be recycled in**
• Concrete gypsum from drywall	• Asphalt paving
• Metals	• Concrete
• Bricks	• Re-milled lumber
• Asphalt from roads and roofing shingles	• Wallboard
• Wood from buildings	
Foundry sand	**Can be recycled in**
• Spent sand used in metal casting	• Road embankments
	• Flowable and structural fill
	• Base and sub-base for road construction

SOURCE: "Industrial Materials," in *Industrial Materials Recycling: Managing Resources for Tomorrow*, U.S. Environmental Protection Agency, Office of Solid Waste and Emergency Response, January 2007, http://www.epa.gov/wastes/conserve/imr/pdfs/ind-mat.pdf (accessed September 7, 2015)

STRIVING FOR "ZERO WASTE"

Some businesses strive to generate no waste that requires land disposal or incineration. This "zero waste" goal is espoused by various organizations. For example, the U.S. Zero Waste Business Council (http://www.uszwbc.org/about-uszwbc/uszwbc-guiding-principles) notes, "Zero Waste means designing and managing products and processes to systematically avoid and eliminate the volume and toxicity of waste and materials, conserve and recover all resources, and not burn or bury them." The private organization operates a certification program that recognizes businesses or communities that achieve greater than 90% diversion of wastes "from landfills, incinerators and the environment." As of November 2015, the council (http://www.uszwbc.org/certification/facilities/certified-facilities) indicates that specific facilities of 11 companies had met the certification requirements. The businesses included Disneyland, Fetzer Vineyards, Raytheon, Sierra Nevada Brewing, and Whole Foods Markets. In "Northrop Grumman Facility Recognized for Leading Waste Diversion Efforts" (AVTimes.com, September 9, 2015), Jim E. Winburn notes that a Northrop Grumman facility in Palmdale, California, was certified by the council in September 2015. The company is an aerospace producer and manufacturer. According to Winburn, the facility achieved greater than 90% waste diversion by creating reusable containers for its airplane parts and by hiring a company to sort and manage its waste materials for recycling.

MUNICIPAL SOLID WASTE RECOVERY

Municipal solid waste (MSW) is the everyday garbage produced by homes and businesses. As described in Chapter 6, the U.S. Environmental Protection Agency (EPA) conducts detailed estimates on the generation

FIGURE 7.1

Reuse of industrial materials in building construction

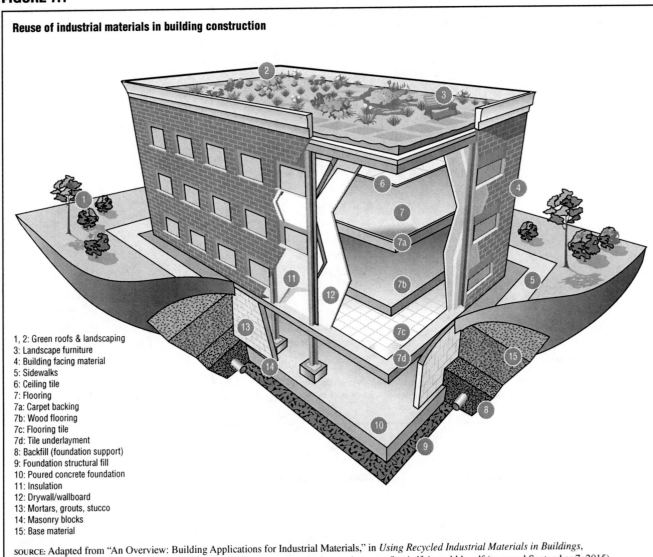

1, 2: Green roofs & landscaping
3: Landscape furniture
4: Building facing material
5: Sidewalks
6: Ceiling tile
7: Flooring
7a: Carpet backing
7b: Wood flooring
7c: Flooring tile
7d: Tile underlayment
8: Backfill (foundation support)
9: Foundation structural fill
10: Poured concrete foundation
11: Insulation
12: Drywall/wallboard
13: Mortars, grouts, stucco
14: Masonry blocks
15: Base material

SOURCE: Adapted from "An Overview: Building Applications for Industrial Materials," in *Using Recycled Industrial Materials in Buildings*, U.S. Environmental Protection Agency, October 2008, http://www.epa.gov/wastes/conserve/imr/pdfs/recy-bldg.pdf (accessed September 7, 2015)

TABLE 7.2

Organic by-products

Animal manure and bedding
Biosolids
Food processing residuals (fruit and vegetable peelings, pulp, pits)
Food scraps
Hatchery wastes
Meat, seafood, poultry and dairy processing wastewater and solids
Mixed refuse (food scraps, paper etc.)
Pharmaceutical and brewery waste
Pulp and paper mill residues
Spent mushroom substrate
Textile residuals
Waste grain, silage
Wood ash
Yardwaste (leaves, grass clippings, woodchips)

SOURCE: Adapted from "Other Organic By-Products," in *Guide to Field Storage of Biosolids*, U.S. Environmental Protection Agency, July 2000, http://water.epa.gov/scitech/wastetech/biosolids/upload/2002_06_28_mtb_biosolids_fsguide_chapter7.pdf (accessed September 7, 2015)

and recovery of this nonhazardous waste stream. The most recent estimates are provided in *Advancing Sustainable Materials Management: Facts and Figures 2013* (September 2015, http://www.epa.gov/wastes/non haz/municipal/pubs/2013_advncng_smm_rpt.pdf), which includes data through 2013. The EPA reports that Americans recycled 87.2 million tons (79.1 million t) of MSW in 2013, accounting for 34.3% of the total MSW generated. (See Figure 7.2.) The recycle rate has more than doubled since 1990, when it stood at 6.4%.

Table 7.3 shows the recycling rates for various components making up the MSW stream in 2013. Overall, paper and paperboard had the highest rate (63.3%), followed by yard trimmings (60.2%). By contrast, recovery rates were low for food wastes and other organic by-products suitable for composting (5%) and plastics (9.2%). Table 7.4 breaks down the MSW stream for 2013 by product category. The highest recovery rate

FIGURE 7.2

Recycling rates for municipal solid waste, 1960–2013

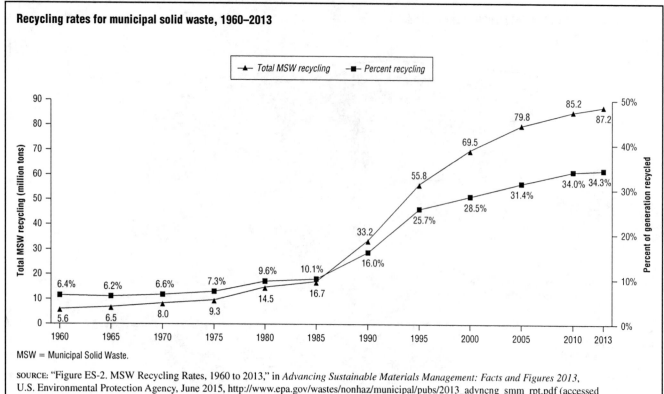

MSW = Municipal Solid Waste.

SOURCE: "Figure ES-2. MSW Recycling Rates, 1960 to 2013," in *Advancing Sustainable Materials Management: Facts and Figures 2013*, U.S. Environmental Protection Agency, June 2015, http://www.epa.gov/wastes/nonhaz/municipal/pubs/2013_advncng_smm_rpt.pdf (accessed September 4, 2015)

TABLE 7.3

Generation, recovery, and discards of materials in municipal solid waste, 2013

Material	Weight generated	Weight recovered	Recovery as percent of generation	Weight discarded
Paper and paperboard	68.60	43.40	63.3%	25.20
Glass	11.54	3.15	27.3%	8.39
Metals				
Steel	17.55	5.80	33.0%	11.75
Aluminum	3.50	0.70	20.0%	2.80
Other nonferrous metals[a]	2.01	1.37	68.2%	0.64
Total metals	**23.06**	**7.87**	**34.1%**	**15.19**
Plastics	32.52	3.00	9.2%	29.52
Rubber and leather	7.72	1.24	16.1%	6.48
Textiles	15.13	2.30	15.2%	12.83
Wood	15.77	2.47	15.7%	13.30
Other materials	4.58	1.31	28.6%	3.27
Total materials in products	**178.92**	**64.74**	**36.2%**	**114.18**
Other wastes				
Food, other[b]	37.06	1.84	5.0%	35.22
Yard trimmings	34.20	20.60	60.2%	13.60
Miscellaneous inorganic wastes	3.93	Negligible	Negligible	3.93
Total other wastes	**75.19**	**22.44**	**29.8%**	**52.75**
Total municipal solid waste	**254.11**	**87.18**	**34.3%**	**166.93**

[a]Includes lead from lead-acid batteries.
[b]Includes recovery of other MSW organics for composting.
Details might not add to totals due to rounding. Negligible = Less than 5,000 tons or 0.05 percent.
Note: Includes waste from residential, commercial, and institutional sources.

SOURCE: "Table ES-2. Generation, Recovery, and Discards of Materials in MSW, 2013," in *Advancing Sustainable Materials Management: Facts and Figures 2013*, U.S. Environmental Protection Agency, June 2015, http://www.epa.gov/wastes/nonhaz/municipal/pubs/2013_advncng_smm_rpt.pdf (accessed September 4, 2015)

TABLE 7.4

Generation, recovery, and discards of materials in municipal solid waste, by category, 2013

[In millions of tons and percent of generation of each product]

Products	Weight generated	Weight recovered	Recovery as percent of generation	Weight discarded
Durable goods				
Steel	15.15	4.06	26.8%	11.09
Aluminum	1.51	Not available	Not available	1.51
Other non-ferrous metals†	2.01	1.37	68.2%	0.64
Glass	2.28	Negligible	Negligible	2.28
Plastics	12.07	0.83	6.9%	11.24
Rubber and leather	6.66	1.24	18.6%	5.42
Wood	6.31	Negligible	Negligible	6.31
Textiles	3.86	0.47	12.2%	3.39
Other materials	1.70	1.31	77.5%	0.39
Total durable goods	**51.55**	**9.28**	**18.0%**	**42.27**
Nondurable goods				
Paper and paperboard	30.03	14.45	48.1%	15.58
Plastics	6.47	0.13	2.0%	6.34
Rubber and leather	1.06	Negligible	Negligible	1.06
Textiles	10.96	1.83	16.7%	9.13
Other materials	3.08	Negligible	Negligible	3.08
Total nondurable goods	**51.60**	**16.41**	**31.8%**	**35.19**
Containers and packaging				
Steel	2.40	1.74	72.5%	0.66
Aluminum	1.80	0.70	38.9%	1.10
Glass	9.26	3.15	34.0%	6.11
Paper and paperboard	38.56	28.95	75.1%	9.61
Plastics	13.98	2.04	14.6%	11.94
Wood	9.46	2.47	26.1%	6.99
Other materials	0.31	Negligible	Negligible	0.31
Total containers and packaging	**75.77**	**39.05**	**51.5%**	**36.72**
Other wastes				
Food, other‡	37.06	1.84	5.0%	35.22
Yard trimmings	34.20	20.60	60.2%	13.60
Miscellaneous inorganic wastes	3.93	Negligible	Negligible	3.93
Total other wastes	**75.19**	**22.44**	**29.8%**	**52.75**
Total municipal solid waste	**254.11**	**87.18**	**34.3%**	**166.93**

Includes waste from residential, commercial, and institutional sources.
†Includes lead from lead-acid batteries.
‡Includes recovery of other MSW organics for composting.
Details might not add to totals due to rounding. Negligible = less than 5,000 tons or 0.05 percent.

SOURCE: "Table ES-3. Generation, Recovery, and Discards of Products in MSW by Material, 2013," in *Advancing Sustainable Materials Management: Facts and Figures 2013*, U.S. Environmental Protection Agency, June 2015, http://www.epa.gov/wastes/nonhaz/municipal/pubs/2013_advncng_smm_rpt.pdf (accessed September 4, 2015)

(51.5%) was for containers and packaging. This was followed by nondurable goods (31.8%), other wastes— food, yard trimmings, and miscellaneous inorganic wastes (29.8%), and durable goods (18%).

Figure 7.3 compares the recycling rates of selected products in the MSW stream in 2013. Nearly all lead-acid batteries (99%), which are used in automobiles, were recycled. Other products with relatively high recovery rates were steel cans (70.6%), newspapers and mechanical papers (67%), yard trimmings (60.2%), and aluminum beer and soda cans (55.1%).

Paper

The paper industry has been at the leading edge of the recycling revolution. Used paper-based products can

be de-inked in chemical baths and reduced to a fibrous slurry that can be reformulated into new paper products. Paper can undergo this process several times before the fibers become too damaged for reuse. Paper products vary greatly in the type (hardwood versus softwood) and length of fibers that are used to make them. Recycled papers must typically be sorted into particular usage categories (e.g., newsprint or fine writing papers) before being reprocessed.

Table 7.5 shows EPA estimates of the tons of paper (and paperboard) products recovered in selected years between 1960 and 2013. Overall, the recovery rate in 2013 was 63.3%. By contrast, only about 17% of paper and paperboard was recovered in 1960.

FIGURE 7.3

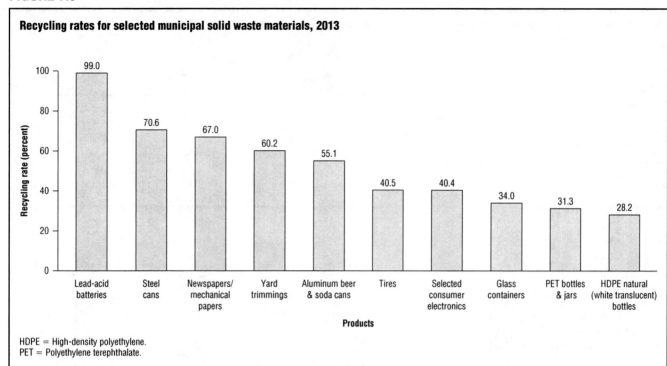

Recycling rates for selected municipal solid waste materials, 2013

HDPE = High-density polyethylene.
PET = Polyethylene terephthalate.

SOURCE: "Figure 3. Recycling Rates of Selected Products, 2013," in *Advancing Sustainable Materials Management: 2013 Fact Sheet*, U.S. Environmental Protection Agency, June 2015, http://www.epa.gov/wastes/nonhaz/municipal/pubs/2013_advncng_smm_fs.pdf (accessed September 4, 2015)

Glass

Waste glass can be melted down and formed into new glass products over and over without losing its structural integrity. Virgin raw materials, such as sand, limestone, and soda ash, are added as needed to formulate new glass products. However, colored glass cannot be easily decolorized, as paper is de-inked. This means that glass products must be sorted by color before reprocessing.

Table 7.5 shows EPA estimates of the tons of glass products recovered in selected years between 1960 and 2013. Most glass that becomes MSW is from bottles and jars that are manufactured for food and drink products. Glass recovery increased throughout the 1980s and early 1990s and then leveled off between 2 million and 4 million tons (1.8 million to 3.6 million t) per year. The recovery rate for glass in 2013 was 27.3%. This compares with a 1.5% recovery rate in 1960.

Metals

Table 7.5 shows EPA estimates of the tons of metal products recovered in selected years between 1960 and 2013. Ferrous metals (iron and steel) are primarily used in durable goods such as appliances, furniture, and tires. Aluminum is used extensively in drink and food cans and packaging materials. Lead, zinc, and copper fall under the category "other nonferrous metals." They are found in batteries, appliances, and consumer electronics.

Metals recovery was relatively flat until the mid-1980s, when it began increasing dramatically. (See Table 7.5.) Recovery leveled off during the latter part of the first decade of the 21st century. Recovery rates differed greatly from metal to metal in 2013. About two-thirds (68.2%) of other nonferrous metals in the MSW stream were recovered, compared with only 33% of ferrous and 20% of aluminum. In 1960 metals recovery was virtually nonexistent.

Plastics

Plastic products are manufactured from chemical resins that are molded into various shapes. There are dozens of resins in common use, each with a different chemical formulation. Although waste plastic products can be melted down and reformulated into new products, sorting by resin type must first be performed.

As shown in Figure 6.4 in Chapter 6, in 1960 there were virtually no plastic products in MSW. In 2013 the MSW stream contained 32.5 million tons (29.5 million t) of plastic products. This massive increase in generation has been accompanied by low rates of recovery. Only 9.2% of all plastic products generated in MSW in 2013 were recovered. (See Table 7.5.)

Consumer Electronics

Computers and other electronic devices contain materials that are valuable for reuse, particularly metals, plastics, and glass. The most common metals in personal

TABLE 7.5

Recovery of municipal solid waste, by material, selected years 1960–2013

[In thousands of tons and percent of generation of each material]

Materials	1960	1970	1980	1990	2000	2005	2009	2011	2012	2013
					Thousands of tons					
Paper and paperboard	5,080	6,770	11,740	20,230	37,560	41,960	42,500	45,900	44,360	43,400
Glass	100	160	750	2,630	2,880	2,590	3,000	3,180	3,210	3,150
Metals										
Ferrous	50	150	370	2,230	4,680	5,020	5,330	5,450	5,530	5,800
Aluminum	Neg.	10	310	1,010	860	690	690	720	710	700
Other nonferrous	Neg.	320	540	730	1,060	1,280	1,380	1,430	1,390	1,370
Total metals	**50**	**480**	**1,220**	**3,970**	**6,600**	**6,990**	**7,400**	**7,600**	**7,630**	**7,870**
Plastics	Neg.	Neg.	20	370	1,480	1,780	2,130	2,660	2,800	3,000
Rubber and leather	330	250	130	370	820	1,050	1,370	1,330	1,270	1,240
Textiles	50	60	160	660	1,320	1,830	1,980	2,010	2,230	2,300
Wood	Neg.	Neg.	Neg.	130	1,370	1,830	2,200	2,350	2,410	2,470
Other**	Neg.	300	500	680	980	1,210	1,310	1,370	1,330	1,310
Total materials in products	**5,610**	**8,020**	**14,520**	**29,040**	**53,010**	**59,240**	**61,890**	**66,400**	**65,240**	**64,740**
Other wastes										
Food	Neg.	Neg.	Neg.	Neg.	680	690	850	1,270	1,740	1,840
Yard trimmings	Neg.	Neg.	Neg.	4,200	15,770	19,860	19,900	19,300	19,590	20,600
Miscellaneous inorganic wastes	Neg.	Neg.	Neg.	Neg.	Neg.	Neg.	Neg.	Neg.	Neg.	Neg.
Total other wastes	**Neg.**	**Neg.**	**Neg.**	**4,200**	**16,450**	**20,550**	**20,750**	**20,570**	**21,330**	**22,440**
Total MSW recovered—weight	**5,610**	**8,020**	**14,520**	**33,240**	**69,460**	**79,790**	**82,640**	**86,970**	**86,570**	**87,180**
					Percent of generation of each material					
Paper and paperboard	16.9%	15.3%	21.3%	27.8%	42.8%	49.5%	62.1%	65.6%	64.6%	63.3%
Glass	1.5%	1.3%	5.0%	20.1%	22.6%	20.7%	25.5%	27.7%	27.7%	27.3%
Metals										
Ferrous	0.5%	1.2%	2.9%	17.6%	33.1%	33.0%	33.5%	33.0%	32.9%	33.0%
Aluminum	Neg.	1.3%	17.9%	35.9%	27.0%	20.7%	20.1%	20.5%	20.2%	20.0%
Other nonferrous	Neg.	47.8%	46.6%	66.4%	66.3%	68.8%	71.5%	70.8%	70.2%	68.2%
Total metals	**0.5%**	**3.5%**	**7.9%**	**24.0%**	**34.8%**	**34.3%**	**34.8%**	**34.4%**	**34.2%**	**34.1%**
Plastics	Neg.	Neg.	0.3%	2.2%	5.8%	6.1%	7.1%	8.3%	8.8%	9.2%
Rubber and leather	17.9%	8.4%	3.1%	6.4%	12.3%	14.4%	18.3%	17.5%	16.8%	16.1%
Textiles	2.8%	2.9%	6.3%	11.4%	13.9%	15.9%	15.2%	15.3%	15.6%	15.2%
Wood	Neg.	Neg.	Neg.	1.1%	10.1%	12.4%	14.1%	14.9%	15.2%	15.7%
Other**	Neg.	39.0%	19.8%	21.3%	24.5%	28.2%	28.0%	29.5%	29.0%	28.6%
Total materials in products	**10.3%**	**9.6%**	**13.3%**	**19.8%**	**29.7%**	**32.0%**	**35.9%**	**37.6%**	**36.9%**	**36.2%**
Other wastes										
Food, other[a]	Neg.	Neg.	Neg.	Neg.	2.2%	2.1%	2.4%	3.5%	4.8%	5.0%
Yard trimmings	Neg.	Neg.	Neg.	12.0%	51.7%	61.9%	59.9%	57.3%	57.7%	60.2%
Miscellaneous inorganic wastes	Neg.	Neg.	Neg.	Neg.	Neg.	Neg.	Neg.	Neg.	Neg.	Neg.
Total other wastes	**Neg.**	**Neg.**	**Neg.**	**6.8%**	**25.4%**	**29.9%**	**28.7%**	**27.8%**	**28.7%**	**29.8%**
Total MSW recovered—(%)	**6.4%**	**6.6%**	**9.6%**	**16.0%**	**28.5%**	**31.4%**	**33.8%**	**34.7%**	**34.5%**	**34.3%**

*Recovery of postconsumer wastes; does not include converting/fabrication scrap.
**Recovery of electrolytes in batteries; probably not recycled.
Neg = Less than 5,000 tons or 0.05 percent.
[a]Includes recovery of paper and mixed MSW for composting.
Details may not add to totals due to rounding.

SOURCE: "Table 2. Recovery of Municipal Solid Waste, 1960 to 2013," in *Advancing Sustainable Materials Management: Facts and Figures 2013*, U.S. Environmental Protection Agency, June 2015, http://www.epa.gov/wastes/nonhaz/municipal/pubs/2013_advncng_smm_rpt.pdf (accessed September 4, 2015)

computers are aluminum, steel, and copper. Small amounts of precious metals, such as gold, palladium, platinum, and silver, are also found in computer circuit boards. Some of the metals used in personal computers (antimony, arsenic, cadmium, chromium, cobalt, lead, mercury, and selenium) are classified as hazardous by the Resource Conservation and Recovery Act and cannot be disposed of in MSW landfills. This is discussed further in Chapter 8.

The primary source of plastics in electronic devices is computer casings. Plastic can be melted down to produce new materials or used as a fuel in certain industrial processes. Most of the glass content of computers is in monitors, both the older types containing cathode-ray tubes (CRTs) and the newer liquid crystal display (LCD) and light-emitting diode (LED) monitors. CRT glass contains lead, which is a hazardous material. Likewise, older LCD monitors contain mercury, another hazardous material; however, many newer models are mercury free. LED monitors contain neither mercury nor lead. LCD and LED monitors and television screens pose their own recycling challenges, however, mainly because they contain very thin layers of materials that are difficult to separate.

The EPA reports in *Advancing Sustainable Materials Management: Facts and Figures 2013* that 3.1 million tons (2.8 million t) of consumer electronic products entered the MSW stream in 2013. This included selected products, such as televisions, compact disc and digital videodisc players, video cameras, stereo systems, telephones, and computer equipment. Nearly 1.3 million tons (1.2 million t) were recovered for recycling, providing a recycling rate of 40.4%. (See Figure 7.3.) The electronic recycling rate was only 10% in 2000; thus, the rate more than quadrupled during the following 13 years.

The EPA's Sustainable Materials Management Electronics Challenge program (2015, http://www.epa.gov/epawaste/conserve/smm/electronics/index.htm) is a partnership between the agency and consumer companies that manufacture and/or sell electronic goods and companies that provide mobile services, such as cell phone service. Participants in the program offer the public various opportunities for dropping off or mailing in unwanted electronic products. These products are typically reused, refurbished, or have their valuable components (e.g., gold, lead, or copper) recovered. This reduces the amount of electronic waste requiring disposal and decreases the risks from heavy metals and other toxic chemicals within the products leaching into the environment after disposal.

The electronics challenge program encourages manufacturers to use reverse supply chain methods to reduce MSW generation. A supply chain is the series of activities and feedstocks that go into manufacturing a final product. In "The Reverse Supply Chain" (HBR.org, February 2002), V. Daniel R. Guide Jr. and Luk N. Van Wassenhove define the reverse supply chain as "the series of activities required to retrieve a used product from a customer and either dispose of it or reuse it." High consumer demand for electronic products makes them particularly attractive candidates for reverse supply chain methods that result in reusable products. For example, cell phone and computer manufacturers acquire used products and refurbish them for resale. Guide and Wassenhove note that these companies "target customers who cannot afford the new products but who would jump at the chance to buy used versions at lower prices."

MSW Recycling Programs

The successful recycling of any product within MSW depends on the success of three key components in the recycling process:

- Collection and sorting of the products to be recycled
- Processing and manufacturing technologies to convert waste materials into new products
- Consumer demand for recycled products and those containing recycled materials

Lack of any one of these components seriously jeopardizes recovery efforts for a particular material within the MSW stream. The following discussion is based on information provided by the EPA in *Advancing Sustainable Materials Management: Facts and Figures 2013*.

CURBSIDE PROGRAMS. Curbside programs are those in which recyclable items are collected from bins placed outside residences. According to the EPA, an industry study in 2011 found there were more than 9,800 curbside recycling collection programs in the United States that year. Overall, 70% of the U.S. population had access to curbside recycling programs.

Some municipalities offer reward programs to encourage curbside recycling. These programs typically provide residents with points based on the number of pounds of materials they place in their recycling bins for curbside pickup. The points can be redeemed for items such as gift certificates to restaurants or stores.

Drop-off centers for recyclable materials are operated by various entities, including cities, grocery stores, charitable organizations, and apartment complexes. Typically, they accept a broader range of materials than curbside collection programs. The EPA notes that the American Forest and Paper Association estimated in 2010 that more than 21,000 U.S. communities had drop-off centers.

Buy-Back Centers and Deposit Systems

Two systems provide a cash incentive to encourage recycling. These are buy-back centers and deposit programs. Buy-back centers are typically businesses that pay cash for recovered materials, such as scrap metal, aluminum cans, or paper.

Deposit programs charge consumers a deposit or fee on beverage containers at the time of purchase, ranging typically from 5 cents to 10 cents per container. The deposit can be redeemed if the container is returned empty for reuse. The EPA reports that in 2011 there were 10 states operating deposit-type programs: California, Connecticut, Hawaii, Iowa, Maine, Massachusetts, Michigan, New York, Oregon, and Vermont. Deposit amounts vary by state.

Materials Recovery Facilities

Materials recovery facilities (MRFs) sort collected recyclables, process them, and ship them to companies that can use them to produce new or reformulated products.

For example, an MRF may sort and crush various types of glass recovered from curbside programs and then ship the processed glass to a bottle factory, where it can be used to produce new bottles.

The EPA notes that in 2013 there were 797 MRFs operating in the United States, which processed more than 140,000 tons (127,006 t) of materials per day.

COMMERCIAL RECYCLABLES COLLECTION. According to the EPA, commercial establishments are responsible for the largest quantity of MSW recycled in the United States. The most commonly recycled materials in the business sector are old corrugated containers and office papers. Grocery stores and other retail outlets are the primary recyclers of old corrugated containers, which are typically picked up by paper dealers. Likewise, many businesses collect used office paper, which they turn over to paper dealers.

The Role of Government in MSW Recycling

The oldest recycling law in the United States is the Oregon Recycling Opportunity Act, which was passed in 1983 and went into effect in 1986. The act established curbside residential recycling opportunities in large cities and set up drop-off depots in small towns and rural areas. A growing number of states require that many consumer goods sold must be made from recycled products. In addition, many states have set recycling/recovery goals for their municipal waste.

For recycling programs to work, there must be markets for recycled products. To help create demand, some states require that newspaper publishers use a minimum proportion of recycled paper. Many states require that recycled materials be used in making products such as telephone directories, trash bags, glass, and plastic containers. All states have some kind of "buy recycled" program that requires them to purchase recycled products when possible.

The states also use other incentives for recycling. Some states provide financial assistance, incentive money, or tax credits or exemptions for recycling businesses. Furthermore, almost all states bar certain recyclable materials (such as car and boat batteries, grass cuttings, tires, used motor oil, glass, plastic containers, and newspapers) from entering their landfills.

The federal government helps create a market for recycled goods as well. The Resource Conservation and Recovery Act requires federal procuring agencies to purchase recycled-content products that are designated by the EPA in its overall Comprehensive Procurement Guidelines (CPG; http://www.epa.gov/epawaste/conserve/tools/cpg/index.htm). EPA guidance regarding the purchase of recycled-content products is also included in the Recovered Materials Advisory Notices, which are published periodically and include recommended recycled-content ranges for CPG products that are commercially available.

The EPA also has created a computer model that can calculate the environmental benefits of recycling in terms of reduced emissions of greenhouse gases (GHG). As is explained in Chapter 3, emissions of GHG, such as carbon dioxide and methane, into the atmosphere are believed to be contributing to global warming and associated climate change. These emissions are primarily associated with the combustion of fossil fuels in power plants and transportation vehicles. In *Advancing Sustainable Materials Management: Facts and Figures 2013* the EPA notes that its Waste Reduction Model compares GHG emissions for various waste management practices. Table 7.6 shows the calculated benefits for 2013 from recovering (rather than landfilling or incinerating) various MSW components. For example, the recovery of 43 million tons (39 million t) of paper and paperboard resulted in a GHG benefit of 149 million metric tons of carbon dioxide equivalent. This was equivalent to taking 31 million cars (and hence their emissions) off the road. According to the EPA, the total 87 million tons (78.9 million t) of MSW that was recovered during 2013 equated to a reduction of more than 186 million metric tons of carbon dioxide equivalent. This was comparable to removing more than 39 million passenger vehicles from the road.

THE HISTORY AND CURRENT STRENGTH OF MSW RECYCLING

As with any business, recycling is subject to the cyclical highs and lows of supply and demand. During the early years of recycling the economy was unable to use all the plastic, paper, and other materials that were recovered. It was difficult for private recycling companies to make a profit. Instead of earning money from recycling, the programs cost them money. Some cities even started dumping their recycled materials into landfills because they could not sell them. Eventually, markets grew for some recycled materials, particularly in the paper sector. Market growth has been helped by the widespread public support that recycling receives.

Figure 7.4 shows that the recovery of materials in MSW grew dramatically during the 1990s compared with previous decades. After 2000, however, the proportion of recovered MSW grew much more slowly. Some analysts believe recycling rates for MSW have reached a plateau and cannot easily be increased because of the supply-and-demand imbalance in recycled-content markets. They prefer to focus on source reduction (the reduction of the amount of municipal waste produced originally).

One method for reducing MSW generation is a principle called extended producer responsibility (EPR). EPR regulations require manufacturers and producers to take some responsibility for the final disposition of their products. This

TABLE 7.6

Greenhouse gas benefits associated with recovery of specific municipal solid waste materials, 2013

[In millions of tons, MMTCO₂E and in numbers of cars taken off the road per year]

Material	Weight recovered (millions of tons)	GHG benefits MMTCO₂E	Numbers of cars taken off the road per year
Paper and paperboard	43.00	149.00	31 million
Glass	3.20	1.00	210 thousand
Metals			
Steel	5.80	9.50	2 million
Aluminum	0.70	6.40	1.3 million
Other nonferrous metals[†]	1.37	5.90	1.2 million
Total metals	**7.87**	**21.80**	**4.5 million**
Plastics	3.00	3.60	760 thousand
Rubber and leather[‡]	1.24	0.60	127 thousand
Textiles	2.30	5.80	1.2 million
Wood	2.47	3.80	798 thousand
Other wastes			
Food, other[a]	1.84	1.70	308 thousand
Yard trimmings	20.60	1.04	220 thousand

[†]Includes lead from lead-acid batteries. Other nonferrous metals calculated in WARM as mixed metals.
[‡]Recovery only includes rubber from tires.
[a]Includes recovery of other MSW organics for composting.
GHG = Greenhouse gas; MMT CO₂ E = Million metric tons of carbon dioxide equivalent.
Includes materials from residential, commercial, and institutional sources. These calculations do not include an additional 1.32 million tons of MSW recovered that could not be addressed in the WARM model. Recently WARM assumptions and data have been revised. MMTCO₂E is million metric tons of carbon dioxide equivalent.

SOURCE: "Table ES-4. Greenhouse Gas Benefits Associated with Recovery of Specific Materials, 2013," in *Advancing Sustainable Materials Management: Facts and Figures 2013*, U.S. Environmental Protection Agency, June 2015, http://www.epa.gov/wastes/nonhaz/municipal/pubs/2013_advncng_smm_rpt.pdf (accessed September 4, 2015)

provides an incentive for products and their packaging to be more recoverable and contain less toxic materials. EPR is a cornerstone of recycling requirements in Canada, Japan, and the European Union, and is beginning to play a larger role in the United States. The Electronics Take Back Coalition (2015, http://www.electronicstakeback.com/promote-good-laws/state-legislation) notes that as of 2015, 25 states had passed legislation mandating electronic waste recycling. For example, the New York State Department of Environmental Conservation (2015, http://www.dec.ny.gov/chemical/65583.html) indicates that New York "requires manufacturers to provide free and convenient recycling of electronic waste to most consumers in the state."

COMPOSTING

Composting is a recovery method in which plant-based waste materials are isolated and allowed to decompose, producing an organic-rich substance that is suitable for use as a soil amendment. Typical compost wastes include grass and garden cuttings, leaves, and kitchen refuse, such as potato peelings, coffee grounds, and eggshells. Meat scraps and other animal-based wastes are not recommended for composting because they can attract scavenging animals.

The natural decomposition of a pile of organic waste can be a long process. Composters can accelerate the process through a variety of techniques, including layering plant wastes with manure or soil, watering the compost, and turning or churning it with garden implements

to provide more oxygen. These methods can produce a usable compost material within a few months.

Gardeners mix compost with the soil to loosen the structure of the soil and provide it with nutrients, or spread it on top of the soil as a mulch to keep in moisture. Because compost adds nutrients to the soil, slows soil erosion, and improves water retention, it is an alternative to the use of chemical fertilizers. Compost created on a large scale is often used in landscaping, land reclamation, and landfill cover and to provide high-nutrient soil for farms and nurseries.

Yard waste is especially suitable for composting because of its high moisture content. Over the past few decades composting yard trimmings has become an accepted waste management method in many U.S. locations. The practice got a huge boost beginning in the late 1980s, when many states banned yard trimmings from disposal facilities. In *Advancing Sustainable Materials Management: Facts and Figures 2013*, the EPA states that in 2013 there were approximately 3,560 publicly operated yard-trimming composting programs in the United States. An unknown amount of backyard composting also takes place. Table 7.7 and Table 7.8 are lists compiled by the EPA of materials that can be composted and should not be composted, respectively. Some organic materials are not suitable for composting because they cause odors, attract pests, pose a threat to human health, or are harmful in some way to the environment.

FIGURE 7.4

Recovery and discards of municipal solid waste, 1960–2013

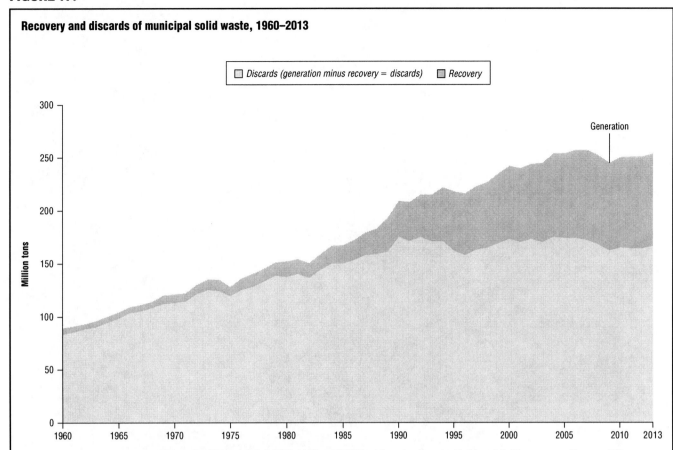

SOURCE: "Figure 11. Recovery and Discards of Materials in MSW, 1960 to 2013," in *Advancing Sustainable Materials Management: Facts and Figures 2013*, U.S. Environmental Protection Agency, June 2015, http://www.epa.gov/wastes/nonhaz/municipal/pubs/2013_advncng_smm_rpt.pdf (accessed September 4, 2015)

TABLE 7.7

Materials that can be composted

Greens:

- Uncooked or cooked fruits and vegetables
- Bread and grains
- Coffee grounds and filters
- Grass clippings
- Paper tea bags with the staple removed, if there is one.
- Hair and fur
- Chicken, rabbit, cow, horse manure

Browns:

- Cotton or wool rags
- Dryer and vacuum cleaner lint
- Eggshells
- Nut shells
- Fireplace ashes (from wood burning)
- Sawdust
- Hay and straw
- Yard trimmings (e.g., leaves, branches, twigs)
- Houseplants
- Used potting soil
- Wood chips
- Leaves
- Shredded newspaper
- Cardboard rolls
- Clean paper

SOURCE: "What to Add," in *Backyard Composting: It's Only Natural*, U.S. Environmental Protection Agency, October 2009, http://www.epa.gov/wastes/conserve/tools/greenscapes/pubs/compost-guide.pdf (accessed September 7, 2015)

TABLE 7.8

Materials that should not be composted

- Aluminum, tin or other metal
- Glass
- Dairy products (e.g., butter, milk, sour cream, yogurt) & eggs
- Fats, grease, lard, or oils
- Greasy or oily foods
- Meat or seafood scraps
- Pet wastes (e.g., dog or cat feces, soiled cat litter)
- Soiled diapers
- Plastic
- Stickers from fruits or vegetables (to prevent litter)
- Black walnut tree leaves or twigs
- Yard trimmings treated with chemical pesticides
- Roots of perennial weeds
- Coal or charcoal ash
- Firestarter logs
- Treated or painted wood

SOURCE: "What Not to Add," in *Backyard Composting: It's Only Natural*, U.S. Environmental Protection Agency, October 2009, http://www.epa.gov/wastes/conserve/tools/greenscapes/pubs/compost-guide.pdf (accessed September 7, 2015)

CHAPTER 8
HAZARDOUS AND RADIOACTIVE WASTE

The most toxic and dangerous waste materials produced in the United States are those classified by the government as hazardous or radioactive.

WHAT IS HAZARDOUS WASTE?

Hazardous waste is dangerous solid waste. The federal government's definition of solid waste includes materials one would ordinarily consider solid, as well as sludges, semisolids, liquids, and even containers of gases. The vast majority of hazardous waste is generated by industrial sources. Small amounts come from commercial and residential sources.

Officially, hazardous waste is defined by the federal government as a waste that is either listed as such in regulations issued by the U.S. Environmental Protection Agency (EPA) or that exhibits one or more of the following characteristics: corrosivity, ignitability, reactivity, or toxicity. (See Figure 8.1.) In 2015 the EPA had a list of more than 1,500 hazardous wastes. The list is published in the Code of Federal Regulations (CFR; November 3, 2015, http://www.ecfr.gov/cgi-bin/ECFR?page=browse) under Title 40, Section 261.31–33.

Because of its dangerous characteristics, hazardous waste requires special care when being stored, transported, or discarded. Most hazardous wastes are regulated under Subtitle C of the Resource Conservation and Recovery Act (RCRA). The EPA has the primary responsibility for permitting facilities that treat, store, and dispose of hazardous waste. The states can adopt more stringent regulations if they wish.

Contamination of the air, water, and soil with hazardous waste can frequently lead to serious health problems. Exposure to some hazardous wastes is believed to cause cancer, degenerative diseases, mental retardation, birth defects, and chromosomal changes. Although most scientists agree that exposure to high doses of hazardous waste is dangerous, there is less agreement on the danger of exposure to low doses.

INDUSTRIAL HAZARDOUS WASTE

Every two years since 1991 the EPA, in partnership with the states, has conducted an inventory of the nation's industrial hazardous waste. As of November 2015, the 2013 inventory had been completed, but the results had not been published in a comprehensive report. The most recent report available was published in December 2012 and included data from 2011 (http://www3.epa.gov/epawaste/inforesources/data/br11/index.htm).

As shown in Table 8.1, 34.3 million tons (31.1 million t) of RCRA hazardous waste was generated in 2011. Texas was, by far, the leading generator among the states, accounting for nearly 15.7 million tons (14.2 million t) or 45.7% of the total. The 10 industries that generated the largest amounts of hazardous waste in 2011 were:

- Basic chemical manufacturing—18.9 million tons (17.2 million t)

- Petroleum and coal products manufacturing—6.6 million tons (6 million t)

- Waste treatment and disposal—2 million tons (1.8 million t)

- Pesticide, fertilizer, and other agricultural chemical manufacturing—1.6 million tons (1.5 million t)

- Iron and steel mills and ferroalloy manufacturing—1.4 million tons (1.2 million t)

- Nonferrous metal (except aluminum) production and processing—995,300 tons (902,900 t)

- Coating, engraving, heat treating, and allied activities—255,500 tons (231,800 t)

- Resin, synthetic rubber, and artificial synthetic fibers and filaments—228,400 tons (207,200 t)

FIGURE 8.1

Types of hazardous waste

- Corrosive—A corrosive material can wear away (corrode) or destroy a substance. For example, most acids are corrosives that can eat through metal, burn skin on contact, and give off vapors that burn the eyes.

- Ignitable—An ignitable material can burst into flames easily. It poses a fire hazard; can irritate the skin, eyes, and lungs; and may give off harmful vapors. Gasoline, paint, and furniture polish are ignitable.

- Reactive—A reactive material can explode or create poisonous gas when combined with other chemicals. For example, chlorine bleach and ammonia are reactive and create a poisonous gas when they come into contact with each other.

- Toxic—Toxic materials or substances can poison people and other life. Toxic substances can cause illness and even death if swallowed or absorbed through the skin. Pesticides, weed killers, and many household cleaners are toxic.

SOURCE: "What Kinds of Hazardous Waste Are There?" in *Fast Flash I: Hazardous Substances and Hazardous Waste*, U.S. Environmental Protection Agency, August 9, 2011, http://www.epa.gov/superfund/students/clas_act/haz-ed/ff_01.htm (accessed September 7, 2015)

- Pharmaceutical and medicine manufacturing— 214,300 tons (194,400 t)

- Other chemical product and preparation manufacturing— 188,700 tons (171,200 t)

METHODS OF MANAGING HAZARDOUS WASTE

Before the 1970s most industrial hazardous waste was dumped in landfills, stored on-site, burned, or discharged into surface waters with little or no treatment. Since the Pollution Prevention Act of 1990, industrial waste management follows a hierarchy introduced by the EPA that advocates source reduction first, followed by recycling or reuse, and then treatment. (See Figure 8.2.) Source reduction is an activity that prevents the generation of waste initially—for example, a change in operating practices or raw materials. The second choice is recycling, followed by energy recovery. If none of these methods is feasible, then treatment before disposal is recommended.

A variety of chemical, biological, and thermal processes can be applied to neutralize or destroy toxic compounds in hazardous waste. For example, microorganisms

TABLE 8.1

Resource Conservation and Recovery Act hazardous waste generated, by state, 2011

State	Rank	Hazardous waste quantity Tons generated	Percentage
Texas	1	15,683,405	45.7
Lousiana	2	4,399,520	12.8
Mississippi	3	1,828,886	5.3
Ohio	4	1,617,758	4.7
Kansas	5	1,238,342	3.6
New Mexico	6	1,042,387	3.0
Arkansas	7	922,732	2.7
Indiana	8	888,054	2.6
Illinois	9	675,534	2.0
Alabama	10	578,348	1.7
California	11	534,704	1.6
North Dakota	12	455,868	1.3
Hawaii	13	425,644	1.2
Minnesota	14	357,412	1.0
Washington	15	333,960	1.0
Pennsylvania	16	308,720	0.9
New Jersey	17	290,456	0.8
Wisconsin	18	289,401	0.8
Michigan	19	282,895	0.8
Missouri	20	251,015	0.7
Georgia	21	211,127	0.6
Arizona	22	202,942	0.6
Florida	23	198,406	0.6
New York	24	186,483	0.5
Kentucky	25	142,246	0.4
South Carolina	26	140,496	0.4
Oregon	27	93,180	0.3
Tennessee	28	89,352	0.3
North Carolina	29	83,114	0.2
Virginia	30	74,803	0.2
West Virginia	31	62,334	0.2
Iowa	32	51,013	0.1
Utah	33	49,726	0.1
Oklahoma	34	44,294	0.1
Maryland	35	44,250	0.1
Delaware	36	43,307	0.1
Puerto Rico	37	37,335	0.1
Massachusetts	38	35,554	0.1
Nebraska	39	35,425	0.1
Colorado	40	31,801	0.1
Connecticut	41	24,967	0.1
Nevada	42	9,839	0.0
Rhode Island	43	8,619	0.0
Montana	44	5,883	0.0
Wyoming	45	4,079	0.0
New Hampshire	46	3,949	0.0
Idaho	47	3,742	0.0
Alaska	48	2,524	0.0
Maine	49	2,406	0.0
Vermont	50	1,978	0.0
South Dakota	51	1,347	0.0
Virgin Islands	52	1,251	0.0
District of Columbia	53	1,137	0.0
Guam	54	86	0.0
Navajo Nation	55	23	0.0
Trust territories	56	14	0.0
Total		**34,334,072**	**100.0**

Note: Columns may not sum due to rounding.

SOURCE: Adapted from "Exhibit 1.2. Rank Ordering of States Based on Quantity of RCRA Hazardous Waste Generated and Number of Hazardous Waste Generators, 2011," in *National Analysis: The National Biennial RCRA Hazardous Waste Report (Based on 2011 Data)*, U.S. Environmental Protection Agency, December 10, 2012, http://www.epa.gov/epawaste/inforesources/data/br11/national11.pdf (accessed September 7, 2015)

and chemicals can remove hazardous hydrocarbons from contaminated water. State and federal regulations require the pretreatment of most hazardous wastes before they are

FIGURE 8.2

Waste management hierarchy

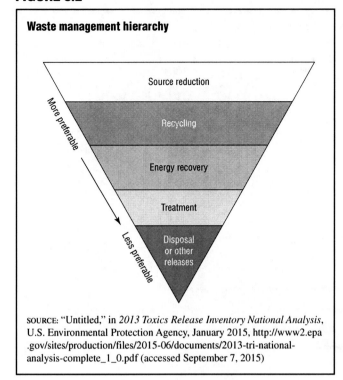

SOURCE: "Untitled," in *2013 Toxics Release Inventory National Analysis*, U.S. Environmental Protection Agency, January 2015, http://www2.epa .gov/sites/production/files/2015-06/documents/2013-tri-national-analysis-complete_1_0.pdf (accessed September 7, 2015)

FIGURE 8.3

Typical class I injection well

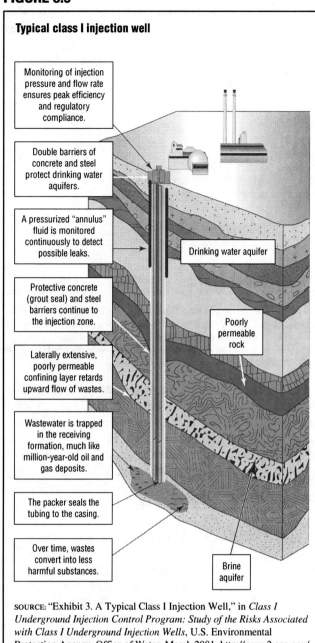

SOURCE: "Exhibit 3. A Typical Class I Injection Well," in *Class I Underground Injection Control Program: Study of the Risks Associated with Class I Underground Injection Wells*, U.S. Environmental Protection Agency, Office of Water, March 2001, http://www2.epa.gov/ sites/production/files/2015-07/documents/study_uic-class1_study_ risks_class1.pdf (accessed September 7, 2015)

discarded in landfills. These treated materials can only be placed in specially designed land disposal facilities. Besides land disposal, hazardous wastes may be injected under high pressure into underground wells that are thousands of feet deep. (See Figure 8.3.) Hazardous waste can also be burned in incinerators. As waste is burned, however, hot gases are released into the atmosphere, carrying toxic materials not consumed by the flames. In 1999 the federal government imposed a ban on new hazardous waste incinerators.

Table 8.2 lists the management methods that were used in 2011 for RCRA hazardous wastes. Nearly 23 million tons (20.7 million t), or 58.6% of the total, was managed through deep well or underground injection. The total amount of hazardous waste managed in 2011 was higher than the amount generated because the facilities also managed wastes that were generated before 2011.

FEDERAL REGULATION OF HAZARDOUS WASTES

The Toxics Release Inventory

The Toxics Release Inventory (TRI; http://www2 .epa.gov/toxics-release-inventory-tri-program) was established under the Emergency Planning and Community Right-to-Know Act of 1986. Under the program certain industrial facilities using specific toxic chemicals must report annually on their waste management activities and toxic chemical releases. These releases are to air, land, or water. According to the EPA, in "Learn about the Toxics Release Inventory" (http://www2.epa.gov/toxics-release-

inventory-tri-program/learn-about-toxics-release-inventory), more than 650 toxic chemicals are on the TRI list. The Pollution Prevention Act of 1990 requires the EPA to collect data on toxic chemicals that have been recycled, treated, or combusted for energy recovery.

Manufacturing facilities, federal facilities, and facilities involved in metal and coal mining, electric utilities that burn coal or oil, chemical wholesale distributors, petroleum terminals, RCRA Subtitle C hazardous water treatment and disposal facilities, and solvent recovery services have to report under the TRI program, but only if they have 10 or more full-time employees and use certain thresholds of toxic chemicals.

TABLE 8.2

Management of Resource Conservation and Recovery Act hazardous waste, by method, 2011

Management method	Tons managed	Percentage of quantity	Number of facilities*	Percentage of facilities*
Deepwell or underground injection	22,852,829	58.6	41	3.0
Other disposal	3,612,247	9.3	341	24.6
Aqueous organic treatment	2,848,612	7.3	40	2.9
Other treatment	1,990,520	5.1	300	21.6
Energy recovery	1,563,267	4.0	68	4.9
Landfill/surface impoundment	1,291,650	3.3	53	3.8
Metals recovery	1,039,554	2.7	106	7.6
Incineration	1,009,814	2.6	132	9.5
Aqueous inorganic treatment	702,769	1.8	108	7.8
Fuel blending	651,974	1.7	90	6.5
Stabilization	613,251	1.6	79	5.7
Sludge treatment	395,316	1.0	26	1.9
Solvents recovery	255,219	0.7	383	27.6
Other recovery	184,533	0.5	64	4.6
Land treatment/application/farming	16,376	0.0	14	1.0
Total	**39,027,932**	**100.0**	**1,389**	

*Column may not sum because facilities may have multiple handling methods.
Notes: Columns for these exhibits may not sum due to rounding. Facilities reporting storage-only and their quantity managed are excluded.

SOURCE: "Exhibit 2.6. Management Method, by Quantity of RCRA Hazardous Waste Managed, 2011," in *National Analysis: The National Biennial RCRA Hazardous Waste Report (Based on 2011 Data)*, U.S. Environmental Protection Agency, December 10, 2012, http://www.epa.gov/epawaste/inforesources/data/br11/national11.pdf (accessed September 7, 2015)

As of November 2015, the most recently published TRI report was released in January 2015. In *2013 Toxics Release Inventory National Analysis* (http://www2.epa.gov/toxics-release-inventory-tri-program/2013-tri-national-analysis-introduction), the EPA summarizes data for 2013. As shown in Table 8.3, 25.6 billion pounds (11.6 billion kg) of TRI chemicals were waste managed in 2013 by 21,598 TRI facilities. The breakdown by management method is shown in Figure 8.4. Overall, 36% of the waste was recycled, 37% was treated, 16% was released to the environment, and 11% was used for energy recovery. The EPA reports that 4.1 billion pounds (1.9 billion kg) of TRI chemicals were released in 2013. (See Table 8.3.) The vast majority of the releases (3.7 billion pounds [1.7 billion kg]) were on-site releases. The remaining 410 million pounds (186 million kg) were off-site releases. Figure 8.5 shows the distribution of releases to the environment in 2013. Nearly two-thirds (66%) of the disposed waste went to on-site land disposal. Another 19% was released to the air on-site. Much smaller percentages went to on-site surface water discharges (5%) and off-site disposal or other releases to the environment (10%).

A breakdown of disposed and released wastes by industry in 2013 is provided in Figure 8.6. The metal mining industry was responsible for nearly half (47%) of the releases, followed by electric utilities (13%), chemicals production (12%), and primary metals (8%). The EPA (2015, http://www2.epa.gov/sites/production/files/2015-06/2013-tri-na-ch5-where-you-live_0.xlsx) notes that the states with the highest releases were Alaska (970.6 million pounds [440.3 million kg]), Utah (525.5 million pounds [238.4 million kg]), and Nevada (369.7 million pounds [167.7 million kg]).

TABLE 8.3

Toxics Release Inventory Program, 2013

Number of TRI facilities:	**21,598**
Production-related waste managed:	**25.63 billion lb**
Recycled	9.23 billion lb
Energy recovery	2.91 billion lb
Treated	9.49 billion lb
Disposed of or otherwise released	4.00 billion lb
Total disposal or other releases:	**4.14 billion lb**
On-site	**3.74 billion lb**
Air	0.77 billion lb
Water	0.21 billion lb
Land	2.75 billion lb
Off-site	**0.41 billion lb**

lb = Pounds; TRI = Toxics Release Inventory.

SOURCE: "Quick Facts for 2013," in *2013 Toxics Release Inventory National Analysis*, U.S. Environmental Protection Agency, January 2015, http://www2.epa.gov/sites/production/files/2015-06/documents/2013-tri-national-analysis-complete_1_0.pdf (accessed September 7, 2015)

As shown in Figure 8.7, the amount of TRI releases declined from 2003 to 2009 and then began to rise again. The number of facilities with TRI releases decreased between 2003 and 2013.

The Resource Conservation and Recovery Act

The RCRA, which was first enacted by Congress in 1976 and expanded by amendments in 1980, 1984, 1992, and 1996, was designed to manage the disposal, incineration, treatment, and storage of waste in landfills, surface impoundments, waste piles, tanks, and container storage areas. It regulates the production and disposal of hazardous

FIGURE 8.4

Management of Toxics Release Inventory production-related wastes, by method, 2013

[25.63 billion pounds]

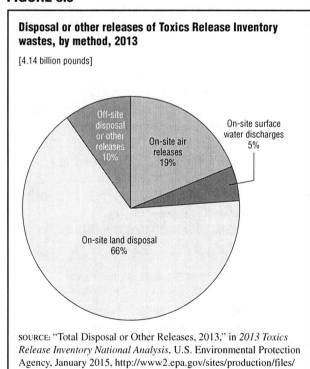

SOURCE: "Production-Related Waste Managed, 2013," in *2013 Toxics Release Inventory National Analysis*, U.S. Environmental Protection Agency, January 2015, http://www2.epa.gov/sites/production/files/2015-06/documents/2013-tri-national-analysis-complete_1_0.pdf (accessed September 7, 2015)

FIGURE 8.5

Disposal or other releases of Toxics Release Inventory wastes, by method, 2013

[4.14 billion pounds]

Off-site disposal or other releases 10%
On-site air releases 19%
On-site surface water discharges 5%
On-site land disposal 66%

SOURCE: "Total Disposal or Other Releases, 2013," in *2013 Toxics Release Inventory National Analysis*, U.S. Environmental Protection Agency, January 2015, http://www2.epa.gov/sites/production/files/2015-06/documents/2013-tri-national-analysis-complete_1_0.pdf (accessed September 7, 2015)

FIGURE 8.6

Disposal or other releases of Toxics Release Inventory wastes, by industry, 2013

[4.14 billion pounds]

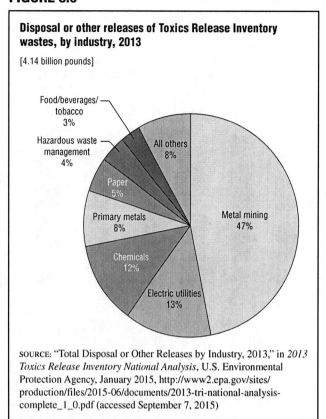

Food/beverages/tobacco 3%
Hazardous waste management 4%
All others 8%
Paper 5%
Primary metals 8%
Chemicals 12%
Metal mining 47%
Electric utilities 13%

SOURCE: "Total Disposal or Other Releases by Industry, 2013," in *2013 Toxics Release Inventory National Analysis*, U.S. Environmental Protection Agency, January 2015, http://www2.epa.gov/sites/production/files/2015-06/documents/2013-tri-national-analysis-complete_1_0.pdf (accessed September 7, 2015)

waste operations to take corrective action to clean up the waste they have released into the environment.

The RCRA imposes design and maintenance standards for waste disposal facilities, such as the installation of liners to prevent waste from leaking into groundwater. Land disposal facilities in operation after November 1980 are regulated under the act and are required to meet RCRA standards or close. Owners of facilities that ceased operation before November 1980 are required to clean up any hazardous waste threats their facilities still pose. Abandoned sites and those that owners cannot afford to clean up under the RCRA are usually referred to the national Superfund program.

The Comprehensive Environmental Response, Compensation, and Liability Act and the Superfund

The Comprehensive Environmental Response, Compensation, and Liability Act (CERCLA) of 1980 established the Superfund program to pay for cleaning up highly contaminated hazardous waste sites that had been abandoned or where a sole responsible party could not be identified. Originally a $1.6 billion, five-year program, the Superfund was focused initially on cleaning up leaking dumps that jeopardized groundwater.

During the original mandate of the Superfund, only six sites were cleaned up. When the program expired in 1985, many observers viewed it as a billion-dollar fiasco

waste and provides guidelines and mandates to improve waste disposal practices. The EPA also has the authority under the RCRA to require businesses with hazardous

FIGURE 8.7

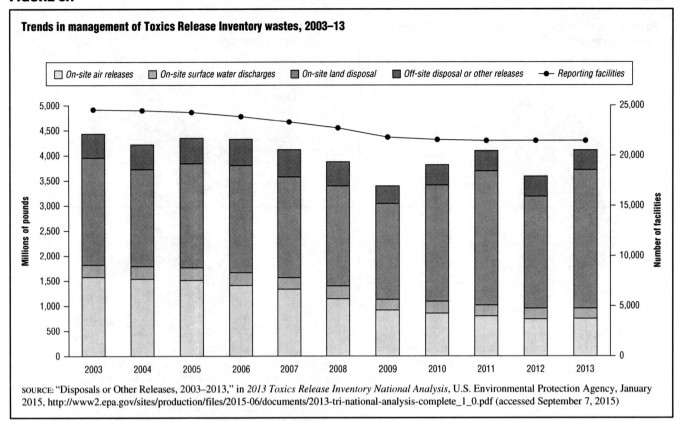

Trends in management of Toxics Release Inventory wastes, 2003–13

Legend: On-site air releases · On-site surface water discharges · On-site land disposal · Off-site disposal or other releases · Reporting facilities

SOURCE: "Disposals or Other Releases, 2003–2013," in *2013 Toxics Release Inventory National Analysis*, U.S. Environmental Protection Agency, January 2015, http://www2.epa.gov/sites/production/files/2015-06/documents/2013-tri-national-analysis-complete_1_0.pdf (accessed September 7, 2015)

rampant with scandal and mismanagement. Nonetheless, the negative publicity surrounding the program increased public awareness of the magnitude of the cleanup job in the United States. Consequently, in 1986 and later in 1990 the Superfund was reauthorized.

THE NATIONAL PRIORITIES LIST. CERCLA requires the government to maintain a list of hazardous waste sites that pose the highest potential threat to human health and the environment. This list is known as the National Priorities List (NPL) and includes hazardous waste sites in the country that are being cleaned up under the Superfund program. The NPL constitutes Appendix B to the National Oil and Hazardous Substances Pollution Contingency Plan, 40 CFR Part 300, which the EPA promulgated pursuant to Section 105 of CERCLA.

The NPL is constantly changing as new sites are officially added (finalized) and other sites are deleted (removed). Table 8.4 shows NPL site actions and milestones achieved by fiscal year (FY; October through September) between 1983 and 2015. These data were reported in May 2015, so only data for nine months are included for FY 2015.

As of August 28, 2015, there were 1,320 sites on the NPL. (See Table 8.5.) Another 1,173 had been declared as "construction completed." The EPA determines construction completed when all physical construction of cleanup actions are completed, all immediate threats have been addressed, and all long-term threats are under control. This does not mean that a site has met its cleanup goals. It simply means that the engineering/construction phase of site cleanup is completed. The EPA had deleted 389 sites from the NPL as of August 28, 2015. According to the EPA, in "National Oil and Hazardous Substances Pollution Contingency" (*Federal Register*, vol. 61, no. 21, January 31, 1996), sites are deleted when the agency determines that "no further Fund-financed CERCLA response action is appropriate." Beginning in FY 1996 the EPA started designating "partial deletions" to indicate that portions of NPL sites had reached the deletion criteria. As shown in Table 8.5, there were 51 "proposed" sites under consideration for the NPL as of August 28, 2015.

FUNDING FOR SUPERFUND. Funding for the Superfund program has historically come from three major sources: responsible parties, a so-called Superfund tax, and monies appropriated from the federal government's general fund. In addition, there is interest earned on the fund balance.

The EPA is authorized to compel parties responsible for creating hazardous pollution (such as waste generators, waste haulers, site owners, or site operators) to clean up the sites. In "Superfund Remedial Annual Accomplishments: 2014" (October 14, 2015, http://www2.epa.gov/superfund/superfund-remedial-annual-accomplishments),

TABLE 8.4

National Priorities List site actions and milestones, fiscal years 1983–2015

[As of May 27, 2015]

Action	2015	2014	2013	2012	2011	2010	2009	2008	2007	2006	2005	2004	2003	2002	2001	2000	1999
Proposed sites	6	16	9	18	35	8	23	17	17	10	12	26	14	9	45	40	37
Final sites	3	21	9	24	25	20	20	18	12	10	18	11	20	19	29	39	43
Deleted sites	5	14	7	11	7	7	8	9	7	7	18	16	9	17	30	19	23
Construction completion list (CCL) sites	9	8	14	22	22	18	20	30	24	40	40	40	40	42	47	87	85
Partial deletion sites	1	3	1	0	2	3	3	3	2	1	5	3	6	5	3	5	3
Partial deletion actions	2	4	2	2	3	5	3	3	3	3	5	7	7	7	4	5	3

Action	1998	1997	1996	1995	1994	1993	1992	1991	1990	1989	1988	1987	1986	1985	1984	1983
Proposed sites	34	20	27	9	36	52	30	23	25	64	246	71	45	317	0	552
Final sites	17	18	13	31	43	33	0	7	300	101	0	99	170	3	132	406
Deleted sites	20	32	34	25	13	12	2	9	1	10	5	0	8	0	0	5
Construction completion list (CCL) sites	87	88	64	68	61	68	88	12	8	10	12	3	8	3	0	5
Partial deletion sites	7	6	0	0	0	0	0	0	0	0	0	0	0	0	0	0
Partial deletion actions	7	6	0	0	0	0	0	0	0	0	0	0	0	0	0	0

Notes: A fiscal year is October 1 through September 30. The policy to allow partial deletions at sites was implemented in fiscal year 1996. The total number of partial deletion sites represents the number of sites that have had partial site deletions. Some sites have had multiple partial deletions. The total number of partial deletion actions represents the number of partial deletion actions that have occurred at all of the sites and may include multiple partial deletions at a single site.

SOURCE: "Number of NPL Site Actions and Milestones by Fiscal Year," in *National Priorities List (NPL): Number of NPL Site Actions and Milestones by Fiscal Year*, U.S. Environmental Protection Agency, May 27, 2015, http://www.epa.gov/superfund/sites/query/queryhtm/npfy.htm (accessed September 7, 2015)

TABLE 8.5

National Priorities List summary as of August 28, 2015

	Non-federal (general)	Federal	Total
Status			
Proposed sites	47	4	51
Final sites	1,163	157	1,320
Deleted sites	372	17	389
Milestone			
Partial deletions	43	19	62*
Construction completions	1,097	76	1,173

*81 partial deletions have occurred at these 62 sites.
Note: Sites that have achieved these milestones are included in one of the three National Priorities List status categories.

SOURCE: "NPL Site Totals by Status and Milestone," in *National Priorities List (NPL): NPL Site Totals by Status and Milestone*, U.S. Environmental Protection Agency, August 28, 2015, http://www.epa.gov/superfund/sites/query/queryhtm/npltotal.htm (accessed September 7, 2015)

the EPA notes that it received Superfund program commitments of more than $453.7 million from private responsible parties for FY 2014. The EPA obtains the money through fines, penalties, and cost recoveries (money recovered through legal settlements with the responsible parties). If responsible parties cannot be found, or if a settlement cannot be reached, public monies finance the cleanup. After completing a cleanup, the EPA can take action against the responsible parties to recover costs. In "Superfund Remedial Annual Accomplishments: 2014," the EPA indicates that in FY 2014 responsible parties agreed to reimburse the agency for $57.7 million in past costs related to cleanup work at Superfund sites.

The Superfund tax was set up as part of the original Superfund legislation of 1980. It was financed by dedicated taxes collected from companies in the chemical and crude oil industries and a special income tax on corporate profits. This system was extremely unpopular with many corporations, which argued that environmentally responsible companies should not have to pay for the mistakes of others. The tax was eliminated in 1995. By the end of FY 2003 the Superfund tax monies had been exhausted. As of November 2015, several bills had been introduced in Congress to reinstate the tax, but none had been passed. Reinstating the tax is a controversial issue. Advocates argue that it is unfair for all U.S. taxpayers to have to pay to clean up hazardous waste sites. Opponents counter that it is unfair to tax corporations that are complying with environmental rules for the sins of polluting companies.

The third primary source of money for the Superfund program is money appropriated from the federal government's general fund. This means that all U.S. taxpayers assume some of the financial burden to clean up hazardous waste sites. After the depletion of the Superfund tax

fund in FY 2003, general appropriation funds became the only government source of money for the program. The U.S. Government Accountability Office (GAO) reports in *Superfund: EPA's Costs to Remediate Existing and Future Sites Will Likely Exceed Current Funding Levels* (June 22, 2010, http://www.gao.gov/new.items/d10857t .pdf) that appropriations averaged about $1.2 billion per year between FY 1981 and FY 2009; nearly $1.3 billion was appropriated in FY 2009. An additional $600 million was appropriated to the Superfund program through the American Recovery and Reinvestment Act of 2009. The EPA (http://www2.epa.gov/planandbudget/archive#Budget Summary) requested the following amounts for the Superfund program in its budgets for FY 2010 to FY 2015 (a breakdown of the EPA budget request for FY 2016 is shown in Table 1.6 in Chapter 1):

- FY 2010—$1.3 billion
- FY 2011—$1.3 billion
- FY 2012—$1.2 billion
- FY 2013—$1.2 billion
- FY 2014—$1.2 billion
- FY 2015—$1.2 billion
- FY 2016—$1.2 billion

THE FEDERAL AGENCY HAZARDOUS WASTE COMPLIANCE DOCKET. CERCLA requires the EPA to maintain a list of federal lands or facilities (for example, military bases) that are contaminated or potentially contaminated with hazardous waste. The Federal Agency Hazardous Waste Compliance Docket (the Docket) is regularly reported in the *Federal Register*. As of November 2015, the latest Docket (http://www.gpo.gov/fdsys/pkg/FR-2015-08-17/pdf/2015-20248.pdf) was published in July 2015 and included 2,323 federal sites. The GAO is the investigatory arm of the U.S. Congress. In *Hazardous Waste Cleanup: Numbers of Contaminated Federal Sites, Estimated Costs, and EPA's Oversight Role* (September 11, 2015, http://www.gao.gov/assets/680/672464.pdf), the GAO indicates that the number of contaminated or potentially contaminated federal sites is actually much higher.

The GAO notes that the federal government owns more than 700 million acres (280 million ha) of land. Much of it is located in the western United States and is managed by the Bureau of Land Management (BLM), an agency within the Interior Department. According to the GAO, the BLM knows of 4,722 sites on its land with "confirmed or likely contamination." In addition, the BLM has identified more than 30,000 abandoned mines on its land that have not yet been assessed for contamination. (See Figure 8.8.) The GAO further states that the BLM "estimated that there may be approximately 100,000 abandoned mines that had not yet been inventoried in

California, Nevada, and Utah." A full inventory of abandoned mine sites by the BLM is expected to take "decades." In addition, the U.S. Forest Service estimates that its lands hold between 27,000 and 39,000 abandoned mines, and approximately 20% of these mines "may pose some level of risk to human health or the environment."

The GAO indicates that officials with the Interior Department and the U.S. Department of Agriculture "believed that abandoned mines should not be listed on EPA's Docket because the agencies did not cause the contamination and, therefore, the sites should not be considered federal sites." However, the EPA disagrees with this opinion. The GAO recommends that the federal agencies work together to ensure that contaminated or potentially contaminated sites on federal lands are identified and assessed.

Abandoned mine sites have received heightened public attention since August 2015, when a spill of contaminated water occurred at the defunct Gold King mine in Colorado. That mine is located on private land along the headwaters of the upper Animas River. The EPA (http://www2.epa.gov/region8/upper-animas-mining-district) notes that it previously investigated the upper Animas River to assess the possibility of listing the watershed on the NPL. The agency states that a 2008 investigation "indicated that the area would qualify [for listing], although after receiving additional community input, EPA again postponed efforts to include the area on the NPL." As a result, state and local agencies in Colorado were responsible for the cleanup of the watershed. Nevertheless, the EPA indicates that its Superfund Remedial Program "contributed resources" to assist in these efforts.

HAZARDOUS WASTE FROM SMALL BUSINESSES AND HOUSEHOLDS

A small percentage of hazardous waste comes from thousands of small-quantity generators—businesses that produce less than 2,200 pounds (1,000 kg) of hazardous waste per month. Common generators are dry-cleaning facilities, furniture-making plants, construction companies, and photo processors. Typical hazardous wastes include spent solvents, leftover chemicals, paints, and unused cleaning chemicals. Hazardous wastes from small-quantity generators and households are regulated under Subtitle D of the RCRA.

Household hazardous waste includes solvents, paints, cleaners, stains, varnishes, pesticides, motor oil, and car batteries. Because of the relatively low amount of hazardous substances in individual products, household hazardous waste is not regulated as a hazardous waste. Since the

FIGURE 8.8

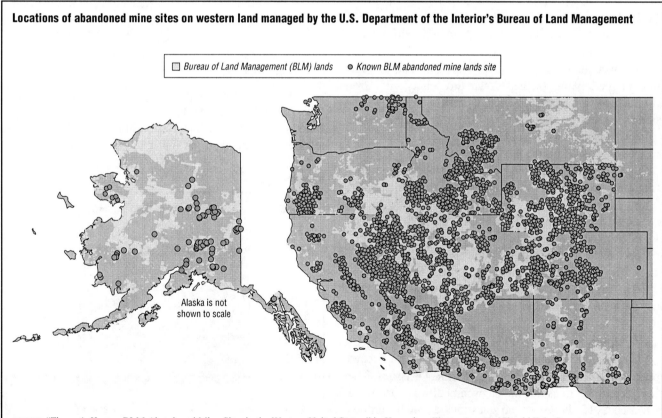

Locations of abandoned mine sites on western land managed by the U.S. Department of the Interior's Bureau of Land Management

☐ Bureau of Land Management (BLM) lands   ⊙ Known BLM abandoned mine lands site

Alaska is not shown to scale

SOURCE: "Figure 1. Known BLM Abandoned Mine Sites in the Western United States," in *Hazardous Waste: Agencies Should Take Steps to Improve Information on USDA's and Interior's Potentially Contaminated Sites*, U.S. Government Accountability Office, January 2015, http://www.gao.gov/assets/670/667959.pdf (accessed September 10, 2015)

1980s many communities have held special collection days for household hazardous waste to ensure that it is disposed of properly.

Universal Wastes

Universal wastes are a federally defined subset of hazardous wastes that are produced in small amounts by many generators. According to the EPA, in "Universal Wastes" (December 21, 2012, http://www.epa.gov/waste/hazard/wastetypes/universal/index.htm), the federal list of universal wastes includes batteries, pesticides, mercury-containing equipment (e.g., thermostats), and lamps (e.g., fluorescent bulbs). Although these wastes sometimes wind up in the municipal waste stream, they contain worrisome components, such as heavy metals, that pose an environmental hazard. Thus, the EPA regulates them separately from other hazardous wastes with simpler streamlined requirements that are designed to encourage generators to recycle or dispose of the wastes properly. The EPA's universal waste regulations are published in 40 CFR 273 and apply only to businesses, not to residential generators. The states are allowed to adopt the federal universal waste regulations or add to them, as they see fit.

In December 2008 the EPA proposed adding pharmaceuticals to the federal list of universal wastes. This ruling would apply to pharmacies; hospitals; physician, dentist, and veterinarian offices; and similar facilities. The EPA hoped that a centralized collection process for unwanted or unused pharmaceuticals would help prevent the environmental problems associated with the disposal of pharmaceuticals into municipal landfills and sewage systems (i.e., being flushed down the toilet). In "Proposed Rule: Management Standards for Hazardous Waste Pharmaceuticals" (September 28, 2015, http://www2.epa.gov/hwgenerators/proposed-rule-management-standards-hazardous-waste-pharmaceuticals), the EPA notes that its 2008 proposal attracted numerous public comments indicating great concern about how the new rule would be implemented. After consideration, the agency (http://www.gpo.gov/fdsys/pkg/FR-2015-09-25/pdf/2015-23167.pdf) "concluded that the universal waste program is not appropriate for managing hazardous waste pharmaceuticals." The EPA crafted a revised proposal that was published in September 2015. As of November 2015, the rule had not been finalized.

Public Opinion on Hazardous Waste

The Gallup Organization regularly polls Americans about their attitudes regarding environmental issues. The most recent poll to assess the environment was conducted in March 2015; however, no questions about hazardous waste were included. Gallup notes in *Environment* (2015, http://www.gallup.com/poll/1615/environment.aspx) that in March 2014 participants were asked to express their level of worry about "contamination of soil and water by toxic waste." Just over half (53%) of survey respondents expressed a great deal of concern about the contamination of soil and water by toxic waste. This value was down from a high of 69% in 1989. In 2014, 24% of respondents indicated a fair amount of concern about the issue, and 17% worried only a little about it. Another 5% were not at all worried about the problem.

RADIOACTIVE WASTE

Radioactive waste results from the mining, processing, and use of radioactive materials for commercial, military, medical, and research purposes. In *2014–2015 Information Digest* (August 2014, http://www.nrc.gov/reading-rm/doc-collections/nuregs/staff/sr1350/v26/sr1350v26.pdf), the U.S. Nuclear Regulatory Commission (NRC) defines radioactivity as "the property possessed by some elements (such as uranium) of spontaneously emitting energy in the form of radiation as a result of the decay (or disintegration) of an unstable atom." As the decay or disintegration takes place, the nucleus of an unstable atom emits nuclear radiation in the form of alpha particles, beta particles, neutrons, or gamma rays. They are examples of ionizing radiation because they can displace or remove electrons from other materials with which they come into contact. Thus, high doses of ionizing radiation can damage skin or tissue. As shown in Figure 8.9 alpha and beta particles are relatively weak; neutrons and gamma rays, however, can pass through (and hence damage) the human body. X-rays, a nonnuclear ionizing form of radiation, can also pass through the human body.

Humans purposely produce nuclear radiation by artificially breaking apart atomic nuclei. Such a process is called nuclear fission. The fission of uranium 235 (U-235) releases several neutrons that can penetrate other U-235

FIGURE 8.9

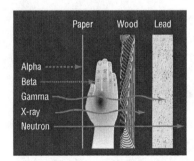

Radiation types and their penetrating capacities

SOURCE: "Untitled," in *2014–2015 Information Digest*, U.S. Nuclear Regulatory Commission, August 2014, http://www.nrc.gov/reading-rm/doc-collections/nuregs/staff/sr1350/v26/sr1350v26.pdf (accessed September 7, 2015)

nuclei. In this way the fission of a single U-235 atom can begin a cascading chain of nuclear reactions. If this series of reactions is regulated to occur slowly, as it is in nuclear power plants, the energy emitted can be captured for a variety of uses, such as generating electricity. If this series of reactions is allowed to occur all at once, as in a nuclear bomb, the energy emitted is explosive. (Plutonium-239 can also be used to generate a chain reaction similar to that of U-235.)

In general, the U.S. Department of Energy (DOE) is responsible for managing radioactive waste that is associated with the nation's military and defense operations. The NRC has primary responsibility for managing radioactive wastes that are produced by other sources. Some state agencies have also been authorized to regulate aspects of radioactive waste management within their jurisdictions. The EPA regulates the release of radioactive materials to the environment.

Nuclear Power Plants

The primary commercial source of radioactive waste is associated with electricity generation at nuclear power plants. These plants rely on controlled slow fission reactions with nuclear fuel pellets to produce heat to create steam. Figure 8.10 shows the locations of the nation's 99 operational nuclear power plants as of February 2015. Nuclear power plant construction was robust through the 1970s and then ceased. The drop-off is attributed to a variety of factors including construction and regulatory difficulties, availability of cheap supplies of natural gas, and public opposition to nuclear power. Opposition grew dramatically following an emergency at the Three Mile Island nuclear power plant near Harrisburg, Pennsylvania. On March 28, 1979, equipment failures, design problems, and operator errors led to a partial meltdown in the nuclear core of one of the reactors. A meltdown occurs when cooling of the nuclear fuel rods is inadequate and the fuel overheats and melts, releasing radioactivity to the atmosphere.

Although no one was directly injured or killed by the accident, it did expose a substantial population of nearby residents to radioactive gases. The NRC indicates in the fact sheet "Three Mile Island Accident" (August 2009, http://www.nrc.gov/reading-rm/doc-collections/fact-sheets/3mile-isle.pdf) that approximately 2 million people in the area were exposed to an average dose of 1 millirem. This is roughly one-sixth the amount of radiation that is associated with a full set of chest x-rays.

Public fears about nuclear power were rekindled in 1986, when an explosion occurred at a nuclear power plant near the town of Chernobyl in the Soviet Union (now Ukraine). During the early morning hours of April 26, 1986, operators decided to test one of the reactors to see what would happen if the station lost electrical power. A combination of design flaws and operator errors during the test resulted in a massive power surge that overheated and ruptured some of the fuel rods. The resulting explosions destroyed the nuclear reactor core and ripped the roof off the reactor building, sending radioactive debris and smoke into the atmosphere.

Dozens of people, mostly plant workers, died during the explosions or soon thereafter from acute radiation poisoning. Hundreds, possibly thousands, more people died later as a result of exposure to radiation that was released by the accident. More than 100,000 people were evacuated from the surrounding area. The Chernobyl disaster left a long-lasting negative public perception about nuclear power.

However, during the latter part of the first decade of the 21st century high fuel prices and concerns about the contribution of fossil fuels to global warming prompted new interest in nuclear power in the United States. In response, President Barack Obama (1961–) made nuclear power a key element of his energy policy. In *Blueprint for a Secure Energy Future* (March 30, 2011, http://www.whitehouse.gov/sites/default/files/blueprint_secure_energy_future.pdf), the White House notes that in 2010 it issued a conditional loan guarantee for two new nuclear power units at the existing Plant Vogtle site near Augusta, Georgia. They were the first new nuclear power units ordered since the late 1970s.

The burgeoning support for nuclear power in the United States suffered a setback in March 2011, when an earthquake and tsunami seriously damaged Japan's Fukushima Daiichi nuclear power plant, one of the largest nuclear power plant facilities in the world. Loss of sufficient cooling water allowed fuel rod temperatures in several of the reactors to rise to dangerous levels. Subsequent explosions caused further structural damage. Some radioactive gases were released into the atmosphere, and tens of thousands of people in the region surrounding the plant had to be evacuated.

The long-term public health consequences of the disaster, such as higher cancer rates, remain to be seen. In February 2013 the World Health Organization (WHO) released its predictions in *Health Risk Assessment from the Nuclear Accident after the 2011 Great East Japan Earthquake and Tsunami, Based on a Preliminary Dose Estimation* (http://www.who.int/ionizing_radiation/pub_meet/fukushima_risk_assessment_2013/en/index.html). Overall, the WHO notes, "This health risk assessment concludes that no discernible increase in health risks from the Fukushima event is expected outside Japan. With respect to Japan, this assessment estimates that the lifetime risk for some cancers may be somewhat elevated above baseline rates in certain age and sex groups that were in the areas most affected." The WHO cautions, however, that its estimates are based on preliminary data

FIGURE 8.10

Locations of commercial operating nuclear power reactors, 2015

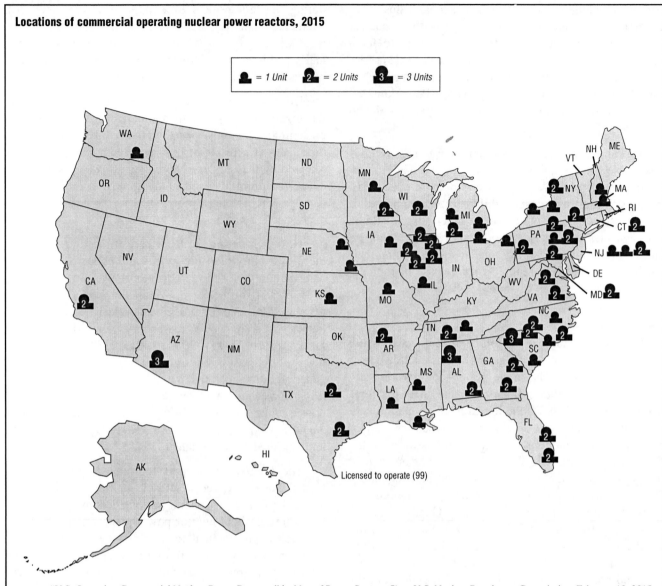

SOURCE: "U.S. Operating Commercial Nuclear Power Reactors," in *Map of Power Reactor Sites*, U.S. Nuclear Regulatory Commission, February 18, 2015, http://www.nrc.gov/reactors/operating/map-power-reactors.html (accessed September 7, 2015)

and that scientific knowledge is limited on the effects of low-level radiation on human health.

Following the Fukushima incident, the NRC ordered a task force to examine the causes of the accident and recommend ways in which the U.S. nuclear power industry should respond to prevent a similar occurrence. In July 2011 the task force released *Recommendations for Enhancing Reactor Safety in the 21st Century: The Near Term Task Force Review of Insights from the Fukushima Dai-Ichi Accident* (http://pbadupws.nrc.gov/docs/ML11 18/ML111861807.pdf). Overall, the task force notes that "in light of the low likelihood of an event beyond the design basis of a U.S. nuclear power plant and the current mitigation capabilities at those facilities, the Task Force concludes that continued operation of these plants and continued licensing activities do not pose an imminent risk to the public health and safety." However, the task

force does provide specific recommendations that are designed to improve the NRC's regulatory framework and its oversight of plant safety performance; strengthen protection methods against earthquakes and floods at nuclear power plants; enhance mitigation capabilities at the plants, for example, through design changes and improved on-site emergency response procedures; and strengthen plant emergency preparedness measures, particularly in regards to total loss of electrical power. In "What Are the Lessons Learned from Fukushima?" (April 17, 2015, http://www.nrc.gov/reactors/operating/ops-experience/japan-dashboard/priorities.html), the NRC describes its responses to the various recommendations made by the task force. For example, the commission instigated a rulemaking "to enhance the capability to maintain plant safety during a prolonged loss of electrical power."

In February 2012 the NRC approved the license for the two planned new reactors at Plant Vogtle. A month later the agency approved a license for two new nuclear reactors at the Virgil C. Summer power plant in Jenkinsville, South Carolina. Since that time, both projects have been plagued by construction delays and cost overruns. As of November 2015, the four new nuclear units were expected to be operational in 2019 or 2020. The NRC (http://www.nrc.gov/reactors/new-reactors/col.html) indicates that, as of November 2015, it had received applications for 18 new commercial nuclear reactor projects. Besides the Plant Vogtle and Summer projects, construction had been approved for one other project—Fermi Unit 3 for the Detroit Edison Company (now DTE Energy) in Michigan. According to JC Reindl, in "Regulators OK Fermi 3, but DTE Has No Plans to Build It" (Freep.com, May 1, 2015), DTE Energy "has no immediate plans to build Fermi 3, and sought the approval as a long-term planning option."

Military and Defense Sources

The U.S. government maintained an active program for nuclear weapons development from the early 1940s through the 1980s. It began with development of the atomic bomb during World War II (1939–1945). During the first three decades following the development of the atomic bomb, nuclear waste management received little attention from government policy makers. Beginning in the 1970s public concern about the environmental and health risks of stockpiled nuclear materials led to political action. Over the next decade nuclear weapons production was curtailed. When the Soviet Union collapsed in 1991, the DOE ceased nearly all production of new nuclear weapons. In addition, it began a major undertaking to dismantle and destroy many of the nuclear weapons that had been created.

In 1989 the DOE formed a new program that was eventually directed by the Office of Environmental Management (EM) to oversee the massive and expensive effort to clean up more than 100 former nuclear weapons facilities. The GAO estimates in *Nuclear Waste: Better Performance Reporting Needed to Assess DOE's Ability to Achieve the Goals of the Accelerated Cleanup Program* (July 2005, http://www.gao.gov/new.items/d05764.pdf) that the DOE spent more than $60 billion on environmental management between 1989 and 2001. Billions more dollars have been spent since then. In *Budget for Fiscal Year 2016* (February 2015, http://www.energy.gov/sites/prod/files/2015/02/f19/FY2016BudgetinBrief.pdf), the DOE indicates that the enacted budgets for environmental management for FY 2014 and FY 2015 were $5.8 billion and $5.9 billion, respectively. The agency's request for FY 2016 was $5.8 billion. The DOE notes that as of February 2015, the EM had completed cleanup at 91 sites. Most of the remaining 16 sites are massive

projects that are expected to take decades to complete. The following projected completion dates are taken from the EM's FY 2016 budget request (February 2015, http://www.energy.gov/sites/prod/files/2015/02/f19/FY2016BudgetVolume5.pdf).

- Brookhaven National Laboratory, New York—2019
- Energy Technology Engineering Center, California—2017
- Hanford Site, Washington—2070
- Idaho National Engineering and Environmental Laboratory, Idaho—2042 to 2050
- Lawrence Livermore National Laboratory, California—2020
- Los Alamos National Laboratory, New Mexico—Undetermined
- Moab: Uranium Mill Tailings Remedial Action Project, Utah—2025
- Nevada National Security Site, Nevada—2030
- Oak Ridge Reservation, Tennessee—2046
- Paducah Gaseous Diffusion Plant, Kentucky—2047
- Portsmouth Gaseous Diffusion Plant, Ohio—2044 to 2052
- Sandia National Laboratories, New Mexico—2020
- Savannah River Site, Georgia—2042
- Separations Process Research Unit, New York—2018
- Waste Isolation Pilot Plant (WIPP), New Mexico—2035 to 2039
- West Valley Demonstration Project, New York—2040 to 2045

It should be noted that WIPP is a repository for radioactive wastes from other sites. It is described in detail later in this chapter.

The Hanford Site is believed to be the largest environmental cleanup project in the world. It is located in southeastern Washington along the Columbia River and covers 586 square miles (1,518 square km). It began operations in 1944 as the nation's first plutonium production facility for the nuclear weapons program. According to the DOE (http://www.hanford.gov/page.cfm/About HanfordCleanup), the facility produced millions of tons of solid waste and hundreds of billions of gallons of liquid waste. The agency notes, "These liquid wastes were disposed of by pouring them onto the ground or into trenches or holding ponds. Unintentional spills of liquids also took place." The site closed during the late 1980s, leaving behind tons of disintegrating nuclear fuel rods and contaminated sludge, soil and groundwater.

The cleanup at Hanford (which began during the 1980s) has proved to be difficult and very expensive. In December 2012 the GAO issued a scathing report about the project's problems. In *Hanford Waste Treatment Plant: DOE Needs to Take Action to Resolve Technical and Management Challenges* (http://www.gao.gov/assets/660/650931.pdf), the GAO notes that the DOE is constructing a waste treatment plant (WTP) to handle millions of gallons of liquid waste. However, as of 2012 the WTP budget had tripled since 2000 to $13.4 billion, and the projected completion date slipped by nearly a decade to 2019. The GAO again addressed the WTP in May 2015 in *Hanford Waste Treatment: DOE Needs to Evaluate Alternatives to Recently Proposed Projects and Address Technical and Management Challenges* (http://www.gao.gov/assets/680/670080.pdf). The GAO states, "Significant technical and management challenges continue to affect the WTP and hinder its completion." The DOE has proposed two treatment facilities to treat some waste while it continues to struggle with completing the WTP. The new projects are expected to cost "at least $1 billion and take 6 to 8 years to construct." However, the GAO is highly critical of these estimates noting, "DOE's preliminary cost and schedule estimates for constructing the two proposed facilities are not reliable because they do not meet industry best practices for reliable cost and schedule estimates."

Classes of Radioactive Waste

Federal and state agencies classify radioactive wastes based on their radioactivity, sources, and methods of management. These classifications differ from agency to agency, and there is sometimes overlap between classes. Major classes defined by the federal government are as follows:

- Uranium mill tailings—remnants from uranium mining, which was extensively practiced in the western United States in the decades following World War II. By the 1980s the United States imported most of the uranium it needed for nuclear power and weapons production. As a result, the vast majority of domestic uranium mines and processing facilities ceased operating. The DOE is responsible for cleaning up abandoned mill-tailing sites that were associated primarily with nuclear weapons production. The NRC oversees the cleanup operations to ensure that they meet environmental standards set by the EPA. The NRC notes in "Fact Sheet on Uranium Mill Tailings" (March 2015, http://www.nrc.gov/reading-rm/doc-collections/fact-sheets/mill-tailings.html) that as of 2015, 20 sites were undergoing cleanup operations.

- High-level radioactive waste (HLW)—this is waste that requires isolation from living things for thousands of years. The prime example is spent nuclear fuel

from commercial reactors. During the Cold War (1947–1991), the DOE reprocessed spent nuclear fuel at several locations for defense purposes. In 1992 the agency discontinued the program due to a lack of demand for the fuel. As a result, significant amounts of spent nuclear fuel remain in storage at some DOE facilities. As of 2015 no permanent long-term storage facility existed for HLW; therefore, it was stored on-site at the locations where it was generated or transported to other approved sites for temporary storage. (See Figure 8.11.) The GAO indicates in *Commercial Spent Nuclear Fuel: Observations on the Key Attributes and Challenges of Storage and Disposal Options* (April 11, 2013, http://www.gao.gov/assets/660/653731.pdf) that approximately 77,200 tons (70,000 t) was stored in 2013 and that this total is expected to more than double by 2055. Figure 8.12 shows the storage of commercial spent nuclear fuel (in metric tons) by state through 2013. Illinois had the largest amount (10,207.4 tons [9,260 t]), followed by Pennsylvania (7,120.9 tons [6,460 t]), and South Carolina (4,931.7 tons [4,474 t]).

- Low-level radioactive waste (LLW)—LLW includes items such as protective clothing, tools, equipment, rags, mops, and animal carcasses used in radiation research. Until the 1960s the United States dumped LLW into the ocean. Thereafter, various storage sites were developed around the country. As of 2015 four commercial LLW sites were operating in South Carolina, Texas, Utah, and Washington. In "Low-Level Waste Disposal Statistics" (April 13, 2015, http://www.nrc.gov/waste/llw-disposal/licensing/statistics.html), the NRC reports that in 2011 LLW disposal totaled 1.8 million cubic feet (50,970 cubic m). The wastes are enclosed in canisters buried underground, as shown in Figure 8.13.

- Transuranic waste (TRU)—waste that consists of chemical elements with an atomic number greater than that of uranium (92) and therefore are beyond (trans-) uranium. With the exception of plutonium, which is found in extremely small amounts in nature, all the TRU elements are artificially produced (made by humans). TRU waste remains radioactive for up to tens of thousands of years. Until 1999 all of the wastes were in temporary storage at various DOE facilities around the country. In 1999 the DOE began moving the wastes to WIPP.

Geologic Repositories for Radioactive Waste

The United States has been working for decades to establish permanent storage facilities for HLW and TRU waste. These facilities are geological repositories; that is, storage facilities constructed deep underground in ancient geological formations that are relatively dry and not subject

FIGURE 8.11

Spent nuclear fuel storage installations, 2014

▲ Site-specific license (15)   ● General license (56)

34 States have at least one ISFSI

Alabama
- Browns Ferry
- Farley

Arizona
- Palo Verde

Arkansas
- Arkansas Nuclear

California
- ▲ Diablo Canyon
- ▲ Rancho Seco
- San Onofre
- ▲ Humboldt Bay

Colorado
- ▲ Fort St. Vrain

Connecticut
- Haddam Neck
- Millstone

Florida
- St. Lucie
- Turkey Point

Georgia
- Hatch
- Vogtle

Idaho
- ▲ DOE: TMI-2 (Fuel Debris)
- ▲ Idaho Spent Fuel Facility

Illinois
- Braidwood
- Byron
- ▲ GE Morris (Wet)
- Dresden
- La Salle
- Quad Cities
- Zion

Iowa
- Duane Arnold

Louisiana
- River Bend
- Waterford

Maine
- Maine Yankee

Maryland
- ▲ Calvert Cliffs

Massachusetts
- Yankee Rowe

Michigan
- Big Rock Point
- Palisades
- Cook

Minnesota
- Monticello
- ▲ Prairie Island

Mississippi
- Grand Gulf

Nebraska
- Cooper
- Ft. Calhoun

New Hampshire
- Seabrook

New Jersey
- Hope Creek
- Salem
- Oyster Creek

New York
- Indian Point
- FitzPatrick
- Ginna
- Nine Mile Point

North Carolina
- Brunswick
- McGuire

Ohio
- Davis-Besse
- Perry

Oregon
- ▲ Trojan

Pennsylvania
- Limerick
- Susquehanna
- Peach Bottom

South Carolina
- ▲ Oconee
- ▲ Robinson
- Catawba

Tennessee
- Sequoyah

Texas
- Comanche Peak

Utah
- ▲ Private Fuel Storage

Vermont
- Vermont Yankee

Virgina
- ▲ Surry
- ▲ North Anna

Washington
- Columbia

Wisconsin
- Point Beach
- Kewaunee
- LaCrosse

ISFSI = Independent Spent Fuel Storage Installation.
DOE = U.S. Department of Energy.
TMI = Three Mile Island.

SOURCE: "Figure 45. Licensed and Operating Independent Spent Fuel Storage Installations by State," in *2014–2015 Information Digest*, U.S. Nuclear Regulatory Commission, August 2014, http://www.nrc.gov/reading-rm/doc-collections/nuregs/staff/sr1350/v26/sr1350v26.pdf (accessed September 7, 2015)

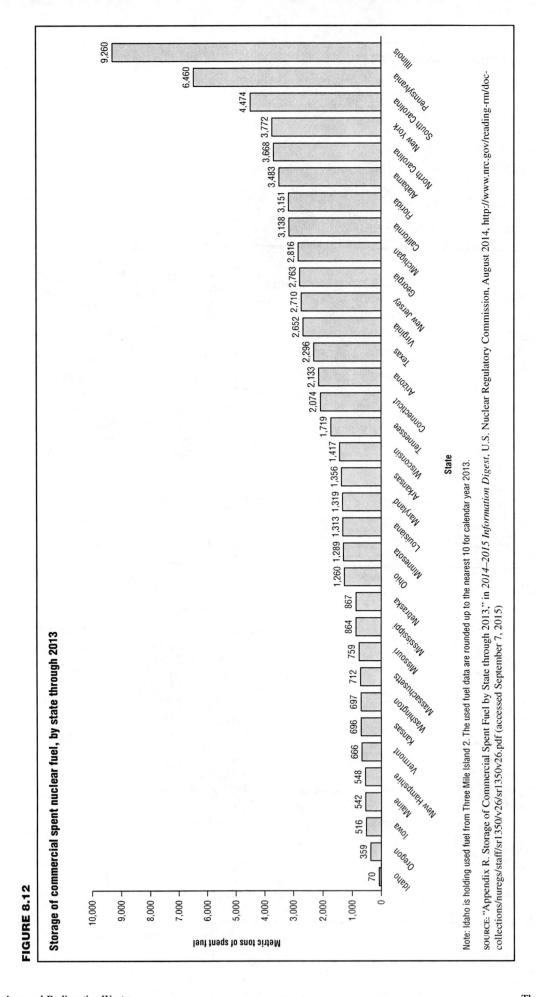

FIGURE 8.12

Storage of commercial spent nuclear fuel, by state through 2013

Note: Idaho is holding used fuel from Three Mile Island 2. The used fuel data are rounded up to the nearest 10 for calendar year 2013.

SOURCE: "Appendix R. Storage of Commercial Spent Fuel by State through 2013," in *2014–2015 Information Digest*, U.S. Nuclear Regulatory Commission, August 2014, http://www.nrc.gov/reading-rm/doc-collections/nuregs/staff/sr1350/v26/sr1350v26.pdf (accessed September 7, 2015)

FIGURE 8.13

Low-level waste disposal facility

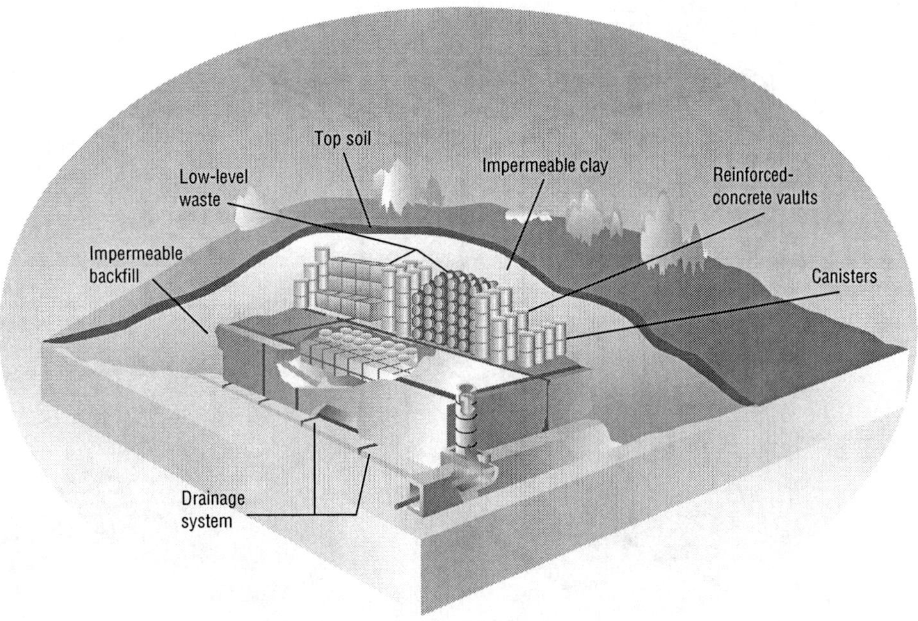

Top soil

Low-level
waste

Impermeable clay

Reinforced-
concrete vaults

Impermeable
backfill

Canisters

Drainage
system

SOURCE: Adapted from "Figure 42. Low-Level Waste Disposal," in *2014–2015 Information Digest*, U.S. Nuclear Regulatory Commission, August 2014, http://www.nrc.gov/reading-rm/doc-collections/nuregs/staff/sr1350/v26/sr1350v26.pdf (accessed September 7, 2015)

to earthquakes or other stresses. WIPP is an example of a geologic repository for radioactive waste.

Engineers working on permanent storage facilities have designed barrier systems that combine multiple physical barriers with chemical controls to provide a high level of long-term containment for radioactive waste. Radioactive waste is chemically treated for long-term storage and placed into steel drums. The drums are then placed in a concrete container. Many of these drum-filled concrete containers, which are surrounded with a special chemically treated backfill material, are placed in a larger concrete container deep underground. The rock surrounding this large concrete container must have low groundwater flow. The multiple barriers, chemical conditions, and geologic conditions under which the wastes are stored ensure that the wastes dissolve slowly and pose little danger to the groundwater.

THE WASTE ISOLATION PILOT PLANT. WIPP became the world's first deep depository for nuclear waste when it received its first shipment in March 1999. The large facility is located in a desert region near Carlsbad, New Mexico. It was designed for permanent storage of the nation's TRU waste. WIPP is 2,150 feet (655 m) below the surface in the salt beds of the Salado Formation. The layout is depicted in Figure 8.14.

In February 2014 the facility suffered two serious incidents. On February 5, 2014, a salt haul truck caught fire in an underground area. (See Figure 8.15.) Nine days later a radioactive release occurred in Room 7 of the underground waste disposal area. (See Figure 8.15.) In *Waste Isolation Pilot Plant Recovery Plan, Revision 0* (September 30, 2014, http://www.wipp.energy.gov/Special/WIPP%20Recovery%20Plan.pdf), the DOE indicates that 86 personnel in the mine at the time of the fire were safely evacuated. Seven of them were evaluated for smoke inhalation, and one of the victims received treatment for that condition. In regard to facility damage, the agency states, "the soot and smoke from the fire adversely affected key equipment and facilities of the WIPP repository, which has resulted in a widespread cleanup effort throughout the underground and identification of deficiencies in WIPP's emergency response, maintenance, and other operational procedures."

Details on the radioactive release at WIPP were reported by the DOE in April 2015 in *Accident Investigation Report: Phase 2: Radiological Release Event at the Waste Isolation Pilot Plant, February 14, 2014* (http://www.energy.gov/sites/prod/files/2015/04/f21/WIPP%20Rad%20Event%20Report%20Phase%202%2004.16.2015.pdf). The agency concludes that the release occurred because of a chemical reaction between organic materials and nitrate salts inside

FIGURE 8.14

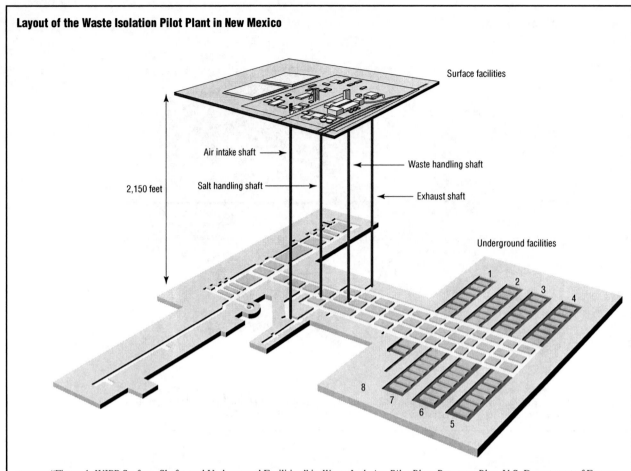

Layout of the Waste Isolation Pilot Plant in New Mexico

SOURCE: "Figure 1. WIPP Surface, Shafts, and Underground Facilities," in *Waste Isolation Pilot Plant Recovery Plan*, U.S. Department of Energy, September 30, 2014, http://www.wipp.energy.gov/Special/WIPP%20Recovery%20Plan.pdf (accessed September 7, 2015)

a storage drum. The resulting pressure buildup popped open the lid of the drum and "propelled" TRU waste into the storage area. An airflow monitoring system sensed the release and set off an alarm. The facility's ventilation system was activated to capture the contaminated air; however, "a small portion" leaked from the system and "exhausted directly to the atmosphere." The DOE's investigation revealed that the drum, which had come from the Los Alamos National Laboratory (LANL) in New Mexico, contained "incompatible materials." The DOE states, "If LANL had adequately developed and implemented repackaging and treatment procedures that incorporated suitable hazard controls and included a rigorous review and approval process, the release would have been preventable."

In *Waste Isolation Pilot Plant Recovery Plan, Revision 0*, the DOE indicates that no employees were below ground when the release occurred. The leaking ventilation system did allow contaminated air to escape from the facility. The agency notes, "Slightly elevated levels of

airborne radioactive concentrations were detected outside the WIPP facility after the release occurred."

The WIPP ceased accepting new waste shipments following the February 2014 incidents and began implementing new safety measures outlined in the facility's recovery plan. As of November 2015, the DOE (http://www.wipp.energy.gov/wipprecovery/recovery.html) indicated that the facility was scheduled to resume "limited" operations in early 2016.

According to the DOE, in "Shipment & Disposal Information" (February 11, 2014, http://www.wipp.energy.gov/shipments.htm), through February 2014 WIPP had received 11,894 shipments of TRU wastes totaling nearly 3.2 million cubic feet (91,000 cubic m). The total amount of TRU waste that can be deposited at WIPP is capped by the Waste Isolation Pilot Plant Land Withdrawal Act of 1992 at 6.2 million cubic feet (175,570 cubic m). It is estimated that WIPP will reach its full capacity in the late 2020s or early 2030s.

FIGURE 8.15

Locations of two 2014 incidents at the Waste Isolation Pilot Plant

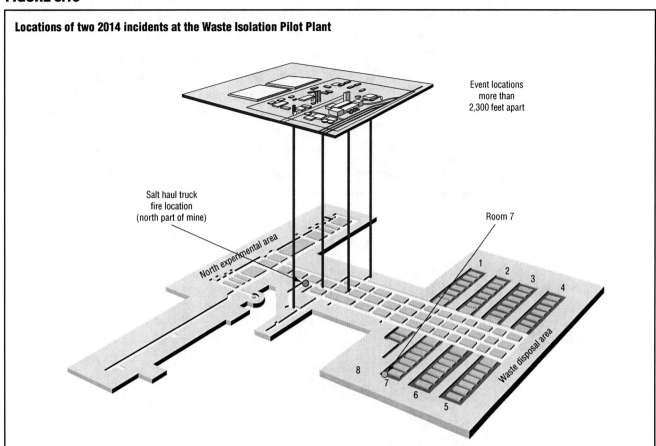

Event locations
more than
2,300 feet apart

Salt haul truck
fire location
(north part of mine)

North experimental area

Room 7

1 2 3 4

8 7 6 5

Waste disposal area

SOURCE: "Figure 4. Location of the Two Incidents at WIPP in February 2014," in *Waste Isolation Pilot Plant Recovery Plan*, U.S. Department of Energy, September 30, 2014, http://www.wipp.energy.gov/Special/WIPP%20Recovery%20Plan.pdf (accessed September 7, 2015)

YUCCA MOUNTAIN. For decades the centerpiece of the federal government's geologic disposal plan for spent nuclear fuel and other HLW was the Yucca Mountain site in Nevada. The site is approximately 100 miles (161 km) northwest of Las Vegas, Nevada, on federal lands within the Nevada Test Site in Nye County. The mountain is located in a remote desert region.

The Nuclear Waste Policy Act of 1982 required the U.S. secretary of energy to investigate the site and, if it was suitable, to recommend to the president that the site be established. In February 2002 President George W. Bush (1946–) received such a recommendation and approved it. Despite opposition from the Nevada governor Kenny Guinn (1936–2010), the project was subsequently approved by the U.S. House of Representatives and the U.S. Senate. In July 2002 President Bush signed the Yucca Mountain resolution into law.

In June 2008 the DOE submitted a license application for the facility to the NRC. Licensing documents are available from the NRC at http://www.nrc.gov/waste/hlw-disposal/yucca-lic-app.html.

Development of the Yucca Mountain repository was plagued by legal setbacks and political controversy.

Nevada lawmakers, in particular, were vehemently opposed to it. President Obama also did not support the project and did not provide funding for it in his proposed federal budgets. In March 2010 the DOE filed a motion with the NRC to withdraw its license application. Some analysts complain the decision was driven solely by political motives. The GAO explains in *Commercial Spent Nuclear Fuel: Observations on the Key Attributes and Challenges of Storage and Disposal Options* (April 11, 2013, http://www.gao.gov/assets/660/653731.pdf) that lack of support from Nevada legislators and the Obama administration proved to be insurmountable challenges for the project. The GAO states, "DOE officials did not cite technical or safety issues with the Yucca Mountain repository project when the project's termination was announced but instead stated that other solutions could achieve broader support."

The DOE created a panel called the Blue Ribbon Commission on America's Nuclear Future to recommend steps for future action. In January 2012 the commission (http://cybercemetery.unt.edu/archive/brc/20120620220827/http://brc.gov/sites/default/files/documents/brc_finalreport_jan2012.pdf) issued its final report, noting, "This nation's failure to come to grips with the nuclear waste issue has already proved damaging and costly, and it will be more damaging and more costly the longer it continues." The commission recommends legislative and administration policy changes as the first steps toward finding a permanent solution to the nation's HLW disposal problem.

In January 2013 the DOE released *Strategy for the Management and Disposal of Used Nuclear Fuel and High-Level Radioactive Waste* (http://energy.gov/sites/prod/files/Strategy%20for%20the%20Management%20and%20Disposal%20of%20Used%20Nuclear%20Fuel%20and%20High%20Level%20Radioactive%20Waste.pdf). The report lays out the Obama administration's plan for future HLW management and disposal as follows:

• Begin operating a pilot interim storage facility by 2021 that will accept used nuclear fuel from reactor sites that have been shut down

• Make available by 2025 a larger interim storage facility "that will have sufficient capacity to provide flexibility in the waste management system and allows for acceptance of enough used nuclear fuel to reduce expected government liabilities"

• Make available by 2048 a geologic repository

Implementation of the plan is dependent on the passage of authorizing legislation and budget approvals from Congress.

CHAPTER 9

WATER ISSUES

Water is precious for many reasons. It is an essential resource for sustaining human, animal, and vegetable life. Agriculture is absolutely dependent on water to produce food crops and livestock. Water is crucial to tourism, navigation, and industry. Enormous amounts are used to generate power, mine materials, and produce goods. Water is an ingredient, a medium, and a means of conveyance or cooling in most industrial processes. Water supplies a vital habitat for many of the earth's creatures, from the whale to the tadpole. There are entire ecosystems that are water based.

All these competing uses put an enormous strain on the earth's water supply. Overall, the amount of water on the earth remains constant, simply passing from one stage to another in a circular pattern known as the hydrologic cycle. (See Figure 9.1.) Water in the atmosphere condenses and falls to the earth as precipitation, such as rain, sleet, or snow. Precipitation seeps into the ground, saturating the soil and refilling underground aquifers; it is drawn from the soil by vegetation for growth and returned into the air by plant leaves through the process of transpiration; and some precipitation flows into surface waters such as rivers, streams, lakes, wetlands, and oceans. Moisture evaporates from surface water back into the atmosphere to repeat the cycle.

Humans have interrupted the hydrologic cycle to accommodate the many water demands of modern life. Flowing rivers and streams are dammed up. Groundwater and surface water are pumped from their sources to other places. Water is either consumed or discharged back to the environment, usually not in the same condition. Water quality becomes increasingly important. There are two primary issues when it comes to water: availability and suitability.

WATER AVAILABILITY

Water covers nearly three-fourths of the planet; however, the vast majority of it is too salty to drink or nourish crops and too corrosive for many industrial processes. In general, saline water is defined as water that contains at least 1,000 milligrams of salt per liter of water. No cheap and effective method for desalinating large amounts of ocean water has been discovered. This makes freshwater an extremely valuable commodity. Although the overall water supply on the earth is enormous, freshwater is not often in the right place at the right time in the right amount to serve all the competing needs.

Overall Water Use in 2010

Every five years since 1950 the U.S. Geological Survey (USGS) has collected comprehensive data on water use in the United States. As of November 2015 the most recent report available was published in 2014 and includes data through 2010.

Molly A. Maupin et al. of the USGS find in *Estimated Use of Water in the United States in 2010* (November 2014, http://pubs.usgs.gov/circ/1405/pdf/circ1405.pdf) that in 2010 an estimated 355 billion gallons of water per day (Bgal/d; 1.3 trillion L/d) were withdrawn from surface water and groundwater sources. (See Table 9.1.) Nearly half of the water—161 Bgal/d (609.5 billion L/d) or 45%—was withdrawn for generation of thermoelectric power. Maupin et al. note that nearly all (94%) of the water that was withdrawn for thermoelectric power generation in 2010 was used for once-through cooling purposes. In other words, the water was withdrawn, traveled through the facility, and discharged back to its source. This is considered a nonconsumptive use of water because little to none of the water is actually consumed. (Some very small amounts may be consumed by evaporation, leaks, or minor uses in facility equipment.)

As shown in Table 9.1, irrigation was the second-largest water withdrawal in 2010, accounting for 115 Bgal/d (435.3 billion L/d), or 32% of the total amount. Much of this water was consumed. It was absorbed by

FIGURE 9.1

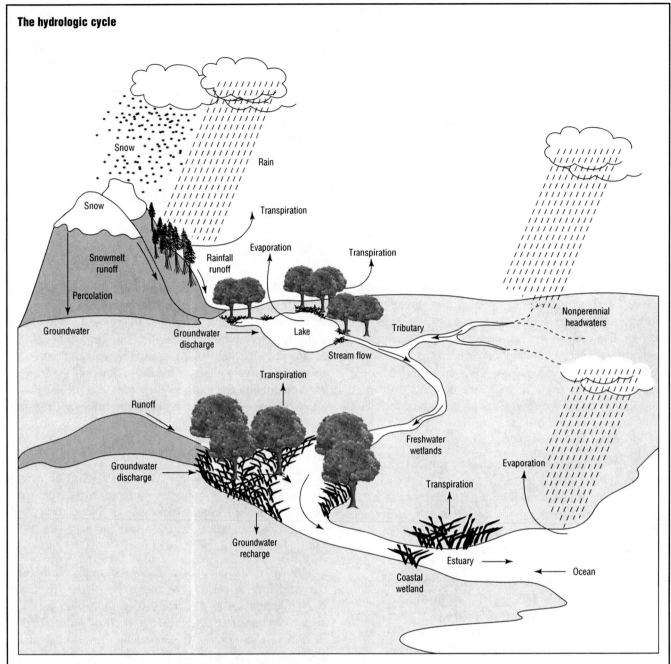

The hydrologic cycle

SOURCE: "The Water Cycle," in *National Water Quality Inventory: 1998 Report to Congress*, U.S. Environmental Protection Agency, June 2000, http://water.epa.gov/lawsregs/guidance/cwa/305b/upload/2000_07_05_305b_98report_chap1.pdf (accessed September 8, 2015)

growing vegetation, ran off into surface waters, trickled down to groundwater, evaporated from the ground, or evaporated from vegetation (a process called transpiration). Thus, irrigation is a large consumptive use of freshwater.

Public water supply is another major consumptive use of freshwater. In 2010, 42 Bgal/d (159 billion L/d), or 12% of the total withdrawn, went to public water supply. (See Table 9.1.) This is water that was withdrawn from water sources by public and private water suppliers that provided water to at least 25 people or via a minimum of 15 connections. The water was potable (fit to drink) and used

in homes, offices, and commercial and industrial facilities for a variety of purposes.

As shown in Table 9.1, minor uses of water in 2010 included miscellaneous industrial uses (including commercial and mining), livestock and aquaculture applications, and self-supplied domestic water (from private wells). Complete data were not available for all minor uses in 2010.

Freshwater use amounted to 306 Bgal/d (1.2 trillion L/d), or 86% of total water withdrawals in 2010, when

TABLE 9.1

Trends in estimated water use, selected years 1950–2010

[Water-use data are in billion gallons per day (thousand million gallons per day) and are rounded to two significant figures for 1950–80, and to three significant figures for 1985–2005. Percentage change is calculated from unrounded numbers. Geographic extent: 1950, 48 States and District of Columbia, and Hawaii; 1955, 48 States and District of Columbia; 1960 and 1975–2005, 50 States and District of Columbia, Puerto Rico, and U.S. Virgin Islands; 1965–70, 50 States and District of Columbia, and Puerto Rico]

	Year													Percentage change 2005 to 2010
	1950	1955	1960	1965	1970	1975	1980	1985	1990	1995	2000	2005	2010	
Population, in millions	150.7	164	179.3	193.8	205.9	216.4	229.6	242.4	252.3	267.1	285.3	300.7	313	4
Total withdrawals	**180**	**240**	**270**	**310**	**370**	**420**	**430**	**397**	**404**	**398**[a]	**413**	**409**[a]	**355**	**−13**
Public supply	14	17	21	24	27	29	33	36.6[a]	38.7[a]	40.2	43.3[a]	44.3[a]	42.0	−5
Rural domestic and livestock														
Self-supplied domestic	2.1	2.1	2.0	2.3	2.6	2.8	3.4	3.32	3.39	3.39	3.58	3.71[a]	3.60	−3
Livestock	1.5	1.5	1.6	1.7	1.9	2.1	2.2	2.23	2.25	2.28	2.39[a]	2.15[a]	2.00	−7
Irrigation	89	110	110	120	130	140	150	135	134	130	139	127[a]	115	−9
Thermoelectric power	40	72	100	130	170	200	210	187	194	190	195	201	161	−20
Other														
Self-supplied industrial	37	39	38	46	47	45	45	25.8[a]	22.5[a]	21.6[a]	19.7	18.1[a]	15.9	−12
Mining	c	c	c	c	c	c	c	c	3.44	4.93	3.59[a]	4.16[a]	3.83[a]	5.32	39
Commercial	c	c	c	c	c	c	c	1.23	2.39	2.89	b	b	b	
Aquaculture	c	c	c	c	c	c	c	2.24	2.24[a]	3.23[a]	5.78[a]	8.84[a]	9.42	7
Source of water														
Ground														
Fresh	34	47	50	60	68	82	83	73.4	79.4[a]	76.3[a]	84.4[a]	78.9[a]	76.0	−4
Saline	b	0.6	0.4	0.5	1.0	1.0	0.93	0.66	1.22	1.11	2.48[a]	1.51[a]	3.29	118
Surface														
Fresh	140	180	190	210	250	260	280	263	256[a]	261	265	270	230	−15
Saline	10	18	31	43	53	69	71	59.6	67.1[a]	59.7	61.0	59.4[a]	45.0	−24

[a]Revised data values.
[b]Data not available.
[c]Included in self-supplied industrial category.

SOURCE: Molly A. Maupin et al., "Table 14. Trends in Estimated Water Use in the United States, 1950–2010," in *Estimated Use of Water in the United States in 2010*, U.S. Department of the Interior, U.S. Geological Survey, November 2014, http://pubs.usgs.gov/circ/1405/pdf/circ1405.pdf (accessed September 8, 2015)

groundwater and surface water sources are combined. (See Table 9.1.) Freshwater provides the majority of water that is used for public water supply, domestic self-supply (private wells), irrigation, livestock watering, aquaculture, thermoelectric power generation, and industrial purposes. Most of the freshwater—230 Bgal/d (870.6 trillion L/d) or 86%—was obtained from surface water sources, such as rivers and lakes. As shown in Figure 9.2, surface water has been the primary source of the nation's freshwater for decades.

Water Use Trends between 1950 and 2010

Table 9.1 shows trends in the U.S. population and water withdrawals between 1950 and 2010. The population rose from 150.7 million in 1950 to 313 million in 2010, an increase of nearly 108%. By contrast, water withdrawals went from 180 Bgal/d (681.4 billion L/d) in 1950 to 355 Bgal/d (1.6 trillion L/d) in 2010, an increase of 97%. In 1950 the per capita (per person) water withdrawal was 1,194 gallons per day (4,520 L/d). This value climbed steadily over the years, reaching a peak in 1975 of 1,940 gallons per day (7,344 L/d) per person. Per capita use has since declined and was 1,134 gallons per day (4,393 L/d) per person in 2010.

Historically, freshwater has accounted for the vast majority of all water used. (See Table 9.1.) In 1950

freshwater comprised 97% of total withdrawals. The percentage has gradually decreased and was 86% in 2010.

Groundwater

Groundwater is water that fills pores or cracks in subsurface rocks. When rain falls or snow melts on the earth's surface, water may run off into lower land areas or lakes and streams. Some is caught and diverted for human use. What is left absorbs into the soil, where it can be used by vegetation, seeps into deeper layers of soil and rock, or evaporates back into the atmosphere. (See Figure 9.3.)

An aquifer is an underground formation that contains enough water to yield significant amounts when a well is drilled into it. Aquifers vary from a few feet thick to tens or hundreds of feet thick. They can be located just below the earth's surface or thousands of feet beneath it, and one aquifer may be only a part of a large system of aquifers that feed into one another. They can cover a few acres of land or many thousands of square miles. Because runoff water can easily seep down to the water table (the boundary between saturated and unsaturated soils), aquifers are susceptible to contamination.

Modern technological developments allow massive quantities of water to be pumped out of the ground. When large amounts of water are removed from the ground,

FIGURE 9.2

Trends in population and withdrawals of fresh groundwater and surface water, selected years 1950–2010

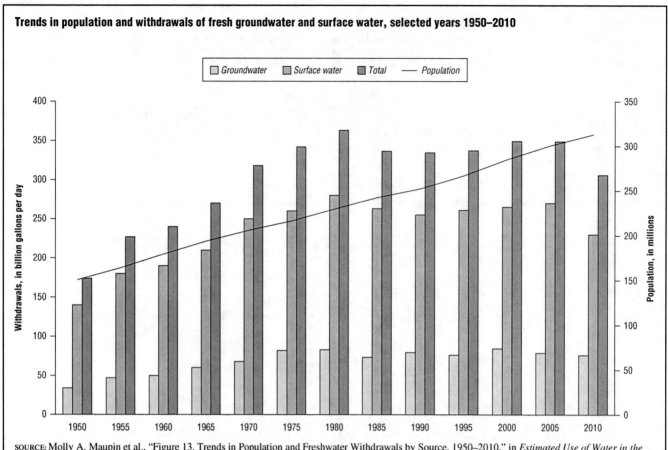

SOURCE: Molly A. Maupin et al., "Figure 13. Trends in Population and Freshwater Withdrawals by Source, 1950–2010," in *Estimated Use of Water in the United States in 2010*, U.S. Department of the Interior, U.S. Geological Survey, November 2014, http://pubs.usgs.gov/circ/1405/pdf/circ1405.pdf (accessed September 8, 2015)

FIGURE 9.3

Groundwater in the hydrologic cycle

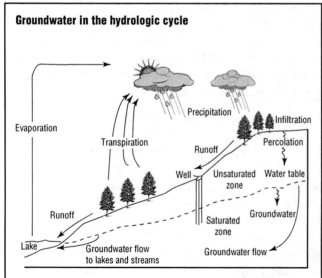

SOURCE: "Ground Water in the Hydrologic Cycle," in *Guide for Industrial Waste Management*, U.S. Environmental Protection Agency, Office of Solid Waste and Emergency Response, June 1999, http://www.epa.gov/osw/nonhaz/industrial/guide/pdf/chap7a.pdf (accessed September 8, 2015)

underground aquifers can become depleted much more quickly than they can naturally be replenished. Removal of groundwater also disturbs the natural filtering process that occurs as water travels through rocks and sand.

WATER QUALITY CONSIDERATIONS

Water is a fundamental need in every society. Families use water for drinking, cooking, and cleaning. Industry needs it to make chemicals, prepare paper, and clean factories and equipment. Cities use water to fight fires, clean streets, and fill public swimming pools. Farmers water their livestock, clean barns, and irrigate crops. Hydroelectric power plants use water to drive generators, and thermonuclear power plants need it for cooling. Water quality is important to all users, as differing levels of quality are required for different uses. Although some industrial users can tolerate water containing high levels of contaminants, drinking water requirements are extremely strict.

CLEAN WATER ACT

On June 22, 1969, the Cuyahoga River in Cleveland, Ohio, burst into flames, the result of oil and debris that had accumulated on the river's surface. This episode thrust the problem of water pollution into the public consciousness. Many people became aware—and wary—of the nation's polluted waters, and in 1972 Congress passed the Federal Water Pollution Control Act, commonly known as the Clean Water Act (CWA).

The objective of the CWA was to "restore and maintain the chemical, physical, and biological integrity of the nation's waters." It called for ending the discharge of all pollutants into the navigable waters of the United States to achieve "wherever attainable, an interim goal of water quality which provides for the protection and propagation of fish, shellfish, and wildlife and provides for recreation in and on the water."

The CWA includes five titles as follows:

- Title I—Research and Related Programs

- Title II—Grants for the Construction of Treatment Works

- Title III—Standards and Enforcement

- Title IV—Permits and Licenses

- Title V—General Provisions

Clean Water Act Jurisdiction

Since its original passage, the scope of the water bodies subject to the CWA has been the subject of much litigation. The law gives the U.S. Environmental Protection Agency (EPA) jurisdiction over "waters of the United States." This term has traditionally been interpreted to include navigable waters (waters that can be traversed by boat). The CWA's applicability to streams and small wetlands is a matter of extreme controversy.

The U.S. Supreme Court has rendered three decisions on the definition of "waters of the United States": *United States v. Riverside Bayview Homes, Inc.* (474 U.S. 121 [1985]), *Solid Waste Agency of Northern Cook County v. U.S. Army Corps of Engineers* (531 U.S. 159 [2001]), and *Rapanos v. United States* (547 U.S. 715 [2006]). However, it is widely agreed that these decisions do not provide clear-cut guidance. According to Jason Miller of the U.S. Fish and Wildlife Service (FWS), in *Our Wetlands and Streams after Rapanos/Carabell … Does the Clean Water Act Still Protect Them?* (July 2008, http://www.fws.gov/habitatconservation/rapanos_carabell/Post_Rapanos_pres_web.pdf), these decisions have been interpreted to mean that federal jurisdiction applies to wetlands that are adjacent to waters that are permanent, relatively permanent, standing, or flowing. In addition, it applies to wetlands that have a "significant nexus" to navigable waters.

In 2007 the EPA finalized a guidance document that informed its staff how to use these definitions to determine which waters are subject to federal jurisdiction. In 2011 the agency prepared *Draft Guidance on Identifying Waters Protected by the Clean Water Act* (http://water.epa.gov/lawsregs/guidance/wetlands/upload/wous_guidance_4-2011.pdf), which was a revised guidance document on the subject.

After a period of public comment and consideration, the EPA and the U.S. Army Corps of Engineers (ACE) collaborated to draft a regulation to more clearly define the scope of the water bodies subject to the CWA. The ACE was involved because Section 404 of the law grants the ACE the authority to regulate developments that change waterways in certain ways, for example, dredging out bottom sediment from a river or dumping dirt into a swamp to fill it. In June 2015 the new regulation, called the Clean Water Rule (https://www.federalregister.gov/articles/2015/06/29/2015-13435/clean-water-rule-definition-of-waters-of-the-united-states), was published. In "Clean Water Rule Protects Streams and Wetlands Critical to Public Health, Communities, and Economy" (May 27, 2015, http://yosemite.epa.gov/opa/admpress.nsf/0/62295CDDD6C6B45685257E52004FAC97), the EPA notes that in addition to covering navigable waters, the rule also covers tributaries to them and their headwaters. Waters "next to" rivers and lakes and their tributaries are also included, as are small wetlands (such as prairie potholes), that "impact downstream waters." The Clean Water Rule went into effect in August 2015.

Critics decried the rule as a grievous overreach of power by the EPA and ACE. Numerous lawsuits were filed. In September 2015, 13 states (Alaska, Arizona, Arkansas, Colorado, Idaho, Missouri, Montana, Nebraska, Nevada, New Mexico, North Dakota, South Dakota, and Wyoming) obtained an injunction from a district court in North Dakota halting enforcement of the rule in their states. Another lawsuit was filed by 18 states (Alabama, Florida, Georgia, Indiana, Kansas, Kentucky, Louisiana, Michigan, Mississippi, North Carolina, Ohio, Oklahoma, South Carolina, Tennessee, Texas, Utah, West Virginia, and Wisconsin). In October 2015 the U.S. Court of Appeals for the 6th Circuit granted a stay of the rule, making it unenforceable nationwide. In *State of Ohio, et al. v. U.S. Army Corps of Engineers, et al.* (October 10, 2015, http://www.ca6.uscourts.gov/opinions.pdf/15a0246p-06.pdf), the court notes that "a stay temporarily silences the whirlwind of confusion that springs from uncertainty about the requirements of the new Rule and whether they will survive legal testing."

Environmental groups were sorely disappointed by the decision. For example, in "Sierra Club Responds to Court Ruling Endangering American Waterways" (October 9, 2015, http://content.sierraclub.org/press-releases/2015/10/sierra-club-responds-court-ruling-endangering-american-waterways), the Sierra Club states, "The Clean Water Rule is a necessary step forward to restore protections to our nation's rivers, streams and wetlands to ensure that we do not return to the days of when our waters were so polluted they literally caught on fire."

Water Quality Standards

Under Title III, Section 305(b) of the CWA, the states are required to assess the condition of their waters and report the extent to which the waters support the basic goals of the CWA and state water quality standards. Water quality standards are designed to protect designated uses (such as drinking water supply).

Title III, Section 303(d) requires the states to identify any of their water bodies not meeting water quality standards. The states may then set a total maximum daily load (TMDL) for each of the problematic water bodies. According to the EPA, in "Impaired Waters and Total Maximum Daily Loads" (August 14, 2015, http://water .epa.gov/lawsregs/lawsguidance/cwa/tmdl/index.cfm), a TMDL is basically the maximum amount of a particular pollutant that can be released into a water body without impairing its quality below that of the applicable water quality standard. TMDL calculations result in loading and reduction goals. For example, it might be determined that a river impaired by a pollutant needs to receive no more than 20 pounds (9.1 kg) per year of that pollutant from all dischargers in the future to improve and meet the applicable water quality limit. In this case, 20 pounds per year is the loading goal. Assuming that the river currently receives 40 pounds (18.1 kg) per year of the pollutant means that discharges of the pollutant must be reduced by 50%. This is the reduction goal.

TMDL analyses provide numerical goals that are pollutant-specific and water body–specific. Figure 9.4 shows that as of September 2015, over 68,000 TMDLs had been completed around the country that addressed more than 71,000 causes of water impairment. Achieving TMDL goals can be accomplished through various means. The options differ depending on whether the dischargers are point sources or nonpoint sources.

FIGURE 9.4

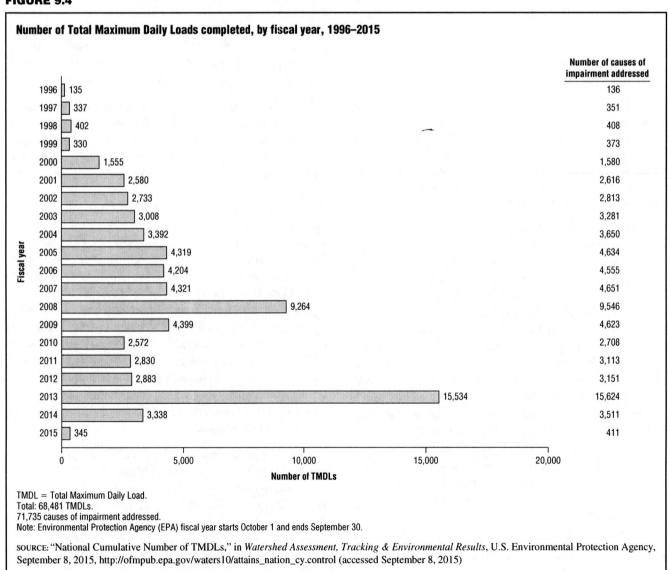

Number of Total Maximum Daily Loads completed, by fiscal year, 1996–2015

Fiscal year	Number of TMDLs	Number of causes of impairment addressed
1996	135	136
1997	337	351
1998	402	408
1999	330	373
2000	1,555	1,580
2001	2,580	2,616
2002	2,733	2,813
2003	3,008	3,281
2004	3,392	3,650
2005	4,319	4,634
2006	4,204	4,555
2007	4,321	4,651
2008	9,264	9,546
2009	4,399	4,623
2010	2,572	2,708
2011	2,830	3,113
2012	2,883	3,151
2013	15,534	15,624
2014	3,338	3,511
2015	345	411

TMDL = Total Maximum Daily Load.
Total: 68,481 TMDLs.
71,735 causes of impairment addressed.
Note: Environmental Protection Agency (EPA) fiscal year starts October 1 and ends September 30.

SOURCE: "National Cumulative Number of TMDLs," in *Watershed Assessment, Tracking & Environmental Results*, U.S. Environmental Protection Agency, September 8, 2015, http://ofmpub.epa.gov/waters10/attains_nation_cy.control (accessed September 8, 2015)

Point Source Management

Point sources are those that disperse pollutants from a specific source or area, such as a sewage drain or an industrial discharge pipe. (See Figure 9.5.) Pollutants commonly discharged from point sources include bacteria (from wastewater treatment plants and sewer overflow), toxic chemicals, and heavy metals (from industrial plants). Point sources are regulated under the National Pollutant Discharge Elimination System (NPDES). Any facility using point sources to discharge to receiving waters must obtain an NPDES permit for them. States can operate their own NPDES-permitting program if they have been authorized to do so by the EPA. In "Specific State Program Status" (2015, http://water.epa.gov/polwaste/npdes/basics/NPDES-State-Program-Status.cfm), the EPA indicates that as of 2015 most states had received that authorization.

NPDES permits include monitoring and reporting requirements and set specific limits on the amounts and types of pollutants that can be discharged to water bodies. The limits take into account any TMDLs that have been set for the water bodies. The EPA (http://www.epa.gov/enviro/facts/pcs-icis/search.html) allows the public to access NPDES permit information, including any reported violations of the permit limits, via the Permit Compliance System and the Integrated Compliance Information System databases on the Envirofacts website.

Nonpoint Source Management

Nonpoint sources are those that are spread out over a large area and have no specific outlet or discharge point. (See Figure 9.5.) These include agricultural and urban runoff, runoff from mining and construction sites, and

FIGURE 9.5

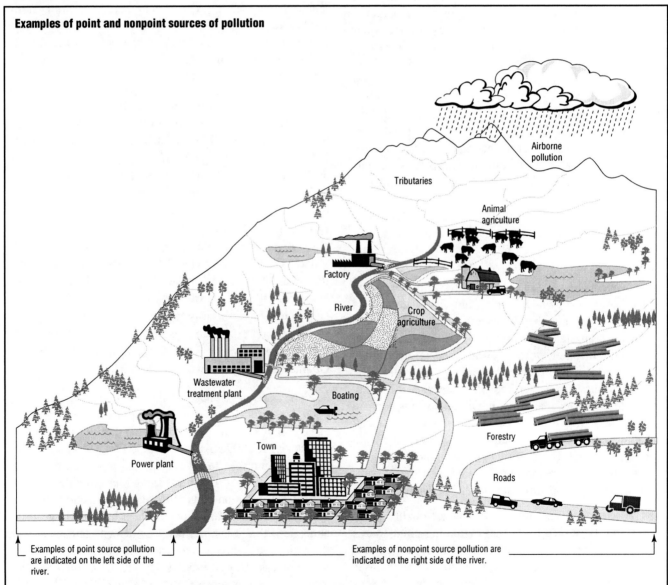

Examples of point and nonpoint sources of pollution

Examples of point source pollution are indicated on the left side of the river.

Examples of nonpoint source pollution are indicated on the right side of the river.

SOURCE: "Figure 3. Examples of Point and Nonpoint Sources of Pollution," in *Water Quality: Key EPA and State Decisions Limited by Inconsistent and Incomplete Data*, U.S. General Accounting Office, March 2000, http://www.gao.gov/archive/2000/rc00054.pdf (accessed September 8, 2015)

accidental or deliberate spills. Nonpoint sources are much more difficult to regulate than point sources, but are increasingly blamed for contributing significantly to water pollution. Data presented later in this chapter show that sources such as agriculture and urban-related runoff and stormwater are blamed by the states as primary probable causes of water impairment.

Nonpoint source management at the federal level is not addressed directly in the CWA. However, Title III, Section 319(b) of the law does require each state to establish a "management program for controlling pollution added from nonpoint sources to the navigable waters within the State and improving the quality of such waters." For example, California (September 2, 2015, http://www.waterboards.ca.gov/water_issues/programs/nps) operates an extensive Nonpoint Source Pollution Control Program.

In addition, nonpoint source management is achieved through nonregulatory measures, such as by encouraging voluntary practices by dischargers and by private water protection organizations that promote community actions. For example, the Iowa chapter of the Sierra Club recommends in "Protecting Iowa's Water Quality: Point and Non-point Sources of Pollution" (April 21, 2015, http://www.sierraclub.org/sites/www.sierraclub.org/files/sce/iowa-chapter/water/WaterQuality.pdf) that citizens, businesses, and local governments take measures to prevent or slow rainfall runoff from their properties, such as by using rain barrels or detention ponds. The organization notes, "These techniques hold water on the landscape longer and will serve to filter pollutants rather than allowing them to rush into water bodies."

Watershed Management

In "Watersheds" (January 16, 2013, http://water.epa.gov/type/watersheds/index.cfm), the EPA defines a watershed as an "area that drains to a common waterway, such as a stream, lake, estuary, wetland, aquifer, or even the ocean." In other words, a watershed is determined geologically and hydrologically, rather than politically. Figure 9.6 shows a watershed example and the many issues and processes that affect it. Obviously, a watershed can include both point sources and nonpoint sources that contribute to water impairment. Watersheds are delineated by the USGS and assigned unique 12-digit numbers that identify the region, subregion, basin, subbasin, watershed, and subwatershed. (See Table 9.2.)

The EPA believes the nation's water quality problems cannot be solved by further regulating point-source discharges. Instead, the agency advocates a comprehensive approach that crosses jurisdictional boundaries and addresses all the air, water, land, social, and economic issues that affect a particular watershed. The EPA actively encourages the participation of private

environmental and conservation groups in watershed protection. The agency's Adopt Your Watershed program (http://water.epa.gov/action/adopt/index.cfm) provides a database that includes information about each of the nation's more than 2,600 watersheds. The database identifies thousands of local and regional groups that engage in activities to further watershed protection and improvement.

THE CHESAPEAKE BAY WATERSHED. The Chesapeake Bay is a massive estuary (an area where ocean and freshwater come together) located on the upper East Coast. (See Figure 9.7.) The estuary is fed by rivers and streams in multiple states and the District of Columbia; thus, the Chesapeake Bay watershed is enormous. Its water quality has long been a source of concern. During the late 1970s Congress ordered the EPA to conduct a comprehensive study of the watershed. Ben A. Franklin reports in "Chesapeake Bay Study Citing Pollution Threats" (NYTimes.com, September 27, 1983) that the $27 million study took seven years to complete and revealed significant deterioration since the 1960s in the bay's water quality and ecological health. These problems were forecast to worsen as the area's population continued to grow.

Over the decades various federal-state programs have been implemented in an effort to improve the watershed, but have failed to achieve desired goals. In early January 2009 a large group of plaintiffs sued the EPA alleging the agency had failed to meet its obligations under the CWA and federal-state agreements to restore and preserve the bay's water quality and ecological resources. The case, Fowler v. EPA (No. 1:09-CV-00005-CKK), reflects the name of one of the plaintiffs, the former Maryland state senator C. Bernard Fowler (1924–). Another major plaintiff was the Chesapeake Bay Foundation (http://www.cbf.org), a nonprofit organization whose stated mission is to "Save the Bay, and Keep It Saved." The lawsuit was filed during the waning days of the administration of George W. Bush (1946–); only weeks later Barack Obama (1961–) was sworn in as president.

The case never reached the courtroom. On May 15, 2009, President Obama issued Executive Order 13508, Chesapeake Bay Protection and Restoration (http://www.gpo.gov/fdsys/pkg/FR-2009-05-15/pdf/E9-11547.pdf), which established a committee to investigate and report on the major challenges involved in protecting and restoring the bay and outline the pollution control strategies and actions that the EPA should take in response. In May 2010 the EPA announced that it had reached a settlement agreement with the plaintiffs. In the press release "EPA Reaches Settlement in Chesapeake Bay Lawsuit" (May 11, 2010, http://yosemite.epa.gov/opa/admpress.nsf/0/ac46af32562521d48525772000591133?OpenDocument), the agency notes that it agreed to do the following:

FIGURE 9.6

Land drawing demonstrating watershed approach for the management of water resources

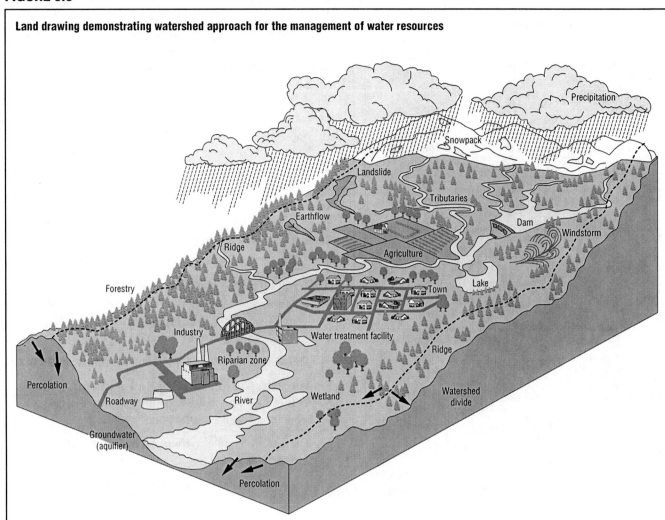

SOURCE: "Figure 1. The Area Hydrologically Defined by a Watershed Is Affected by Many Processes and Issues. A 'Watershed Approach' Coordinates Their Management," in *Protecting and Restoring America's Watersheds: Status, Trends and Initiatives in Watershed Management*, U.S. Environmental Protection Agency, Office of Water, June 2001, http://www.epa.gov/owow/protecting/restore725.pdf (accessed September 8, 2015)

TABLE 9.2

Watershed boundary definitions and examples

Definition	Example
A region, the largest drainage basin, contains the drainage area of a major river or the combined drainage areas of several rivers.	Mid-Atlantic (02)
Subregions divide regions and include the area drained by a river system.	Chesapeake Bay watershed (0207)
Basins divide or may be equivalent to subregions.	Potomac River watershed (020700)
Subbasins divide basins and represent part or all of a surface-drainage basin, a combination of drainage basins, or a distinct hydrologic feature.	Monocacy watershed (0207009)
Watersheds divide subbasins and usually range in size from 40,000 to 250,000 acres.	Monocacy River watershed (0207000905)
Subwatersheds divide or may be equivalent to watersheds and usually range in size from 10,000 to 40,000 acres.	Double Pipe Creek subwatershed (020700090502)

SOURCE: "Breaking down the Watershed," in *Handbook for Developing Watershed Plans to Restore and Protect Our Waters*, U.S. Environmental Protection Agency, March 2008, http://water.epa.gov/polwaste/nps/upload/2008_04_18_NPS_watershed_handbook_handbook.pdf (accessed September 8, 2015)

- Establish a "stringent" TMDL for the entire watershed

- Expand its review of permits in the watershed

- Initiate a rulemaking to prepare new national regulations on concentrated animal feeding operations (CAFOs) and urban and suburban stormwater

- Establish a publicly available system for tracking and monitoring the EPA's progress toward reducing pollution in the Chesapeake Bay watershed

The EPA calls the Chesapeake Bay TMDL "the largest and most complex [TMDL] ever developed in the nation,

FIGURE 9.7

Map of Chesapeake Bay region

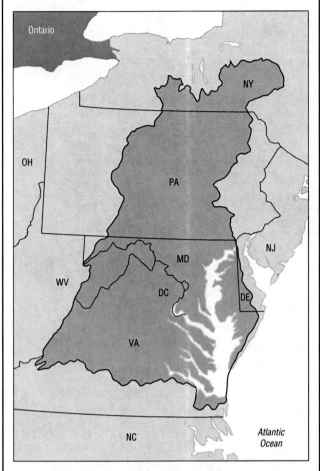

SOURCE: "Map," in *Fact Sheet: Chesapeake Bay Total Maximum Daily Load (TMDL)*, U.S. Environmental Protection Agency, August 26, 2013, http://www.epa.gov/reg3wapd/pdf/pdf_chesbay/BayTMDLFactSheet8_26_13.pdf (accessed September 8, 2015)

pollution-from-animal-operations), the Chesapeake Bay Foundation and the EPA announced in June 2013 that they had revised the original settlement agreement to eliminate the requirement for a new national CAFO regulation. The Chesapeake Bay Foundation explains it agreed to the change because it feared that such a regulation would be subject to numerous and lengthy court challenges. Instead, the foundation agreed to allow the EPA to conduct a series of investigations and inspections related to CAFO management and then decide whether any revisions to the existing CAFO rules are warranted. Some environmental groups were extremely disappointed in the outcome and accused the Obama administration of giving in to pressure from the agricultural industry, which was staunchly opposed to tighter CAFO regulation.

THE NATION'S WATER QUALITY

As noted earlier, Title III, Section 305(b) of the CWA requires each state to report water quality data to the EPA. These data must indicate:

- The water quality of all navigable waters in the state

- The extent to which the waters provide for the protection and propagation of marine animals and allow recreation in and on the water

- The extent to which pollution has been eliminated or is under control

- The sources and causes of the pollution

The act stipulates that the states must submit this information to the EPA on a biennial basis (every two years). Under Title III, Section 303(d) of the CWA, states are required to submit to the EPA a separate list of waters that are considered to be impaired and requiring pollution controls.

National Surface Water Quality Database

Since 2002 the EPA has electronically collected state water quality data on surface waters and compiled it in the database Watershed Assessment, Tracking, and Environmental Results (WATERS; http://iaspub.epa.gov/tmdl_waters10/attains_nation_cy.control). As of 2015 most states had submitted WATERS data through 2012; thus, the following discussion of national water quality assumes 2012 as the reporting year.

In general, the states assess surface water quality in rivers and streams, lakes, ocean shoreline, and estuaries. Because of the tremendous resources required to assess all water bodies, only a small portion of each water body type is actually assessed for each reporting period.

Surface water bodies are rated on quality as follows:

- Good—meets applicable water quality standards and designated uses

involving pollution sources throughout a 64,000-square-mile watershed that includes six states and the District of Columbia." In December 2010 the agency (http://www.epa.gov/reg3wapd/tmdl/ChesapeakeBay/tmdlexec.html) finalized the TMDL. It requires massive load reductions in nitrogen, phosphorus, and sediment to water bodies in Delaware, Maryland, New York, Pennsylvania, Virginia, West Virginia, and the District of Columbia. According to the EPA (September 30, 2015, http://www2.epa.gov/chesapeake-bay-tmdl/frequently-asked-questions-faqs-about-chesapeake-bay-tmdl), full implementation of the required pollution control measures is expected by 2025.

As explained later in this chapter, CAFOs are operations that house large numbers of livestock. Some CAFOs are required to be permitted under the NPDES. According to the press release "CBF and EPA Reach New Agreement to Reduce Pollution from Animal Operations" (http://www.cbf.org/news-media/newsroom/fed/2013/06/05/cbf-and-epa-reach-new-agreement-to-reduce-

- Threatened—qualifies for "good" rating, but is expected to degrade in the near future

- Impaired—fails to meet applicable water quality standards and designated uses

Table 9.3 provides a summary of the ratings for the different types of water bodies that were assessed by the states. It should be noted that the percentage of total waters assessed varied widely from only 1.2% of wetland acreage to 88.1% of the open waters of the Great Lakes as measured in square miles. Overall, the data indicate significant problems with impairment. For example, 581,347 river and stream miles (935,587 km) out of 1.1 million miles (1.8 million km) total or 54% were impaired. Likewise, 13 million lake, reservoir, and pond acres (excluding the Great Lakes; 5.3 ha) out of 18.8 million acres (7.2 million ha) total or 69% were impaired.

The EPA categorizes the many different (and sometimes overlapping) state-designated uses of water bodies into nine broad classes:

- Aesthetic value—water bodies valued for their aesthetic qualities, for example, beautiful scenery

- Agricultural—water bodies supporting the irrigation of agricultural land and the watering of livestock and wildlife

- Aquatic life harvesting—water bodies supporting the growth of harvestable aquatic life, such as fish and shellfish

- Exceptional recreational or ecological significance—water bodies supporting rare, threatened, or endangered species; serving as exceptional habitats; or being outstanding natural resource waters in some other way

- Fish, shellfish, and wildlife protection and propagation—water bodies supporting aquatic life and other wildlife

that use them as part of their habitats; the spawning of salmon and other fish species; the migration of various species of aquatic organisms; and commercial and sport fishing

- Public water supply—water bodies serving as sources of public water supplies

- Industrial—water bodies supporting industrial operations

- Recreation—water bodies supporting recreational activities, such as boating and swimming

- Other—water bodies supporting other uses not specified, for example, navigational uses

In 2012 the two designated use classes with the highest levels of impairment for each water body type were:

- Rivers and streams—Aquatic life harvesting (70.5% impaired) and fish, shellfish, and wildlife protection and propagation (42.6% impaired). (See Table 9.4.)

- Lakes, reservoirs, and ponds—Aquatic life harvesting (76.8% impaired) and fish, shellfish, and wildlife protection and propagation (43.5% impaired). (See Table 9.5.)

- Bays and estuaries—Aquatic life harvesting (82.7% impaired) and fish, shellfish, and wildlife protection and propagation (60.9% impaired). (See Table 9.6.)

- Coastal shoreline—Other uses (100%) and aquatic life harvesting (93.5%). (See Table 9.7.)

- Ocean and near coastal—Aquatic life harvesting (93% impaired) and fish, shellfish, and wildlife protection and propagation (59.5% impaired). (See Table 9.8.)

- Wetlands—Aquatic life harvesting (99.2% impaired) and agricultural (67.2% impaired). (See Table 9.9.)

TABLE 9.3

Water bodies assessed for water quality, 2012

	Size of water							
	Rivers and streams (miles)	Lakes, reservoirs, and ponds (acres)	Bays and estuaries (square miles)	Coastal shoreline (miles)	Ocean and near coastal (square miles)	Wetlands (acres)	Great Lakes shoreline (miles)	Great Lakes open water (square miles)
Good waters	493,292	5,631,978	7,574	901	616	574,085	78	62
Threatened waters	7,657	145,572						
Impaired waters	581,347	13,008,063	27,515	7,262	1,058	678,981	4,353	53,270
Total assessed waters	**1,082,296**	**18,785,613**	**35,089**	**8,163**	**1,674**	**1,253,066**	**4,431**	**53,332**
Total waters	**3,533,205**	**41,666,049**	**87,791**	**58,618**	**54,120**	**107,700,000**	**5,202**	**60,546**
Percent of waters assessed	30.6	45.1	40.0	13.9	3.1	1.2	85.2	88.1

Note: Incomplete state reported information may lead to discrepancies and/or missing information in these reports. Compilation of state-level data; while most data are from 2012, some data are from 2006, 2008, 2010, or 2014.

SOURCE: "Assessed Waters of United States," in *Watershed Assessment, Tracking & Environmental Results*, U.S. Environmental Protection Agency, September 8, 2015, http://ofmpub.epa.gov/waters10/attains_nation_cy.control (accessed September 8, 2015)

TABLE 9.4

Percentage of rivers and streams supporting designated uses, 2012

[Waters assessed for more than one designated use are included in multiple designated use groups below]

Designated use group	Miles assessed	Percent good	Percent threatened	Percent impaired
Fish, shellfish, and wildlife protection and propagation	851,132	56.9	0.6	42.6
Recreation	454,459	59.0	1.4	39.7
Agricultural	394,607	96.1	0.1	3.8
Aquatic life harvesting	279,176	28.7	0.9	70.5
Public water supply	201,800	77.0	0.2	22.8
Industrial	198,273	97.8	0.0	2.2
Other	85,956	97.9	0.0	2.1
Aesthetic value	28,790	92.8	0.0	7.2
Exceptional recreational or ecological significance	4,541	80.2	0.0	19.8

Note: Compilation of state-level data; while most data are from 2012, some data are from 2006, 2008, 2010, or 2014.

SOURCE: Adapted from "National Summary: Designated Use Support in Assessed Rivers and Streams," in *Watershed Assessment, Tracking & Environmental Results*, U.S. Environmental Protection Agency, September 8, 2015, http://ofmpub.epa.gov/waters10/attains_nation_cy.control (accessed September 8, 2015)

TABLE 9.5

Percentage of lakes, reservoirs, and ponds supporting designated uses, 2012

[Waters assessed for more than one designated use are included in multiple designated use groups below]

Designated use group	Acres assessed	Percent good	Percent threatened	Percent impaired
Fish, shellfish, and wildlife protection and propagation	11,148,096	55.3	1.1	43.5
Aquatic life harvesting	9,935,475	22.0	1.3	76.8
Recreation	8,507,012	82.1	1.5	16.4
Public water supply	6,193,162	78.7	1.8	19.5
Agricultural	5,976,377	95.9	0.0	4.1
Industrial	3,251,743	99.9	0.0	0.1
Other	2,474,382	87.2	0.0	12.8
Aesthetic value	1,212,475	62.6	0.0	37.4
Exceptional recreational or ecological significance	229	84.3	0.0	15.7

Note: Compilation of state-level data; while most data are from 2012, some data are from 2006, 2008, 2010, or 2014.

SOURCE: Adapted from "National Summary: Designated Use Support in Assessed Lakes, Reservoirs, and Ponds," in *Watershed Assessment, Tracking & Environmental Results*, U.S. Environmental Protection Agency, September 8, 2015, http://ofmpub.epa.gov/waters10/attains_nation_cy .control (accessed September 8, 2015)

- Great Lakes shoreline—Aquatic life harvesting (100% impaired) and recreation (67.8% impaired). (See Table 9.10.)

- Great Lakes open water—Aquatic life harvesting (100% impaired) and fish, shellfish, and wildlife protection and propagation (98.5% impaired). (See Table 9.11.)

Table 9.12 lists the general impairment causes reported by the states. Although dozens of factors were involved, the most highly reported causes across multiple water body types were mercury, nutrients, organic enrichment/oxygen depletion, pathogens, and polychlorinated biphenyls. Table 9.13 identifies the probable sources of the impairment causes listed in Table 9.12. For many water bodies, the states could not determine specific sources, so they put the blame on "unknown" sources. The two leading impairment sources were agriculture and atmospheric deposition.

MERCURY. As shown in Table 9.12, mercury was the primary cause of impairment for several water body types in 2012, particularly lakes, reservoirs, and ponds. More than 8.2 million acres (3.3 million ha) of lakes, reservoirs, and ponds were deemed impaired due to mercury. According to the EPA, in "Specific State Causes of Impairment That Make Up the National Mercury Cause of Impairment Group for Threatened and Impaired Lakes, Reservoirs, and Ponds" (2015, http://iaspub.epa.gov/ tmdl_waters10/attains_nation_cy.cause_detail?p_cause _group_name=MERCURY), this impairment factor was evidenced by widespread mercury detection in fish tissue. Mercury is said to bioaccumulate, meaning that

TABLE 9.6

Percentage of bays and estuaries supporting designated uses, 2012

[Waters assessed for more than one designated use are included in multiple designated use groups below]

Designated use group	Square miles assessed	Percent good	Percent threatened	Percent impaired
Aquatic life harvesting	25,423	17.3	0.0	82.7
Fish, shellfish, and wildlife protection and propagation	21,001	39.1	0.0	60.9
Recreation	14,567	71.1	0.0	28.9
Agricultural	3,789	96.6	0.0	3.4
Industrial	3,223	100.0	0.0	0.0
Other	3,167	100.0	0.0	0.0
Public water supply	187	75.0	0.0	25.0
Aesthetic value	67	76.6	0.0	23.4

Note: Compilation of state-level data; while most data are from 2012, some data are from 2006, 2008, 2010, or 2014.

SOURCE: Adapted from "National Summary: Designated Use Support in Assessed Bays and Estuaries," in *Watershed Assessment, Tracking & Environmental Results*, U.S. Environmental Protection Agency, September 8, 2015, http://ofmpub.epa.gov/waters10/attains_nation_cy.control (accessed September 8, 2015)

it builds up in the tissues of the organisms that consume it. The chemical mostly reaches water bodies via atmospheric deposition. As described in Chapter 2, mercury is present in fossil fuels, such as coal, and enters the atmosphere when the fuels are burned.

NUTRIENTS. Nutrients are substances that nourish vegetation; nitrogen and phosphorus and compounds that contain them (such as phosphate and nitrate) are prime examples. Excess levels of these nutrients can stimulate

TABLE 9.7

Percentage of coastal shoreline supporting designated uses, 2012

[Waters assessed for more than one designated use are included in multiple designated use groups below]

Designated use group	Miles assessed	Percent good	Percent threatened	Percent impaired
Aquatic life harvesting	7,123	6.5	0.0	93.5
Recreation	1,687	77.0	0.0	23.0
Fish, shellfish, and wildlife protection and propagation	916	45.6	0.0	54.4
Aesthetic value	235	100.0	0.0	0.0
Industrial	30	83.3	0.0	16.7
Other	4	0.0	0.0	100.0

Note: Compilation of state-level data; while most data are from 2012, some data are from 2006, 2008, 2010, or 2014.

SOURCE: Adapted from "National Summary: Designated Use Support in Assessed Coastal Shoreline," in *Watershed Assessment, Tracking & Environmental Results*, U.S. Environmental Protection Agency, September 8, 2015, http://ofmpub.epa.gov/waters10/attains_nation_cy.control (accessed September 8, 2015)

TABLE 9.8

Percentage of ocean and near coastal waters supporting designated uses, 2012

[Waters assessed for more than one designated use are included in multiple designated use groups below]

Designated use group	Square miles assessed	Percent good	Percent threatened	Percent impaired
Recreation	1,126	97.2	0.0	2.8
Fish, shellfish, and wildlife protection and propagation	919	40.5	0.0	59.5
Aquatic life harvesting	888	7.0	0.0	93.0
Other	376	46.7	0.0	53.3
Agricultural	201	100.0	0.0	0.0

Note: Compilation of state-level data; while most data are from 2012, some data are from 2006, 2008, 2010, or 2014.

SOURCE: Adapted from "National Summary: Designated Use Support in Assessed Ocean and Near Coastal," in *Watershed Assessment, Tracking & Environmental Results*, U.S. Environmental Protection Agency, September 8, 2015, http://ofmpub.epa.gov/waters10/attains_nation_cy.control (accessed September 8, 2015)

TABLE 9.9

Percentage of wetlands supporting designated uses, 2012

[Waters assessed for more than one designated use are included in multiple designated use groups below]

Designated use group	Acres assessed	Percent good	Percent threatened	Percent impaired
Fish, shellfish, and wildlife protection and propagation	1,242,467	51.4	0.0	48.6
Recreation	1,044,435	92.9	0.0	7.1
Public water supply	480,668	100.0	0.0	0.0
Aquatic life harvesting	121,894	0.8	0.0	99.2
Agricultural	53,605	32.8	0.0	67.2
Industrial	18,460	100.0	0.0	0.0
Other	985	100.0	0.0	0.0

Note: Compilation of state-level data; while most data are from 2012, some data are from 2006, 2008, 2010, or 2014.

SOURCE: Adapted from "National Summary: Designated Use Support in Assessed Wetlands," in *Watershed Assessment, Tracking & Environmental Results*, U.S. Environmental Protection Agency, September 8, 2015, http://ofmpub.epa.gov/waters10/attains_nation_cy.control (accessed September 8, 2015)

TABLE 9.10

Percentage of Great Lakes shoreline supporting designated uses, 2012

[Waters assessed for more than one designated use are included in multiple designated use groups below]

Designated use group	Miles assessed	Percent good	Percent threatened	Percent impaired
Aquatic life harvesting	4,064	0.0	0.0	100.0
Agricultural	3,131	100.0	0.0	0.0
Industrial	3,131	100.0	0.0	0.0
Other	3,131	100.0	0.0	0.0
Fish, shellfish, and wildlife protection and propagation	865	33.1	0.0	66.9
Recreation	816	32.2	0.0	67.8
Public water supply	336	100.0	0.0	0.0

Note: Compilation of state-level data; while most data are from 2012, some data are from 2006, 2008, 2010, or 2014.

SOURCE: Adapted from "National Summary: Designated Use Support in Assessed Great Lakes Shoreline," in *Watershed Assessment, Tracking & Environmental Results*, U.S. Environmental Protection Agency, September 8, 2015, http://ofmpub.epa.gov/waters10/attains_nation_cy.control (accessed September 8, 2015)

algae growth in water bodies, which can reduce oxygen concentrations to dangerous levels for aquatic creatures, such as fish and shellfish. In 2012 nutrients were one of the top causes of impairment for lakes, reservoirs, and ponds and for rivers and streams. (See Table 9.12.) Significant nitrogen and phosphorus sources include sewage/wastewater treatment plants, septic tanks, fertilizer, animal wastes, and certain industrial discharges. Nitrogen also makes its way into water bodies via atmospheric deposition.

ORGANIC ENRICHMENT/OXYGEN DEPLETION. Water bodies containing excessive nutrients and/or pathogens (disease-causing microorganisms, such as bacteria) can become overly rich in organic material, such as plant and algal growth. This process is called eutrophication and

occurs through various mechanisms. High nutrient concentrations spur the growth of algae mats and aquatic plants. As they die off, they are degraded by aerobic (oxygen-gobbling) bacteria that thrive and multiply. Likewise, excessive algae mats on the water surface can block sunlight to underlying aquatic plants, causing them to die. The aerobic bacteria that flourish in this environment lower the dissolved oxygen content of the water, which is harmful to aquatic species, such as fish and invertebrate. As these creatures die, they perpetuate the cycle by further raising the organic content of the water. Aerobic bacteria also feast on fecal matter, which can enter water bodies via sewage and animal waste, such as from livestock.

TABLE 9.11

Percentage of Great Lakes open water supporting designated uses, 2012

[Waters assessed for more than one designated use are included in multiple designated use groups below]

Designated use group	Square miles assessed	Percent good	Percent threatened	Percent impaired
Aquatic life harvesting	39,184	0.0	0.0	100.0
Industrial	39,031	100.0	0.0	0.0
Agricultural	39,031	100.0	0.0	0.0
Other	39,031	100.0	0.0	0.0
Fish, shellfish, and wildlife protection and propagation	14,300	1.5	0.0	98.5
Recreation	151	100.0	0.0	0.0
Public water supply	151	100.0	0.0	0.0

Note: Compilation of state-level data; while most data are from 2012, some data are from 2006, 2008, 2010, or 2014.

SOURCE: Adapted from "National Summary: Designated Use Support in Assessed Great Lakes Open Water," in *Watershed Assessment, Tracking & Environmental Results*, U.S. Environmental Protection Agency, September 8, 2015, http://ofmpub.epa.gov/waters10/attains_nation_cy.control (accessed September 8, 2015)

As shown in Table 9.12, oxygen enrichment/oxygen depletion was the leading cause of impairment to wetlands in 2012 and negatively impacted numerous other water body types.

PATHOGENS. As noted earlier, pathogens are disease-causing microorganisms. One of the most commonly measured pathogens in water bodies is *Escherichia coli* (*E. coli*), which is a type of fecal coliform. The latter is a group of bacteria with common characteristics that are found in the fecal matter of humans and animals. High pathogen levels are problematic for several reasons. First, they pose a threat to public health in water supplies that are used by humans for drinking water or recreational activities. Second, they can trigger organic enrichment/oxygen depletion problems. Pathogens make their way into water bodies via sewage and animal wastes, such as from livestock. In 2012 pathogens were among the leading causes of impairment to multiple types of water bodies, particularly rivers and streams. (See Table 9.12.)

TABLE 9.12

Causes of impairment in assessed water bodies, 2012

	Size of assessed waters with listed causes of impairment							
Cause of impairment group	Rivers and streams (miles)	Lakes, reservoirs, and ponds (acres)	Bays and estuaries (square miles)	Coastal shoreline (miles)	Ocean and near coastal (square miles)	Wetlands (acres)	Great Lakes shoreline (miles)	Great Lakes open water (square miles)
Algal growth	6,013	908,061	1,474	93	0	4,631	191	
Ammonia	11,658	215,221	41	22	1	31		
Biotoxins	2,150	19,589						
Cause unknown	46,052	42,798	1,827			1,000		
Cause unknown—fish kills	678	9,412				1,034		
Cause unknown—impaired biota	42,464	57,780	341	74		1,214		
Chlorine	754	3,208	5					
Dioxins	5,044	109,156	4,351		9	212	3,471	38,862
Fish consumption advisory	9,916	539,504	3,084			1,000	285	14,087
Flow alteration(s)	42,580	189,938	3			4,387	202	
Habitat alterations	67,230	319,965	2		10	2,104	170	
Mercury	103,617	8,229,414	14,143	6,461	281	315,437	2,194	29,968
Metals (other than mercury)	76,583	1,306,148	1,878	60	15	101,695		
Noxious aquatic plants	354	82,502	1,668			940		
Nuisance exotic species	1,422	752,707	763		35	2,454	307	25
Nuisance native species	127	100,137	4					
Nutrients	110,100	3,575,728	3,605	131	7	67,955	380	
Oil and grease	3,014	31,485	101	95				
Organic enrichment/ oxygen depletion	89,869	1,457,774	5,422	437	579	462,402	138	13,867
Other cause	11,380	196,023	3,428				19	
Pathogens	177,529	549,577	7,021	1,043	80	72,397	621	
Pesticides	19,128	494,234	1,847	36	52	169	2,483	29,661
pH/acidity/caustic conditions	28,645	1,000,236	73	143	7	881		
Polychlorinated biphenyls (PCBs)	80,882	2,988,021	8,313	50	531	933	4,064	39,183
Radiation	692	48						
Salinity/total dissolved solids/ chlorides/sulfates	36,700	820,733	44			74,484		
Sediment	119,339	789,055	224	5		10,786	319	
Taste, color and odor	854	26,529	7					
Temperature	68,807	240,684	145	96	1	14,900		
Total toxics	10,708	15,405	336		29	13		192
Toxic inorganics	7,607	6,152	6			28,053	5	
Toxic organics	4,990	31,337	719		14	256		
Trash	1,692	5,097	436			320	3	
Turbidity	46,581	1,341,862	895	331	24	3,915		

Note: Compilation of state-level data; while most data are from 2012, some data are from 2006, 2008, 2010, or 2014.

SOURCE: "National Causes of Impairment," in *Watershed Assessment, Tracking & Environmental Results*, U.S. Environmental Protection Agency, September 8, 2015, http://ofmpub.epa.gov/waters10/attains_nation_cy.control (accessed September 8, 2015)

TABLE 9.13

Probable sources of impairment to assessed water bodies, 2012

Probable source group	Size of assessed waters with probable sources of impairments							
	Rivers and streams (miles)	Lakes, reservoirs, and ponds (acres)	Bays and estuaries (square miles)	Coastal shoreline (miles)	Ocean and near coastal (square miles)	Wetlands (acres)	Great Lakes shoreline (miles)	Great Lakes open water (square miles)
Agriculture	139,340	1,514,974	3,122	113		275,384	620	4,373
Aquaculture	340	4,620	0	5				
Atmospheric deposition	99,971	4,893,737	8,369	388	269	200,741	3,411	53,270
Commercial harbor and port activities	52		495		0			
Construction	12,434	338,935	4	4	4	1,000	18	
Groundwater loadings/withdrawals	270	88,429	0					
Habitat alterations (not directly related to hydromodification)	35,161	277,281	2,231			33	90	
Hydromodification	60,280	830,801	1,752	140	7	76,147	231	
Industrial	17,896	525,037	4,332	94	4	196,192	72	
Land application/waste sites			1					
Land application/waste sites/tanks	10,331	56,773	85	4		680	11	
Legacy/historical pollutants	6,256	765,478	1,873	8		212	867	13,991
Military bases	20	2,639						
Municipal discharges/sewage	62,700	667,755	5,434	370	114	72,341	305	
Natural/wildlife	54,615	1,063,821	3,543	1	1	70,825	0	
Other	10,691	1,036,515	4,847			237		25
Recreation and tourism (non-boating)	1,811	224,059	10	0	5			
Recreational boating and marinas	142	143,419	794	106	8	72,320		
Resource extraction	30,439	719,525	780	0		97,748		
Silviculture (forestry)	19,334	182,327	0					
Spills/dumping	3,398	198,491	3,164	13	2	6	18	
Unknown	113,413	3,469,116	8,604	497	116	344,313	144	310
Unspecified nonpoint source	50,748	882,527	4,005	121	4	63,958	6	
Urban-related runoff/stormwater	66,616	776,034	3,396	273	379	66,393	99	13,867

Note: Compilation of state-level data; while most data are from 2012, some data are from 2006, 2008, 2010, or 2014.

SOURCE: "National Probable Sources Contributing to Impairments," in *Watershed Assessment, Tracking & Environmental Results*, U.S. Environmental Protection Agency, September 8, 2015, http://ofmpub.epa.gov/waters10/attains_nation_cy.control (accessed September 8, 2015)

POLYCHLORINATED BIPHENYLS. Polychlorinated biphenyls (PCBs) are a group of synthetic organic chemicals that were widely used in the United States through the 1970s as lubricants and coolants for electrical equipment. After scientists became aware of their toxic nature, the chemicals fell into disfavor. However, the damage was already done. PCBs are very long-lasting in the environment because they are not biodegradable. Also, like mercury, they bioaccumulate in the tissues of aquatic organisms. Eating contaminated fish and other aquatic creatures is one of the ways in which humans are exposed to PCBs. In "Polychlorinated Biphenyls" (April 8, 2013, http://www3.epa.gov/epawaste/hazard/tsd/pcbs/about.htm), the EPA explains that PCBs continue to enter the environment as old electrical equipment leaks or is landfilled or incinerated. PCBs can enter water bodies via atmospheric deposition. As shown in Table 9.12, PCBs were a major impairment cause for several different water body types in 2012, including lakes (especially the Great Lakes), reservoirs, and ponds.

AGRICULTURE. In 2012 agricultural operations were singled out by the states as one of the top identifiable sources of impairment to assessed water bodies. (See Table 9.13.) This is primarily due to the harmful effects of nutrients, which are associated with fertilizers and livestock waste. The latter is also a source of pathogens. As described in Chapter 6, manure production at large livestock facilities can be massive. Runoff from manure stockpiles or fields treated with the waste poses a threat to water quality.

The EPA explains in *NPDES Permit Writers' Manual for Concentrated Animal Feeding Operations* (February 2012) that it regulates CAFOs that discharge to water bodies. CAFOs are a subset of animal feeding operations (AFOs), which the agency defines as facilities that stable, confine and feed, or maintain livestock for at least 45 days per year in noncrop-related areas. AFOs fall under federal CWA regulation when they are deemed CAFOs. This distinction is made on a case-by-case basis and depends on numerous factors, including the number of animals involved and how wastes are managed. As of 2012, the EPA estimates that there were approximately 20,000 CAFOs in the United States. CAFOs that discharge to water bodies must obtain NPDES permits.

ATMOSPHERIC DEPOSITION. Atmospheric deposition is explained in detail in Chapter 5, which concerns acid rain. Many chemicals that become airborne, such as the emissions from smokestacks, can fall back to the earth and impact water quality. These chemicals include organic compounds, such as PCBs, and metals, such as mercury. As shown in Table 9.13, atmospheric deposition was a leading source of impairment to water bodies in 2012. This was particularly true for lakes, reservoirs, and ponds in that atmospheric deposition was blamed by the states for impairing 4.9 million acres (2 million ha) of these water bodies. Obviously, the key to controlling atmospheric deposition lies in controlling the facilities that emit the offending chemicals. Chapter 2 and Chapter 5 describe the various regulatory programs that are designed to control air pollutants that contribute to the problem.

Other Major Sources of National Water Quality Data

The data collected by the states under Title III, Sections 303(d) and 305(b) of the CWA provide one perspective on the nation's overall water quality. Other perspectives can be obtained through scientifically rigorous sampling programs that are overseen by the EPA and the USGS.

EPA NATIONAL AQUATIC RESOURCE SURVEYS. The EPA relies on probability-based studies that are conducted at various sites around the country using nationally consistent methods and designs. This approach is used in the National Aquatic Resources Surveys (NARS; http://www2.epa.gov/national-aquatic-resource-surveys), which are collaborations between the EPA and other federal agencies, state agencies, and other public and private partners. The NARS assess four aquatic resources: rivers and streams; lakes, ponds, and reservoirs; coastal waters; and wetlands. As of November 2015, the most recent NARS reports on these resources were:

- Rivers and streams: *Draft National Rivers and Streams Assessment 2008–2009: A Collaborative Survey* (February 28, 2013, http://www2.epa.gov/national-aquatic-resource-surveys/national-rivers-and-streams-assessment) with data through 2009 and *Wadeable Streams Assessment: A Collaborative Survey of the Nation's Streams* (December 2006, http://water.epa.gov/type/rsl/monitoring/streamsurvey/index.cfm) with data through 2004.

- Lakes, ponds, and reservoirs: *National Lakes Assessment: A Collaborative Survey of the Nation's Lakes* (April 2010, http://www2.epa.gov/national-aquatic-resource-surveys/national-lakes-assessment) with data through 2007.

- Coastal waters: *National Coastal Condition Report IV* (April 2012, http://water.epa.gov/type/oceb/assessmonitor/nccr/index.cfm) with data through 2006.

As of November 2015, the EPA (http://www2.epa.gov/national-aquatic-resource-surveys/national-wetland-condition-assessment-2011-results), notes that the first NARS report on wetlands had not yet been published even though the associated field work was completed in 2011.

Some of the major highlights from the published NARS reports regarding noncoastal waters are presented in this section. Coastal waters are addressed later in this chapter.

In *Draft National Rivers and Streams Assessment 2008–2009* (NRSA), the EPA presents data collected during the summers of 2008 and 2009 at 1,924 rivers and streams of various sizes and types around the country. The results are compared with those of reference water bodies, which the agency describes as the "least-disturbed" rivers and streams in the ecological regions studied. One of the goals of the NRSA was to determine the stressors that are negatively impacting rivers and streams. The indicators that were examined during the assessment included biological indicators (e.g., aquatic life), chemical indicators (e.g., phosphorus), physical indicators (e.g., streambed sediments), and human health indicators (e.g., mercury in fish tissue). The most widespread stressors measured during the NRSA were phosphorus and nitrogen levels, riparian condition as evidenced by vegetation cover and disturbance, excess sedimentation (which can indicate erosion problems), fish habitat, salinity, and acidification. Nationally, phosphorus was found at high levels (as compared with reference water bodies) in 39.9% of the river and stream miles sampled. Likewise, nitrogen levels were high, when compared with least-disturbed conditions, in 27.7% of river and stream miles. Other stressors that negatively affected at least 20% of river and stream miles on a national basis were riparian vegetation cover (23.8%) and riparian disturbance (20.1%). There were regional differences between the various stressors.

The older *Wadeable Streams Assessment* includes data collected in 2004 at 1,392 small streams and rivers around the country. According to the EPA, in the fact sheet "The Wadeable Streams Assessment: A Collaborative Survey of the Nation's Streams" (October 25, 2006, http://water.epa.gov/type/watersheds/monitoring/upload/2007_10_25_monitoring_wsa_factsheet_10_25_06.pdf), these water bodies were compared with "the best available reference sites in their regions." Just over a quarter (28%) of the streams and rivers received a "good" rating. Another quarter were rated "fair," whereas 42% were rated "poor," and 5% were not assessed.

The EPA describes in the fact sheet "National Lakes Assessment" (April 2010, http://water.epa.gov/type/lakes/upload/nla_survey_fact_sheet.pdf) its "first-ever baseline study of the condition of the nation's lakes." A total of 1,028 lakes, ponds, and reservoirs at least 3.3 feet (1 m) deep and 10 acres (4 ha) in size were sampled in 2007. It should be noted that this study did not include the Great Lakes or the Great Salt Lake. The sampled water bodies were assessed for a variety of indicators to determine their overall biological health. More than half

(56%) of the water bodies were rated "good," based on a taxa loss of less than 20%. The EPA explains that "this rating is based on an index of phytoplankton and zooplankton taxa loss—the percentage of taxa observed compared to those that are expected, based on conditions at least-disturbed lakes." Another 21% of water bodies were rated "fair" for taxa loss, and 22% were rated "poor." The EPA also assessed the water bodies for specific stressors, which are conditions that "increase the likelihood (i.e., relative risk)" of poor biological health. More than one-third (35.9%) of the lakes were rated "poor" for lakeshore habitat conditions. This particular stressor poses a relatively high risk (three out of five) to the biological condition of the water bodies.

USGS WATER QUALITY DATA SOURCES. The USGS (http://water.usgs.gov/owq) collects water quality data at surface water and groundwater sampling locations around the country. The results are provided in various databases, including the National Water Information System (http://waterdata.usgs.gov/nwis/qw), the National Stream Quality Accounting Network (http://water.usgs.gov/nasqan), and the National Water-Quality Assessment (NAWQA; http://water.usgs.gov/nawqa) databases.

The USGS also publishes reports that summarize collected data on selected topics. For example, in *The Quality of Our Nation's Waters: Water Quality in Principal Aquifers of the United States, 1991–2010* (2015, http://pubs.usgs.gov/circ/1360/pdf/circ1360report.pdf), Leslie A. DeSimone, Peter B. McMahon, and Michael R. Rosen summarize the results from nine regional USGS assessments of the nation's groundwater quality. The studies focused on principal aquifers, particularly those that supply large amounts of drinking water. In total, 6,600 wells were sampled, and 1.3 million chemical analyses were performed. The researchers found that groundwater in 22% of the sampled wells contained at least one chemical constituent at levels higher than human-health benchmarks for drinking water. Most of these constituents were believed to be naturally occurring, for example, arsenic or radon that dissolved from underground rock formations into the groundwater. One troublesome constituent was linked with anthropogenic (human-based) sources. Nitrate was detected at levels above human-health benchmarks in more than 1% of the sampled wells. As noted earlier, nitrate is a nutrient associated with sewage/wastewater treatment plants, septic tanks, fertilizer, animal wastes, and certain industrial discharges.

COASTAL WATERS

As shown in Table 9.3, only 13.9% of the nation's coastal shoreline miles were assessed in 2012 as part of Title III, Sections 303(d) and 305(b) of the CWA analyses performed by the states. Overall, 7,262 miles (89%;

11,687 km) out of 8,163 miles (13,137 km) of coastal shoreline miles were deemed impaired. The primary causes of impairment were mercury, pathogens, and oxygen enrichment/oxygen depletion. (See Table 9.12.)

Since 2001 the EPA has published four NARS reports on the country's coastal areas. As of November 2015, the most recent report, *National Coastal Condition Report IV*, was published in April 2012. The EPA compiles data collected by various federal and state agencies and assigns rating scores to coastal areas based on water and sediment quality, coastal habitat condition, benthic health (the condition of bottom-dwelling organisms), and fish tissue contaminants. The numerical rating scale extends from less than 2 (poor) to greater than 4 (good). Overall, the national coast was rated in fair condition with a score of 3. Regionally, the southeastern coast of Alaska (score of 5), Guam (score of 4.8), and the U.S. Virgin Islands (score of 4), and the West Coast (score of 3.8) received the highest ratings, while the Northeast Coast (score of 2.6), the Gulf Coast (score of 2.4), and the Great Lakes (score of 2.2) earned the lowest scores.

Hypoxic Coastal Waters

Hypoxia is a low-oxygen condition that poses a severe danger to fish, crustaceans, and other aquatic life. As described earlier, nutrient pollution—an excess of nitrogen and phosphorus that encourages excessive algae growth—is one of the primary causes of organic enrichment/oxygen depletion. Figure 9.8 shows the minimum oxygen requirements for various sea creatures inhabiting the Chesapeake Bay, one of two U.S. water bodies, along with the Gulf of Mexico, in which hypoxia has been extensively studied.

Each year the National Oceanic and Atmospheric Administration (NOAA) reports the size of the Gulf of Mexico hypoxic "dead zone." Agricultural sources, such as crop fertilization and livestock wastes, are the primary sources believed responsible for excessive nitrogen and phosphorus concentrations flowing into the Gulf from the Mississippi and Atchafalaya Rivers. In "2015 Gulf of Mexico Dead Zone 'Above Average'" (August 4, 2015, http://www.noaanews.noaa.gov/stories2015/080415-gulf-of-mexico-dead-zone-above-average.html), NOAA indicates that the dead zone measured 6,474 square miles (16,767.6 square km) in 2015, up from 5,052 square miles (13,084.6 square km) in 2014. Both measurements are well above the goal of 1,930 square miles (5,000 square km), which was set by the interagency Mississippi River/Gulf of Mexico Hypoxia Task Force in 2008 in *Gulf Hypoxia Action Plan 2008* (http://water.epa.gov/type/watersheds/named/msbasin/upload/2008_8_28_msbasin_ghap2008_update082608.pdf). It was originally hoped that the goal would be realized by 2015. According to NOAA, "nutrients from the Mississippi River watershed are

FIGURE 9.8

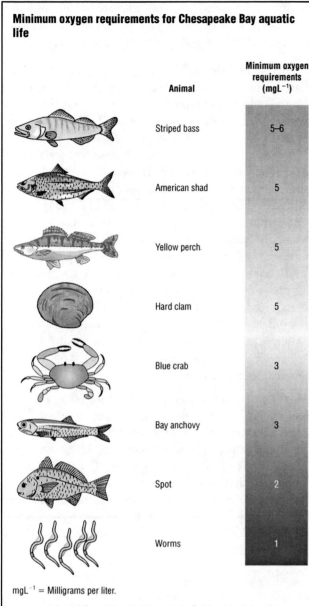

Minimum oxygen requirements for Chesapeake Bay aquatic life

Animal	Minimum oxygen requirements (mgL⁻¹)
Striped bass	5–6
American shad	5
Yellow perch	5
Hard clam	5
Blue crab	3
Bay anchovy	3
Spot	2
Worms	1

mgL⁻¹ = Milligrams per liter.

SOURCE: Adapted from "Box 3. Hypoxia Definition," in *Scientific Assessment of Hypoxia in U.S. Coastal Waters*, Committee on Environment and Natural Resources, Interagency Working Group on Harmful Algal Blooms, Hypoxia, and Human Health of the Joint Subcommittee on Ocean Science and Technology, September 2010, http://www.whitehouse.gov/sites/default/files/microsites/ostp/hypoxia-report.pdf (accessed September 11, 2015)

continuing to affect the nation's coastal resources and habitats in the Gulf."

Beaches

In 2000 Congress passed the Beaches Environmental Assessment and Coastal Health (BEACH) Act. It established a program of federal grants to state and local governments to facilitate water quality monitoring at the nation's beaches. However, funding for the program ceased in fiscal year (FY) 2013. In *FY 2013: EPA Budget in Brief* (February 2012, (http://yosemite.epa.gov/sab/ sabproduct.nsf/2B686066C751F34A852579A4007023C2/ $File/FY2013_BIB.pdf), the EPA notes that state and local governments have established beach monitoring programs that "can continue without federal support."

The BEACH Act requires the EPA to collect information from coastal states regarding beach closings because of environmental problems. The information is reported in the EPA's Beach Advisory and Closing Online Notification database (http://watersgeo.epa.gov/ beacon2/beacon.html). The public can search the database to learn about any current or previous warnings or closures at particular beaches. Such information is also available from state and local agencies. For example, San Diego County (http://www.sdbeachinfo.com) in California monitors environmental conditions at dozens of beaches along its coastline. As of November 2015, roughly 3 miles (4.8 km) of beaches were closed due to sewage-contaminated runoff near the southern border of the county. In May 2015 officials in Los Angeles temporarily closed miles of beaches after large amounts of tar-based globs washed ashore. It was suspected that the tar balls originated from a spill of crude oil from a ruptured pipeline near Santa Barbara, California.

OCEAN PROTECTION

Throughout history humans have used the oceans virtually as they pleased. Ocean waters have long served as highways and harvest grounds. Now, however, humankind is at a threshold. Marine debris (garbage created by humans) is a problem of global proportions and is extremely evident in countries such as the United States, where there is extensive recreational and commercial use of coastal waterways.

U.S. ocean protection laws date back to 1972, when the Marine Protection, Research, and Sanctuaries Act was passed to regulate intentional ocean disposal of materials and to authorize research. Title 1 of the act, known as the Ocean Dumping Act, prohibits all ocean dumping, except that allowed by permits, in any ocean waters under U.S. jurisdiction by any U.S. vessel or by any vessel sailing to or from a U.S. port. The act bans the dumping of radiological, chemical, and biological warfare agents, high-level radioactive waste, and medical waste. In 1997 Congress amended the act to ban the dumping of municipal sewage sludge and industrial waste.

Oil Pollution Act

In 1989 the oil freighter *Exxon Valdez* ran into a reef in Prince William Sound, Alaska, spilling more than 11 million gallons (41.6 million L) of oil into one of the richest and most ecologically pristine areas in North America. An oil slick the size of Rhode Island killed wildlife and marine species. A $5 billion damage penalty was levied against Exxon, whose ship captain was found to be at fault in the wreck. (The U.S. Supreme Court cut the amount to $507.5 million in 2008.)

In response to the *Exxon Valdez* oil spill, Congress passed the Oil Pollution Act of 1990, which went into effect in 1993. The law requires companies that are involved in storing and transporting petroleum to have standby plans for cleaning up oil spills on land or in water. The law makes the U.S. Coast Guard responsible for approving cleanup plans and procedures for coastal and seaport oil spills, while the EPA oversees cleanups on land and in inland waterways. In addition, oil tankers must be built with double hulls to better secure the oil in the event of a hull breach.

In April 2010 an explosion aboard an offshore drilling platform in the Gulf of Mexico killed 11 workers and resulted in the largest oil spill in U.S. history. Leased by the BP oil company, the Deepwater Horizon platform was located approximately 50 miles (80 km) off the coast of Louisiana. An estimated 4.9 million barrels of oil spewed into the Gulf before the damaged well head was eventually capped. Although a massive response effort was launched to mitigate (to relieve or reduce in harshness) the ecological and economic damages of the spill, thousands of aquatic birds and other creatures were believed to have died. In addition, fishing and shellfish harvesting were temporarily banned in large areas of the Gulf.

The Oil Pollution Act of 1990 limits to $75 million the total liability of responsible parties for economic damages suffered by residents, businesses, and local governments in a spill area. Following the BP oil spill some legislators introduced bills that would have retroactively raised the liability limit under the act. However, these bills failed to gain widespread support in Congress and were not passed. The spill spawned a number of lawsuits against and between BP and its owner and operator partners. A detailed examination of the spill's effects on the area's wetlands is presented in Chapter 11.

Marine Debris

The Marine Debris Research, Prevention, and Reduction Act became law in 2006. It created the Marine Debris Research, Prevention, and Reduction Program within NOAA and the Coast Guard to help identify, determine sources of, and reduce or prevent marine debris and its adverse impacts on the marine environment and navigation safety. In "Discover the Issue" (October 9, 2015, http://marinedebris.noaa.gov/discover-issue), the NOAA defines marine debris as "any persistent solid material that is manufactured or processed and directly or indirectly, intentionally or unintentionally, disposed of or abandoned into the marine environment or the Great Lakes."

Ocean current patterns can cause marine debris to become concentrated in accumulation areas known as "garbage patches." For example, the Great Pacific Garbage Patch lies in the Pacific Ocean between Hawaii and the western coast of the United States. According to NOAA, the "garbage patch" is not one continuous large pile of marine debris. Instead, the agency notes, "While higher concentrations of litter items can be found in this area, along with other debris such as derelict fishing nets, much of the debris is actually small pieces of floating plastic that are not immediately evident to the naked eye." Ingestion of these microplastics can harm marine life. The NOAA indicates that the microplastics originate from a variety of sources, including discarded plastic shopping bags and containers that break down over time.

The problem of marine debris took on added significance following the devastating earthquake and tsunami that struck Japan in March 2011. According to NOAA (http://marinedebris.noaa.gov/current-efforts/emergency-response/japan-tsunami-marine-debris), the Japanese government estimates that approximately 5 million tons (4.5 million t) of debris was swept off the land into the ocean. Although about 70% of the debris is believed to have sunk off the Japanese coast, the remainder—roughly 1.5 million tons (1.4 million t)—floated out to sea. Pieces of the debris have since washed up onto U.S. and Canadian shores. The NOAA Marine Debris Program (http://marinedebris.noaa.gov) tracks and maps marine debris locations and advises people and government agencies on what to do with debris that washes ashore.

DRINKING WATER
Drinking Water Legislation

The Safe Drinking Water Act (SDWA) of 1974 mandated that the EPA establish and enforce minimum national drinking water standards for all public water systems—community and noncommunity—in the United States. The law also required the EPA to develop guidelines for water treatment and to set testing, monitoring, and reporting requirements. Congress intended that, after the EPA had set regulatory standards, each state or U.S. territory would run its own drinking water program. The EPA established the Primary Drinking Water Standards by setting the maximum contamination levels for contaminants that are known to be detrimental to human health. All public water systems in the United States are required to meet primary standards. Secondary standards cover nonhealth-threatening aspects of drinking water, such as odor, taste, staining properties, and color. Secondary standards are recommended but not required.

Over the decades the SDWA has been amended several times. For example, in 1986 amendments banned the use of lead pipe and lead solder in new public drinking water systems and in the repair of existing systems.

The Lead Contamination Control Act of 1988 added further restrictions after the dangers of ingesting lead became better understood. In 1996 Congress passed a number of significant amendments to the SDWA. The law changed the relationship between the federal government and the states in administering drinking water programs by giving states greater flexibility and more responsibility.

The EPA and state health or environmental departments regulate public water supplies. Public supplies are required to ensure that the water meets certain government-defined health standards. The SDWA governs this regulation. The law mandates that all public suppliers test their water regularly to check for the existence of contaminants and treat their water supplies constantly to take out or reduce certain pollutants to levels that will not harm human health.

Private water supplies, usually wells, are not regulated under the SDWA. System owners are solely responsible for the quality of the water that is provided from private sources. However, many states have programs that are designed to help well owners protect their water supplies. Usually, these state-run programs are not regulatory but provide safety information. This type of information is vital because private wells are often shallower than those used by public suppliers. The shallower the well, the greater the potential for contamination.

Incidence of Disease Caused by Tainted Water

It is difficult to know how many illnesses are caused by contaminated water. People may not know the source of many illnesses and may attribute them to food (which may also have been in contact with polluted water), chronic illness, or other infectious agents. Since 1971 the Centers for Disease Control and Prevention and the EPA have collected and reported data that relate to waterborne-disease outbreaks. As of November 2015, the most recent historical data were presented and analyzed by Karlyn D. Beer et al. in "Surveillance for Waterborne Disease Outbreaks Associated with Drinking Water—United States, 2011–2012" (*Morbidity and Mortality Weekly Report*, vol. 64, no. 31, August 14, 2015). The results indicate that there were 32 outbreaks between 2011 and 2012 in water intended for drinking. They caused 431 people to become ill and killed 14 people.

Milwaukee: The Nation's Worst Drinking Water Disaster

In April 1993 more than 400,000 residents of Milwaukee, Wisconsin, became victims of what is considered to be the worst drinking water disaster the nation has experienced. Microscopic parasites called *Cryptosporidium* flourished in the city water supply, causing an outbreak of cryptosporidiosis, a diarrheal disease. At least 40 deaths resulted. City and state public health officials conducted an extensive review of the outbreak's effects and causes, and their results were published by William R. Mac Kenzie et al. in "A Massive Outbreak in Milwaukee of *Cryptosporidium* Infection Transmitted through the Public Water Supply" (*New England Journal of Medicine*, vol. 331, no. 3, July 21, 1994).

According to Mac Kenzie et al., the city was served by two water treatment plants in 1993, both of which accessed water from Lake Michigan. Both plants used a multistep treatment process that included chlorination, other chemical treatments, and filtration. *Cryptosporidium* are resistant to chlorine and other typical chemical treatments because they have a hard outer shell. They also require very fine filtration for removal. Thus, they were able to move unimpeded through the system and into the public drinking water supply. Although one of the plants did notice unusually high levels of turbidity (cloudiness) in the raw water before the outbreak, biological organisms were not suspected as the cause until later. This oversight and mechanical problems at the plants were later blamed for allowing the outbreak to occur. The original source of the parasites could not be determined, but suspected sources included cattle ranches, slaughterhouses, and sewage treatment plants that discharged to waters draining into Lake Michigan.

In *Global Issues in Water, Sanitation, and Health: Workshop Summary* (2009, http://www.ncbi.nlm.nih.gov/books/NBK28462/pdf/TOC.pdf), Jeffrey P. Davis, William R. Mac Kenzie, and David G. Addiss discuss the lessons learned from the disaster, including shortcomings in the Milwaukee water system. After the disaster, the city changed the intake location for one of its treatment plants and updated its filter. Monitors and alarms were installed to warn of high turbidity levels. In addition, the researchers note that the city "adopted very stringent water quality standards." Lastly, the city installed ozonization systems to treat incoming water with ozone before chlorination. Ozone is a molecule that contains three oxygen atoms and effectively kills *Cryptosporidium* spores.

In "National Primary Drinking Water Regulations: Long Term 2 Enhanced Surface Water Treatment Rule" (*Federal Register*, vol. 71, no. 3, January 5, 2006), the EPA indicates that it finalized the Long Term 2 Enhanced Surface Water Treatment Rule, which imposes new regulations on public water systems that use surface water bodies as their intake water sources. Among other measures, the rule mandates monitoring and control processes that are designed to "protect public health from illness due to *Cryptosporidium* and other microbial pathogens."

PUBLIC OPINION ABOUT WATER ISSUES

Each year the Gallup Organization conducts an annual poll on environmental topics. As shown in Table

TABLE 9.14

Public concern about pollution of drinking water, selected years 1990–2015

HOW MUCH DO YOU PERSONALLY WORRY ABOUT POLLUTION OF DRINKING WATER?

	Great deal	Fair amount	Only a little	Not at all	No opinion
	%	%	%	%	%
2015 Mar 5–8	55	22	15	8	*
2014 Mar 6–9	60	22	13	5	*
2013 Mar 7–10	53	26	14	6	—
2012 Mar 8–11	48	30	15	6	*
2011 Mar 3–6	51	26	16	7	*
2010 Mar 4–7	50	27	17	6	*
2009 Mar 5–8	59	25	11	5	*
2008 Mar 6–9	53	28	13	6	*
2007 Mar 11–14	58	24	12	5	*
2006 Mar 13–16	54	27	12	7	*
2004 Mar 8–11	53	24	17	6	*
2003 Mar 3–5	54	25	15	6	—
2002 Mar 4–7	57	25	13	5	*
2001 Mar 5–7	64	24	9	3	*
2000 Apr 3–9	72	20	6	2	*
1999 Apr 13–14	68	22	7	3	*
1991 Apr 11–4	67	19	10	3	1
1990 Apr 5–8	65	22	9	4	*

*Less than 0.5%.

SOURCE: "I'm going to read you a list of environmental problems. As I read each one, please tell me if you personally worry about this problem a great deal, a fair amount, only a little, or not at all. First, how much do you personally worry about: pollution of drinking water?" in *Environment*, The Gallup Organization, 2015, http://www.gallup.com/poll/1615/Environment.aspx#1 (accessed August 28, 2015). Copyright © 2015 Gallup, Inc. All rights reserved. The content is used with permission; however, Gallup retains all rights of republication.

TABLE 9.15

Public concern about pollution of rivers, lakes, and reservoirs, selected years 1989–2015

I'M GOING TO READ YOU A LIST OF ENVIRONMENTAL PROBLEMS. AS I READ EACH ONE, PLEASE TELL ME IF YOU PERSONALLY WORRY ABOUT THIS PROBLEM A GREAT DEAL, A FAIR AMOUNT, ONLY A LITTLE, OR NOT AT ALL. FIRST, HOW MUCH DO YOU PERSONALLY WORRY ABOUT: POLLUTION OF RIVERS, LAKES, AND RESERVOIRS?

	Great deal	Fair amount	Only a little	Not at all	No opinion
	%	%	%	%	%
2015 Mar 5–8	47	32	15	6	*
2014 Mar 6–9	53	28	15	3	*
2013 Mar 7–10	46	32	16	6	*
2012 Mar 8–11	48	31	17	4	*
2011 Mar 3–6	46	33	16	6	*
2010 Mar 4–7	46	32	18	4	*
2009 Mar 5–8	52	31	13	4	*
2008 Mar 6–9	50	34	12	4	—
2007 Mar 11–14	53	31	13	3	*
2006 Mar 13–16	51	33	11	5	*
2004 Mar 8–11	48	31	16	5	*
2003 Mar 3–5	51	31	13	5	—
2002 Mar 4–7	53	32	12	3	*
2001 Mar 5–7	58	29	10	3	*
2000 Apr 3–9	66	24	8	2	*
1999 Apr 13–14	61	30	7	2	*
1999 Mar 12–14	55	30	12	3	*
1991 Apr 11–14	67	21	8	3	1
1990 Apr 5–8	64	23	9	4	—
1989 May 4–7	72	19	5	3	1

*Less than 0.5%.

SOURCE: "I'm going to read you a list of environmental problems. As I read each one, please tell me if you personally worry about this problem a great deal, a fair amount, only a little, or not at all. First, how much do you personally worry about: pollution of rivers, lakes, and reservoirs?" in *Environment*, The Gallup Organization, 2015, http://www.gallup.com/poll/1615/Environment.aspx#1 (accessed August 28, 2015). Copyright © 2015 Gallup, Inc. All rights reserved. The content is used with permission; however, Gallup retains all rights of republication.

9.14, 55% of those asked in March 2015 expressed a great deal of concern about pollution of drinking water, compared with 22% who expressed a fair amount of concern. Another 15% indicated only a little concern and 8% expressed no concern. The percentage of poll respondents indicating a great deal of concern about pollution of drinking water has dropped dramatically in recent years, from a high of 72% in April 2000.

Table 9.15 shows the results related to pollution of rivers, lakes, and reservoirs. In March 2015 nearly half (47%) of respondents expressed a great deal of concern about pollution of rivers, lakes, and reservoirs, compared with 32% who expressed a fair amount of concern. Another 15% indicated only a little concern, and 6% expressed no concern. The percentage of poll respondents indicating a great deal of concern about this problem declined considerably since the question was first posed in May 1989. At that time nearly three-quarters (72%) of those asked expressed a great deal of concern about pollution of rivers, lakes, and reservoirs.

CHAPTER 10

TOXINS IN EVERYDAY LIFE

The Swiss-born chemist Paracelsus (1493?–1541) once stated that "it is the dose that makes the poison." Many of the substances naturally found in the environment or released by modern, industrialized society are poisonous at certain dosages. These substances may be found in the home, workplace, or backyard, in the food and water people eat and drink, and in medications and consumer products.

WHY ARE TOXINS TOXIC?

A toxin is a substance (bacterial, viral, chemical, metal, fibrous, or radioactive) that poisons or harms a living organism. A toxin may cause immediate, short-term symptoms such as gastroenteritis, or cause harm after long-term exposure such as living in a lead- or radon-contaminated home for many years. Some toxins can have both immediate and long-term effects: living in an environment with poor air quality may trigger an acute asthma attack, or, after many years of exposure, it may contribute to lung cancer. Although the effects of a toxin may not show up for years, these effects may, nevertheless, be serious.

Toxins are often grouped according to their most harmful effect on living creatures. These categories include carcinogens, mutagens, and teratogens:

- A carcinogen is any substance that causes cancerous growth.

- A mutagen is an agent capable of producing genetic change.

- A teratogen is a substance that produces malformations or defective development.

The risks posed by environmental contamination may not be blatantly obvious. For example, people or animals that are exposed to contaminants may suffer damage to their immune systems and have difficulty recovering from infectious diseases. However, tracing the problem to environmental pollutants can be difficult.

GOVERNMENT LEGISLATION

Toxins that can be encountered in everyday life are regulated under a variety of federal and state laws. The following are the major pieces of federal legislation.

The Pure Food and Drug Act was originally passed in 1906 and substantially strengthened in 1938 by passage of its replacement, the Federal Food, Drug, and Cosmetic Act. This act was amended during the 1950s and 1960s to tighten restrictions on pesticides (a category that includes insecticides and herbicides), food additives, and drugs. Responsibility for enforcement of the act lies with the U.S. Food and Drug Administration (FDA) under the U.S. Department of Health and Human Services. The FDA oversees food supplies, human and veterinary drugs, biological products (such as vaccines and blood supplies), medical devices, cosmetics, and electronic products that emit radiation.

In 1947 Congress passed the Federal Insecticide, Fungicide, and Rodenticide Act. Although it was originally enforced by the U.S. Department of Agriculture (USDA), authority passed to the U.S. Environmental Protection Agency (EPA) after its creation in 1970. The act was strengthened and expanded by major amendments over the next few decades, particularly in 1996. The act provides the EPA with primary control over pesticide distribution, sale, and use. The states also have authority to regulate pesticides and can do so at more restrictive levels than what the EPA requires. The EPA studies the environmental and health effects of pesticide use and requires some users to register when purchasing pesticides. All pesticides that are to be marketed in the United States must first be registered with the EPA. According to the Technology Sciences Group, Inc., in "Registrations & Approvals: Pesticides—U.S. Pesticide

Regulation" (2015, http://www.tsgusa.com/capabilities/pesticides/us-pesticide-regulation.htm#.Vh0xjytKB-9), "Once an EPA registration is issued, registration must be obtained from every state and territory where the product will be distributed or sold."

The Federal Hazardous Substances Labeling Act was passed in 1960. The U.S. Consumer Product Safety Commission (CPSC) administers the law as it applies to household products. The commission has jurisdiction over approximately 15,000 consumer products that pose a fire, electrical, chemical, or mechanical hazard. Household products (such as cleaners) that contain hazardous chemicals must warn consumers about their potential hazards.

The Toxic Substances Control Act (TSCA) was enacted by Congress in 1976. It gives the EPA authority to track the thousands of industrial chemicals that are produced or imported into the United States. The EPA screens the chemicals and can require that industries test chemicals that may pose a hazard to the environment or human health. The EPA can ban chemicals it deems too risky. The EPA indicates in "About the TSCA Chemical Substance Inventory" (October 8, 2015, http://www2.epa.gov/tsca-inventory/about-tsca-chemical-substance-inventory#howare) that more than 85,000 chemicals are tracked and controlled by the agency under the TSCA. Primary responsibility for administering the TSCA lies with the EPA's Office of Pollution Prevention and Toxics.

In 1984 a deadly cloud of chemicals was released from the Union Carbide pesticide plant in Bhopal, India, following an explosion in the plant. The methyl isocyanate gas killed approximately 3,000 people and injured 200,000 others. Shortly after, a similar chemical release occurred in West Virginia, where a cloud of gas sent 135 people to the hospital with eye, throat, and lung irritation complaints. There were no fatalities. Such incidents fueled the demand by workers and the general public for information about hazardous materials in their areas. As a result, Congress passed the Emergency Planning and Community Right-to-Know Act of 1986.

The act established, among other things, the Toxics Release Inventory (TRI; http://www2.epa.gov/toxics-release-inventory-tri-program), a public database that contains information on toxic chemical releases by various facilities. More than 650 toxic chemicals are on the TRI list.

RISK MANAGEMENT

In general, the risks that are associated with toxin exposures are assessed by scientists using the following five-step approach:

1. Identify the hazard—gather and evaluate data on the hazards to human health of exposure to specific substances. This step typically involves research into the ways in which substances affect living tissues and cells, for example, using laboratory animals.

2. Determine the dose response—calculate a numerical relationship between the amount of exposure (the dose) and the extent of harm. There may be many different dose responses for a single substance, depending on how the exposure occurs. The duration and pathway of exposure are key variables. Pathways include inhalation into the lungs, dermal (skin) contact, and ingestion (swallowing).

3. Assess the exposure—ascertain information about the population that has been or will likely be exposed to particular substances.

4. Characterize the risk—use data from the first three steps to determine the likelihood that harm is going to occur to a population from a particular exposure to a particular substance.

5. Manage the risk—impose regulatory or other control measures to minimize the known risks that are associated with particular exposures to toxic substances by vulnerable populations.

The science of risk management is quite complex. Table 10.1 presents some of the common terms and acronyms that are used by the EPA to characterize exposure and risk data.

Sources of Public Data

The prevalence and biological effects of some chemical toxins have been studied extensively. Experts acknowledge, however, that there are many toxins for which few data are available. In general, data on the generation, usage, and levels of chemicals in the environment (air, water, soil, and so on) are much more plentiful than data on the known effects of chemicals to human health. This raises difficulties for regulatory agencies that wish to set health-based limits on particular toxins. It also makes it harder for the public to determine whether a particular exposure is harmful or not.

TOXICS RELEASE INVENTORY. In *2013 Toxics Release Inventory National Analysis* (January 2015, http://www2.epa.gov/toxics-release-inventory-tri-program/2013-tri-national-analysis-introduction), the EPA states that 21,598 facilities released 4.1 billion pounds (1.9 billion kg) of TRI chemicals in 2013. Figure 8.5 in Chapter 8 shows the distribution of releases to the environment in 2013, and Figure 8.6, also in Chapter 8, shows the breakdown by industry that year.

AMERICAN ASSOCIATION OF POISON CONTROL CENTERS. Since 1983 the American Association of Poison Control Centers has maintained a national database on poison exposure. The National Poison Data System

TABLE 10.1

Exposure and risk management terms

Acronym (If any)	Term	Definition
	Acute exposure	Exposure by the oral, dermal, or inhalation route for 24 hours or less.
	Short-term exposure	Repeated exposure by the oral, dermal, or inhalation route for more than 24 hours, up to 30 days.
	Subchronic exposure	Repeated exposure by the oral, dermal, or inhalation route for more than 30 days, up to approximately 10% of the life span in humans
	Chronic exposure	Repeated exposure by the oral, dermal, or inhalation route for more than approximately 10% of the life span in humans
LED_{10}	Lower limit on effective dose $_{10}$,	The 95% lower confidence limit of the dose of a chemical needed to produce an adverse effect in 10 percent of those exposed to the chemical, relative to control.
LOAEL	Lowest-observed-adverse-effect	The lowest exposure level at which there are biologically significant increases in frequency or severity of adverse effects between the exposed population and its appropriate control group.
LOEL or LEL	Lowest-observed-effect level	In a study, the lowest dose or exposure level at which a statistically or biologically significant effect is observed in the exposed population compared with an appropriate unexposed control group.
NOAEL	No-observed-adverse-effect level	The highest exposure level at which there are no biologically significant increases in the frequency or severity of adverse effect between the exposed population and its appropriate control; some effects may be produced at this level, but they are not considered adverse or precursors of adverse effects.
NOEL	No-observed-effect level	An exposure level at which there are no statistically or biologically significant increases in the frequency or severity of any effect between the exposed population and its appropriate control.
RfC	Reference concentration	An estimate (with uncertainty spanning perhaps an order of magnitude) of a continuous inhalation exposure to the human population (including sensitive subgroups) that is likely to be without an appreciable risk of deleterious effects during a lifetime.
RfD	Reference dose	An estimate (with uncertainty spanning perhaps an order of magnitude) of a daily oral exposure to the human population (including sensitive subgroups) that is likely to be without an appreciable risk of deleterious effects during a lifetime.

SOURCE: Adapted from "IRIS Glossary," in *Integrated Risk Information System (IRIS)*, U.S. Environmental Protection Agency, August 31, 2011, http://ofmpub .epa.gov/sor_internet/registry/termreg/searchandretrieve/glossariesandkeywordlists/search.do?details=&glossaryName=IRIS%20Glossary (accessed September 8, 2015)

(http://www.aapcc.org/data-system) presents information from dozens of poison control centers around the country. According to James B. Mowry et al., in *2013 Annual Report of the American Association of Poison Control Centers' National Poison Data System (NPDS): 31st Annual Report* (2014, https://aapcc.s3.amazonaws.com/pdfs/annual_reports/2013_NPDS_Annual_Report.pdf), in 2013 U.S. poison centers handled nearly 3.1 million calls. The majority of the calls—2.3 million—involved human exposures. The substances most frequently involved in exposures were painkillers, cosmetics and personal care products, and household cleaning substances.

THE NATIONAL REPORT ON HUMAN EXPOSURE TO ENVIRONMENTAL CHEMICALS. The Centers for Disease Control and Prevention (CDC) regularly updates a report that assesses the exposure of the U.S. population to environmental chemicals based on biomonitoring results. Biomonitoring involves collecting and analyzing bodily samples, such as blood, urine, breast milk, and hair, to measure the concentrations of particular chemical substances. This is also known as determining the "body burden" of chemicals.

The CDC defines environmental chemicals as chemicals that are present in air, water, food, soil, dust, or other environmental media (including consumer products). The report includes data on the blood and urine levels of various chemical substances. The *First National Report on Human Exposure to Environmental Chemicals*

was published in 2001 and covers 27 chemicals. The *Second National Report on Human Exposure to Environmental Chemicals*, released in 2003, provides data for 116 chemicals. The *Third National Report on Human Exposure to Environmental Chemicals* was published in 2005 and includes biomonitoring data for 148 chemicals. The *Fourth National Report on Human Exposure to Environmental Chemicals* (http://www.cdc.gov/exposurereport/pdf/FourthReport.pdf) was published in 2009 and includes all previously published data plus data for 75 previously untested environmental chemicals. Overall, the chemicals fall into the following categories:

- Metals (such as lead and mercury)

- Pesticides (including insecticides and herbicides)

- Phthalates (a class of chemicals that are used in many consumer products, including adhesives, detergents, oils, solvents, soaps, shampoos, and plastics)

- Phytoestrogens (naturally occurring plant-based chemicals with hormonal effects)

- Polycyclic aromatic hydrocarbons (chemicals resulting from incomplete combustion of fossil fuels)

- Polychlorinated compounds (chlorine-containing organic chemicals that are used in a wide variety of industrial and commercial products)

- Cotinine (a component of tobacco smoke)

The CDC (2015, http://www.cdc.gov/exposurereport) maintains a listing of supplemental data published since

2009 that provide biomonitoring results for these and other chemicals. The CDC notes that its reports do not assess the potential harmfulness of the chemicals examined. The reports provide scientists with biomonitoring data so that research priorities can be set to determine human health effects for particular exposure levels.

OTHER BIOMONITORING STUDIES. The Minnesota Department of Health (MDH) operates a public health tracking system (http://www.health.state.mn.us/tracking) that collects data on chemical exposures and related health trends and uses the information to set public health priorities. In *Environmental Health Tracking and Biomonitoring: Connecting Environment, Exposure, and Public Health* (January 2013, http://www.health.state.mn.us/divs/hpcd/tracking/pubs/ehtblegreport2013.pdf), the MDH describes some of the major results from the program. The agency notes that it found "elevated" mercury levels in 10% of the newborns it tested in one study. The MDH has also tested small numbers of subjects for concentrations of arsenic, cotinine, and organic chemicals, such as perfluorochemicals, bisphenol A, and paraben. The results have been used to further the agency's public health programs and to justify larger biomonitoring studies devoted to environmental chemical exposures.

Biomonitoring has also become a popular tool for individuals to publicize their concerns about the widespread nature of toxins.

In 2006 *National Geographic* magazine paid laboratories to test blood and urine samples from one of its journalists, David Ewing Duncan, for more than 300 chemicals. Duncan describes the results in "The Pollution Within" (NationalGeographic.com, October 2006). He notes that scientists detected numerous toxins within his body, including dichloro-diphenyl-trichloroethane (DDT), the pesticides chlordane and heptachlor, polychlorinated biphenyls (PCBs), phthalates, perfluorinated acids, dioxins, mercury, and polybrominated diphenyl ethers (commonly used in flame retardants). Although the dosages for most of the chemicals were extremely low, Duncan notes that toxicologists know very little about the additive or combined effects of mixtures of chemical toxins in the human body.

The Commonweal Biomonitoring Resource Center collaborates with the Environmental Working Group in the Human Toxome Project. The project (2015, http://www.ewg.org/sites/humantoxome) provides biomonitoring results obtained from individuals of various ages and sexes for a wide variety of chemicals. It also offers information on the health effects (or concerns) that are associated with various chemical groups.

INTEGRATED RISK INFORMATION SYSTEM. The most sophisticated source of publicly available data regarding human exposure to toxins is the EPA electronic database Integrated Risk Information System (IRIS; http://www2.epa.gov/iris). IRIS contains information on the human health effects that are associated with exposure to environmental substances. There are many thousands of chemicals in use in the United States; as of November 2015, however, the IRIS database included health hazard information for only about 570 chemicals.

CHEMICAL TOXINS

Chemical toxins are the broadest and most common type of toxic substances that people are likely to encounter in their daily lives. These toxins can be found in a variety of products. The following are the primary sources:

- Household cleaners, solvents, adhesives, and paints
- Fertilizers and pesticides
- Metal, fibrous, and wooden building materials
- Plastics and electronics

In addition, people can be exposed daily to chemicals that are purposely introduced to their environment. These releases may have beneficial purposes (e.g., chlorination and fluoridation of public water supplies) or they may be consequences of industrial, commercial, or residential processes.

Information on some selected chemical toxins follows.

Lead

Lead is a naturally occurring metal. It was commonly used in many industries before the 1970s. Exposure to even low levels of lead can severely impact human health. Lead was once commonly used in many products, including gasoline and paint. Although these uses have been phased out, millions of older residences around the country were painted at one time with paints containing lead. Painted surfaces pose little danger as long as the paint remains undamaged. The greatest hazard is when chips of paint flake off or when renovations are performed that involve sanding or stripping paint.

Other household products that may contain unacceptable levels of lead include ceramics and crystal ware, miniblinds, weights used for draperies, wheel balances, fishing lures, seams in stained-glass windows, linoleum, batteries, solder, ammunition, and plumbing. Test kits and laboratories that test for lead can check questionable items and locations for the presence of the heavy metal.

The CDC also warns about the lead content in toys and trinkets that are imported from other countries. In "Toys" (October 15, 2013, http://www.cdc.gov/nceh/lead/tips/toys.htm), the CDC explains that lead can be present in plastics and paints that are used in toy manufacture. In 2003 a child died from lead poisoning after swallowing a piece of toy jewelry. In 2006 another child died after swallowing a small charm from a toy bracelet. Both incidents prompted massive recalls of the items involved. The CPSC is a federal government agency that is charged with protecting American consumers from unsafe products. As of November 2015, the CPSC (http://www.cpsc.gov/en/Recalls) listed 323 recalls that had been issued since 2001 on consumer products due to lead concerns. The majority of the recalled products are toys and toy jewelry. In 2007 millions of toys were recalled by manufacturers because of the presence of lead-containing paint that had been applied in Chinese factories.

Most of the lead in water comes from lead pipes and lead solder in plumbing systems. By 1993 all large public water supply systems were required to add substances such as lime or calcium carbonate to their water lines to reduce the corrosion of older pipes, which releases lead.

BLOOD LEAD LEVELS. Lead is highly toxic and can harm the brain, kidneys, bone marrow, and central nervous system. Infants, children, and pregnant women can experience serious health effects with levels as low as 10 micrograms of lead per deciliter of blood. (See Figure 10.1.) At high levels of exposure (now rare in the United States), lead can cause mental retardation, convulsions, and even death.

The CDC monitors blood lead levels (BLLs) of children and adults. Figure 10.2 shows the number of children aged five years and younger tested between 1997 and 2013 and determined to have elevated BLLs (more than 10 micrograms per deciliter). The graph illustrates that about 0.5% of the approximately 2 million children tested in 2013 had elevated BLLs.

REDUCING LEAD EXPOSURE. In 1971 Congress passed the Lead-Based Poisoning Prevention Act, restricting residential use of lead paint in structures that were constructed or funded by the federal government. The phase-out of leaded fuel in automobiles began during the 1970s.

The Lead Contamination Control Act of 1988 banned the sale of lead-lined drinking water coolers and authorized the CDC to create and expand programs at the state and local levels for screening BLLs in infants and children and referring those with elevated BLLs for treatment.

In 1992 Congress amended the TSCA to add Title IV (Lead Exposure Reduction). Title IV directs the EPA to address the general public's exposure to lead-based paint through regulations, education, and other activities. A particular concern of Congress and the EPA is the potential lead exposure risk that is associated with housing renovation. The law directs the EPA to publish lead hazard information and make it available to the general public, especially to those undertaking renovations.

FIGURE 10.1

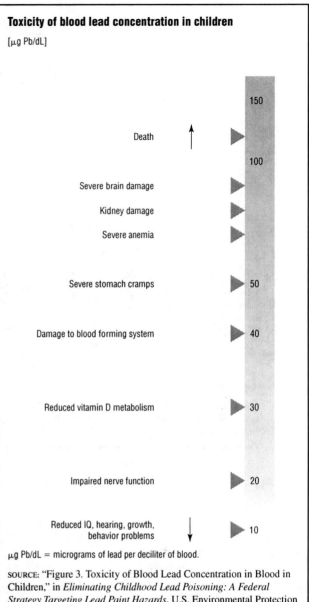

Toxicity of blood lead concentration in children

[μg Pb/dL]

μg Pb/dL = micrograms of lead per deciliter of blood.

SOURCE: "Figure 3. Toxicity of Blood Lead Concentration in Blood in Children," in *Eliminating Childhood Lead Poisoning: A Federal Strategy Targeting Lead Paint Hazards*, U.S. Environmental Protection Agency, President's Task Force on Environmental Health Risks and Safety Risks to Children, February 2000, http://www.cdc.gov/nceh/lead/about/fedstrategy2000.pdf (accessed September 8, 2015)

Also in 1992 Congress passed the Residential Lead-Based Paint Hazard Reduction Act, which is known as Title X. The law requires sellers and landlords to disclose information about lead-based paint hazards to buyers and leasers. The law also stopped the use of lead-based paint in federal structures and set up a framework to evaluate and remove lead-based paint from buildings nationwide. In 1996 Congress once again amended the TSCA, adding Section 402a to establish and fund training programs for lead abatement and to set up requirements and training of technicians and lead-abatement professionals.

As noted earlier, manufacturers recalled millions of toys in 2007 because of the presence of lead paint. In 2008 Congress passed the Consumer Product Safety

FIGURE 10.2

Concentrations of lead measured in blood of children aged less than 5, 1997–2013

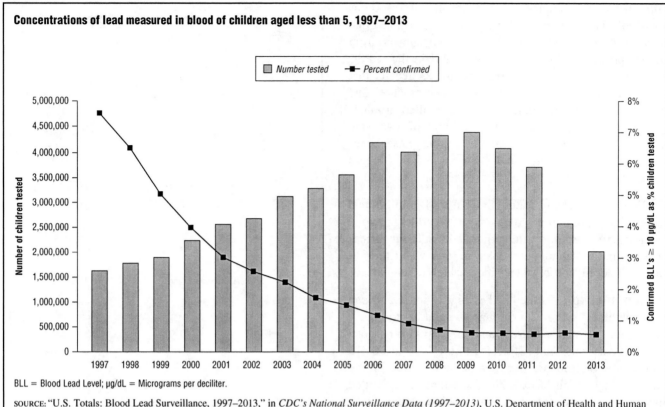

BLL = Blood Lead Level; µg/dL = Micrograms per deciliter.

SOURCE: "U.S. Totals: Blood Lead Surveillance, 1997–2013," in *CDC's National Surveillance Data (1997–2013)*, U.S. Department of Health and Human Services, Centers for Disease Control and Prevention, March 9, 2015, http://www.cdc.gov/nceh/lead/data/stateconfirmedbyyear_1997_2013.pdf (accessed September 8, 2015)

Improvement Act. It supplements the extensive Consumer Product Safety Act (CPSA), which was enacted during the 1970s and has been amended several times. The new law covers consumer products for both children and non-children. Children's products sold after August 2011 must not exceed 100 parts per million of lead. The law (http://www.cpsc.gov/en/Business--Manufacturing/Testing-Certification) also includes lead-testing requirements for U.S. manufacturers and importers of covered products. However, complaints from business groups prompted the CPSC to delay implementation of these requirements until 2013.

Following successful test results the manufacturer, importer, or private labeler of a children's product must prepare a written Children's Product Certificate that certifies that the product complies with applicable safety rules. In "FAQs—Certification and Third Party Testing" (2015, http://www.cpsc.gov/en/Business--Manufacturing/Testing-Certification/Childrens-Product-Certificate), the CPSC indicates that the certificate must do the following:

- Accompany each product or shipment of products

- Be furnished to retailers and distributors either physically or electronically (for example, by being posted on a website)

- Be provided to the CPSC, upon request

The CPSC notes, "It is a violation of the CPSA to fail to furnish a Children's Product Certificate, to issue a false certificate of conformity under certain conditions, and to otherwise fail to comply with section 14 of the CPSA. A violation of the CPSA could lead to a civil penalty and possibly criminal penalties and asset forfeiture." A certificate of conformity is a general certificate that is used for non-children's products. According to the CPSC (2015, http://www.cpsc.gov/en/Business--Manufacturing/Testing-Certification/General-Certificate-of-Conformity), a General Certificate of Conformity is a certificate "in which the manufacturer or importer certifies that its non-children's (general use) product complies with all applicable consumer product safety rules (or similar rules, bans, standards, or regulations under any law enforced by the Commission for that product.)"

RADIATION

Radiation is energy that travels in waves or particles. Radiation exposure comes from natural and human-made sources. People are exposed to natural radiation from outer space (cosmic radiation), the earth (terrestrial radiation and radon), and their own bodies (from naturally occurring radioactive elements). According to the U.S. Nuclear Regulatory Commission (NRC), in "Exposure" (July 23, 2015, http://www.nrc.gov/reading-rm/basic-ref/glossary/exposure.html), these sources account for

TABLE 10.2

Human-made sources of radiation

In general, the following man-made sources expose the public to radiation (the significant radioactive isotopes are indicated in parentheses):

- Medical sources (by far, the most significant man-made source)
  - Diagnostic x-rays
  - Nuclear medicine procedures (iodine-131, cesium-137, and others)
- Consumer products
  - Building and road construction materials
  - Combustible fuels, including gas and coal
  - X-ray security systems
  - Televisions
  - Fluorescent lamp starters
  - Smoke detectors (americium)
  - Luminous watches (tritium)
  - Lantern mantles (thorium)
  - Tobacco (polonium-210)
  - Ophthalmic glass used in eyeglasses
  - Some ceramics

SOURCE: "Members of the Public," in *Man-Made Sources*, U.S. Nuclear Regulatory Commission, October 10, 2014, http://www.nrc.gov/about-nrc/radiation/around-us/sources/man-made-sources.html (accessed September 8, 2015)

FIGURE 10.3

Common radon reduction method for homes

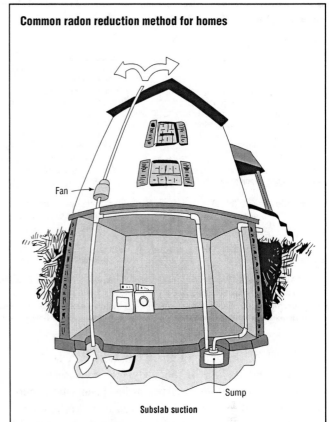

SOURCE: "Subslab Suction," in *Consumer's Guide to Radon Reduction: How to Fix Your Home*, U.S. Environmental Protection Agency, March 2013, http://www.epa.gov/radon/pdfs/consguid.pdf (accessed September 8, 2015)

approximately half of the average person's radiation exposure. Human-made sources, such as those listed in Table 10.2, include medical devices, electromagnetic equipment, and consumer products. The NRC estimates that these sources account for the other half of a person's average radiation exposure.

Radon

Radon is an invisible, odorless radioactive gas formed by the decay of uranium in rocks and soil. This gas seeps from underground rock into the basements and foundations of structures via cracks in foundations, pipes, and sometimes through the water supply. Because it is naturally occurring, it cannot be entirely eliminated from the environment. When radon is inhaled into the lungs, it undergoes radioactive decay by releasing particles that damage the deoxyribonucleic acid in the lung tissue.

In "Basic Radon Facts" (February 2013, http://www2.epa.gov/sites/production/files/2014-08/documents/basic_radon_facts.pdf), the EPA recommends that people have testing done to determine the radon level in their homes. The agency recommends that homes with radon levels at or above 4 picocuries per liter (pCi/L) be fixed to reduce the radon levels. The radon content in most homes can be reduced with devices such as specially designed sumps and fans that suck radon away from the foundation of a home and discharge it harmlessly above the roof. (See Figure 10.3.)

INDOOR AIR TOXINS

Indoor air pollution has become a serious problem in the United States. Although most people think of outdoor air when they think of air pollution, studies now reveal that indoor environments are not safe havens from air pollution. Modern indoor environments contain a variety of pollution sources, including building materials and consumer products. (See Table 10.3.) People and pets also contribute to airborne pollution. Improvements in home and building insulation and the widespread use of central air conditioning and heating systems have largely ensured that any contaminant present indoors will not be diluted by outside air and, therefore, will become more concentrated.

Asbestos

Asbestos is the generic name for several fibrous minerals that are found in nature. Long and thin fibers are bundled together to make asbestos, which is an excellent thermal and electrical insulator. The physical properties that give asbestos its resistance to heat and decay have long been linked to adverse health effects in humans. Asbestos is found in mostly older homes and buildings, primarily in indoor insulation. Other sources include materials used for construction and industrial purposes, such as roof coatings and pipeline wraps.

Asbestos tends to break into microscopic fibers. These tiny fibers can remain suspended in the air for long periods of time and can easily penetrate body tissues

TABLE 10.3

Sources and health effects of indoor air pollutants

Pollutant	Example sources	Primary health effects
Biological pollutants	Dust mites, fungi, bacteria, and pests such as cockroaches and mice	Allergic reactions (from inflammation to asthma). Infections and toxic reactions can also occur.
Volatile organic compounds (VOCs) including benzene, dichlorobenzene, ethyl benzene, chloroform, formaldehyde, methyl tertiary butyl ether, perchloroethylene, tetrachloroethene, toluene, and xylenes	Personal care products, cleaning products, paints, pesticides, building materials, and furniture	Effects vary by chemical, but include eye and respiratory irritation, rashes, headaches, nausea, vomiting, shortness of breath, and cancer.
Asbestos	Older insulation, building materials, some vinyl floor tiles, shingles, and heat-resistant fabrics	Lung cancer, mesothelioma, and (with occupational exposures) asbestosis.
Incomplete combustion products, including particulates and carbon monoxide	Solid fuels, for example, wood used for home heating	Particulate matter effects include respiratory irritation, respiratory infections, bronchitis, and lung cancer. Carbon monoxide exposure can cause low birth weight, headaches, nausea, dizziness, and death.
Polychlorinated biphenyls (PCBs)	Consumer products, including caulking in older buildings, paints, plastics, adhesives, and lubricants	PCBs have been shown to cause several adverse effects in animals, including cancer and immune, reproductive, nervous, and endocrine system effects. Human studies provide evidence supporting these effects.
Polybrominated biphenyl ethers (PBDEs), which are used as flame retardants	Consumer products, including upholstery, construction materials, and electrical appliances	Animal research suggests PBDEs can cause neurodevelopmental, kidney, thyroid, and liver toxicity and can disrupt endocrine systems.

SOURCE: Adapted from "The Sources and Effects of Indoor Pollutants Include," in *Our Built and Natural Environments: A Technical Review of the Interactions among Land Use, Transportation, and Environmental Quality, Second Edition*, U.S. Environmental Protection Agency, June 2013, http://www2.epa.gov/sites/production/files/2014-03/documents/our-built-and-natural-environments.pdf (accessed September 8, 2015)

when inhaled. Because of their durability, these fibers can lodge and remain in the body for many years. No safe exposure threshold for asbestos has been established, but the risk of disease generally increases with the length and amount of exposure. Diseases that are associated with asbestos inhalation include asbestosis (scarring of the lungs), lung and throat cancers, malignant mesothelioma (a tissue cancer in the chest or abdomen), and nonmalignant pleural disease (accumulation of bloody fluid around the lungs).

Asbestos was one of the first substances regulated under Section 112 of the Clean Air Act (CAA) of 1970 as a hazardous air pollutant. The discovery that asbestos is a strong carcinogen has resulted in the need for its removal or encapsulation (sealing off so that residue cannot escape) from known locations, including schools and public buildings. Many hundreds of millions of dollars have been spent in such cleanups.

Under the CAA asbestos-containing materials must be removed from demolition and renovation sites without releasing asbestos fibers into the environment. Among other safeguards, workers must wet asbestos insulation before stripping the material from pipes and must seal the asbestos debris while it is still wet in leak-proof containers to prevent the release of asbestos dust. The laws of most states have specific requirements for asbestos workers. A number of legal convictions have resulted from improper and illegal asbestos removal.

The Asbestos Hazard Emergency Response Act was signed into law in 1986. It requires public and private primary and secondary schools to inspect their buildings for asbestos-containing building materials. In 1989 the

EPA banned the importation, production, processing, and distribution of many asbestos-containing products in the United States. The ban was challenged in court and partially overturned. As a result, only a handful of asbestos-containing products remain banned. However, the use of asbestos is banned in products that have not traditionally contained it.

TOXINS IN FOOD

The presence of environmental toxins in food has become a topic of major concern in recent years. Chemical pollutants that end up in food can come from air and wastewater emissions or from land sources, such as landfills or farms. Food can also pose a danger to human health if it is contaminated by biological organisms.

Persistent and Bioaccumulative Chemicals

The most worrisome chemical contaminants in food are those that are persistent (resistant to biodegradation) and bioaccumulative, meaning that they are absorbed by lower life forms and become concentrated as they work their way up the food chain. There are four chemical toxins found in food that are particularly noted for their persistent bioaccumulative properties: mercury, pesticides, dioxins, and PCBs.

MERCURY. Mercury is a naturally occurring inorganic element. It is also released by human activities, primarily via waste incineration and fossil fuel combustion. In the environment, inorganic mercury can convert to an organic form called methylmercury. It accumulates in fish and shellfish and works its way up the food chain. Methylmercury accumulates in human tissue when people eat contaminated fish. At certain dosages it can damage the central nervous system, cause severe neurological impairment, and be fatal.

The public is urged to consult local and state fish advisories regarding the safety of fish caught in their area. In "Fish Advisories" (2015, http://www2.epa.gov/fish-tech), the EPA provides links to state advisories. State advisories typically list major water bodies and provide consumption restrictions (if any) for fish that are caught from those waters. Although mercury is the subject of most restrictions, other contaminants are also a concern, including pesticides, dioxins, and PCBs.

PESTICIDES. Water contamination is a primary pathway for pesticides to reach food sources, particularly fish. Other foods can be affected via the use of contaminated irrigation waters. Pesticides are also spread directly on and around ground-grown foods, such as crops and fruit trees.

The FDA notes in *Pesticide Monitoring Program—2009 Pesticide Report* (June 7, 2013, http://www.fda.gov/downloads/Food/FoodborneIllnessContaminants/Pesticides/UCM352872.pdf) that the responsibility for monitoring pesticides in food is divided among three government agencies: the EPA, the USDA, and the FDA. As mentioned earlier, the EPA regulates pesticide use and sets tolerance levels for pesticides. The USDA's Agricultural Marketing Service conducts the Pesticide Data Program, in which a wide range of edible and drinkable commodities are tested for pesticide content. Testing is performed on fresh and processed foods.

In *Pesticide Data Program Annual Summary, Calendar Year 2013* (December 2014, http://www.ams.usda.gov/sites/default/files/media/2013%20PDP%20Anuual%20Summary.pdf), the USDA reports the testing results for calendar year 2013. The agency notes that it tested 10,104 samples, including 100 samples of drinking water and 14 samples of groundwater. More than 40% of all samples had no detectable pesticide residue. Twenty-three (or 0.23%) of the 9,990 non-water samples contained residues exceeding the EPA tolerance levels. Overall, pesticides were detected, but below tolerance levels, in 301 non-water samples for a percentage level of 3%.

Table 10.4 shows the number of pesticides detected per sample by non-water commodity. Commodities for which pesticides were detected in more than 90% of the samples included peaches (97.9%; only 2.1% of samples had no detected pesticides), nectarines (97.2%; 2.8% of samples had no detected pesticides), celery (95.5%; 4.5% of samples had no detected pesticides), and plums (92.9%; 7.1% of samples had no detected pesticides).

Fear of agricultural pesticide usage has contributed to a rise in consumer interest in organic foods. The federal government's National Organic Program defines organic agriculture as that which excludes the use of synthetic fertilizers and pesticides. More important, it strives for low environmental impact and enlists natural biological systems (cover crops, crop rotation, and natural predators) to increase fertility and decrease the likelihood of pest infestation.

DIOXINS AND PCBS. Dioxins are a group of several hundred chlorinated organic compounds with similar chemical structures and biological effects. They are known to damage the major organs and systems of laboratory animals. The chemicals are also linked with adverse effects to the skin and liver in humans. Dioxins are classified as probable human carcinogens.

Dioxin categories include chlorinated dibenzo-p-dioxins, chlorinated dibenzofurans, and some PCBs. Dioxins are most commonly associated with the burning or combustion of other substances. Certain industrial processes, such as chlorine bleaching of pulp and paper, also produce dioxins. They are generated by natural sources, primarily forest fires, and are introduced to the environment by humans through a variety of activities.

PCBs are a group of synthetic organic chemicals that were primarily used as lubricants and coolants in electrical equipment before the 1970s. The manufacture of PCBs was halted in the United States in 1977 because of concerns about their effects on the environment and human health. PCBs are known to cause a variety of serious health problems in laboratory animals, such as liver cancer. They are classified as possible carcinogens in humans.

Since the mid-1990s the USDA has conducted occasional sampling studies to determine the levels of dioxins and dioxin-like compounds in the U.S. domestic meat supply. As of November 2015, the most recent study was performed in 2012–13. In *Dioxin FY 2013 Survey: Dioxins and Dioxin-Like Compounds in the U.S. Domestic Meat and Poultry Supply* (May 2015, http://www.fsis.usda.gov/wps/wcm/connect/da1d623d-3005-4116-bef7-2a61d1ebd543/Dioxin-Report-FY2013.pdf?MOD=AJPERES), the USDA indicates that its survey in the mid-1990s found "low levels of dioxins" in samples taken from the carcasses of cattle, hogs, chickens, turkeys, and miscellaneous livestock. The levels generally declined in subsequent surveys conducted in 2002–03, 2007–08, and 2012–13. The USDA concludes that dioxin levels in hogs, chickens, and turkeys decreased by 20% to 80% between the mid-1990s and 2012–13. However, the levels in cattle either remained flat or declined only slightly.

Biological Contaminants

According to federal officials, foodborne illnesses due to pathogens (disease-causing biological organisms) pose a substantial health burden in the United States. Although the U.S. food supply is among the safest in

TABLE 10.4

Number of pesticides detected per sample, by food commodity, 2013

Commodity (# of samples)	Number of pesticides[a] detected per sample[b]													
	0	1	2	3	4	5	6	7	8	9	10	11	12	13
Fresh fruit and vegetables						Percent								
Bananas (708)	15.1	37.3	38.8	7.8	1.0	—	—	—	—	—	—	—	—	—
Broccoli (708)	63.7	23.4	8.5	3.1	0.8	0.4	—	—	—	—	—	—	—	—
Carrots (712)	34.8	26.8	17.6	11.1	4.1	2.7	1.7	1.1	0.1	—	—	—	—	—
Cauliflower (532)	48.3	44.2	6.8	0.8	—	—	—	—	—	—	—	—	—	—
Celery (708)	4.5	10.3	16.1	20.3	16.7	12.3	10.2	5.5	2.3	1.4	0.4	—	—	—
Green beans (378)	29.6	28.6	18.8	12.4	6.9	2.6	0.5	0.3	0.3	—	—	—	—	—
Mushrooms (532)	50.0	45.9	2.3	1.7	0.2	—	—	—	—	—	—	—	—	—
Nectarines (543)	2.8	10.1	15.8	15.8	16.6	15.8	11.6	6.3	3.5	0.7	0.6	0.2	—	0.2
Peaches (285)	2.1	7.7	15.8	12.6	16.8	7.4	9.8	7.7	4.6	6.0	7.7	1.4	—	0.4
Plums (507)	7.1	45.8	33.9	10.1	1.2	0.8	0.6	0.4	0.2	—	—	—	—	—
Raspberries (652)	29.3	23.8	14.7	12.9	10.4	6.0	2.0	0.5	0.3	0.2	—	—	—	—
Summer squash (709)	47.1	23.0	14.2	7.9	4.4	2.0	1.1	0.3	—	—	—	—	—	—
Winter squash (187)	27.8	34.2	20.3	10.7	3.2	1.6	1.1	1.1	—	—	—	—	—	—
Processed fruit and vegetables														
Apple juice (379)	54.1	13.7	10.6	6.3	6.3	6.3	1.6	0.8	0.3	—	—	—	—	—
Baby food—applesauce (379)	48.8	23.5	17.4	7.7	2.1	0.5	—	—	—	—	—	—	—	—
Baby food—peas (378)	100	—	—	—	—	—	—	—	—	—	—	—	—	—
Grape juice (176)	63.1	17.0	6.3	11.9	1.7	—	—	—	—	—	—	—	—	—
Raspberries, frozen (53)	54.7	13.2	11.3	1.9	—	1.9	3.8	1.9	3.8	5.7	1.9	—	—	—
Percent of total samples	35.4	25.2	15.9	9.0	5.5	3.7	2.5	1.4	0.7	0.4	0.3	0.06	—	0.02
Actual number of samples	3,015	2,150	1,354	768	471	313	211	117	56	35	29	5	—	2
Total number of fruit & vegetable samples = 8,526														
Infant formula products														
Infant formula, dairy-based (177)	100	—	—	—	—	—	—	—	—	—	—	—	—	—
Infant formula, soy-based (179)	99.4	0.6	—	—	—	—	—	—	—	—	—	—	—	—
Actual number of samples	355	1	—	—	—	—	—	—	—	—	—	—	—	—
Dairy product														
Butter (756)	43.8	25.9	15.6	10.2	4.4	0.1	—	—	—	—	—	—	—	—
Actual number of samples	331	196	118	77	33	1	—	—	—	—	—	—	—	—
Fish product														
Salmon (352)	99.1	0.9	—	—	—	—	—	—	—	—	—	—	—	—
Actual number of samples	349	3	—	—	—	—	—	—	—	—	—	—	—	—

[a]Environmental contaminants have been excluded from the count of pesticides detected in this appendix. Parent compounds and their metabolites are combined to report the number of "pesticides" rather than the number of "residues."
[b]Excludes the 14 groundwater and 100 drinking water samples.

SOURCE: "Appendix L. Samples vs. Number of Pesticides Detected per Sample," in *Pesticide Data Program Annual Summary, Calendar Year 2013*, U.S. Department of Agriculture, Agricultural Marketing Service, December 2014, http://www.ams.usda.gov/sites/default/files/media/2013%20PDP%20Anuual%20Summary.pdf (accessed September 8, 2015)

the world, Americans do experience episodes of food poisoning and disease.

Foodborne illnesses became the object of intense public scrutiny following an outbreak of *Escherichia coli* (*E. coli*) in 1993 that killed four people and sickened hundreds. The illness was attributed to undercooked hamburgers from fast-food restaurants. The FDA responded by raising the recommended internal temperature for cooked hamburgers to 155 degrees Fahrenheit (68.3 degrees C). A sampling program was begun to test for *E. coli* in raw ground beef. New labels containing food-handling instructions were required on consumer packages of raw meats and poultry.

Since that time there have been other serious outbreaks of foodborne illnesses that have sickened and killed victims in the United States, including *E. coli* in spinach in 2006, *salmonella* in peanut products in 2009,

and *listeria* in ice cream in spring 2015. According to the CDC (http://www.cdc.gov/listeria/outbreaks/ice-cream-03-15/index.html), as of June 10, 2015, the agency had confirmed that 10 people in four states had been sickened by *listeria* in ice cream, and three of them had died.

Federal and state agencies operate a surveillance program called FoodNet to monitor laboratory-identified foodborne diseases that are related to pathogens. FoodNet data for 2014 are presented in Table 10.5. In total, 19,542 cases of foodborne illnesses were related to monitored pathogens in 2014. The most common were *salmonella* (7,452 cases), *campylobacter* (6,486), and *shigella* (2,801). Overall, foodborne illnesses resulted in 4,445 hospitalizations and 71 deaths during 2014.

In 2010 the federal government launched its Healthy People 2020 initiative, which set specific public health improvement goals to be accomplished by the year

TABLE 10.5

Number of cases of foodborne pathogens causing infection, hospitalizations, and death, by pathogen, 2014

	Cases			Hospitalizations		Deaths	
	No.	Incidence[a]	Objective[b]	No.	(%)	No.	(%)
Bacteria							
Campylobacter	6,486	13.45	8.5	1,080	(17)	11	(0.2)
Listeria	118	0.24	0.2	108	(92)	18	(15.3)
Salmonella	7,452	15.45	11.4	2,141	(29)	30	(0.4)
Shigella	2,801	5.81	N/A[c]	569	(20)	2	(0.1)
STEC O157	445	0.92	0.6	154	(35)	3	(0.7)
STEC non–O157	690	1.43	N/A	104	(15)	0	(0.0)
Vibrio	216	0.45	0.2	40	(19)	2	(0.9)
Yersinia	133	0.28	0.3	30	(23)	1	(0.8)
Parasitic							
Cryptosporidium	1,175	2.44	N/A	217	(18)	4	(0.3)
Cyclospora	26	0.05	N/A	2	(8)	0	(0.0)
Total	**19,542**			**4,445**		**71**	

N/A = not available. STEC = Shiga toxin–producing *Escherichia coli.*
[a]Per 100,000 population.
[b]Healthy People 2020 objective targets for incidence of Campylobacter, *Listeria, Salmonella,* STEC O157, Vibrio, and Yersinia infections per 100,000 population.
[c]No national health objective exists for these pathogens.
Note: Data for 2014 are preliminary.

SOURCE: Stacy M. Crim et al., "Table. Number of Cases of Culture–Confirmed Bacterial and Laboratory–Confirmed Parasitic Infection, Hospitalizations, and Deaths, by Pathogen—Foodborne Diseases Active Surveillance Network, United States, 2014," in *MMWR,* vol. 64, no. 18, U.S. Department of Health and Human Services, Centers for Disease Control and Prevention, May 15, 2015, http://www.cdc.gov/mmwr/pdf/wk/mm6418.pdf (accessed September 8, 2015)

2020. Table 10.6 shows the goals related to food safety, specifically desired reductions in the number of cases of confirmed foodborne infections per 100,000 population. As of May 2015, the results were mixed with decreases in infections due to *E. coli* O157 and *Yersinia,* no changes in the number of infections associated with *listeria* and *salmonella,* and increases in infections due to *campylobacter* and *Vibrio.*

TABLE 10.6

Food safety progress report, 2014

Pathogen	Healthy people 2020 target rate	2014 rate[a]	Change compared with 2006–2008[b]
Campylobacter	8.5	13.45	⬆ 13% increase
E. coli O157[c]	0.6	0.92	⬇ 32% decrease
Listeria	0.2	0.24	No change
Salmonella	11.4	15.45	No change
Vibrio	0.2	0.45	⬆ 52% increase
Yersinia	0.3	0.28	22% decrease ⬇

[a]Culture-confirmed infections per 100,000 population.
[b]2006–2008 were the baseline years used to establish healthy people 2020 targets.
[c]Shiga toxin-producing *Eschericha coli* O157.

SOURCE: Adapted from "2014 Food Safety Progress Report," in *Foodborne Diseases Active Surveillance Network (FoodNet),* U.S. Department of Health and Human Services, Centers for Disease Control and Prevention, May 2015, http://www.cdc.gov/foodnet/pdfs/progress-report-2014-508c.pdf (accessed September 8, 2015)

CHAPTER 11
DEPLETION AND CONSERVATION OF NATURAL RESOURCES

Throughout history humans have relied on the world's natural resources for survival. Early civilizations were dependent on sources of clean water, fertile soils, and wild animals that could be hunted for meat, skins, and fur. As time passed, societies learned to harvest and use other natural resources, primarily wood, metals, minerals, and fossil fuels. For centuries, little thought was given to the consequences of depleting these resources. The supply appeared to be never-ending.

Despite many technological advances, humans in the 21st century are still dependent on some of the same natural resources that sustained the first civilizations. In addition, there is enormous demand for wood, metals, minerals, and other natural materials from which goods are manufactured. Finally, fossil fuels (coal, natural gas, and oil) provide the bulk of the world's power. Since the latter half of the 20th century, scientists have been aware that these natural resources are limited in terms of quantity and quality.

Natural resources are important not only for their practical value and economic worth but also for their contribution to environmental health. For example, forests and wetlands provide habitat for a wide variety of plant and animal life. These ecosystems are also appreciated by humans for their aesthetic appeal and recreational purposes. Developers and industrial entities, however, have an interest in using these lands for different purposes. To balance competing interests, the government has created a number of agencies with responsibility for overseeing the management of natural resources. A list of federal agencies is provided in Table 11.1.

FORESTS

Forests are one of the world's most important natural resources. They not only offer a source of wood, but they also perform a wide range of social and ecological functions. They provide livelihoods for forest workers, protect and enrich soils, regulate the hydrologic cycle, affect local and regional climate through evaporation, and help stabilize the global climate. Through the process of photosynthesis, they absorb carbon dioxide and release the oxygen that humans and animals breathe. They provide habitat for many plant and animal species, are the main source of wood for industrial and domestic heating, and are widely used for recreation.

Status of U.S. Forests

As shown in Table 11.2, forested lands are prevalent in many regions of the United States and constitute from 23.2% to 29.7% of the nation's overall land cover. In 2011 the U.S. Forest Service (FS) published *National Report on Sustainable Forests—2010* (June 2011, http://www.fs.fed.us/research/sustain/docs/national-reports/2010/2010-sustainability-report.pdf), the most recent report on this topic as of November 2015. This report updates a 2003 report on the factors and challenges that are associated with the sustainability of U.S. forests. Overall, the FS focuses its analysis on three "overarching" issues:

- The loss of forestlands and working forests
- The relationship between forests, climate change, and bioenergy development
- Changing forest health and disturbance patterns

Forest Losses

The FS notes in *National Report on Sustainable Forests—2010* that forests cover 751 million acres (303.9 million ha) of the United States. This value is down from an estimated 1 billion acres (404.7 million ha) at the time of European colonization. Widespread deforestation occurred in the eastern United States during the 19th century, when forestland was converted to agricultural land. Most of this conversion was completed by the early 1900s. Since that time U.S. forest acreage has remained relatively constant. However, the FS indicates

TABLE 11.1

Federal agencies that oversee natural resources

Federal agency	Founded	Description
U.S. Army Corps of Engineers	1802	Grants permits for dredging and filling in certain waterways, including many wetlands.
U.S. Department of Agriculture		
Forest Service	1905	Manages more than 193 million acres of public lands in national forests and grasslands.
Natural Resources Conservation Service	1935*	Helps private land owners/managers conserve their natural resources. Participation is voluntary.
U.S. Department of the Interior		
Bureau of Indian Affairs	1824	Manages 55 million acres of land held in trust for American Indians, Indian tribes, and Alaska Natives.
Bureau of Land Management	1812*	Manages 245 million acres of public lands (mostly in the West) and 300 acres of subsurface mineral resources.
Bureau of Reclamation	1902	Provides water and energy to more than 31 million people via hundreds of dams, reservoirs, canals, and power plants it has constructed in 17 western states.
Fish and Wildlife Service	1871*	Conserves, protects and enhances fish, wildlife, plants and their habitats for the benefit of the public.
Bureau of Ocean Energy Management, Regulation and Enforcement	1982	Manages the nation's natural gas, oil and other mineral resources on the outer continental shelf.
National Park Service	1916	Preserves the resources of more than 80 million acres comprising the national park system.
Office of Surface Mining	1977	Oversees surface mining on federal lands and some tribal and state lands.
U.S. Geological Survey	1879	Provides data related to Earth sciences, natural disasters, and management of natural resources.
U.S. Environmental Protection Agency	1970	Develops and enforces regulations that implement environmental laws enacted by Congress.

*Date of founding of predecessor agency that evolved into current agency.

SOURCE: Created by Kim Masters Evans for Gale, © 2015

TABLE 11.2

Land-cover statistics, by region and type, 2007

Land-cover class	Northeast	Southeast	Midwest	Great Plains	Southwest	Northwest	Alaska	Hawaii	United States	Land use class (ca 2007)	United States (ca 2007)
Agriculture	10.9%	23.0%	49.0%	29.7%	5.0%	10.0%	0.0%	4.0%	18.6%	Cropland	18.0%
Grassland, shrub/scrub, moss, lichen	3.4%	7.8%	2.9%	50.5%	65.7%	42.8%	44.9%	33.3%	39.2%	Grassland, pasture, and range	27.1%
Forest	52.4%	38.7%	23.7%	10.7%	19.9%	37.7%	22.4%	22.0%	23.2%[a]	Forest	29.7%[a]
Barren	0.8%	0.3%	0.2%	0.5%	3.7%	1.5%	7.7%	11.2%	2.6%	Special use[b]	13.8%
Developed, built-up	9.6%	7.7%	8.0%	4.0%	2.7%	3.0%	0.1%	6.7%	4.0%	Urban	2.7%
Water, ice, snow	14.9%	7.3%	10.4%	1.9%	1.7%	3.2%	18.5%	21.7%	7.4%	Miscellaneous[c]	8.7%
Wetlands	8.0%	15.2%	5.8%	2.7%	0.7%	1.3%	6.4%	0.3%	5.0%		

[a]Definitional differences in the way certain categories are defined, such as the special uses distinction in the USDA Economic Research Service land use estimates, make direct comparisons between land use and land cover challenging. For example, forest land use (29.7%) exceeds forest cover (23.2%). Forest use definitions include lands where trees have been harvested and may be replanted, while forest cover is a measurement of the presence of trees.
[b]Special uses represent rural transportation, rural parks and wildlife, defense and industrial, plus miscellaneous farm and other special uses.
[c]Miscellaneous uses represent unclassified uses such as marshes, swamps, bare rock, deserts, tundra plus other uses not estimated, classified, or inventoried.

SOURCE: D. G. Brown et al., "Table 13.1. Circa-2001 Land-Cover Statistics for the National Climate Assessment Regions of the United States Based on the National Land Cover Dataset, and Overall United States Land-Use Statistics—Circa 2007," in "Chapter 13: Land Use and Land Cover Change," *Climate Change Impacts in the United States: The Third National Climate Assessment*, U.S. Global Change Research Program, revised October 2014, http://s3.amazonaws.com/nca2014/high/NCA3_Climate_Change_Impacts_in_the_United%20States_HighRes.pdf?download=1 (accessed September 9, 2015)

that the overall statistics on forest acreage do not show the whole picture. U.S. forests have become increasingly fragmented and perforated by human developments via subdivisions, recreational areas, and vacation and retirement homes. The FS explains that this is problematic because "large, contiguous tracts of forest" are optimal for ecosystem health.

Another challenge cited by the FS is the loss of working forests (forests that are actively managed by landowners). As of 2007, almost one-third (33.1%) the nation's forests were federally owned, and 9.2% and 1.5% were owned by state and local governments, respectively. Thus, 43.8% of U.S. forests were publicly

owned. Families and individuals owned 35.1% of U.S. forestlands. The remainder was split between the forest industry (6.8%), other corporations (11.5%), and other noncorporate parties (2.8%).

Forestlands owned by government entities and the forest industry are typically managed to optimize forest health, particularly for timber production. The owners may regularly monitor for diseases or other problems and take corrective actions as needed. According to the FS, private ownership of forests is increasing, and the average tract size per private owner is decreasing—a phenomenon known as parcelization. In addition, the agency reports that private forest owners more often "live farther away from the parcels they own" than in the past. These three factors are contributing to less active management of forestlands. The FS notes, "With the loss of an active management focus and the revenue streams that often accompany it, the survival of these forests and their associated ecosystem services is in question."

Climate Change and Bioenergy Development

Climate and forests are inextricably linked in that climate affects forests, and forests impact climate. The mechanisms and challenges associated with global warming and associated climate change are described in Chapter 3. In brief, increasing concentrations of carbon in the atmosphere due to anthropogenic (human-caused) sources (particularly the combustion of fossil fuels) are believed to be warming the planet and inducing climatic changes. The chief culprit is carbon dioxide, which is emitted in voluminous amounts by power plants, transportation vehicles, and industrial facilities.

Carbon dioxide is also a fertilizing agent for vegetation, including trees. Thus, in *National Report on Sustainable Forests—2010*, the FS indicates that increasing atmospheric carbon dioxide concentrations will likely boost forest growth in some areas. A warming climate will certainly change forest composition in terms of tree and vegetation types. For example, warm-weather species will probably spread into areas that were once too cool to sustain them. In addition, climate change may aggravate three major forest health stressors: drought, wildfires, and insect infestations. However, the linkage is not known with certainty. Although the FS indicates that some of these impacts "may already be occurring," more data are needed to ascertain their exact relationships.

Vegetation mitigates the effect of carbon buildup in the atmosphere by absorbing and storing carbon. This is an example of natural carbon sequestration. According to the FS, annual carbon accumulation in U.S. forests offsets an estimated 11% of the nation's total carbon emissions. Live forests are a major carbon "sink" because they store massive amounts of carbon. Nevertheless, the sequestration capacity of forests is very small when compared with the anthropogenic carbon emissions of the United States. Thus, afforestation (establishing new forest) is not a viable option for offsetting total emissions to any large degree. It is useful on a smaller scale, and plays a key role in the carbon offset markets. As is explained in Chapter 3, the markets allow emitters that are required to reduce their net carbon output a means to offset some of their emissions. For example, countries bound by the Kyoto Protocol (an international agreement that limits the carbon emissions of some countries) can help achieve their goals by planting or expanding forests. The United States is not a party to the Kyoto Protocol. Nevertheless, some U.S. companies, organizations, and other entities choose afforestation as a means to offset their carbon emissions. The FS notes that sales of carbon offsets in the United States totaled $1.7 million in 2007, up from about $600,000 in 2005.

Deforestation (clearing existing forest) has a twofold effect on the carbon cycle. First, it reduces the amount of natural carbon sequestration that can be achieved. Second, it releases carbon stored in the trees and other vegetation into the environment. This release may occur slowly, for example, as felled trees decay, or it can occur rapidly, as during a forest fire. The FS estimates that U.S. forests store 27 times as much carbon as the nation emits into the air each year. Losing large areas of these forests to purposeful deforestation or natural wildfires would release massive amounts of carbon into the atmosphere.

BIOENERGY CONSIDERATIONS. Forest vegetation (or biomass) is combustible and can be purposely burned as a fuel to produce electricity or for other purposes. The FS explains in *National Report on Sustainable Forests—2010* that over the long term, forest biomass combustion is considered carbon-neutral because the carbon released during combustion is assumed equal to that sequestered by subsequent forest regrowth. The agency notes that the combustion of forest products, such as logs and wood chips, generated more than 2.1 quadrillion British thermal units of energy in 2007. This was about 2% of the total energy consumed that year. Whereas biomass combustion for residential, commercial, and industrial applications has decreased since 1989, biomass combustion for electricity production by power plants has grown dramatically. According to the FS, the latter use offsets some of the carbon emissions that would have resulted from burning coal to produce the electricity. The FS notes that increased use of forest biomass for bioenergy may take place in the future and states, "To the extent that these potentials are realized, carbon sequestration and bioenergy production could radically alter the ecological and economic landscape of forest management in our country."

Forest Health

In *National Report on Sustainable Forests—2010*, the FS relies on information it compiled in *America's Forests Health Update 2009* (June 2009, http://www.fs.fed.us/foresthealth/publications/foresthealthupdate2009.pdf). In both reports, the FS focuses on four major forest stressors: fragmentation (which is addressed earlier in this chapter), droughts, wildfires, and pests. The agency indicates that these factors are interrelated, and the effects of the latter three stressors may be aggravated by global warming and associated climate change.

DROUGHTS. In *America's Forests Health Update 2009*, the FS notes that it tracks drought trends in forests using the Palmer Drought Severity Index (PDSI), which is compiled by the National Climatic Data Center. The agency states that "an assessment of monthly PDSI for forested areas of the United States indicates that much of the Interior West was significantly drier during the period from 1996 to 2005, compared to the 110-year average." Prolonged dryness in combination with above-normal temperatures stresses trees, making them more susceptible to wildfires and insect and disease infestation.

WILDFIRES. Before pioneers settled the West, fires occurred frequently, keeping the forest clear of undergrowth. Fuels seldom accumulated, and the fires were generally of low intensity, consuming undergrowth but not igniting the tops of large trees. Disrupting this normal cycle of fire has produced an accumulation of hazardous fuels, which are capable of feeding an increasing number of large, uncontrollable, and catastrophic wildfires. In addition, the threat of wildfires is aggravated by global warming and drought.

The National Interagency Coordination Center at the National Interagency Fire Center compiles wildland fire statistics. Table 11.3 shows the number of wildland fires and the acreage burned annually between 1960 and 2014. In 2014, 63,312 wildland fires burned more nearly 3.6 million acres (5.8 million ha). The number of fires and the affected acreage increased dramatically during the 21st century compared with earlier years. Following the 2000 fire season, the FS collaborated with other agencies to develop a national fire plan. As of November 2015, the most recent plan was published in April 2014. In *A National Cohesive Wildland Fire Management Strategy* (http://www.forestsandrangelands.gov/strategy/documents/strategy/CSPhaseIIINationalStrategyApr2014.pdf), the Wildland Fire Leadership Council addresses three factors that are considered key to dealing with future wildfires:

- Restoring and maintaining resilient landscapes such as by reducing excessive undergrowth in forests

- Creating fire-adapted communities so that humans and their infrastructure can better withstand wildfires without loss of life or property

- Responding to wildfires with a coordinated management plan that takes into account all stakeholders

PESTS. Pests, such as insects and pathogens, can infest huge areas of forests and kill thousands of trees. This is damaging by itself, but it also exaggerates other threats to forests, such as wildfires. Wildfires are more likely to spread quickly and burn hotter when forests contain large numbers of trees that have been weakened or killed by insect damage. Scientists fear that global warming and climate change will result in increased populations of native and nonnative (or exotic) insects that prey on vegetation, thus further stressing forests.

TABLE 11.3

Total number of wildland fires and acreage burned, 1960–2014

[Figures prior to 1983 may be revised as NICC verifies historical data.]

Year	Fires	Acres
2014	63,312	3,595,613
2013	47,579	4,319,546
2012	67,774	9,326,238
2011	74,126	8,711,367
2010	71,971	3,422,724
2009	78,792	5,921,786
2008	78,979	5,292,468
2007	85,705	9,328,045
2006	96,385	9,873,745
2005	66,753	8,689,389
2004	65,461	8,097,880*
2003	63,629	3,960,842
2002	73,457	7,184,712
2001	84,079	3,570,911
2000	92,250	7,393,493
1999	92,487	5,626,093
1998	81,043	1,329,704
1997	66,196	2,856,959
1996	96,363	6,065,998
1995	82,234	1,840,546
1994	79,107	4,073,579
1993	58,810	1,797,574
1992	87,394	2,069,929
1991	75,754	2,953,578
1990	66,481	4,621,621
1989	48,949	1,827,310
1988	72,750	5,009,290
1987	71,300	2,447,296
1986	85,907	2,719,162
1985	82,591	2,896,147
1984	20,493	1,148,409
1983	18,229	1,323,666
1982	174,755	2,382,036
1981	249,370	4,814,206
1980	234,892	5,260,825
1979	163,196	2,986,826
1978	218,842	3,910,913
1977	173,998	3,152,644
1976	241,699	5,109,926
1975	134,872	1,791,327
1974	145,868	2,879,095
1973	117,957	1,915,273
1972	124,554	2,641,166
1971	108,398	4,278,472
1970	121,736	3,278,565
1969	113,351	6,689,081
1968	125,371	4,231,996
1967	125,025	4,658,586
1966	122,500	4,574,389
1965	113,684	2,652,112
1964	116,358	4,197,309
1963	164,183	7,120,768
1962	115,345	4,078,894
1961	98,517	3,036,219
1960	103,387	4,478,188

*2004 fires and acres do not include state lands for North Carolina.
Notes: The National Interagency Coordination Center (NICC) at NIFC compiles annual wildland fire statistics for federal and state agencies. This information is provided through Situation Reports, which have been in use for several decades. Prior to 1983, sources of these figures are not known, or cannot be confirmed, and were not derived from the current situation reporting process. As a result the figures above prior to 1983 shouldn't be compared to later data.

SOURCE: "Total Wildland Fires and Acres (1960–2009)," in *Statistics*, National Interagency Fire Center, 2015, http://www.nifc.gov/fireInfo/fireInfo_stats_totalFires.html (accessed September 10, 2015)

In *National Report on Sustainable Forests—2010* the FS estimates the acreage of forest mortality caused by biotic processes and agents (i.e., insects, diseases, and invasive alien species) from 2003 to 2007 compared with the reference period 1997 to 2002. The acreage afflicted with mortality more than tripled from 12 million acres (4.9 million ha) to 37 million acres (15 million ha). The agency notes that insects of concern in U.S. forests include bark beetles and engraver beetles (also known as ips beetles), which are native species, and gypsy moths, which are nonnative species. Nonnative species can be harmful because they do not have natural predators in their new environment. This allows them to "invade" their new territory and spread quickly.

The FS employs a variety of measures to combat abiotic processes and agents, including the application of insecticides and the release of biological control agents. These agents include insects and pathogens that prey on the nonnative invasive pests.

WETLANDS: FRAGILE ECOSYSTEMS

Marshes, swamps, bogs, estuaries, and bottomlands are specific biosystems with sometimes distinctive characteristics; however, they are commonly grouped together under the term *wetlands*. Wetlands are always or often saturated by enough surface or groundwater to sustain vegetation that is typically adapted to saturated soil conditions, such as cattails, bulrushes, red maples, wild rice, blackberries, cranberries, and peat moss. The Florida Everglades and the coastal Alaskan salt marshes are examples of wetlands, as are the sphagnum-heath bogs of Maine. Because some varieties of wetlands are rich in minerals and nutrients and provide many of the advantages of both land and water environments, they are often dynamic systems that teem with a diversity of species, including many insects, which are a basic link in the food chain.

Wetlands were once regarded as useless swamps, good only for breeding mosquitoes and taking up otherwise valuable space. As a result, much wetland acreage has been lost to development. The U.S. Fish and Wildlife Service (FWS) tracks wetlands status and trends as part of its National Wetlands Inventory (http://www.fws.gov/wetlands/Status-and-Trends/index.html). As of November 2015, the most recent national report from the National Wetlands Inventory program was published in September 2011. In *Status and Trends of Wetlands in the Conterminous United States 2004 to 2009: Report to Congress* (http://www.fws.gov/wetlands/Documents/Status-and-Trends-of-Wetlands-in-the-Conterminous-United-States-2004-to-2009.pdf), Thomas E. Dahl of the FWS estimates that between the 1950s and 1970s, 458,000 acres (185,300 ha) of wetlands were lost annually in the conterminous (the lower 48 states) United States. (See Figure 11.1.) Wetlands continued to be lost annually from the 1970s through the 1990s, but the losses declined over the decades. Between 1998 and 2004 there was a gain of 32,000 acres (12,900 ha) per year. However, this

trend reversed itself between 2004 and 2009, when 13,800 acres (5,600 ha) of wetlands were lost annually.

Chapter 9 describes the water quality data collected by the states and compiled by the U.S. Environmental Protection Agency (EPA) into a national database. Most of the assessments were performed in 2012. As shown in Table 9.3 in Chapter 9, 678,981 acres (274,773.9 ha) of the total 1.3 million acres (0.5 million ha) of assessed wetlands were rated as impaired. In terms of designated uses, the highest percentages of assessed wetlands were impaired for aquatic life harvesting (99.2%) and agricultural use (67.2%). (See Table 9.9 in Chapter 9.) The probable causes and sources of impairment are listed in Table 9.12 and Table 9.13 in Chapter 9. Organic enrichment/oxygen depletion due to natural causes/wildlife and industrial and municipal/sewage discharges were blamed for impairing the largest acreage of wetlands. As noted in Chapter 9, the EPA conducts probability-based sampling studies called National Aquatic Resources Surveys on the nation's aquatic resources. As of November 2015, the agency (http://water.epa.gov/type/wetlands/assessment/survey/index.cfm) indicated that the fieldwork was completed in 2011, but the report had not yet been published.

The Many Roles of Wetlands

Productive wetlands are rich ecosystems that support diverse forms of plants and wildlife. They provide food and habitat for many animals and breeding and nesting areas for aquatic life. They also serve as way stations for migrating birds. Wetlands can temporarily or permanently trap pollutants such as excess nutrients, toxic chemicals, suspended materials, and disease-causing microorganisms—thus cleansing the water that flows over and through them. Some pollutants that become trapped in wetlands are biochemically converted to less harmful forms; other pollutants remain buried there; still others are absorbed by wetland plants and are either recycled through the wetland or carried away from it. (See Figure 11.2.) Wetlands support commercial fishing and are useful for floodwater reduction, shoreline stabilization, and recreational activities.

Wetlands Regulation

Wetlands are affected by two major pieces of federal legislation: the Clean Water Act (CWA) and the Rivers and Harbors Appropriation (RHA) Act of 1899. Regulations carrying out the intent of these acts are promulgated by the EPA and the U.S. Army Corps of Engineers (ACE).

Sections of the CWA regulate activities that affect wetlands, particularly discharges to them of dredged or fill material. These discharges are subject to the requirements of Sections 401 and 404 of the CWA. They are also regulated under many state regulations. The RHA regulates activities that could obstruct navigation of the

FIGURE 11.1

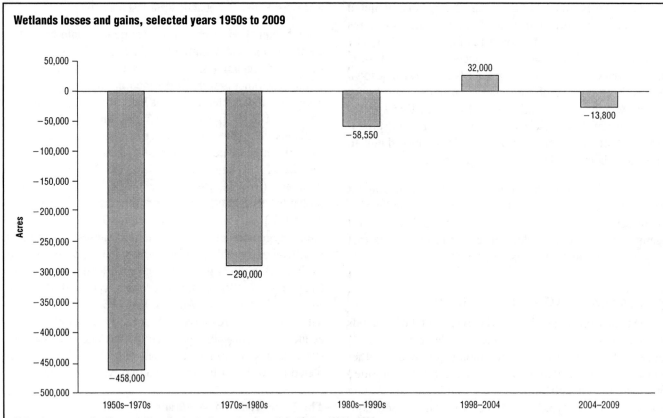

Wetlands losses and gains, selected years 1950s to 2009

Notes: Average annual net loss and gain estimates for the conterminous United States, 1954 to 2009. Estimates of error are not graphically represented.

SOURCE: Thomas E. Dahl, "Figure 19. Average Annual Net Loss and Gain Estimates for the Conterminous United States, 1954 to 2009," in *Status and Trends of Wetlands in the Conterminous United States 2004 to 2009: Report to Congress*, U.S. Department of the Interior, U.S. Fish and Wildlife Service, September 2011, http://www.fws.gov/wetlands/Documents/Status-and-Trends-of-Wetlands-in-the-Conterminous-United-States-2004-to-2009.pdf (accessed September 10, 2015)

country's waterways. For example, the building of dams, bridges, wharves, and piers is regulated, as are excavation and fill activities. The creation of any obstruction requires the approval of the ACE. The restrictions of the RHA apply only to wetlands that are navigable. The federal government defines navigable as a body of water that is subject to tides and/or has been, is, or could likely be used to transport interstate or foreign commerce.

There are other federal laws and programs that are designed to protect wetlands through the use of incentives (e.g., grants) or disincentives (e.g., denial of federal funding for certain projects that affect wetlands). In addition, wetlands are regulated by a host of state and local agencies. Overall, there is no one federal program that oversees all aspects of wetland protection. Furthermore, the existing federal legislation regulates the filling of wetlands but not other activities that could damage them. Critics complain that these policies do not provide adequate protection for wetlands. However, many private landowners, farmers, and developers believe that existing legislation is too restrictive.

During the late 1980s President George H. W. Bush (1924–) set a national goal for eliminating wetland losses

in the short term and achieving net gains in wetlands over the long term. The concept was called no-net-loss. Land developers were encouraged to offset wetland losses by developing or buying shares in wetland mitigation banks. For example, a utility company that wanted to destroy wetlands in one location to build a power plant could develop a larger acreage of wetlands in another suitable location. Wetland banking has become a common means through which wetland losses are offset.

FEDERAL JURISDICTION CONTROVERSY. The wetland restrictions of the CWA are a source of controversy because of confusion over which types of wetlands are subject to the law. The original law did not specifically mention wetlands, but gave the EPA jurisdiction over "waters of the United States." As discussed in Chapter 9, in June 2015 the EPA and the ACE published the Clean Water Rule (https://www.federalregister.gov/articles/2015/06/29/2015-13435/clean-water-rule-definition-of-waters-of-the-united-states) to clarify which water bodies (including wetlands) are subject to federal jurisdiction. The new rule extends coverage to small wetlands that "impact downstream waters" and other wetlands that were not previously

FIGURE 11.2

Wetlands' contribution to improving water quality and reducing storm water runoff

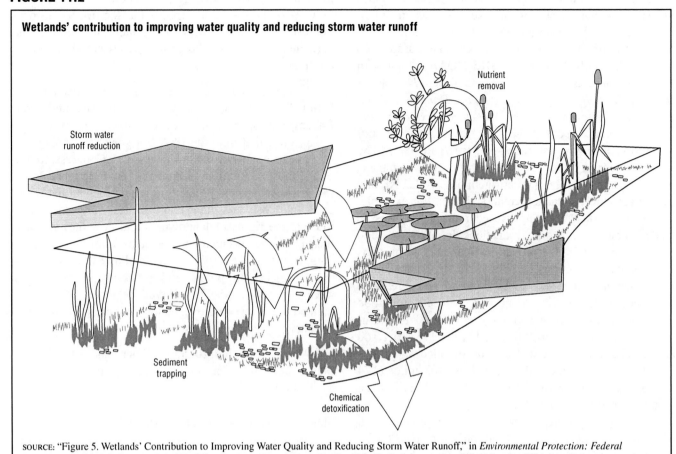

Nutrient removal

Storm water runoff reduction

Sediment trapping

Chemical detoxification

SOURCE: "Figure 5. Wetlands' Contribution to Improving Water Quality and Reducing Storm Water Runoff," in *Environmental Protection: Federal Incentives Could Help Promote Land Use That Protects Air and Water Quality*, U.S. General Accounting Office, October 2001, http://www.gao.gov/new.items/d0212.pdf (accessed September 10, 2015)

covered. As such, the Clean Water Rule aroused much controversy and triggered numerous lawsuits. More than 30 states sued the EPA arguing the new rule is too sweeping in scope. In October 2015 a federal appeals court stayed (temporarily postponed) enforcement of the Clean Water Rule. It remains to be seen if the rule will survive all of the legal challenges against it.

The Gulf Coast's Wetlands

During the first decade of the 21st century the Gulf Coast's wetlands suffered a series of devastating blows from Hurricanes Rita and Katrina in 2005 and the BP Deepwater Horizon oil spill in 2010. As described in Chapter 9, the latter dumped an estimated 4.9 million barrels of oil into the Gulf after an oilrig exploded approximately 50 miles (80 km) off the Louisiana coast. To mitigate (to relieve or reduce in harshness) the environmental damage, numerous measures were employed after the spill, including controlled burns, floating barriers, and chemical dispersants. Nevertheless, some wetland areas in the Gulf were seriously affected.

According to Jonathan L. Ramseur of the Congressional Research Service, in *Deepwater Horizon Oil Spill:*

Recent Activities and Ongoing Developments (April 17, 2015, http://fas.org/sgp/crs/misc/R42942.pdf), nearly 1,100 miles (1,800 km) of shoreline were oiled. The Gulf's wetlands were already stressed by erosion and organic enrichment/oxygen depletion when the spill occurred. Further damage was caused by Hurricane Lee (2011) and Hurricane Isaac (2012).

Ramseur notes that as of December 2014, BP had spent more than $14 billion on cleanup operations. In addition, civil settlements with multiple parties were expected to total in the billions of dollars. In November 2012 the U.S. Department of Justice reached a settlement with BP over criminal charges related to the oil spill. The company agreed to plead guilty to more than a dozen charges and pay $4 billion in fines. More than half of the money ($2.4 billion) was slated to go to the National Fish and Wildlife Foundation (NFWF) "to support restoration efforts in the Gulf states." The NFWF is a private nonprofit organization created by Congress during the 1980s. It works with government and private partners to award grants for conservation projects. Another $100 million of the BP fine was earmarked for the North American Wetlands Conservation Fund. The remainder will go to various federal programs and funds.

The Oil Pollution Act of 1990 requires that a Natural Resource Damage Assessment take place when an oil spill occurs. The National Oceanic and Atmospheric Administration (NOAA) heads the assessment associated with the BP spill. In October 2015 NOAA, along with other federal and state agencies, published *Deepwater Horizon Oil Spill: Draft Programmatic Damage Assessment and Restoration Plan and Draft Programmatic Environmental Impact Statement* (http://www.gulfspill restoration.noaa.gov/restoration-planning/gulf-plan). The report provides a comprehensive overview of the impacts of the spill on wildlife, habitat (including wetlands), and human activities, such as recreational uses. For example, the agencies state, "Oiling caused multiple injuries to marsh habitats, including reductions in above ground biomass and total plant cover in mainland herbaceous salt marshes, reductions in periwinkle snail abundance, reductions in shrimp and flounder growth rates, reduced reproductive success in forage fish, reduced amphipod survival, and reduced nearshore oyster cover. These injuries were observed over 350 to 721 miles (563 to 1,160 km) of shoreline. Increased erosion of oiled shorelines has also been documented over at least 108 miles (174 km) of coastal wetlands." The report also describes the proposed restoration plan for the ecosystems affected by the oil spill. According to the agencies, implementation of the plan will cost about $8.8 billion and be paid for by BP under a proposed legal agreement. As of November 2015, neither the restoration plan nor the legal agreement had been finalized.

BIODIVERSITY

Biological diversity, or biodiversity, refers to the full range of plant, animal, and microbial life and the ecosystems that house them. The loss of biodiversity leads to problems beyond the simple loss of animal and plant variety. When local populations of a species are wiped out, the genetic diversity within that species that enables it to adapt to environmental change is diminished, resulting in a situation of biotic impoverishment. The loss of habitats, the contamination of water and food supplies, poaching, and indiscriminate hunting and fishing have depleted the population of many species. Most scientists agree that prospects for the survival of many species of wildlife, and hence biodiversity, are getting worse.

Worldwide, species loss is monitored by the International Union for Conservation of Nature (IUCN), based in Switzerland. Since 1960 the IUCN has evaluated thousands of plant and animal species for its annual *Red List of Threatened Species* (http://www.iucnredlist.org). The IUCN categorizes species based on their level of risk of extinction in the wild. According to the IUCN (http://cmsdocs.s3.amazon aws.com/summarystats/2015_2_Summary_Stats_Page_Documents/2015_2_RL_Stats_Table_1.pdf), 22,784 species were "threatened with extinction" in 2015. The IUCN

examined 77,340 species for the report. This constituted only 4% of the 1.7 million species that the IUCN considers "described species." Thus, many more species may be classified as threatened as more species are evaluated in the future.

In the United States species loss is tracked at the national level through programs established under the Endangered Species Act (ESA), which was passed in 1973. Since that time the ESA has gone from being one of the least controversial laws passed by Congress, to one of the most contentious. Like other environmental laws, the ESA mandates protection requirements that have economic costs and other consequences. In particular, it impacts the rights of landowners and how they manage their properties if endangered species are present. Critics complain the act overly restricts land and water development projects on public and private properties. ESA advocates believe the law should be more fully implemented and supported by greater funding to help ensure the survival of imperiled species.

As of September 2015, 1,567 species in the United States were listed as endangered or threatened. (See Table 11.4.)

Species Loss: Crisis or False Alarm?

As with most environmental issues, not all experts agree about the threat to species diversity. Some observers believe that extensive damage to species diversity has not been proven and claim that although wild habitats are disappearing because of human expansion, the seriousness of extinction has been exaggerated and is not supported by scientific evidence. They point to the fact that the total number of species and their geographic distribution are unknown. How, they ask, can forecasts be made based on such sketchy data?

Other observers contend that extinctions, even mass ones, are inevitable and occur as a result of great geological and astronomical events that humans cannot affect. They do not believe that disruptions caused by human activity are enough to create the mega-extinction prophesied by people they consider "alarmists."

Furthermore, some critics of the environmental movement believe the needs of humans are being made secondary to those of wildlife. They contend that the ESA protects wildlife regardless of the economic cost to human beings.

The Gallup Organization conducts polls to gauge public opinion on various environmental issues. In "Environment" (2015, http://www.gallup.com/poll/1615/Environment.aspx#1), Gallup notes that in March 2015, 36% of respondents expressed a great deal of worry about the extinction of plant and animal species. Another 28% had a fair amount of worry, and 22% reported "only a little" worry about it; 14% expressed no worry at all about

TABLE 11.4

Number of threatened and endangered U.S. species, as of September 10, 2015

Group	United States*		
	Endangered	Threatened	Total listings
Annelid worms	0	0	0
Snails	34	12	46
Flatworms and roundworms	0	0	0
Sponges	0	0	0
Corals	0	6	6
Mammals	74	25	99
Fishes	93	70	163
Amphibians	20	15	35
Reptiles	14	23	37
Clams	75	13	88
Arachnids	12	0	12
Insects	61	11	72
Crustaceans	22	3	25
Birds	79	21	100
Millipedes	0	0	0
Hydroids	0	0	0
Animal totals	**484**	**199**	**683**
Conifers and cycads	2	1	3
Flowering plants	694	155	849
Ferns and allies	28	2	30
Lichens	2	0	2
Plant totals	**726**	**158**	**884**
Grand totals	**1,210**	**357**	**1,567**

*United States listings include those populations in which the United States shares jurisdiction with another nation.

Notes: 12 animal species (9 in the U.S.) are counted more than once in the above table, primarily because these animals have distinct population segments (each with its own individual listing status).

The U.S. species counted more than once are:

- Frog, mountain yellow-legged (Rana muscosa)
- Salamander, California tiger (Ambystoma californiense)
- Salmon, Chinook (Oncorhynchus (= Salmo) tshawytscha)
- Salmon, chum (Oncorhynchus keta)
- Salmon, coho (Oncorhynchus (= Salmo) kisutch)
- Salmon, sockeye (Oncorhynchus (= Salmo) nerka)
- Sea turtle, loggerhead (Carettacaretta)
- Steelhead (Oncorhynchus (= Salmo) mykiss)
- Sturgeon, Atlantic (Acipenseroxyrinchusoxyrinchus)

There are a total of 602 distinct active (Draft and Final) recovery plans. Some recovery plans cover more than one species, and a few species have separate plans covering different parts of their ranges. This count includes only plans generated by the USFWS (or jointly by the USFWS and NMFS), and only listed species that occur in the United States.

SOURCE: Adapted from "Summary of Listed Species Listed Populations and Recovery Plans as of Thu, 10 Sep 2015 18:46:12 GMT," in *Species Reports*, U.S. Fish and Wildlife Service, September 10, 2015, http://ecos.fws.gov/tess_public/pub/boxScore.jsp (accessed September 10, 2015)

the issue. The proportions of respondents expressing a great deal or a fair amount of worry about the extinction of plant and animal species have decreased somewhat since 2000, when the question was first asked.

THE SPOTTED OWL CONTROVERSY. Environmentalists have long argued with government and industry over the question of logging in the Pacific Northwest. Timber production has economic benefits to society, but environmentalists want to limit logging to aid the health of the ecosystem.

The argument came to a head in 1990, when the spotted owl—which lives only in this particular region—was added to the list of endangered species. The owl's presence halted logging there (following protests by environmental groups) at considerable economic loss to communities and families in the area. Numerous lawsuits ensued while the federal government tried to come up with a compromise that was satisfactory to all the stakeholders involved. The result in 1994 was the Northwest Forest Plan (NWFP), which allowed logging to resume with restrictions on the size, number, and distribution of trees to be cut. The NWFP is implemented by a variety of federal agencies through the Regional Ecosystem Office (REO). The REO notes in "Northwest Forest Plan (NWFP) Overview" (2015, http://www.reo.gov/general/aboutNWFP.htm) that the NWFP covers 24.5 million acres (9.9 million ha) in Oregon, Washington, and Northern California.

In 2015 the FS (http://www.reo.gov/monitoring/reports/20yr-report) published a series of reports that present NWFP data collected since the early 1990s. In *Status and Trends of Northern Spotted Owl Populations and Habitats* (May 2015, http://www.reo.gov/monitoring/reports/20yr-report/NSO%20Habitat%2020yr%20Report%20-%20Draft%20for%20web.pdf), Raymond J. Davis et al. estimate that northern spotted owl nesting and roosting habitat areas declined by 1.5% between 1993 and 2012 on federal lands covered by the NWFP. Wildfire was the primary cause of habitat loss. The 1.5% rate of habitat loss over two decades is lower than the rate of 5% per decade that was expected when the NWFP was implemented. Davis et al. do not include spotted owl population data in their report; however, estimates are available from previous reports. In *Status and Trends of Northern Spotted Owl Populations and Habitats* (October 2011, http://www.fs.fed.us/pnw/pubs/pnw_gtr850.pdf), Davis et al. estimate that spotted owl populations declined between 0.4% and 7.1% annually across the federal study areas between 1994 and 2008.

Fisheries and Aquaculture

Every two years the Food and Agriculture Organization (FAO) of the United Nations publishes an assessment of the world's fish populations. In *State of World Fisheries and Aquaculture, 2014* (2014, http://www.fao.org/3/d1eaa9a1-5a71-4e42-86c0-f2111f07de16/i3720e.pdf), the FAO estimates that 174.2 million tons (158 million t) of fish were captured in the wild or farmed (via aquaculture) worldwide for consumption and other purposes in 2012. Just over half (57%) of the haul was wild-caught fish. The remainder was produced by the aquaculture industry.

The FAO also estimates the status of the world's marine (oceanic) fish stocks as of 2011:

- Fully fished—61.3%, meaning that catches were "at or very close to their maximum sustainable production." This means that there is "no room for further expansion" of the catch of them.

- Overfished—28.8%, meaning that they need "strict management plans to rebuild stock abundance to full and biologically sustainable productivity"

- Underfished—9.9%, meaning that the stocks "have been exposed to relatively low fishing pressure and may have some potential to increase their production"

Fisheries exploitation is important not only for its human effects (i.e., economic and food consumption impacts) but also for its negative impacts on ocean ecology and ecosystems. The aquaculture industry has its own negative environmental impacts, primarily the discharge of biological wastes into water bodies and the transmission of disease from farmed stocks to wild populations. These problems are rooted in the nature of coastal aquaculture, which commonly features heavily concentrated populations of cultivated fish in cages or other facilities. Escapees and circulation of aquaculture water with the ocean at large pose the greatest hazards to natural ecosystems.

MINERALS AND OIL

Materials extracted from the earth are needed to provide humans with food, clothing, and housing and to continually upgrade their standard of living. Some of the materials needed are renewable resources, such as agricultural and forestry products, whereas others are nonrenewable, such as minerals and fossil fuels.

The Clean Air Act, the CWA, and the Resource Conservation and Recovery Act of 1976 regulate certain aspects of mining but, in general, the states are primarily responsible for regulation, which varies widely from state to state. In addition, coastal states wield control over oil and gas recovery within their legally defined offshore waters; jurisdiction varies by state, but in some cases it extends out as far as 10 miles (16.1 km). The federal government has jurisdiction over the waters outside state jurisdiction and extending to the boundary of U.S. territorial waters. State and then federal jurisdiction extend to the edge of the outer continental shelf, which is a gently sloping and relatively shallow underwater plain that extends from the U.S. land mass to the edge of the open sea.

Offshore Drilling

Offshore drilling for oil or gas is accomplished through resource leases that are granted by the state or federal government, depending on the location of the drilling site. This practice has been controversial for decades. In 1969 an oilrig in federal waters off the coast of California suffered a leak that sent hundreds of thousands of gallons of oil into the sea, soiling beaches and harbors near Santa Barbara, California. The resulting negative publicity greatly chilled public and political support for offshore drilling. The *Exxon Valdez* oil spill in 1989 further inflamed public opinion against offshore drilling. As a result, offshore areas along the Atlantic and Pacific Coasts have been off limits for new leases for decades. However, prolific offshore drilling occurs in the Gulf of Mexico.

During the latter part of the first decade of the 21st century public and political opinions against offshore drilling began to change in light of historically high gasoline prices and fears about U.S. dependence on foreign oil. At the federal level, offshore oil and gas leases are administered by the Bureau of Ocean Energy Management (BOEM), which sets five-year plans for lease activities. As explained by the agency in "Proposed Outer Continental Shelf Oil and Gas Leasing Program for 2012–2017" (November 8, 2011, http://www.boem .gov/uploadedfiles/5-year_program_factsheet.pdf) in 2009, as the BOEM began formulating a proposed lease plan for 2012 through 2017 it was considering allowing new leases in previously untapped areas. John M. Broder reports in "Obama to Open Offshore Areas to Oil Drilling for First Time" (NYTimes.com, March 31, 2010) that the administration of President Barack Obama (1961–) would have allowed drilling in previously banned areas along the coasts of the Northeast, the Gulf of Mexico, and northern Alaska. After the massive BP oil spill occurred in April 2010 in the Gulf of Mexico, Obama reversed his decision.

The BOEM (http://www.boem.gov/79-FR-34349) notes that in June 2014 it issued a Request for Information (ROI) regarding lease sales for 2017 through 2022. The agency indicated that it would consider lease sales in the Atlantic Ocean. In "Frequently Asked Questions: Draft Proposed Program" (February 3, 2015, http://www.boem.gov/2017-2022-Frequently-Asked-Questions), the BOEM states that it received more than half a million comments from the public, federal and state agencies, the energy industry, and other parties regarding the ROI. Using this input, the agency published in January 2015 a Draft Proposed Program (http://www.boem.gov/Five-Year-Program-2017-2022) for lease sales for 2017 through 2022. As of November 2015, the proposed lease schedule (http://www.boem.gov/2017-2022-Lease-Sale-Schedule) included a lease sale in 2021 for areas in the mid- and south Atlantic Ocean. According to the BOEM, in "Frequently Asked Questions: Draft Proposed Program," the areas would be at least 50 miles (80 km) off the coasts of Virginia, North Carolina, South Carolina, and Georgia. A comprehensive environmental study called a Programmatic Environmental Impact Statement (PEIS) must be performed before the new five-year plan can be finalized. The BOEM anticipates that a draft PEIS will be published in 2016. The report will detail the expected impacts of oil and gas exploration and production on the targeted lease areas.

In "What's behind U.S. Plan to Open Atlantic to Offshore Drilling?" (NationalGeographic.com, January

28, 2015), Wendy Koch asserts that President Obama's decision to open the Atlantic Ocean to drilling was driven by a political desire to compromise with Republican leaders who favor expanded drilling. As explained in Chapter 1, public opinion polling reveals that Republicans strongly support the development of U.S. energy supplies over environmental protection. (See Table 1.4 in Chapter 1.) However, Koch notes, "Environmentalists oppose opening the Atlantic [Ocean] to oil and gas drilling, citing the ecological risks of spills and climate dangers of expanding fossil fuel use."

Oil in the Arctic

The search for oil has led to the exploration of the Alaskan wilderness. Exploratory oil drillers are focusing their attention on the National Petroleum Reserve in Alaska (NPRA) in the Arctic wilderness. The U.S. Geological Survey (USGS) notes in *U.S. Geological Survey 2002 Petroleum Resource Assessment of the National Petroleum Reserve in Alaska* (May 17, 2005, http://pubs.usgs.gov/fs/2002/fs045-02/index.html) that the NPRA encompasses 23 million acres (9.3 million ha) in northwestern Alaska. (See Figure 11.3.) Geologists believe that northern Alaska holds great stores of oil and natural gas. Environmental groups fear that oil and gas development will seriously harm the area.

In October 2010 the USGS released a report that estimated the volumes of oil and natural gas that are potentially available in the NPRA. In "2010 Updated Assessment of Undiscovered Oil and Gas Resources of the National Petroleum Reserve in Alaska" (http://pubs.usgs.gov/fs/2010/3102/pdf/FS10-3102.pdf), the USGS provides estimates of 896 million barrels of oil and 52.8 trillion cubic feet (1.5 trillion m^3) of natural gas in "conventional undiscovered accumulations."

Transportation of the natural gas to markets would require a new pipeline. There is already a pipeline system in place for oil—the Trans-Alaska Pipeline System, which lies between the NPRA and the Arctic National Wildlife Refuge (ANWR). (See Figure 11.3.) The ANWR (May 20, 2015, http://www.fws.gov/refuge/arctic) is a 19-million-acre (7.7-million-ha) area of pristine wilderness along the Alaskan-Canadian border. It, too, is being considered for oil exploration, a move that is strongly opposed by environmentalists.

The future of the refuge lies in the hands of the federal government. In 2002, following heated debate, the U.S. Senate killed a proposal by the administration of President George W. Bush (1946–) to allow oil companies to drill in the ANWR. The proposal was raised again in subsequent years, particularly during times of

FIGURE 11.3

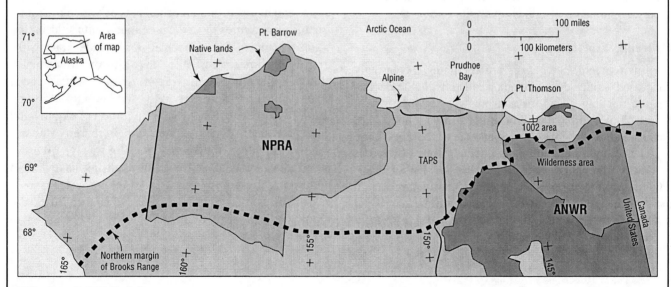

Northern Alaska, showing locations and relative sizes of the National Petroleum Reserve in Alaska and the Arctic National Wildlife Refuge

TAPS = Trans-Alaska Pipeline System.
NPRA = National Petroleum Reserve in Alaska.
ANWR = Arctic National Wildlife Refuge.

SOURCE: "Figure 1. Map of Northern Alaska Showing Locations and Relative Sizes of the National Petroleum Reserve in Alaska (NPRA) and the Arctic National Wildlife Refuge (ANWR)," in *U.S. Geological Survey 2002 Petroleum Resource Assessment of the National Petroleum Reserve in Alaska (NPRA)*, U.S. Department of the Interior, 2002, http://pubs.usgs.gov/fs/2002/fs045-02/figure1.html (accessed September 10, 2015)

high gasoline prices, but was defeated. The Obama administration does not support drilling in the ANWR, and as of November 2015 no federal legislation had been passed that would allow the practice.

The Chukchi Sea lies off the coast of northwestern Alaska and hence northwest of the NPRA shown in Figure 11.3. In "Agency Calls for Arctic Offshore Lease Suggestions" (Associated Press, September 27, 2013), Dan Joling indicates that in 2008 Royal Dutch Shell purchased leases to drill in the Chukchi Sea. This was highly controversial, as environmentalists are staunchly opposed to offshore drilling in the Arctic region. Shell obtained the leases during the Republican administration of Bush. However, Joling notes that "lawsuits and permit requirements held up Arctic offshore drilling until 2012." The article "Shell Halts Chukchi Sea Drilling" (Associated Press, September 9, 2012) notes that in 2012 "it was the first time a drill bit had touched the sea floor in the U.S. Chukchi Sea in more than two decades." Shell's success was short-lived. In "Shell's New Chukchi Plan: Two Rigs Drilling Wells at the Same Time" (ADN.com, August 28, 2014), Yereth Rosen explains, "Plans for drilling in 2013 and 2014 were called off because of equipment and legal woes. Although Shell has spent about $5 billion on its offshore Alaska exploration program, it has yet to drill into any oil-bearing zones." In 2015 Shell tried again after a new drilling plan was approved by the BOEM; however, the results proved disappointing. Erica Martinson reports in "Shell Calls Off Plans for Arctic Oil" (BristolBayTimes.com, October 2, 2015) that the company decided to abandon its efforts "after coming up dry on its $7 billion test well in the Chukchi Sea." According to Martinson, Republican leaders blamed the Obama administration for Shell's decision; low oil prices, however, also likely played a role.

Hydraulic Fracturing

Environmental advocates are becoming increasingly concerned about a drilling method called hydraulic fracturing (or fracking). This method involves the injection of large volumes (up to 1 million gallons [3.8 million L]) of water, sand, and chemicals deep into the earth. (See Figure 11.4.) The high-pressure mixture opens fissures (fractures or cracks) throughout rock formations that harbor oil or natural gas in their pores. Hydraulic fracturing has been in use for decades, but recent technological advancements and high prices for fossil fuels have made the process extremely popular in the oil and gas industry.

Environmental advocates complain that hydraulic fracturing is poorly regulated by the EPA and endangers the quality of groundwater, particularly drinking water wells. The latter claim has been supported by some studies. For example, in "Methane Contamination of Drinking Water Accompanying Gas-Well Drilling and Hydraulic Fracturing" (*Proceedings of the National Academy of Sciences*, vol. 108, no. 20, May 17, 2011), Stephen G. Osborn et al. of Duke University report on samples that were collected from drinking water wells located near active hydraulic fracturing sites in northeastern Pennsylvania and upstate New York. The researchers found abnormally high methane concentrations in drinking water wells located within 0.6 of a mile (1 km) of active hydraulic fracturing operations. Osborn et al. note that chemical analysis of the methane revealed that it had come from deep underground. The researchers speculate that the high-pressure rock drilling technique produced minute cracks in the casing surrounding the injection pathway, allowing upcoming methane to leak into the relatively shallow groundwater aquifers that the drinking water wells access.

In 2010 the EPA began its own comprehensive study regarding the impacts of hydraulic fracturing on drinking water and groundwater. In June 2015 the agency released a draft copy of its report (http://cfpub.epa.gov/ncea/hfstudy/recordisplay.cfm?deid=244651#_ga=1.255067918.740156 32.1444574105) for review by scientists. In other words, the report was not intended for public review or comments. In *Assessment of the Potential Impacts of Hydraulic Fracturing for Oil and Gas on Drinking Water Resources*, the EPA states, "From our assessment, we conclude there are above and below ground mechanisms by which hydraulic fracturing activities have the potential to impact drinking water resources. These mechanisms include water withdrawals in times of, or in areas with, low water availability; spills of hydraulic fracturing fluids and produced water; fracturing directly into underground drinking water resources; below ground migration of liquids and gases; and inadequate treatment and discharge of wastewater." However, the agency goes on to say, "We did not find evidence that these mechanisms have led to widespread, systemic impacts on drinking water resources in the United States." As of November 2015, the report had not been finalized or officially released to the public.

FIGURE 11.4

Hydraulic fracturing

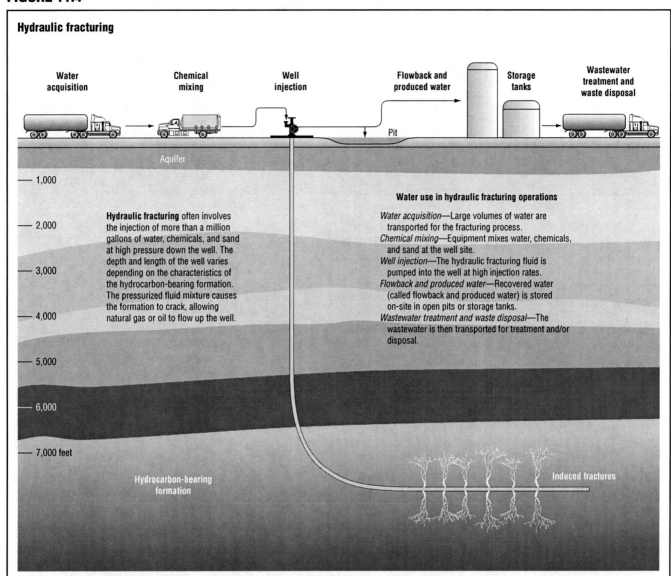

Water acquisition — Chemical mixing — Well injection — Flowback and produced water — Storage tanks — Wastewater treatment and waste disposal

Aquifer

— 1,000

— 2,000

Hydraulic fracturing often involves the injection of more than a million gallons of water, chemicals, and sand at high pressure down the well. The depth and length of the well varies depending on the characteristics of the hydrocarbon-bearing formation. The pressurized fluid mixture causes the formation to crack, allowing natural gas or oil to flow up the well.

— 3,000

— 4,000

— 5,000

— 6,000

— 7,000 feet

Water use in hydraulic fracturing operations

Water acquisition—Large volumes of water are transported for the fracturing process.
Chemical mixing—Equipment mixes water, chemicals, and sand at the well site.
Well injection—The hydraulic fracturing fluid is pumped into the well at high injection rates.
Flowback and produced water—Recovered water (called flowback and produced water) is stored on-site in open pits or storage tanks.
Wastewater treatment and waste disposal—The wastewater is then transported for treatment and/or disposal.

Pit

Hydrocarbon-bearing formation

Induced fractures

SOURCE: "Figure 6a. Illustration of a Horizontal Well Showing the Water Lifecycle in Hydraulic Fracturing," in *Draft Plan to Study the Potential Impacts of Hydraulic Fracturing on Drinking Water Resources*, U.S. Environmental Protection Agency, Office of Research and Development, February 2011, http://yosemite.epa.gov/sab/sabproduct.nsf/0/D3483AB445AE61418525775900603E79/$File/Draft+Plan+to+Study+the+Potential+Impacts+of+Hydraulic+Fracturing+on+Drinking+Water+Resources-February+2011.pdf (accessed September 10, 2015)

IMPORTANT NAMES
AND ADDRESSES

American Lung Association
55 W. Wacker Drive, Ste. 1150
Chicago, IL 60601
1-800-548-8252
URL: http://www.lung.org/

Bureau of Land Management
1849 C St. NW, Rm. 5665
Washington, DC 20240
(202) 208-3801
FAX: (202) 208-5242
URL: http://www.blm.gov/

Bureau of Ocean Management
1849 C St. NW
Washington, DC 20240
(202) 208-6474
URL: http://www.boem.gov/

Centers for Disease Control and Prevention
1600 Clifton Rd.
Atlanta, GA 30329-4027
1-800-232-4636
URL: http://www.cdc.gov/

Environmental Defense Fund
257 Park Ave. South
New York, NY 10010
1-800-684-3322
URL: https://www.edf.org/

Idaho National Laboratory
1955 Fremont Ave.
Idaho Falls, ID 83415
1-866-495-7440
URL: https://www.inl.gov/

National Aeronautics and Space Administration
300 E. St. SW, Ste. 5R30
Washington, DC 20546
(202) 358-0001
FAX: (202) 358-4338
URL: http://www.nasa.gov/

National Atmospheric Deposition Program
Illinois State Water Survey
2204 Griffith Dr.
Champaign, IL 61820-7495
(217) 333-7871
URL: http://nadp.sws.uiuc.edu/

National Audubon Society
225 Varick St.
New York, NY 10014
(212) 979-3000
URL: http://www.audubon.org/

National Environmental Education Foundation
4301 Connecticut Ave. NW, Ste. 160
Washington, DC 20008
(202) 833-2933
FAX: (202) 261-6464
URL: http://www.neefusa.org/

National Interagency Fire Center
3833 S. Development Ave.
Boise, ID 83705-5354
(208) 387-5512
E-mail:
BLM_FA_NIFC_Comments@blm.gov
URL: http://www.nifc.gov/

National Oceanic and Atmospheric Administration
1401 Constitution Ave. NW, Rm. 5128
Washington, DC 20230
(202) 482-3436
URL: http://www.noaa.gov/

National Safety Council
1121 Spring Lake Dr.
Itasca, IL 60143-3201
(630) 285-1121
1-800-621-7615
FAX: (630) 285-1315
E-mail: customerservice@nsc.org
URL: http://www.nsc.org/pages/home.aspx/

National Weather Service Climate Prediction Center
5830 University Research Ct.
College Park, MD 20740
(301) 763-8000
URL: http://www.cpc.ncep.noaa.gov/

Natural Resources Defense Council
40 W. 20th St.
New York, NY 10011
(212) 727-2700
FAX: (212) 727-1773
E-mail: nrdcinfo@nrdc.org
URL: http://www.nrdc.org/

Oak Ridge National Laboratory
1 Bethel Valley Rd.
Oak Ridge, TN 37831
(865) 576-7658
URL: https://www.ornl.gov/

Sierra Club
85 Second St., Second Floor
San Francisco, CA 94105
(415) 977-5500
FAX: (415) 977-5797
E-mail: information@sierraclub.org
URL: http://www.sierraclub.org/

Union of Concerned Scientists
Two Brattle Sq.
Cambridge, MA 02138-3780
(617) 547-5552
FAX: (617) 864-9405
URL: http://www.ucsusa.org/

United Nations Environment Programme
PO Box 30552, 00100
Nairobi, Kenya
(011-254-20) 7621234
FAX: (011-254-20) 7624489/90
E-mail: unepinfo@unep.org
URL: http://www.unep.org/

U.S. Bureau of Reclamation
1849 C St. NW
Washington, DC 20240-0001
(202) 513-0501
FAX: (202) 513-0309
URL: http://www.usbr.gov/

U.S. Department of Agriculture
1400 Independence Ave. SW
Washington, DC 20250
(202) 720-2791
URL: http://www.usda.gov/

U.S. Department of Energy
1000 Independence Ave. SW
Washington, DC 20585
(202) 586-5000
FAX: (202) 586-4403
E-mail: the.secretary@hq.doe.gov
URL: http://www.energy.gov/

U.S. Environmental Protection Agency
1200 Pennsylvania Ave. NW
Washington, DC 20460
(202) 272-0167
URL: http://www.epa.gov/

U.S. Fish and Wildlife Service
4401 N. Fairfax Dr., Rm. 420
Arlington, VA 22203
URL: http://www.fws.gov/

U.S. Food and Drug Administration
10903 New Hampshire Ave.
Silver Spring, MD 20993
1-888-463-6332
URL: http://www.fda.gov/

U.S. Forest Service
1400 Independence Ave. SW
Washington, DC 20250-1111
1-800-832-1355
URL: http://www.fs.fed.us/

U.S. Geological Survey
12201 Sunrise Valley Dr.
Reston, VA 20192
(703) 648-5953
URL: http://www.usgs.gov/

U.S. Global Change Research Program
1800 G St. NW, Ste. 9100
Washington, DC 20006

(202) 223-6262
FAX: (202) 223-3065
URL: http://www.globalchange.gov/

U.S. Government Accountability Office
441 G St. NW
Washington, DC 20548
(202) 512-3000
E-mail: contact@gao.gov
URL: http://www.gao.gov/

U.S. Nuclear Regulatory Commission
Washington, DC 20555-0001
(301) 415-7000
1-800-368-5642
URL: http://www.nrc.gov/

Wilderness Society
1615 M St. NW
Washington, DC 20036
(202) 833-2300
E-mail: action@tws.org
URL: http://www.wilderness.org/

RESOURCES

The U.S. Environmental Protection Agency monitors the status of the nation's environment and publishes a variety of materials on environmental issues. Numerous other U.S. government agencies provided reports and data that were used in the preparation of this book. They included the Bureau of Ocean Energy Management; the Centers for Disease Control and Prevention; the Congressional Budget Office; the Congressional Research Service; the National Aeronautics and Space Administration; Oak Ridge National Laboratory; the U.S. Census Bureau; the U.S. Commission on Civil Rights; the U.S. Consumer Product Safety Commission; the U.S. Department of Agriculture; the U.S. Department of Agriculture, Agricultural Marketing Service; the U.S. Department of Commerce, the National Oceanic and Atmospheric Administration; the U.S. Department of Education; the U.S. Department of Energy; the U.S. Department of Transportation, National Highway Traffic Safety Administration; the U.S. Fish and Wildlife Service; the U.S. Food and Drug Administration; the U.S. Forest Service; the U.S. Geological Survey; the U.S. Global Change Research Program; the U.S. Government Accountability Office; and the U.S. Nuclear Regulatory Commission. The California Air Resources Board provided information about that state's air quality and climate change initiatives and legislation.

Useful international organizations included the Food and Agriculture Organization of the United Nations, the International Union for Conservation of Nature, and the United Nations Environment Programme.

Material from the Gallup Organization's public opinion surveys was extremely useful. Also helpful were the American Association of Poison Control Centers, the American Cancer Society, the American Lung Association, the Environmental Defense Fund, the National Environmental Education and Training Foundation, and the Center for Climate and Energy Solutions.

Various news organizations and journals were helpful for providing timely stories related to the environment, particularly *Biocycle, Chicago Tribune, Geophysical Research Letters, Los Angeles Times, Morbidity and Mortality Weekly Report, National Geographic, Nature, New Scientist, New York Times, Proceedings of the National Academy of Sciences, Recycling Today, Science, USA Today,* and *Waste and Recycling News.*

INDEX

indoor air toxins, 165–166
lead, 162–164, 163*f*, 164*f*
radiation, 164–165, 165*f*, 165*t*
risk management, 160–162
See also Hazardous waste
Trans-Alaska Pipeline System, 181
Transuranic waste, 130, 133–134
Treaties and international agreements
climate change agreements, 57–60
Convention for the Protection of the
Ozone Layer, 75
Convention on Long-Range
Transboundary Air Pollution, 87
Kyoto Protocol, 5, 14, 57–60, 61, 173
Montreal Protocol, 75–79
Trees. *See* Forests
Tropospheric ozone, 46–47, 71, 72*f*
TSCA (Toxic Substances Control Act),
160, 163

U

Ultraviolet (UV) radiation and ozone
depletion, 72–73
UN. *See* United Nations
Underground injection of hazardous waste,
119
Underground nuclear waste storage, 130,
133–136, 133*f*, 134*f*
UNEP. *See* United Nations Environment
Programme
UNFCCC (United Nations Framework
Convention on Climate Change), 57, 59
Union Carbide, 160
United Church of Christ, 15
*United Haulers Association, Inc. v. Oneida-
Herkimer Solid Waste Management
Authority*, 103
United Nations (UN)
climate change agreements, 57
Earth Day, 3
environmental conference of 1972,
13–14
Food and Agriculture Organization,
179
United Nations Economic Commission for
Europe, 87
United Nations Environment Programme
(UNEP)
establishment of, 14
Intergovernmental Panel on Climate
Change, 43–44
Montreal Protocol, 75, 76–77
Project Skyhole Patching, 79
United Nations Framework Convention on
Climate Change (UNFCCC), 57, 59
United States
acid rain, politics of, 86–87
black market trading in ozone-depleting
substances, 79
climate change policies, 60–64
climate change reports, 64–66

electricity net generation by fuel
type, 62*t*
forests, 171
fossil fuel–fired power plants, 63*f*
greenhouse gas emissions trends, 49,
49*f*
Kyoto Protocol, 58
United States, Rapanos v., 141
*United States v. Riverside Bayview Homes,
Inc.*, 141
Universal wastes, 126
Uranium mill tailings, 130
U.S. Army Corps of Engineers, 141,
175–176
*U.S. Army Corps of Engineers, Solid Waste
Agency of Northern Cook County v.*,
141
U.S. Climate Change Research Initiative, 61
U.S. Coast Guard, 155
U.S. Consumer Product Safety Commission
(CPSC), 160
U.S. Department of Agriculture (USDA),
125, 159, 167
U.S. Department of Energy (DOE)
carbon sequestration, 69
ethanol fuel emissions, 37
high-level radioactive waste disposal
plan, 136
nuclear waste treatment plants, 130
nuclear weapons, 129
radioactive waste, 127
Waste Isolation Pilot Plant accident, 134
Yucca Mountain nuclear waste
site, 135
U.S. Department of the Interior, 124, 125
U.S. Energy Information Administration,
49–50
U.S. Food and Drug Administration (FDA),
159, 167
U.S. Forest Service (FS), 171–174, 179
U.S. Geological Survey (USGS), 153, 181
U.S. Global Change Research Program
(USGCRP), 60, 61, 64–66
U.S. Nuclear Regulatory Commission
(NRC), 126, 127, 128, 135, 164
USDA (U.S. Department of Agriculture),
125, 159, 167
USGCRP (U.S. Global Change Research
Program), 60, 61, 64–66
USGS (U.S. Geological Survey), 153, 181
UV (ultraviolet) radiation and ozone
depletion, 72–73

V

Vail, CO, 3
Vegetation and acid rain, 85
Vehicles. *See* Motor vehicles
Vibrio, 169
Vienna Convention, 75
Virgil C. Summer power plant, 129

Vogtle nuclear power plant, 127, 129
Volatile organic compounds (VOCs), 18,
24, 83
Volkswagen Group, 35

W

Warren County, NC, 15
Washington, 129–130
Waste. *See* Hazardous waste; Municipal
solid waste; Nonhazardous waste;
Radioactive waste
Waste Isolation Pilot Plant, 133–134,
134*f*
Waste Isolation Pilot Plant Land
Withdrawal Act, 134
Waste treatment plants, nuclear waste,
130
Waste-to-energy process, 101
Water availability and usage, 137–140,
139*t*
Water quality
acid rain, 84–85
beaches, 154
Clean Water Act, 140–142
climate change effects, 66
coastal waters, 153–154
drinking water, 155–156
environmental movement, 2
hydraulic fracturing, 182
impairment causes, 150(*t*9.12)
impairment sources, 151*t*
lead, 163
National Aquatic Resource Surveys,
152–153
national surface water quality database,
146–152
oceans, 154–155
pesticides in food, 167
point source and nonpoint source
management, 143–144, 143*f*
public opinion, 7, 156–157, 157*t*
standards, 142
surface water supporting
designated uses, by use, 148*t*,
149*t*, 150(*t*9.11)
total maximum daily loads, 142*f*
U.S. Geological Survey water quality
data sources, 153
water bodies assessed for water quality,
147*t*
watershed management, 144–146,
145*f*, 146*f*
wetlands, 175, 177*f*
Water treatment plants, 156
Water vapor, 44–45
Waterborne diseases, 156
Watersheds, 144–146, 145*f*, 146*f*,
153–154
Wells, 156, 182
West Virginia, 160